D1590854

Sejanus

Regent of Rome

John S. McHugh

Pen & Sword
MILITARY

First published in Great Britain in 2020 by
Pen & Sword Military
An imprint of
Pen & Sword Books Ltd
Yorkshire – Philadelphia

Printed and bound in the UK by TJ International Ltd, Padstow, Cornwall.

Pen & Sword Books Limited incorporates the imprints of Atlas, Archaeology,
Aviation, Discovery, Family History, Fiction, History, Maritime, Military, Military
Classics, Politics, Select, Transport, True Crime, Air World, Frontline Publishing,
Leo Cooper, Remember When, Seaforth Publishing, The Praetorian Press,
Wharncliffe Local History, Wharncliffe Transport, Wharncliffe True Crime and
White Owl.

For a complete list of Pen & Sword titles please contact

PEN & SWORD BOOKS LIMITED
47 Church Street, Barnsley, South Yorkshire, S70 2AS, England
E-mail: enquiries@pen-and-sword.co.uk
Website: www.pen-and-sword.co.uk

Or

PEN AND SWORD BOOKS
1950 Lawrence Rd, Havertown, PA 19083, USA
E-mail: Uspen-and-sword@casematepublishers.com
Website: www.penandswordbooks.com

Contents

Maps

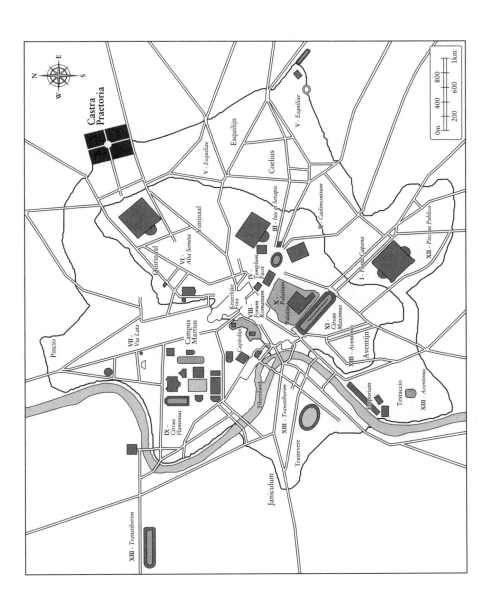

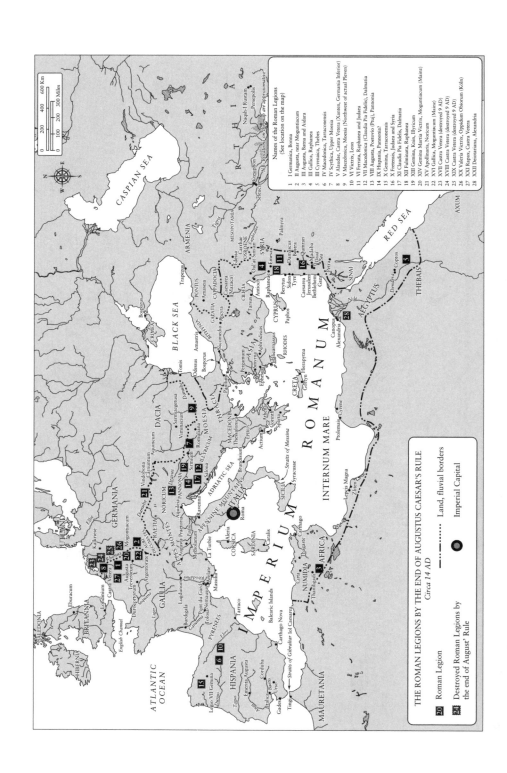

THE ROMAN LEGIONS BY THE END OF AUGUSTUS CAESAR'S RULE
Circa 14 AD

Names of the Roman Legions
(See location on the map)

1 I Germanica, Bonna
2 II Augusta, near Moguntiacum
3 III Augusta, Rama and Aidara
4 III Gallica, Raphanea
5 III Cyrenaica, Thebes
6 IV Macedonica, Tarraconensis
7 IV Scythica, Upper Moesia
8 V Alaudae, Castra Vetera (Xanten, Germania Inferior)
9 V Macedonica, Moesia (Northwest of actual Pleven)
10 VI Victrix, Leon
11 VI Ferrata, Raphanea and Judaea
12 VII Macedonica (Claudia Pia Fidelis), Dalmatia
13 VIII Augusta, Poetovio (Ptuj), Pannonia
14 IX Hispania, Pannonia?
15 X Gemina, Tarraconensis
16 X Fretensis, Judaea and Syria
17 XI Claudia Pia Fidelis, Dalmatia
18 XII Fulminata, Raphanea
19 XIII Gemina, Kaim, Illyricum
20 XIV Gemma Martia Victrix, Moguntiacum (Mainz)
21 XV Apollinaris, Noricum
22 XVI Gallica, Moguntiacum (Mainz)
23 XVII Castra Vetera (destroyed 9 AD)
24 XVIII Castra Vetera (destroyed 9 AD)
25 XIX Castra Vetera (destroyed 9 AD)
26 XX Valeria Victrix, Oppidum Obiorum (Köln)
27 XXI Rapax, Castra Vetera
28 XXII Deiotariana, Alexandria

20 Roman Legion

24 Destroyed Roman Legions by
the end of August Rule

——— Land, fluvial borders

● Imperial Capital

List of Plates

1. Bust of the emperor Tiberius in Ny Carlsberg Glyptotek, Copenhagen. (*Attributed to Cnyborg assumed (based on copyright claims). [Public domain], via Wikimedia Commons*)

2. Antonia the Younger. (*By Rabax63 (Own work) [CC BY-SA 4.0 (https://creativecommons.org/licenses/by-sa/4.0)], via Wikimedia Commons*)

3. Marble portrait of Drusus ca. 21 AD in Louvre, Paris. (© *Marie-Lan Nguyen/Wikimedia Commons – http://creativecommons.org/licenses/by/2.5*)

4. Greek marble bust of Agrippina the Elder. Portrait made in Athens under the reign of Caligula, between 37 and 41 AD, now in the Louvre, Paris. (*Attributed to [GFDL (http://www.gnu.org/copyleft/fdl.html) or CC-BY-SA-3.0 (http://creativecommons.org/licenses/by-sa/3.0/)], via Wikimedia Commons*)

5. Marble bust of Germanicus created on the occasion of the adoption of Germanicus by Tiberius in 4 AD from Córdoba, Spain. (*Attribution GFDL (http://www.gnu.org/copyleft/fdl.html) or CC-BY-SA-3.0 (http://creativecommons.org/licenses/by-sa/3.0/)], via Wikimedia Commons*)

6. Bronze coin of Philadelphia, Lydia, possibly depicting Tiberius Gemellus. Struck in c 35–37 AD showing bare headed Tiberius Gemellus with winged thunderbolt on the obverse (RPC I 3017). (*Attribution Classical Numismatic Group, Inc. http://www.cngcoins.com [GFDL (http://www.gnu.org/copyleft/fdl.html), CC-BY-SA-3.0 (http://creativecommons.org/licenses/by-sa/3.0/) or CC BY-SA 2.5 (http://creativecommons.org/licenses/by-sa/2.5)], via Wikimedia Commons*)

7. Marble bust of Gaius (Caligula) in the Louvre, Paris. (*Attribution By Anonymous - Clio20, CC BY-SA 3.0, https://commons.wikimedia.org/w/index.php?curid=599879, via Wikimedia Commons*)

8. The Great Cameo of France is a sardonyx cameo created around 23 AD. It depicts the imperial family both living and deceased.

The top 'heavenly' layer shows Augustus in the centre in the regalia of *pontifex maximus* with Drusus, the son of Tiberius and Germanicus riding a winged horse. The angelic figure floating before Augustus has been interpreted as Aeneas or his son Julius, the legendary founders of the Julian dynasty. The middle layer is reserved for the living members of the Julio-Claudian house. In the centre the emperor Tiberius sits on his throne with his mother Livia sat alongside him. In front of the emperor stands his heir Nero Caesar, the son of Germanicus and Agrippina. Beside him stands his wife Julia, the daughter of Drusus and Livilla (Livia). Livilla stands slightly behind them with Gaius, the future emperor Caligula. Behind the throne of Tiberius is Drusus Caesar, the second son of Germanicus with his mother Agrippina. Below the imperial family lie figures of defeated and submissive barbarians. (*Attribution GFDL (http://www.gnu.org/copyleft/fdl.html), CC-BY-SA-3.0 (http://creativecommons.org/licenses/by-sa/3.0/) or CC BY-SA 2.5-2.0-1.0 (http://creativecommons.org/licenses/by-sa/2.5-2.0-1.0)], via Wikimedia Commons*)

9. Bronze As struck in 31 AD at Bilbilis with legend TI • CAESAR • DIVI • AVGVSTI • F • AVGVSTVS• showing the image of Sejanus. The obverse carries the legend AV(ligate)GVSTA • BILBILIS • TI • CÆSARE • V [L ÆL]IO • [SEIAN]O, with COS within wreath. The name of Sejanus has been removed as he suffered damnatio memoriae (RPC I 398; NAH 1079-80; SNG Copenhagen 620). (*Attribution by Classical Numismatic Group, Inc. http://www.cngcoins. com, CC BY-SA 3.0, https://commons.wikimedia.org/w/index. php?curid=2385731*)

10. The grotto at the Villa of Tiberius, Sperlonga. (*Attribution by Carole Raddato from FRANKFURT, Germany (Villa of Tiberius, Sperlonga) [CC BY-SA 2.0 (http://creativecommons.org/licenses/by-sa/2.0)], via Wikimedia Commons*)

11. Exterior of grotto from Villa of Tiberius, Sperlonga. (*Attribution by Carole Raddato from FRANKFURT, Germany (Villa of Tiberius at Sperlonga) [CC BY-SA 2.0 (http://creativecommons.org/licenses/by-sa/2.0)], via Wikimedia Commons*)

12. Remains of the Villa of Tiberius, Sperlonga. (*Attribution by Carole Raddato from FRANKFURT, Germany (Villa of Tiberius, Sperlonga) [CC BY-SA 2.0 (http://creativecommons.org/licenses/by-sa/2.0)], via Wikimedia Commons*)

including Sejanus. (*Attribution by Chris 73 – Own work, CC BY-SA 3.0, https://commons.wikimedia.org/w/index.php?curid=6310364*)

22. The view from Via di San Pietro in Carcere looking towards the forum. The Via San Pietro is believed to be the location of the Gemonian Stairs which led from the Capitoline to the Roman forum. The condemned were strangled and their bodies thrown down the stairs where their corpses were left to rot and be abused before being thrown into the river Tibur. (*Attribution by Patrick Nouhailler's…, CC BY-SA 3.0, https://commons.wikimedia.org/w/index.php?curid=53589718*)

23. The Porta Praetoriana in the Aurelian Walls of Rome. The praetorian fortress was built originally on the outskirts of the city. Three of the four masonry walls were later incorporated into the defences of the city by the emperor Aurelian and the gates blocked up. (*Attribution by No machine-readable author provided. Joris assumed (based on copyright claims). - No machine-readable source provided. Own work assumed (based on copyright claims)., Public Domain, https://commons.wikimedia.org/w/index.php?curid=768457*)

24. Northern wall of the Praetorian Fortress. (*Attribution Di Nessun autore leggibile automaticamente. Joris presunto (secondo quanto affermano i diritti d'autore). - Nessuna fonte leggibile automaticamente. Presunta opera propria (secondo quanto affermano i diritti d'autore)., CC BY-SA 3.0, https://commons.wikimedia.org/w/index.php?curid=757164*)

25. Etruscan town of Vulsinii, modern Bolsena with views across the lake. Vulsinii was the birth place of Sejanus' father, Lucius Seius Strabo, and described by Pliny the Elder as the richest town in Tuscany. (*Attribution: https://commons.wikimedia.org/w/index.php?curid=345494*)

26. A carving of a Praetorian guardsman from a triumphal arch for the emperor Trajan found at Pozzuoli, Italy, now located in the Pergamon Museum, Berlin. (*Attribution by Magnus Manske [CC BY-SA (http://creativecommons.org/licenses/by-sa/3.0/)] via Wikimedia Commons*)

27. Roman statue in the Museo archeologico e d'arte della Maremma possibly depicting Drusus Caesar, the son of Germanicus and Agrippina the Elder. (*Attribution by Sailko - Own work, CC BY 3.0, https://commons.wikimedia.org/w/index.php?curid=43773211*)

28. Bust of Gnaeus Domitius Ahenobarbus, the consul of 32 AD and married to Agrippina the Younger. He was the only son of Lucius Domtius Ahenobarbus and Antonia the Elder and descended from Augustus' sister Octavia. (*Attribution by I, Sailko, CC BY-SA 3.0, https://commons.wikimedia.org/w/index.php?curid=9944785*)

key role in securing the throne for her son Tiberius but as her influence with the emperor waned, that of Sejanus grew stronger. After the fall of Agrippina, Livia took Caligula and his sisters Drusilla and Livilla into her care until her death in 29 AD. (*Attribution: Carole Raddato from FRANKFURT, Germany [CC BY-SA 2.0 (https://creativecommons.org/licenses/by-sa/2.0)], via Wikimedia Commons*)

Acknowledgements

To Mary, Patrick and Joseph in acknowledgement of their patience and encouragement. Also to Louise Haysey without whose help I could not have written this.

Chapter 1

Early Years: 20 BC–AD 14

'...we have masters in the form of circumstances, which are legion. And anyone who controls any one of them controls us as well. No one, you realise, fears Caesar himself, it is death, exile, dispossession, jail and disfranchisement that they are afraid of. Nor is Caesar loved, unless by chance he is personally deserving; we love money, a tribuneship, a military command or consulship. But when we love, hate or fear such things, then the people who administer them are bound to become our masters. As a result, we even honour them as gods, because we associate godhead with whatever has the capacity to confer most benefit.' (Epictetus, *Discourses* 4.1.59–61)

Sejanus was feared, loathed, despised and loved, but he was above all else a consummate and immensely gifted politician. At times charming and amiable, always efficient and reliable, but arrogant and cruel when the occasion demanded. He was driven, burning with ambition. He became the master of all through his control of imperial gifts and honours due to the increasing reluctance of Tiberius to fulfil his role as emperor. Tiberius had become increasingly frustrated by the futility of encouraging the Senate to take some responsibility for the governance of the empire, and devastated by cruel fate which had deprived him of his first wife and first love, Vipsania, and then his last love, Drusus, his son. In ancient Rome, power lay in the ability to distribute resources, wealth, offices and honours, with the emperor possessing a virtual monopoly. Sejanus owed his rise to imperial benevolence and his ascendancy to his control over a complex web of favours and obligations that Tiberius delegated to his most trusted of advisors.[1] As Tiberius gradually abdicated his responsibilities, Sejanus filled the space once occupied by his master. So as Tiberius was honoured, loved, feared and loathed as the ultimate arbiter of success and failure, life and death, so too was Sejanus. He is presented in our overwhelmingly hostile sources as a sinister figure, consumed by ambition, who kept to the shadows, using proxies to eliminate his rivals. The poet Juvenal in his tenth satire dwells on the folly of those like Sejanus who pray for power, prestige, wealth and high office, and craved 'nothing else but the top position, sought by every trick in the book. Nothing else but ambitious prayers granted by the malicious gods. Few kings go down to Ceres' son in law [Pluto, god of the underworld] without slaughter and carnage, few tyrants avoid a bloodless death.'[2] There can be no doubt that ambition was his driving force; otherwise, why would a wealthy and well-connected individual who had the resources to live an extremely comfortable life, enter the often-deadly world of courtly politics, especially in the time of Tiberius? However, where did his ambitions end? How did he build his power to become the virtual regent of Rome? Is there a more complex, multi-faceted character behind the stereotyped epitome of evil presented in Tacitus and Dio?

L. Aelius Sejanus was born around 20 BC into a world in flux. It was a time of intense political, social and economic change. So dramatic were these convulsions in the fabric of the old traditional Roman order that the great historian of this period, Ronald Syme, entitled his major work *The Roman Revolution*. Gone was the political dominance of the old Republican aristocracy, decimated by years of civil war, their numbers greatly reduced by battle and proscriptions. The victors in these wars, Julius Caesar and his adopted son Octavian, later honoured with the title Augustus, ensured their own supporters and *amici*, friends, were rewarded. Many were considered 'new men' who were the first in their families to attain the office of consul, which granted nobility. The real genius of Augustus was to create a new order based superficially on republican precedents, but it took political power away from the old senatorial families whilst allowing them to retain the social and economic symbols of their elevated status. Syme observed that the 'primacy of the *nobiles* was a fraud as well as an anachronism – it rested on the support and subsidy of a military leader ... acquired in return for the cession of their power and ambition.'[3] Consulships, landed estates, money, priesthoods and governorships of the prestigious provinces could all be granted by the Princeps, Augustus, the first amongst equals, in return for loyalty (*fides*). This reciprocal exchange was embedded in Roman society in the form of *amicitiae*, which was based on debts of obligation. As a mark of distinction, men with access to the emperor's favour called themselves *amici Caesaris*, friends of the emperor.[4] Tiberius himself was doubly a member of one of the oldest aristocratic families of the Republic. On his father's side, he could trace his descent back to an Appius Claudius, whom it was claimed held a consulship in 493 BC, and from his mother Livia, who was married to Augustus, to the Claudii Puchri. Her father had also been adopted by M. Livius Drusus, the revolutionary tribune of 91 BC and a member of another ancient family.[5] The senatorial aristocracy would have accepted Tiberius as their social equal purely based on the noble blood that ran through his veins. With his adoption by Augustus in AD 4, Tiberius also became a member of the imperial Julian house, and with Augustus' and the Senate's granting of tribunician power, he was publicly recognized as the nominated successor of the emperor.

Sejanus could boast an illustrious and prestigious heritage, but not one that could rank with the great noble families that dominated the Senate. Even Velleius Paterculus, who produced his history in AD 30 at the height of Sejanus' power, could not claim this for him. He is compared to Augustus' great equestrian *amici*, Marcus Agrippa and Statilius Taurus, whose power and status were based not upon their social standing but unfettered access to the emperor and membership of his *consilium*, an informal advisory body made up of his *amici* whose membership was fluid. Velleius flatters Sejanus in his comparison: 'In these men's cases "newness of family" did not obstruct their elevation to multiple consulships, to triumphs, and to numerous priesthoods.'[6] The sources, including Velleius, are frustratingly vague on his origins and extended family. Even the time of his birth can only be conjectured. Sejanus accompanied Gaius, Augustus' grandson and heir, on his visit to the Danube provinces and subsequent embassy to the East in 1 BC.[7] It is probable that Sejanus would have adopted the *toga virilis*, and so entered manhood, just before this. It was traditional for a young male to enter adulthood between the ages of 15 to 17, although this was not fixed. Once he had entered manhood he was eligible for the *tirocinium*, which originally denoted some form of military training. However, the sons of the well-connected would often attach their sons to the entourage of a governor, politician or commander. Sejanus' presence on the staff of the Caesar Gaius in 1 BC suggests he was born around 20 or 19 BC. It was considered a great honour to be attached to the entourage of the young heir to the throne and indicates the influence of his father, Augustus' Praetorian Prefect, Seius Strabo.[8]

L. Seius Strabo was an equestrian from the Etruscan town of Vulsinii, modern Bolsena, nestled on the shores of Lacus Volsiniensis. His grandfather had defeated Pupius Piso in the elections for the curule aedileship in 74 BC and his father was a wealthy landowner and *amicus* of Varro and

Appius Claudius. His main claim to fame was the invention of fois gras. This was not an illustrious family heritage, but the career of Strabo and his son would change that.[9] Juvenal alludes to Sejanus' birth in Vulsinii and ponders that if the Etruscan goddess of Fortune, whose temple was in the town, had shown greater favour to her native son then Rome would have had a different emperor:

'But what of Remus' [Rome's] mob? They are followers of Fortune, as always, and hate those who are condemned. The same crowd, if Nortia had supported her Etruscan, if the aged emperor [Tiberius] had been smothered off his guard, would be hailing Sejanus as Augustus within minutes.'[10]

The Temple of Nortia is today identified with the ruins near to the Florence Gate. However, the original temple ruins probably lie in the old Etruscan site between Chiusi and Vetralla, the city being razed in 264 BC following a slave revolt. There remains in Bolsena a compact amphitheatre, denoting the small size of its Roman population, and some baths, both in a poor state of preservation. Tacitus, betraying the arrogance of the senatorial elite, slanders Sejanus as a 'municipal adulterer'.[11] However, this assessment clearly ignores the position of his father and the multitude of his family connections. By AD 10, L. Seius Strabo was approaching the pinnacle of the equestrian career ladder and as such 'was a leading member of the equestrian order'.[12]

The Praetorian Prefecture to which Strabo was appointed towards the end of Augustus' reign was not at the apex of the equestrian career until the second half of the first century AD. The most prestigious post was that of Prefect of Egypt, probably as this office combined a military, judicial and administrative role with a greater independence than any official based in the capital itself. Furthermore, the Egyptian prefect ruled like a king from the regal palace of the Ptolemies in Alexandria.[13] The post of Praetorian Prefect had been established by Augustus in 2 BC. The Praetorian Guard itself had its origins in the personal bodyguards of Republican generals who disbanded each unit at the end of their campaign. In 27 BC, after the defeat of Mark Antony and Cleopatra's forces at the naval Battle of Actium, Octavian received from the Senate the honorary title of Augustus and used his authority to combine his own Praetorian cohorts with those of his defeated rival to create a permanent body of soldiers loyal solely to him as their commander-in-chief.[14] From its very inception, the Guard was a privileged unit with better rates of pay than the legionaries, lived in the relatively comfortable conditions located in and around the capital and served a shorter length of time.[15] Historians are divided as to the original purpose of the office of Praetorian Prefect. Some suggest that the new post was primarily military, as a commander of the personal bodyguard to counter conspiracies against the life of the emperor and crush the frequent riots that plagued the capital. Others speculate that it was a mainly political role, acting as a visual and at times actual threat to back up the emperor's authority. In all likelihood, it was initially military in purpose, but its political role gradually evolved due the Praetorian Prefect's unfettered access to the emperor.[16]

Between 27 BC and 2 BC, the tribunes of each Praetorian cohort reported directly to Augustus as their commander-in-chief. This was a particularly cumbersome structure, as the emperor's administrative tasks in managing the empire, as well as his political role as the supreme patron granting *beneficia* to his *amici*, would mean it was very difficult to issue commands and oversee the duties of these tribunes. Furthermore, to cater for senatorial sensibilities and reduce the overt military nature of the Principate, only three Praetorian cohorts were lodged in Rome at any one time, with the others stationed in towns around the capital. Praetorian tombstones from the reign of Augustus have been found at Tivoli, Praeneste, Anzio, Terracina and possibly at Nuceria. Another inscription records the death of a Praetorian fighting a fire at Rome's port city of Ostia.[17] This dispersal of cohorts would have added further administrative complications. It is telling that Augustus did not delegate the management of the Praetorians at a much earlier date. A commander of the guards was in a position to undermine the loyalty of the men who patrolled the corridors of the palace, but was also the only higher official armed with a sword in the presence of the emperor. The office of Praetorian Prefect was symbolized by this granting of a sword. The Emperor Trajan, handing a sword to his Praetorian Prefect, Sextus Attius Suburanus, instructed him to: 'Take this sword and use it for me if I rule well, and against me if I rule badly.'[18] The sword not only came to symbolize command of the Praetorian cohorts, but also the use of force to support the authority of the emperor.[19]

The difficulty in appointing a commander of the guard was twofold. Firstly, the status of the commander had to be considered with care, as a senator holding this office would create friction with the Senate itself as the Praetorian Prefect would be answerable not to that body but the emperor himself. Secondly, any official who had unrestricted access to the emperor would have to be trusted implicitly. An aristocrat would have been too great a risk. Augustus' solution was to appoint two Praetorian Prefects from the lesser equestrian class. An equestrian would not possess the necessary social prestige to be acceptable as emperor to the senatorial class, commanders of the legions nor governors of the provinces, as he did not possess sufficient *nobilitas*. Additionally, two appointments were made, which reduced the potential threat, but it is possible that this was also a pragmatic move as the cohorts were so widely distributed. It is also likely that the first two appointments were a senior prefect with a deputy who gained the experience necessary to replace his superior.[20]

Little is known of the Praetorian Prefects appointed before Seius Strabo. The first office-holder in 2 BC was Q. Ostorius Scapula, who held family estates in Liguria. He must have been a high-ranking equestrian who had proved himself loyal to Augustus and completed successful military service during the civil wars or earlier in the reign. A relative, quite possibly his brother P. Ostorius Scapula, was made Prefect of Egypt with control over Rome's grain supply. An inscription suggests that P. Ostorius Scapula was married to a Sallustia Calvina, possibly the daughter of the powerful equestrian *amicus* and close confidant of Augustus, Gaius Sallustius Crispus. Tacitus describes the influence of this man as next to none, saying 'he it was who sustained the burden of secrets of emperors'.[21] Appointments were based on patronage, and it stands testament to the influence Sallustius Crispus held with Augustus as both Ostorii were clearly trusted for their loyalty and ability.[22] His colleague was Publius Salvius Aper, of whom very little is known. An inscription from Brixia, a rich town in Transpadane, from 8 BC records a Lucius Salvius Aper as a local magistrate. He was possibly a close relative.[23] The only other prefect who has left a record from Augustus' reign before the appointment of Seius Strabo is Publius Varius Ligur, who possibly originated from Alba Pompeia in Piedmont.[24]

The power and influence of the Praetorian Prefecture later associated with Sejanus and his successors is clearly not evident from the selection of these men. The creation of these posts in 2 BC coincided with a serious conspiracy that threatened the life of Augustus. His daughter Julia had been married to Tiberius, but they had become estranged and Tiberius had exiled himself to the island of Rhodes. Julia was accused of adultery with several nobles, including Iullus Antonius, the son of Mark Antony and Fulvia, along with aristocrats whose names resonated with the great moments of Rome's illustrious past: Tiberius Sempronius Gracchus, Appius Claudius Pulcher, Cornelius Scipio and Titus Quinctius Crispinus. Adultery was a political act by any member of the imperial family. Julia was the mother of Lucius and Gaius Caesar, heirs of Augustus until their sudden deaths in AD 2 and 4, and Agrippa Postumus, who was aged 10 at the time. Most historians have concluded that there was a genuine and substantial plot to assassinate Augustus as well as her absent husband Tiberius, and for Julia to marry Iullus Antonius. The life of the 18-year-old Gaius would also have been at risk, along with that of his siblings. The subsequent emperor's actions indicated he felt his life had been in danger and the very existence of the Principate threatened. The great noble families no doubt looked for a return to real political power rather than its mere semblance under Augustus. The emperor went into the Senate and denounced his daughter, who was banished to the prison island of Pandateria. She was allowed to return to the mainland two years later, but was confined to the town of Rhegium. Tiberius, in his island exile, was informed of his divorce from his wife by letter. Her lovers and conspirators were found guilty by the Senate and either exiled or executed. Iullus Antonius was allowed the opportunity to take his own life.[25]

Although none of the ancient sources make the connection, it must be more than coincidence that the Praetorian Prefecture was created at a time of a substantial threat to the emperor's life. The post-holders needed to be loyal with a proven record of efficient service, but not men of note. Dio, writing in the third century AD, in his fictitious speech of Augustus' *amicus* Maecenas, urges that the post of Praetorian Prefect return to its original function, merely that of commanding the emperor's *praetorium*. The emperor's *praetorium* would be the command of the imperial bodyguard rather than the many additional administrative tasks associated with this post in the third century. The circumstances surrounding the foundation of the office suggest its function was to protect the life of the emperor and his immediate family. The prestige that later derived from the post was linked to the importance of preserving the life of the emperor and the prefects' proximity to the centre of power, the emperor himself.[26]

L. Seius Strabo was appointed at some point before the death of Augustus, as he supervised the taking of the oath of loyalty to Tiberius. However, he appears to have been the sole prefect at this time.[27] There were several sole Praetorian Prefects in the history of the Empire, including Sejanus himself, his successor Macro, and in the high Empire Perennis under Commodus and Plautianus in the reign of Septimius Severus. All amassed huge power and influence, only to be executed by their emperor. The ancient sources are silent on the logic behind the creation of two Praetorian Prefects and the later reduction to one post at the end of Augustus' reign. Perhaps Strabo had a colleague who had recently died, and no appointment had yet been made. The emperor had been frail for a long time and plans had been made for the dangerous transition between rulers. Tiberius was by nature a suspicious character. Experience had taught him that loyalty had to be proven by actions and not words. Any appointment would have been the choice of both rulers, but Tiberius would have wanted to have had his own men in place. Certainly, Strabo was a close confidant of Augustus, but he was rapidly moved on by Tiberius with promotion to the prefecture of Egypt in AD 15 or 16. Egypt's importance as the breadbasket of Rome, its wealth and three legions meant that Strabo would have been considered by Tiberius to be honest, able and experienced.[28] However, he remained Augustus' choice, and along with many other *amici* of his adopted father, he made way for members of Tiberius' immediate circle of advisors and friends. The late Roman writer Macrobius records an interesting story of Strabo asking Augustus his opinion of the Republican martyr of liberty, Cato the Younger. Clearly, a discussion ensued and the emperor, suitably inspired or irked, wrote a pamphlet on the subject. Suetonius appears to allude to this when he recorded that 'Augustus wrote numerous prose works on a variety of subjects, some of which he read aloud to a group of his closer friends as though in a lecture-hall: The *Reply to Brutus' Eulogy of Cato*, for instance. In this case, however, he tired just before the end – being then already an old man – and handed the last roll to Tiberius, who finished it for him.'[29] This was a highly controversial subject and demonstrates the confidence of the Praetorian Prefect in his friendship with Augustus. Tiberius was not so open-minded.

For such an important figure as Sejanus we are given very little concrete information on his family and connections. Even Velleius appears to be deliberately vague: 'Sejanus was born to a father who was a leading member of the equestrian order, but he is also on his mother's side connected to very illustrious and venerable families that enjoy distinction for their public offices. He has, moreover, brothers, cousins, and an uncle who are former consuls.' Dio also confirms that in AD 31 he had 'numerous relatives' in the Senate.[30] It is thanks to Tacitus that we can identify Quintus Junius Blaesus, the *suffect* consul of AD 10 and governor of Pannonia in AD 14, as his uncle.[31] The office of *suffect* consul was not as prestigious as that of the two ordinary consuls, after whom the year was named. *Suffect* consuls replaced the ordinary consuls who were often asked to resign their posts during the year to enable the emperor to ennoble other deserving members of the Senate. Strangely, when referring to Blaesus a few passages earlier, Velleius makes no mention of his connection with Sejanus; instead he comments with his usual sycophancy that 'one could not tell whether his usefulness in the military sphere exceeded his efficiency in civilian life.'[32]

An inscription, discovered at Volsinii, honours an unnamed prefect of Egypt who constructed baths in his native town. It is commonly agreed that the prefect was Seius Strabo and so must date from around AD 15 or 16, when he became governor of Egypt. Helpfully, the inscription also names his mother as 'Terrentis A.', who has been conclusively identified as a sister of the wife of Gaius Maecenas, Augustus' equestrian *amicus* and advisor whose influence was second only to Marcus Vipsanius Agrippa. However, death removed one and conspiracy the other. Agrippa died in 12 BC, leaving his sons by Julia, Gaius, Lucius and Agrippa Postumus, to be adopted by Augustus. Maecenas, a great patron of the arts, was caught between his loyalty to his emperor and to his wife. He revealed to her the discovery of a conspiracy in 22 BC involving her brother A. Terentius Varro Murena and Fannius Caepio. His wife forewarned Murena, who fled.[33] Both were charged before the Senate, with Tiberius heading the prosecution. Murena was captured and executed without being given the opportunity to defend himself. Maecenas, however, fell from favour. Later, Dio surprisingly records a relationship between the emperor and Maecenas' wife, the guilt on the emperor's part being even greater when Maecenas left him his whole estate in his will when he died in 8 BC.[34] Another influential connection with the Terentias is their half-brother C. Proculeius, who sensibly rejected courtly politics although he remained such a close and trusted friend of Augustus that at one stage the emperor thought of giving his daughter Julia in marriage to him.[35]

The Volsinii inscription also records Strabo's marriage to a Cosconia Gallitta, described as the daughter of a Cornelius Lentulus Maluginensis. Syme identifies this aristocratic lady with the patrician family whose brothers could have been Ser. Lentulus Maluginensis, *suffect* consul in AD 10, and P. Lentulus Scipio, *suffect* consul in AD 2.[36] This would give Sejanus two more consular uncles if Cosconia Gallitta was his mother. However, Velleius states that Sejanus had only one consular uncle, conclusively identified as Junius Blaesus. Furthermore, in AD 22 Ser. Lentulus Maluginensis attempted to become the governor of Asia, despite the fact his priestly duty as *flamen dialis* precluded him from leaving Rome. If, like Blaesus, he was related to the Praetorian Prefect who was approaching the pinnacle of his influence and power, we would have expected him to have benefited from the support of his nephew and received a dispensation. None was forthcoming.[37] The best interpretation of the inscription is that Cosconia Gallita was Strabo's first wife, of whom there were no offspring.

Strabo's second wife and Sejanus' mother can be identified from Junius Blaesus, who must have been her brother. We have no record of her name, but we can assume she was a Junia. Furthermore, Sejanus named his daughter Junilla, no doubt after her grandmother. Blaesus himself was a new man, achieving the *suffect* consulship of AD 10, which interestingly he shared with Ser. Lentulus Maluginensis. It has been conjectured that his fellow consul was the father of Cosconia Gallita, and, if so, perhaps we see here the influence and *amicitiae* on behalf of his past and present wife. The sons of Junius Blaesus became consuls in AD 26 and 28, which would partly account for Velleius' reference to Sejanus' cousins being former consuls.[38]

What we can also ascertain with certainty is that at some point before his rise to prominence, Sejanus was adopted. There can be no doubt that his natural father was L. Seius Strabo, but Sejanus' full nomenclature of L. Aelius Sejanus indicates that he was adopted by a member of the Aelian gens. Another fact to bear in mind is that if Sejanus was adopted into a senatorial family, it would have been unusual for him not to pursue a senatorial career. Historians have offered two possibilities regarding the identity of his adopted father. Firstly Aelius Gallus, Prefect of Egypt in 26–24 BC, is a strong possibility, or secondly there is an Aelius Tubero, from a senatorial family granted patrician status by Augustus.[39] Starting with the latter option, several names stand out from the consular lists as possibly having a connection to Sejanus. Q. Aelius Tubero was an eminent jurist and historian but he never attained the consulship, unlike his sons. The consul of 11 BC who bore his name and was probably the brother of Sex. Aelius Catus, the consul in AD 4, as the age between their consulships make it unlikely they were father and son. Their sister was probably an Aelia, who was married to L. Cassius Longinus, with their offspring being L. Cassius Longinus, ordinary consul in AD 30, and C. Cassius Longinus, a *suffect* consul in the same year. According to Adams, Q. Aelius Tubero, the jurist, possibly adopted Sejanus. A number of problems exist with this hypothesis. Firstly, why would a senator with at least two grown-up male offspring adopt another? Secondly, Sejanus would have been expected to follow a senatorial career in the footsteps of his illustrious brothers. Finally, it is hard to see how these prominent senators and close relations could survive the fall of Sejanus, and yet our sources are silent on their fate. Aelia Paetina, who was married to Claudius in AD 28, may have been the daughter of Q. Aelius Tubero, the consul of 11 BC, or, more probably, Sex. Aelius Catus, the consul of AD 4. Claudius divorced her at some point after AD 31, suggesting some connection with Sejanus, but as Claudius later considered remarrying her, the connection appears to be a tenuous one. A more likely scenario is that Junia was previously married to the jurist Q. Aelius Tubero, who had been previously married to a Sulpicia, with whom he had a number of children. Later, possibly on the death of Q. Aelius Tubero, Junia married Seius Strabo, making his two sons the stepbrothers of Sejanus.[40]

The name of the *suffect* consul of AD 18, L. Seius Tubero, also causes a problem. In AD 16 he had fought as a legate of Germanicus in his campaign beyond the Rhine, and by AD 24 he is described as a prominent noble and close *amicus* of Tiberius who in failing health had been accused of treason, along with the ageing Gnaeus Lentulus, to the great discomfort of the emperor.[41] Sumner and Syme suggest he was a further son of the elder Q. Aelius Tubero who was adopted by Junia and her second husband, L. Seius Strabo. If he was awarded his consul at 42, the earliest age permitted, then he was slightly older than Sejanus. Perhaps he was a young child when Junia married Strabo, and with the boy's natural father dead such a solution appeared both logical and humane.[42] An alternative but less satisfactory hypothesis is suggested by Adams and followed by Sealey, in that Strabo's first wife was not a Junia but an Aelia, the daughter of the elder Q. Aelius Tubero, the child from this first marriage being the consul of AD 18. However, we are faced by Tacitus' description of Seius Tubero as a 'prominent noble', which can hardly have been the case if his father was an equestrian, no matter how illustrious his career and commanding his influence. The familial relationship also ignores the position of Junius Blaesus as Sejanus' uncle, unless we assume Strabo was married three times.[43]

The evidence makes a better fit if L. Aelius Gallus, Prefect of Egypt in 26–24 BC, is assumed to be the adoptive father of L. Aelius Sejanus. Firstly, he is an equestrian, which would make Sejanus' choice of career through equestrian posts logical. Secondly, in AD 31, as news of the sudden fall of Sejanus spread through the streets of Rome and the rabid mob hunted down his friends and relatives, an Aelius Gallus hid in the gardens of Sejanus' *amicus* Pomponius Secundus.[44] Clearly, he was a relative of the deceased Prefect of Egypt, but his fear and flight are only understandable if the rioters were aware of a close connection to the fallen Praetorian Prefect. Sejanus had three children[45] identified by the *Fasti Ostiensis*, discovered in 1929, which preserves their names as Strabo (Sejanus), Capito Aeli(nus) and Junilla Seianai. Syme identifies the eldest as the fugitive given shelter by Pomponius Secundus, his full nomenclature there being Aelius Gallus Strabo.[46] This connection would also provide Sejanus with another brother, as Aelius Gallus had a daughter, Aelia Galla, who married a Postumus, probably the senator C. Propertius Postumus.[47] Adoption by Aelius Gallus would be logical in that he appears to have had no male offspring, and his wealth and name would add lustre to the *dignitas* of both Strabo and his son. However, the political influence of Aelius Gallus would have been limited as he had ended his prefecture of Egypt in disgrace. Augustus ordered Gallus south into Arabia Felix in order to conclude treaties or subdue the inhabitants into acceptance of Roman might. The expedition is well documented by Gallus' *amicus*, the geographer Strabo, who could not hide the ineptitude and military incompetence of his patron. The Roman army was devastated by six months of heat, hunger and defeats brought about by the treachery of their guide. The mission was a complete failure, with the greater part of the Roman force lost, Gallus was recalled to Rome in ignominy. The disgrace associated with the name of Gallus perhaps explains why Velleius, in his brief summary of Sejanus' connections, makes no mention of his adoption. Sejanus' son, Capito Aeli(nus), would appear from his nomenclature to have been adopted by a Capito, possibly C. Fonteius Capito Aelianus, the consul of AD 12 and proconsul of Asia in AD 23/24, but he had sons of his own, making the adoption appear unlikely. A more likely candidate is C. Ateius Capito, a famous jurist and the consul of AD 5 AD and *curator aquarum* from AD 13–22, when death ended his tenure of this post.[48]

In 1 BC the young Sejanus 'became a follower of Gaius Caesar', perhaps as a military tribune.[49] It is possible that Strabo used his connections with either Gaius or Augustus to gain this appointment for his son. However, Strabo's position and office at this time are unknown. His mother was connected to the Junii, but her brother was a decade away from his consulship. Maecenas had died in 8 BC, and it has to be doubted that the Terentias were still alive or commanded any influence. Perhaps the family connection to Q. Aelius Tubero was employed. Both Dio and Tacitus allude to another powerful patron who propagated the rise of Sejanus: Marcus Gabius Apicius. Dio describes Sejanus as 'formerly a favourite' of this Roman gourmet, whose vast wealth allowed him to advance luxurious living to a point where it even offended the sensibilities of the Roman elite. Tacitus adds a few salacious details about how Sejanus developed this connection, for it was 'not without a rumour that he had disposed of his virtue at a price to Apicius, a rich man and a prodigal'.[50] Ignoring the less savoury aspect of Tacitus' account, the historian is clearly alluding to Apicius' influence in acquiring the position on Gaius' staff. The hope would have been that Sejanus would come to the imperial heir's attention and a bond of friendship would be established with the Caesar.

Banquets were an extension of Roman political life, and Apicius' banquets were spectacular. A century later, Pliny wrote in disgust at the money spent by this obsessive gastronome on entertaining his guests: 'Apicius, the deepest abyss of all the prodigals, taught that flamingo's tongue has superb flavour.' Pliny continued that Apicius was 'born to enjoy every extravagant luxury that could be contrived'.[51] Another story relates how Apicius left his villa at Minturnae in Campania, where he had been dining on giant prawns, when he learnt that the prawns in Libya were bigger. Arriving off the African coast, he could see from the ship that in fact he had been misled, and without disembarking, returned home confident in the supreme quality of his own seafood dishes.[52] Roman formal banquets, or *convivia*, were a statement of status and influence as much as the villa or townhouse they were set in or the clothes worn by the hosts. Food was presented on gold and silver platters, and guests counted the number of courses and dishes that were served, and commented on the quality of the entertainment provided. Invitation to such occasions was a recognition of *amicitiae* and was a great honour; the closer to the host you were sat, the greater that honour. Banquets allowed the guests or host to make requests or pass on petitions with a greater chance of success than could be expected in the crowded morning *salutatio*, where there was little or no opportunity for a private conversation.[53]

Apicius' status and influence should not be underestimated, despite being an equestrian from the municipalities. He moved in the very highest of circles. A story retold by Seneca tells how Tiberius was walking through a fish market accompanied by Apicius and Publius Octavius when he spotted a large red mullet and wagered which of his companions would buy it. The bidding went past 5,000 sesterces before Apicius deferred.[54] Another story in Pliny has Apicius persuading Tiberius' son Drusus never to eat *cymae*, which are the tops of cabbages, as they were too common a food for a man of his social standing.[55] The consuls of AD 28, including L. Junius Blaesus, the son of Junia's brother, also dined at Apicius' villa, with Blaesus and the Roman historian Asconius Pedianus engaging with their host in a discussion on gastronomy.[56] Syme also suggests that Apicius was an *amicus* of Gaius. If so, he would have enjoyed sampling the culinary pleasures of the eastern provinces during his travels; however, it is difficult to imagine him relishing the difficulties of the journey.[57] Both Dio and Tacitus recognize the importance of Apicius in furthering the career of Sejanus, a relationship that appears to have been cemented with the marriage of Sejanus to his daughter, Apicata.[58]

Gaius had been invested with proconsular imperium and sent out in 1 BC to tour the legions on the Danube and the Balkans, accompanied by a large entourage. The purpose of this expedition was to provide the Caesar with the opportunity to learn how to rule, as well as be seen by the legions he was one day expected to command.[59] His chief advisor was Marcus Lollius (consul in 21 BC), a close *amicus* of Augustus. His experience in both the military and administrative sphere was meant to be instructive. He had fought at the Battle of Actium, been a governor in Gallia Comata and Macedonia, where he successfully subdued a Thracian tribe, and then as governor of Galatia in Asia Minor he incorporated that newly acquired territory into the administration of the Empire. However, his record was not entirely blemish-free. In 17 BC, during his governorship of Gaul, a number of Germanic tribes crossed the Rhine and inflicted a minor defeat on the Roman forces commanded by Lollius. Tiberius, accompanied by Augustus, came north to rectify the situation. Tiberius replaced Lollius in command of the Gallic legions and led them to victory. Lollius believed the glory of the successful conclusion of the war should have been his, and he never forgave Tiberius. Lollius now used his position to poison the mind of Gaius against his adopted father, Tiberius, who remained in an enforced exile on Rhodes. Another important figure sent to advise the young heir was P. Sulpicius Quirinius, a close *amicus* of Tiberius. Quirinius had defeated the Marmaridae, an African tribe inhabiting the lands south of Cyrene, for which he was probably rewarded with the consulship of 12 BC. He then spent time as governor of Galatia in successfully campaigning against the Homonadenses, who lived in the mountainous regions of the province, and was rewarded with a triumph in Rome.[60] Sejanus would have learnt much from these two men, and especially from Lollius' errors of judgement. Also on the expedition was the historian Velleius Paterculus, who held the post of military tribune attached to one of the legions accompanying Gaius.[61]

News from the East now provided the young heir with the opportunity to develop his diplomatic experience. The new Parthian king had deposed the ruler of Armenia, a kingdom over which Augustus claimed sovereignty. Augustus looked to a political solution rather than war, and Gaius was dispatched to broker an agreement with the Parthians. The party now travelled from the Balkan provinces to Athens, where they were met by the leading men of every town in a formal welcoming ceremony, the *adventus*. There was no war, so their pace was leisurely.[62] From Athens, their next stop was either Samos or Chios, depending on the source.[63] Tiberius now travelled to pay his respects to his stepson from his island exile on

Rhodes. Although Tiberius had at first retired to this island retreat at his own initiative – to the disgust of Augustus, who felt he had abandoned his responsibilities – he now found that his position had become increasingly dangerous when his frequent requests to return to Rome were refused. Tiberius probably hoped to persuade Gaius to use his influence with Augustus to allow him to return to the capital. His hopes were to be dashed. M. Lollius had worked his poison on the young and impressionable Gaius. Sejanus was probably a witness to the formal reception Tiberius was granted. Suetonius describes the meeting as 'chilly', perhaps an understatement when compared to Dio's description of the audience where Tiberius 'humiliated himself and grovelled at the feet, not only of Gaius, but also of all the associates of Gaius'.[64] Sejanus' lowly position meant he would merely have been an observer of the dishonour done to the once-powerful deputy to the emperor.[65]

Tiberius' position soon deteriorated further. His enemies circled their vulnerable prey. A letter was sent to the emperor informing him of a rumour that some centurions whom Tiberius had appointed had returned to their units from leave and were distributing treasonous messages. Tiberius received a letter from Augustus describing these allegations. A desperate Tiberius sent letters protesting his innocence to Augustus, requesting someone be sent to observe his actions and provide proof of his innocence. On a later occasion Gaius and his *amici* were invited to a banquet where Tiberius' name cropped up, and a guest rose to say that if Gaius gave the order he would sail straight to Rhodes and 'fetch back the Exile's head' – for he had come to be known simply as 'the Exile'. This incident brought home to Tiberius that his situation was not only worrying but perilous, and he pleaded most urgently for a recall to Rome, 'Livia supporting him with equal warmth'.[66] For Sejanus, the lessons of courtly politics must have been instructive. Tiberius had absented himself from the centre of power and patronage. He no longer had access to the emperor and could no longer act as a broker of imperial *beneficia*. Consequently, many of his *amici* deserted him.[67] Furthermore, the public withdrawal of imperial *amicitiae* had often proved fatal. All were aware that Tiberius was isolated, with only his mother Livia to defend him at court. Sejanus, described universally in the ancient sources as astute and highly intelligent, would not make the same mistake, positioning himself at the centre of power in the shadow of the emperor's *auctoritas*, becoming indispensable to his patron by becoming an *amicus Caesaris*. The philosopher Epictetus warns his readers of the hardships of being an *amicus Caesaris*, attending the early-morning *salutatio* at the palace or enduring the humiliation of dining with the emperor as a social inferior. Sejanus embraced these privations.[68]

Leaving Tiberius behind to his fate, Gaius and his entourage set sail for Syria. In AD 2 embassies were exchanged with the Parthian king and a meeting arranged on the banks of the Euphrates. No doubt Sejanus was a witness to these events, described intimately by Velleius, who many years later remembered it in vivid detail. Gaius 'met with the king of the Parthians, a young man of very tall stature, on an island situated in the middle of the Euphrates, each leader attended by a retinue of the same size. This spectacle was truly glorious and memorable – the Roman army standing on one bank, with that of the Parthians opposite them on the other side, while two of the most eminent leaders of their respective empires and of the world came together – and it was my luck to set eyes on it as a military tribune in the early stages of my career ... It was the Parthian who dined first with Gaius on our bank, and later Gaius dined with the king on the bank held by the enemy.'[69] The vast armies, drawn up on either bank in full battle array, made a lasting impression upon the junior officer as he stood before the ranks of the legionaries from his own legion. We are not told what impression this display made upon the young Sejanus. Years later the Praetorian Prefect was to intimidate the Senate by inviting them to a parade of the Guard displayed in full battle array. Perhaps the meeting with the Parthian king had been instructive to the young man.

The thaw in relations between the Romans and Parthians was the saving of Tiberius and precipitated the demise of his enemy M. Lollius. For unknown reasons, the Parthians made known to Gaius that Lollius had been accepting bribes from them. Gaius confronted his advisor, whom he dismissed from his service. With the loss of imperial favour, Lollius took a draft of poison a few days later. Tiberius was never one to forgive or forget. Many years later Tiberius composed a panegyric in praise of Sulpicius Quirinius, who took Lollius' place as the main guardian and advisor to Gaius. He moved from lauding his *amicus* to attacking the memory of his dead tormentor, 'whom he accused of instigating the cross-grained and provocative attitude of Gaius Caesar'.[70] Quirinius assiduously courted Tiberius' favour, paying him due respect in his island exile. Livia at last prevailed upon her husband's obstinacy and Augustus requested Gaius' permission to allow his stepfather to return to Rome. With Lollius now gone, the young Caesar acquiesced but on condition that Tiberius refrain from entering public life. Tiberius returned meekly to the capital and after probably attending the ceremony celebrating the entry of his natural son Drusus into manhood, he retired to a private life in his house in the Gardens of Maecenas, well away from the centre of the city.[71] However, fortune's wheel would turn once more, propelling the reluctant émigré to the forefront of imperial politics.

Gaius had been establishing his credentials as future emperor by campaigning in Arabia, perhaps against the Nabatean Arabs. We do not know if Sejanus took part. During AD 2, the young Caesar received the news of the death of his brother Lucius at Massilia in Gaul.[72] The two had grown up together, and it must have been a heavy emotional blow. His duties took precedence over his personal loss, so he entered Armenia at the head of an army to return the kingdom to Roman suzerainty after the collapse of diplomacy. However, whilst laying siege to a small town, he was tricked into a meeting where he was attacked and wounded. The wound festered, and Gaius went into a slow mental and physical decline. Velleius criticizes Gaius' advisors for his deterioration as the emperor found 'his mental functioning to be less beneficial to the state. Nor was there any shortage of people around him to encourage his vices with sycophancy – adulation is always there as the companion of great fortune – and the upshot was that he was induced to prefer the prospect of growing old in some far-off and truly remote corner of the world over returning to Rome.'[73] Velleius would never criticize these advisors if Sejanus had been numbered amongst them, as in AD 30, when his history was completed, Sejanus was at the height of his powers. As his mental and physical condition weakened, Gaius requested permission from Augustus to retire from public life and remain in Syria. The emperor impressed upon him the need to return to Rome. As Sejanus was attached to the entourage of Gaius, he probably accompanied the rapidly fading Caesar as he boarded a trading vessel to Lycia. The journey was probably too much for him, and Gaius died at Limyra, a small city on the south-east coast of Asia Minor, on 21 February AD 4.[74] Sejanus would have accompanied the body home, where it was laid to rest in the Mausoleum of Augustus.

With both Gaius and Lucius dead, Augustus' plans for the succession lay in ruins. He was 66 years old and could not be expected to live much longer. One direct descendant remained in the person of Agrippa Postumus, the youngest brother of Gaius and Lucius, who at 16 years of age was thought too young to be considered as the heir apparent. However, Augustus adopted him, indicating that he remained a possible successor. The emperor needed an experienced and capable helmsman to guide the Empire upon his death, but he also wanted a direct descendant to ultimately hold the tiller. Tiberius was consequently thrust back into public life. He was also adopted by Augustus, but he had to agree to adopt Germanicus in turn, despite the fact he had a natural son of his own, Drusus, whose mother Vipsania, Augustus had forced him to divorce in 11 BC. Tiberius put duty to the state before his own personal considerations. The adoption of Germanicus was probably undertaken more willingly as he was the son of Tiberius' brother Nero Claudius Drusus and Antonia the Younger, the daughter of Mark Antony and Augustus' sister Octavia. The tenuous bloodline to Augustus would be made far stronger by Germanicus' marriage to Augustus' granddaughter Agrippina the Elder, the daughter of Julia and Marcus Agrippa. Their children would be able to claim direct descent from Augustus. Clearly, Tiberius was Augustus' reluctant choice of successor, but his hand had been forced by fate and the expectation of the emperor's imminent death. Tiberius was given *proconsular imperium* and the *tribunicia potestas* for a ten-year period, making his legal powers equal to those held by Augustus. Obedient after his experiences on Rhodes, Tiberius accepted these arrangements, which made him co-regent and heir, but he was essentially the guardian and regent for his adopted son Germanicus. There were those who knew from their previous treatment of Tiberius that their future chances of advancement, honours and other *beneficia* were seriously threatened under the prospective Principate of Tiberius. Attempts were made to undermine Tiberius' legitimacy by suggesting that his ascendancy was a result of the scheming of his mother. Gossip was spread suggesting both Gaius and Lucius were poisoned by Livia; hardly credible but clearly indicating an opposition to the succession of Tiberius. [75] In AD 7 Tiberius' position was strengthened by the fall from favour of Agrippa Postumus, who was banished to the island of Planasia.

Agrippa Postumus had increasingly become a threat to the succession and the position of Tiberius as heir. Dio describes him as 'slavishly boorish' in that he had a 'violent disposition' and 'acted immoderately'. Tacitus calls him 'uncouth' and 'stupidly ferocious', a description mirrored by Suetonius, who calls him 'vulgar and brutal'. However, Agrippa Postumus had legitimate grievances as, despite being Augustus' grandson and adopted son, 'he often reproached Augustus himself for not giving him the inheritance his father [Agrippa] had left him'. When his father had died, the part of his estate left to his son in his will was retained by Augustus. This was perfectly legal as the emperor was his father through adoption and so entitled to retain his son's inheritance until he became an adult. However, as he entered manhood and the vast wealth that should have been his remained out of reach, his frustrations and anger grew. Furthermore, it was clear to all that what he felt was his birth right as the direct descendant of the emperor had been usurped by the position of Tiberius. His claim to the throne was better than that of Tiberius, or indeed that of Germanicus. Postumus clearly blamed Livia.

Events came to a head in AD 6. An uprising had begun in the previous year in Illyricum and Tiberius had been sent to crush it. The campaign was extremely difficult as the terrain supported the effective use of guerrilla warfare. Tiberius requested additional soldiers, but it was Germanicus who was preferred to take command of the reinforcements.[76] The slight was too much for Agrippa Postumus, who is included by Suetonius in a list of conspirators against Augustus. Salacious propaganda attacking Augustus was distributed in Rome by a Junius Novatus, an act referred to by Velleius as an example of Postumus' 'reckless behaviour' that 'alienated the feelings of the man who was both his father and grandfather'. Novatus was probably one of a group of young men who had previously attached themselves to the conspiracy of his mother Julia, and they looked to restore their fortunes by supporting the aspirations of Postumus. Novatus was punished with a fine but Postumus was disinherited and exiled to a villa near the town of Surrentum on the Campanian coast. There it appears his behaviour worsened, and in AD 7 he was placed under tight guard on the prison island of Planasia, halfway between the coast of Tuscany and Corsica.[77]

In AD 8 his sister Julia the Younger was exiled to the island of Tremirus in the Adriatic for having an affair with the aristocrat Decimus Junius Silanus, their child being disowned and, on the orders of Augustus, exposed. Silanus went into voluntary exile when the imperial friendship was withdrawn, whilst the poet Ovid was also implicated and exiled to the Greek city of Tomis on the Black Sea coast. Julia's husband L. Aemilus Paulus had been previously executed for treason. The charge of adultery was often employed to hide the politically embarrassing reality of conspiracy within the imperial house, as implied by the extensive list of accomplices associated with the fall of both Julias. Marriage was an official part of dynastic policy, so adultery was in itself a political act. The number of conspiracies involving direct descendants of Augustus after the adoption of Tiberius must be more than a coincidence, and are more likely to have been a reaction to Augustus' plans for the succession. There remained those who still looked to Agrippa Postumus, Julia the Elder and Julia the Younger as the legitimate heirs, and whilst they remained alive there continued a threat to the planned succession of Tiberius. Suetonius refers to a failed plot late in the reign of Augustus by the otherwise unknown Audasius and Epicadus to release Postumus and his sister Julia and bring them to the legions.[78]

Frustratingly, our sources fail to describe the whereabouts of Sejanus from the death of Gaius in the East to his appointment to the Praetorian Prefecture in AD 14. In a letter written by Sejanus to Tiberius in AD 25, the Praetorian Prefect provides a clue as to his roles in these years. It is evident that he had access to both emperors, as he states that 'owing to the benevolence of the prince's father Augustus, followed by so many expressions of approval from Tiberius, he had formed the habit of carrying his hopes and his vows to the imperial ears as to the gods'. From Sejanus' appointment as Prefect of the Guard, we must assume that Tiberius knew him well and trusted his loyalty. Furthermore, the command of the nine Praetorian cohorts suggests he must have had substantial military experience. Tiberius' campaigns in Germany and Pannonia would have provided such an opportunity.[79]

According to Josephus, Sejanus was a friend of Tiberius' brother Nero Claudius Drusus, who campaigned in Germany from 14 BC to his death in the summer of 9 BC. Most equestrians started their careers as a *praefectus cohortis*, *tribunus militum* or *praefectus alae*. However, Strabo's connections may have allowed his son to avoid these junior posts and instead, Sejanus may have joined the general's staff as a tribune, but his youth would have precluded extensive military experience. Tacitus records that Tiberius Sextus Vistilius, who also was a close friend of Nero Claudius Drusus, had 'transferred to his own retinue'. The likeliest time for this to take place was when he took over his brother's campaign beyond the Rhine in 8 BC. This may also have been the time Sejanus joined Tiberius' staff as a junior officer. It is unlikely that it was Tiberius who then appointed Sejanus to Gaius' embassy to the East, as he was an exile on Rhodes from 6 BC until AD 2. The influence of Apicius may have been at work. Restored to favour in AD 4, Tiberius now moved against the Marcomanni, who threatened Germany, Pannonia and Noricum from their position in modern Bohemia. Plans for a substantial operation beyond the Danube turned to dust in AD 6 when a huge revolt spread from Pannonia to Dalmatia and Illyria. A rapid peace treaty was concluded with the Marcomanni, but the campaign against the rebels took a heavy toll and Roman losses were substantial. Veterans were recalled to the legions and reinforcements were dispatched from Italy by Germanicus. Augustus recognized the threat posed by the revolt, writing to his heir with fulsome praise: 'Your summer campaigns, dear Tiberius, deserve my heartiest of praise; I am sure no other man alive could have conducted them more capably than yourself in the face of so many difficulties and the war-weariness of the troops. All those who served with you agree with me that Ennius' well-known line about Quintius Fabius Cunctator should be amended in your favour: "alone he saved by his watchful eye."'[80]

In AD 7 disaster was narrowly averted when five legions brought from the East were ambushed in the Volcean Marshes near Sirmium. They managed to extricate themselves, but significant losses were incurred. The survivors joined Tiberius' five legions, creating a massive force of ten legions, supplemented with over seventy auxiliary cohorts, ten cavalry cohorts and more than 10,000 veterans. These forces burnt, ravaged and destroyed the land held by the rebels, using famine as their weapon. AD 8 saw some of the rebel leaders defeated, captured or betrayed until their last major stronghold at Andretium was besieged and stormed. Tiberius had shown himself to be a remarkable general and was awarded a triumph, while Germanicus and other commanders were also honoured. However, five days after reports reached Rome of Tiberius' final subjugation of the revolt, news also came of the destruction of three legions in Germany. P. Quinctilius Varus, tricked by Arminius, the supposed allied leader of Cherusci, led his unwitting column into the depths of the Teutoburg Forest, where they were massacred, almost to a man. Tiberius had to abandon his triumph and was sent to restore the situation with the remaining Rhine legions and others drawn from Rhaetia, Spain and Illyricum. The dream of a frontier resting on the Elbe was abandoned, but by AD 12 Tiberius was able to return to Rome for his delayed Pannonian triumph.[81]

Logic suggests that Sejanus held some military posts during these campaigns. In his letter to Tiberius in AD 25, he acknowledges the debt he owed to the patronage of both Augustus and Tiberius. Furthermore, in AD 14, after being appointed to the Praetorian Prefecture alongside his father Seius Strabo, he accompanied Tiberius' son Drusus to Pannonia to suppress the mutiny of its three legions, the VIII Augusta, XIX Hispana and XV Apollinaris. All three had been involved in the suppression of the revolt in Pannonia, Dalmatia and Illyricum.[82] Our sources suggest Sejanus accompanied Drusus as his uncle, Junius Blaesus, was the governor of Pannonia. It is difficult to understand how this familial link could have been of any benefit to Drusus unless the loyalty of Blaesus was questioned, which it clearly wasn't. A more likely but unsubstantiated theory is that Sejanus had served as an officer in one or more of the Pannonian legions and it was thought by Tiberius that he could use his influence, knowledge and experience of these soldiers to help resolve this extremely dangerous situation. The formalized equestrian career structure evolved only gradually through the first century. It was only in the second half of the century that the equestrian *cursus honorum* became established. The usual career path for an *eques* consisted of three military posts, followed by procuratorial positions in Italy and the provinces, and then promotion to 'secretarial' positions with the emperor, including the *ab epistulis Graecis* or *Latinis,* then the most prestigious offices of Prefect of the Vigiles, the Annona, Egypt and the Praetorian Prefecture. This, however, was in the future and the equestrian career at the turn of the first century was in a state of flux.[83]

Sejanus' rise has as much to with his own abilities as with the network of *amicitiae* he and his father had developed. Tacitus provides an insight into his character which is tainted in part by his own senatorial prejudices and subsequent events; Sejanus 'was a man hardy by constitution, fearless by temperament; skilled to conceal himself and to incriminate his neighbour; cringing at once and insolent; orderly and modest to outward view, at heart possessed by a towering ambition, which impelled him at whiles to lavishness and luxury, but oftener to industry and vigilance'.[84] Surprisingly, the obsequious account of Velleius supports Tacitus' estimation: 'Sejanus himself has a great capacity for work and loyal service, and his physique matches his mental vigour. He is a man who combines old–time gravity with cheery light-heartedness, and one who, when he is in action, seems to be at ease.' He continues that 'in appearance and lifestyle he is relaxed, but his mind never sleeps.'[85] Clearly, he was a man who was widely respected even by his opponents. The supreme politician, he was all things to all men. Both friends and enemies recognized his abilities, efficiency, intelligence and capacity for hard work. There can be little doubt that he was highly ambitious; however, this had to be balanced by the fact his appointment to the Praetorian Prefecture suggests his loyalty was not questioned by Tiberius. Dio proposes the close relationship between the emperor and Sejanus was based on the similarity of their characters.[86] This does appear surprising, as Tiberius is often described as cold and withdrawn, whereas Sejanus could, when circumstances dictated, be 'relaxed', 'light-hearted' and 'cheery'. Ability was not enough, though, in Imperial Rome. Many an able man's career would fade into obscurity without powerful patrons and *amici.* Sejanus' career would have been supported by his family, possibly including the senatorial Tubero and his uncle Junius Blaesus. Dio suggests the early part of his career was supported by Apicius, which is confirmed by his marriage to Apicata.[87] His father's appointment to the Praetorian Prefecture in the later part of Augustus' reign would have placed him in a position to press his son's case in private conversations with the emperor. However, Sejanus' greatest patron was Tiberius himself. Tacitus wonders how this man who was so private and solitary, 'a man inscrutable to others became to Sejanus alone unguarded and unreserved'.[88] That trust would have taken years to develop, a trust no doubt assiduously cultivated by the young Sejanus.

Chapter 2

Crisis: AD 14

Tiberius would often 'declare that he was holding a wolf by the ears'. (Suetonius, *Tiberius* 25)

The death of Augustus had long been anticipated and prepared for. Despite this, a serious crisis developed that threatened the succession of Tiberius and propelled Sejanus to the forefront of imperial politics. In AD 13 the Senate passed a law giving Tiberius equal *imperium* to that of Augustus throughout the Empire, and Augustus had made his final adjustments to his will. Important positions in both Rome and the provinces were placed in the hands of men whose loyalty to the Principate or Tiberius was unquestionable. Germanicus, as the adopted son of Tiberius, held the command of the eight legions on the Rhine, as well as administrative control over Gaul. Seius Strabo was the Praetorian Prefect at the emperor's side, with his brother-in-law Q. Junius Blaesus governor of Pannonia with command over its legions. Many of the legionaries along the northern frontier had served under Tiberius over the previous decade. Marcus Aemilius Lepidus, the consul of 6 AD who had served as a commander under Tiberius in the suppression of the revolt in Pannonia and Illyricum, held Spain. His loyalty was further strengthened by the betrothal of his daughter Aemelia Lepida to Drusus, Germanicus' son. The senatorial province of Africa was held by Augustus' *amicus* L. Nonius Asprenas, who was married to a daughter of L. Calpurnius Piso the Pontifex, a close *amicus* of Tiberius. L. Calpurnius Piso was City Prefect with command over the urban cohorts. This was an important office, as rioting was expected to erupt when news of the death of Augustus reached the streets of the capital. The grain supply, so important in ensuring the compliance of Rome's populace, was placed in the hands of C. Turranius, who had held the prefecture of Egypt up to 2/1 BC. He was an experienced administrator and subsequently held the prefecture of the Annona for the whole of Tiberius' reign.[1] The important province of Syria was governed by Q. Caecilius Metellus Creticus Silanus, a close *amicus* of

Germanicus, who had betrothed his daughter to Nero, the eldest son of Germanicus.[2]

Never before in the history of Rome had imperial power been passed from one ruler to another. Augustus was the undisputed ruler of Rome, his position hidden behind a façade of Republican powers and widespread acceptance of his *auctoritas*, an authority based upon his social and political standing. Tiberius was his recognized successor; however, he was a member of the Julian house only through adoption. The blood of Augustus did not run through his veins. For some, he was an upstart, the legitimate heirs being Germanicus or Agrippa Postumus. Other potential opponents, it was feared, would look to a restoration of the Republic and the renewal of real political power in the hands of the senatorial nobility. Rioting, revolt and political crisis were anticipated.[3]

Augustus had become increasingly frail. The Senate had regularly met in the Temple of Apollo, which had been incorporated into the palace complex, yet the emperor had still not been able to attend. Instead, the preparation of senatorial business had been delegated to a small committee of advisors consisting of the leading nobles and *amici* of Augustus, who then put their decisions to the vote of the full Senate for approval. This clearly undermined the authority of that eminent body, but the realities of Augustus' failing health excluded any other option. Seius Strabo may have been a member of this committee, but our sources are silent on its composition. During the summer of AD 14, a rumour was spread that the 76-year-old emperor had made a secret visit to his grandson Agrippa Postumus on his prison island of Planasia and had become reconciled with him. This occurred at the very moment Augustus' health had taken a turn for the worse, and to add substance to the story it was alleged the aged noble Fabius Maximus had accompanied him. Maximus had recently died and some suggested that he had taken his own life. Furthermore, at her husband's funeral, his understandably distraught wife was supposedly heard to blame herself 'for the cause of her husband's destruction'. Most historians have dismissed the idea that such a did take place. Planasia lies south-west of the island of Elba in the Tyrrhenian Sea, and would involve a difficult sea voyage at a time when 'the malady of Augustus began to take a graver form'. Another rumour suggested his wife Livia was poisoning her husband.[4] Opponents of Tiberius' succession were hard at work undermining the legitimacy of the recognized heir in favour of a man who had a direct bloodline to Augustus. This 'visit' would have been used to legitimize the succession of Agrippa Postumus as having been sanctioned by Augustus. Julia the Elder, Augustus' disgraced daughter and Tiberius' ex-wife, remained in the town of Rhegium in the toe of Italy. Her daughter Julia the Younger, the sister of Agrippa Postumus and Germanicus' wife Agrippina, remained on the island of Tremirus in the Adriatic. Whilst these three lived, the enemies of Tiberius would look to the restoration of their position.[5]

Augustus' health improved sufficiently to allow him to travel to the imperial villas in Campania and so escape the heat of Rome. The country air appears to have aided a recovery, as he then travelled to the island of Capri, located just to the south of the Bay of Naples, for a few days, and then on 1 August journeyed to Neapolis to attend a gymnastic festival held in his honour. Livia and Tiberius had accompanied him. The party then moved on to Beneventum, where Tiberius left to take up the governorship of Illyricum, whilst Augustus and Livia set off back to Rome. Augustus had for a number of days been suffering from pains in his abdomen, which now grew significantly worse, forcing them to stop at an imperial villa at Nola, once owned by Augustus' natural father Octavius. Augustus asked to be laid in the room in which his father had died. The end was drawing near. Urgent messages were sent to Tiberius requesting his return. The sources are contradictory on the question of whether Tiberius managed to return in time to speak to his adopted father before he died.[6] The news of the emperor's death was delayed. Livia placed Praetorians around the villa, restricting access and regularly issuing optimistic notices on the health of the now-deceased emperor. On 19 August Tiberius and Livia were ready to simultaneously announce the death of the first emperor and the accession of his successor.[7]

Tiberius was, upon his arrival at Nola, already exercising sole imperial power. This was signified 'by calling on the Praetorians to provide him with a bodyguard; which was to be Emperor in fact and appearance'.[8] The guard had become the very symbol of the emperor's position as they represented his position as the ultimate arbiter of life and death. The words of the Greek Stoic Epictetus encapsulate the fear engendered by the position of the emperor as commander of these soldiers: 'Show me the swords of the guards. See how big they are, and how sharp. What then do these big swords do? They kill.' The philosopher elaborates:

> What makes the tyrant formidable? The guards, you say, and their swords, and the men of the bedchamber and those who exclude

them who would enter. Why then if you bring a boy [child] to the tyrant when he is with his guards, is he not afraid; or is it because the child does not understand these things? If then any man does understand what guards are and that they have swords, and comes to the tyrant for this very purpose because he wishes to die on account of some circumstance and seeks to die easily by the hand of another, is he afraid of the guards? No, for he wishes for the thing which makes the guards formidable.[9]

Tiberius had been recognized long before as co-regent, possessing equal *imperium* to Augustus and *tribunicia potestas*. His military record gave him an *auctoritas* that far eclipsed that of any potential rival. Yet he was a Claudian and his position as heir came through adoption, unlike Agrippa Postumus or his own adopted son Germanicus. He remained vulnerable, but he acted quickly to secure the throne.

Messengers were dispatched to the commanders of the legions and provincial governors in the name of the new emperor and to the Senate in Rome.[10] Upon receipt of the news, the soldiers were to take the oath of loyalty to Tiberius. Velleius, a contemporary, describes the atmosphere in the capital that greeted the announcement of Augustus' death. It was characterized by 'alarm in the Senate, the anxiety of the people, the apprehension in Rome, the fine line that we saw drawn between safety and disaster'.[11] The Senate was summoned by the consuls and the oath of loyalty taken to the new emperor. The vow, taken before the gods, was made in order of status: 'The consuls, Sextus Pompeius and Sextus Appuleius, first took the oath of allegiance to Tiberius Caesar. It was taken in their presence by Seius Strabo and Gaius Turranius, chiefs respectively of the Praetorian cohorts and the corn department. The senators, the soldiers, and the populace followed.'[12] The order reflects the increased importance of the equestrian post-holders of these offices, who ranked above the senatorial ex-consuls and almost all serving magistrates in the capital, their position only eclipsed by the serving consuls. Seius Strabo had probably accompanied Augustus and Livia on their visit to Campania with a proportion of the guard. Tiberius, fearing rioting in the streets of the capital or opposition from prominent senators and equestrians, must have ordered his Praetorian Prefect to return to take command of the remaining cohorts and use their fearsome presence to ensure order and unquestioned obedience to the new regime.

According to Tacitus, the loyalty of a number of leading nobles was questioned by Augustus when discussing possible rivals for the Principate on his death. Tacitus writes:

> [He considered] those who were competent and disinclined, who were inadequate and willing, or who were at once able and desirous – had described Manius Lepidus [Marcus Aemilius Lepidus][13] as capable but disdainful, Asinius Gallus as eager and unfit, Lucius Arruntius as not undeserving and bold enough to venture, should the opportunity arise. The first two names are not disputed; in some versions Arruntius is replaced by Gnaeus Piso.[14]

Marcus Lepidus could trace his ancestry back to the Scipios who achieved fame in the defeat of Hannibal and the destruction of Carthage, but was surely trusted by Tiberius, under whose command he had served in Illyria. In AD 14 he controlled the three legions in northern Spain, a responsibility he would never have been given if there was any question over his loyalty. His daughter was engaged to Drusus, the son of Germanicus, and he continued to hold prestigious posts under Tiberius and remained influential with the emperor. Velleius describes him as 'closest to the name and station of the Caesars'. Capable but disdainful is probably an accurate description of him. Asinius Gallus was loathed by Tiberius. An *amicus* of Augustus, he had married Vipsania, Tiberius' first wife whom Augustus had forced him to divorce in order to marry Julia the Elder. Tiberius was devoted to Vipsania and ultimately despised Julia. To add insult to injury, Gallus had tried to adopt Tiberius and Vipsania's son Drusus. Tiberius would never forgive. Added to this, Asinius Gallus had been governor of Asia during Tiberius' enforced exile on Rhodes and there is no mention of a deferential visit by the governor. Tiberius was also never one to forget a social and political slight. Finally, there is Gallus' abrasive personality: he was proud and arrogant to a fault. The accession of Tiberius ended his career. He held no further offices, nor was he granted any further honours. Strive as he might to regain imperial favour and be acknowledged as the leading noble of the Senate, his star fell on 19 August AD 14 and it would never rise again. Eager and unfit is probably an apt description of him. L. Arruntius had been ennobled through his father's consulship, an office he then shared with Marcus Lepidus in AD 6. He was one of the most highly respected members of the Senate and possessed enormous wealth. He was honoured with the governorship of Hispania Citerior in AD 25, but he was refused permission to travel to his province due to the suspicions of the emperor. His influence and independence made him a figure of hate to both Sejanus and his successor in the office of Praetorian Prefect, Macro. Tiberius gave this powerful noble the status he desired without providing him with the opportunity to use the resources of the state and army to move against him. Tiberius heeded Augustus' advice to the letter.[15]

According to Tacitus, Gnaeus Calpurnius Piso's name is included in the list of potential rivals in some of his sources instead of Lucius Arruntius. Piso came from an ancient and illustrious noble family, the Calpurnii Pisones. Alongside his brother Lucius Caplurnius Piso, also known as Piso the Augur, he was a close *amicus* of both Augustus and Tiberius. Gnaeus had been honoured by Augustus by sharing the consulship of 7 BC with Tiberius. He then held the governorships of Africa and Hispania Tarraconensis. His tenure of both posts was marked by arrogance, brutality and cruelty. In Africa, Seneca criticises Cn. Piso for unjustly putting to death two soldiers and a centurion, whilst in AD 20 he stood accused of 'intrigue and cupidity' during his administration of Spain. An impulsive, arrogant and self-serving figure emerges, a judgement that is borne out by subsequent events. Despite this, Tiberius clearly trusted him, appointing him to the governorship of Syria in AD 17 in order to keep a close rein on his adopted son Germanicus. At the opening address of Cn. Piso's trial in AD 20 the emperor refers to him as his *amicus*. His loyalty to Tiberius was never questioned, but he lacked the acumen to understand his restricted role as an aristocratic noble in the Principate. He continued to behave and act as though the aristocracy retained their political independence, as had existed under the Republic. He would pay a heavy price for his naivety.[16]

The threat that the aristocracy posed was demonstrated by the fate of some of their children. Lucius Arruntius' adopted son Lucius Arruntius Camillus Scribonianus used his governorship of Dalmatia to revolt against the emperor Claudius in AD 41. Marcus Aemilius Lepidus, as well as having a daughter married to Germanicus' son Drusus, had a son of the same name who was married to Germanicus' daughter Drusilla at some point after AD 33. He was a close *amicus* of the emperor Gaius, known to history as Caligula, who named him as his heir in AD 37 but was executed two years later charged with conspiring against him.[17] In AD 16 the noble Marcus Scibonius Libo Drusus was charged with treason, his claim to the throne based primarily on his noble ancestry with supporters 'pointing to his great-grandfather Pompey, to his great-aunt Scribonia (at one time the consort of Augustus), to his cousinship with the Caesars, and his mansion crowded with ancestral portraits'. Members of the senatorial aristocracy would pose a threat to many emperors throughout the history of Imperial Rome.[18]

The declaration of Augustus' death moved the opponents of Tiberius to act. Clemens, a slave of Agrippa Postumus, was tasked with catching a ship to Planasia and there rescuing his master from captivity and bringing him to the legions on the Rhine; a similar plan that had been unsuccessfully attempted before Augustus' death.[19] However, unbeknown to Agrippa's supporters, a death warrant had been issued and was now on its way to the island prison. Clemens boarded a slow merchant ship, which delayed his arrival. Agrippa had already been executed by the time he arrived. However, the loyal slave managed to acquire the funerary ashes and, returning to the mainland, he embarked on an even more ambitious plan. Clemens played upon his similarity to his dead master and, growing his beard, posed as Agrippa Postumus in towns and cities, presenting himself as the rightful heir to Augustus. In this, he had the support of 'many in the imperial household, as well as equites and senators, who were said to have given him the support of their wealth and the benefit of their advice'. Over the next two years the backing for the imperial imposter grew.[20]

In the meantime, Tiberius and Livia made their way to Rome from Nola accompanying the body of Augustus, which was carried in relay by magistrates from each town they passed through. During the heat of the day the body lay in a basilica or temple, the funeral procession only moving at night. Tiberius walked behind the coffin, accompanying his adopted father for his final journey. The emperor issued an edict using his tribunician powers summoning the Senate to meet on the day after Augustus' body reached Rome. There would be no opportunity for debate or posturing. There was to be only one item on the agenda: the arrangements for the funeral.[21]

Augustus' body was laid in state in the palace on 4 September and a formal period of mourning was declared. According to the epigraphical record for the funeral of Tiberius in AD 37, cremations traditionally took place four days after the body entered the capital, which in the case of Augustus would have taken place on 8 September. Tiberius feared a recurrence of the chaos that attended the funeral of Julius Caesar, where the mob snatched firebrands from the pyre to run through the streets, hunting down his assassins. The contemporary historian Velleius Paterculus describes the state of concern of many in the capital, with 'alarm in the Senate, the anxiety of the people, the apprehension in Rome, the fine line that we saw drawn between safety and disaster … we feared the destruction of the world'.[22]

At some point before the funeral of Augustus, probably as the emperor entered Rome, Tiberius received disastrous news from the governor of Pannonia, Junius Blaesus, whose legions had rebelled. Based on the information in Tacitus, where a messenger in AD 69 travelled a distance of 1,000 miles from Cologne to Rome in eight days, it is possible to roughly calculate the time when this news reached Rome. Based on the *Histories*, a messenger could be expected to travel 125 miles per day. The distance from Nola, where Augustus died, to Emona in Pannonia, the approximate site of the legions' summer camp, the news of Augustus' death would arrive around the evening of 24 August. Junius Blaesus would have informed the assembled soldiers and called for a period of official mourning. Tacitus appears to suggest the mutiny took two to three days to develop. Blaesus tried at first to control the rebellious soldiers, so perhaps by the evening of 30 August he decided that he had lost control and sent a messenger to Rome to request assistance from Tiberius. Allowing for the 467 miles of the return journey, the new emperor would have been informed of the news he had dreaded around the evening of 3 September on the outskirts of the capital. The crisis had begun.[23]

Tiberius must have been surprised by these events; these were, after all, the legions he had commanded in his suppression of the Pannonians and Illyrians between AD 6 and 9. The grievances of the legionaries do appear legitimate. Many had served for a significant period beyond their minimum of twenty years in a province that had only recently been conquered for Rome. Furthermore, their reward on retirement, should they live that long, was land amongst their recently subdued foes that was little more than a swamp. They also demanded an increase in pay to a denarius a day, and a maximum sixteen-year term of service, like the Praetorians who lived in comfort in and around the capital. Others resented the brutality of some centurions or the loss of their meagre pay in bribes to alleviate the unjust demands of their superior officers or deductions made for their tent, equipment, clothes and weapons. The crisis precipitated by the death of Augustus and the perceived weak position of Tiberius afforded them the opportunity to successfully present their grievances to the new emperor.[24] Soon after the Rhine legions, under the command of Germanicus, also rebelled, making similar demands.

This was the situation that led to the appointment of Sejanus as joint Praetorian Prefect alongside his father. Tiberius would have summoned his advisors, the imperial *consilium*. The fledgling Principate of Tiberius teetered on the edge of destruction. The situation in Rome demanded the presence of the emperor, as he feared that the funeral of Augustus would spark an outbreak of rioting. He was also aware that some members of the Senate supported the imperial claims of Agrippa Postumus, a problem that was in the process of being permanently solved. However, others could offer themselves to the rebellious legions as an alternative imperial candidate. After all, the two conspiracies to free Agrippa had looked to present him to the legions. If Tiberius journeyed to the Danube to resort order, then those legions on the Rhine would feel insulted. Also, if he failed to quell the revolt, the damage to his *auctoritas* would probably be fatal. Germanicus, Tiberius' adopted son, was a direct descendant of Augustus, as was his wife Agrippina, and was already near the German provinces, but Tiberius remained suspicious of his motives and loyalty. However, to recall Germanicus would test his loyalty to the limit, especially as he had the potential support of the Rhine legions. There was no alternative but to trust in the allegiance of his heir.

The situation on the Danube was more pressing, as Rome was only a relatively short march away from the three rebellious legions. Junius Blaesus, the governor of Pannonia, lacked the authority to restore order. Tiberius decided to send his 26-year-old son Drusus to deal with the rebellion. He had held the office of quaestor in AD 10 but, apart from this minor post, had little military or political experience. It was essential that he was provided with experienced and tested men whose loyalty to Tiberius was beyond question. Tacitus says:

> [He was] provided with a staff of nobles and two Praetorian cohorts. He had no instructions that could be called definite: he was to suit his measures to the emergency. Drafts of picked men raised the cohorts to abnormal strength. In addition, a large part of the Praetorian horse was included, as well as the flower of the German troops, who at that time formed the imperial bodyguard. The commandant of the household troops, Aelius Sejanus, who held the office jointly with his father and exercised a remarkable influence over Tiberius, went in attendance, to act as monitor to the young prince and to keep before the eyes of the rest the prospects of peril or reward.[25]

Tacitus appears to have telescoped Sejanus' future power and influence. The new Praetorian Prefect must have been with Tiberius in Rome, but in what capacity? Clearly, the emperor trusted his loyalty and ability as he placed him next to his son in such a dangerous and hazardous situation. Furthermore, there can be little doubt that his father Strabo used his unrestricted access to the emperor to induce Tiberius into promoting his son. Drusus was probably already well-acquainted with Sejanus as both were connected with Apicius and no doubt attended his dinner parties.[26] It is possible that Strabo used the emperor's concern that there would be unrest in the capital to press the case for his own retention at Tiberius' side whilst urging the appointment of another Praetorian Prefect to take command of the powerful force of guards that would be sent north. Tiberius issued an edict warning the populace 'not to repeat the enthusiastic excesses which on a former day had marred the funeral of the deified Julius, by desiring Augustus to be cremated in the Forum rather than in the Field of Mars, his appointed resting place'.[27]

Tacitus uses the word '*rector*' to describe Sejanus' role in Drusus' party, denoting his position as a guide. Yet whatever previous experience Sejanus had gained since his attendance of Gaius' mission to the East, he could never at this stage of his career possess the *auctoritas* to act as a restraining influence on a prince of the imperial house. Furthermore, the passage refers to a staff of nobles who were to act as Drusus' *consilium* and Sejanus could not be considered a member of this class. In fact, Sejanus is not mentioned again in Tacitus' account of the revolt, suggesting he had a minimal role in subsequent events. Sejanus was simply the 'commandant of the household troops', whose very presence would focus the minds of Drusus' aristocratic advisors on the necessity of success as, in the words of Epictetus, they could see 'the swords of the guards'. Failure to crush the revolt would be fatal for the careers and possibly the lives of many in this small party.[28]

There does appear to have been a puzzling delay in the sending of reinforcements to assist Blaesus. The funeral of Augustus probably took place on 8 September, with a eulogy delivered by both Tiberius and Drusus. Drusus was present as consul designate in the senatorial debate on 17 September that was to grant Augustus divine honours and discuss Tiberius' constitutional position. In the meantime, news from Pannonia would have been circulating in the houses of senators and on the streets of the capital. It is likely the revolt of the Rhine legions was also known. The likelihood of some opportunist taking advantage of this situation, as the northern legions had done, was high. The absence of Drusus might have been the catalyst for panic as, in all likelihood, Tiberius had played down the seriousness of the situation. To outward appearance the emperor wished to present a façade of an orderly succession. The fact that the crisis was not even discussed in the Senate suggests this was indeed the case. The funeral of Augustus took place without incident. It was a magnificent affair, with the two Praetorian Prefects taking a prominent part. Dio provides a vivid description:

> There was a couch made of ivory and gold and adorned with coverings of purple and gold. In it his body was hidden, in a coffin down below; but a wax image of him in triumphal garb was visible. This image was borne from the palace by the officials elected for the following year, and another of gold from the Senate house, and still another upon a triumphal chariot. Behind these came the images of his ancestors, and of his deceased relatives (except that of Caesar, because he had been numbered among the demigods) and those of other Romans who had been prominent in any way, beginning with Romulus himself. An image of Pompey the Great was also seen, and all the nations he had acquired, each represented by a likeness which bore some local characteristic, appeared in procession. After these followed all other objects mentioned above. When the couch had been placed in full view on the rostra of the orators, Drusus read something from that place; and from the other rostra, that is the Julian, Tiberius.[29]

At this point in the text, Dio gives full rein to his oratorical abilities by composing a fictitious speech delivered by the new emperor. The account of the funerary rites then continues:

> Afterwards the same men as before took up the couch and carried it through the triumphal gateway, according to a decree of the Senate. Present and taking part in the funeral procession were the Senate and the equestrian order, their wives, the Praetorian Guard, and practically all others who were in the city at that time. When the body had been placed on the pyre in the Campus Martius, all the priests marched round it first; and then the knights, not only those belonging to the equestrian order but the others as well, and the infantry from the garrison ran round it; and they cast upon it all the triumphal decorations that any of them had ever received from him for any deed of valour. Next the centurions took torches, conformably to a decree of the Senate, and lighted the pyre from beneath. So it was consumed, and an eagle released from it flew

aloft, appearing to bear his spirit to heaven. When these ceremonies had been performed, all the other people departed; but Livia remained on the spot for five days in company with the most prominent knights, and gathered up his bones and placed them in his tomb.[30]

This glorious pageantry not only honoured the founder of the political settlement that had now entered a moment of crisis, but it also formed a visual statement of Tiberius' claim to be the rightful successor that went beyond the legal powers he already possessed. The significant role of the Praetorians and urban cohorts was a less than subtle assertion of the real nature of Tiberius' authority. Nothing could be allowed to interfere with this powerful piece of imperial propaganda. An official period of mourning was then decreed that had a deep religious importance which all were expected to observe. A march north by the guard would not have been appropriate.

Still, Drusus and Sejanus waited. The period of mourning only lasted a few days for men, but the meeting of the Senate on 17 September was too important to delay. This was the date set for the deification of Augustus and a senatorial discussion, initiated by the emperor, on its role under the new regime. Drusus as consul elect was present.[31] The ancient sources portray Tiberius at first refusing the principate, because, they suggest, he was merely dissembling, feigning reluctance to test the loyalty of the senators. However, he was already emperor holding tribunician power and since AD 13 holding equal *imperium* to that held by Augustus. As the imperial successor he had already issued orders to the governors of the provinces and commanders of the legions using these powers. Tiberius was, however, a reluctant emperor; he baulked at the enormity of the task of administering an empire stretching from the sands of the Sahara to the flowing waters of the Rhine and Danube. What Tiberius was asking for was the Senate to take a share of this burden and lift some of the responsibility from his shoulders. However, leading senators, including C. Asinius Gallus and L. Arruntius, doubting his sincerity, opposed his request. As the debate continued, Tiberius was left emotionally drained as frustration turned to anger. At one point he was reduced to complete silence. Gallus realized his oratorical independence had caused offence and obsequiously tried to extricate himself. Some senators became increasingly impatient until Q. Haterius stood to ask Tiberius how long he intended to leave Rome without a head of state. Wearied by it all and abandoning his plan for the

Senate to take a greater responsibility for the administration of the Empire, Tiberius withdrew.[32]

Tiberius' suspicions of the leading senators, particularly Asinius Gallus and Lucius Arruntius, appeared to have been confirmed. His mood was further darkened a few days later when Q. Haterius, in fear for his life after his public expression of his frustrations, sought an audience with Tiberius in the palace. The emperor appears to have been with his mother. The desperate senator threw himself at the feet of the emperor in supplication, but accidentally tripped him. Tiberius fell on his face. The Praetorian Guards leapt upon the assailant, whose life was only saved by the intervention of Livia. As Praetorian Prefect, it is likely Strabo was there as the *praetorium*, or headquarters, of the guard was in the palace itself. This incident reflects the tension at this time of crisis.[33]

Sejanus was at this time marching rapidly towards Pannonia at the head of a small but elite force of Praetorians and German cavalry. A lunar eclipse that occurred when Drusus was at the summer camp of the three rebellious legions can be dated to 27 September. If we assume Drusus left for Pannonia on the morning of 18 September after the senatorial debate and arrived on the morning of the 27th in the region of Emona, a distance of 467 miles was covered in nine days, which would demand an impossible pace of over 50 miles a day for a soldier. It is generally accepted that a Roman infantryman could march a distance of 18–20 Roman miles a day over a sustained period. The only logical conclusion is that the Praetorian cohorts had already set out in advance, with Sejanus at their head. This makes sense on a number of levels. Tiberius and his *consilium* would have known about the revolt around the evening of 3 September. Are we to believe they did nothing, knowing that three legions were devastating a province that had only recently been subdued and were within a two-week march of Rome? This would have been utter folly. Furthermore, the Praetorian infantry, marching at 20 miles a day, could have reached the legionary camp in twenty-three days, in other words by 27 September if the force set out on 4 September, the morning after the desperate message arrived from Blaesus. As Tiberius felt he required the experienced Strabo at his side, the need for a second Praetorian Prefect became apparent, especially as Drusus would not at first be at the head of the force. The equestrian appointee would need to be present in Rome, possessing military experience and considered utterly loyal to Tiberius. Sejanus was the singular beneficiary of the crisis.[34]

Drusus raced north on the morning of 18 September, probably using the horses of the *cursus publicus*, travelling at 100–125 miles a day. He would have reached Sejanus and the Praetorian cohorts around 21 September. They were greeted with a scene of chaos. The three Pannonian legions had unified their forces in the one camp. The surrounding regions had been pillaged and the town of Nauportus sacked. Many of the legionary tribunes had been ejected from the camp and some of the centurions murdered, while others were in hiding. Junius Blaesus survived virtually alone inside the camp; his household and bodyguard of gladiators were held in irons and some had been tortured. The situation remained precarious. Some of the mutineers had attempted to kill their commander.[35] As the son of the emperor, Drusus should have been greeted by the serried ranks of legionaries in full battle array proudly wearing their awards for bravery and distinguished service, with the legionary eagles and standards standing alongside the legionary commanders and officers.[36] Instead, without the order and organization that would have been instilled by the centurions, the Caesar was met by a seething mass of discontent as 'the legions met him, ostensibly to mark their loyalty; but the usual demonstrations of joy and glitter of decorations had given place to repulsive squalor and to looks that aimed at sadness and came close to insolence.'[37]

As Praetorian Prefect, Sejanus would have ridden at the front of the column just behind Drusus. The moment that Drusus entered the camp the gates were shut behind him, leaving the main force of Praetorians outside. Sejanus must have feared the worst. Drusus held his nerve and advanced towards the tribunal to address the soldiers, who now surrounded the small party as one great mass. The speech should have been heard in respectful silence; however, Drusus had to raise his hand in order to calm the crowd. The *auctoritas* derived from Drusus' position as the son of the emperor was all that prevented the group being taken hostage: 'One moment, the mutineers would glance back at their thousands, and a roar of truculent voices followed; the next, they saw the Caesar and trembled: vague murmurings, savage yells and sudden stillness marked a conflict of passions which left them alternately terrified and terrible.'[38]

Gradually the noise level subsided to allow Drusus to read a letter from Tiberius that reminded the soldiers of their shared campaigns and asked for time to put their requests before the Senate. The mutineers had selected a centurion named Clemens to represent them. He ascended the tribunal to present their demands to Drusus, who asked for time to send these to Rome. This was not what the soldiers wanted to hear, but Drusus had not been empowered to grant their demands. Shouts interrupted the Caesar's plea. Questions were fired at him: 'Why had he come, if he was neither to raise the pay of the troops nor to ease their burdens – if, in short, he had no leave to do kindness?' Others asked that, as commander-in-chief, would the emperor defer to the Senate battle orders or executions for ill-discipline? 'Or were rewards to depend on many masters, punishments to be without control?'[39]

The anger of the soldiers now broke the surface and the storm was unleashed. The soldiers looked to provoke a confrontation with those Praetorians who had managed to enter the camp. This they felt would allow them to resort to arms, using the excuse of being provoked by Drusus' escort. Sejanus had instilled a resolute discipline amongst the Praetorians and they did not rise to the provocations. The mutineers' anger was now directed at Gnaeus Lentulus, a noble whom they believed 'was hardening Drusus' heart' and was highly critical of the actions of the three legions. Drusus' position as the emperor's son made attacks on him treasonous, whereas Sejanus was probably unknown to many of the legionaries despite his recent promotion to the Praetorian Prefecture. Lentulus, sometimes called Lentulus the Augur, the consul of 14 BC, was 67 years old and was renowned for his 'military fame'. A close *amicus* of both Augustus and Tiberius, he had served in Pannonia during the revolt in AD 4 and later in Moesia, where he fought across the Danube against the Getae. He remained a powerful figure on the political stage until his death in AD 25. Tacitus honours him with a brief epitaph: 'Lentulus, over and above his consulate and the triumphal distinctions he had won against the Getae, could claim the glories, first of honest poverty gallantly carried, then of a great fortune innocently acquired and temperately employed.' There can be little doubt where this wealth originated. As a *Caesaris amicus*, he would have benefitted from the regular grant of imperial *beneficia* in the form of estates, honours and offices of state. Seneca is far less flattering in his description of him, saying he possessed 'a barren mind, and a spirit no less feeble. He was the greatest of misers, but freer with coins than talk, so dire was his poverty of speech. He owed all his advancement to Augustus.' His experience, *dignitas* and *auctoritas* made him Drusus' principal advisor, and not Sejanus. For this reason, he became the target of the legionaries' anger and frustration.[40]

Drusus had now withdrawn to the camp's *principia* or *praetoria*, the headquarters or commander's tent. There he would have listened to advice from his staff, which would have included Sejanus and his uncle Blaesus. It was probably felt that Lentulus' life was now in danger and his presence was creating further tensions. Sejanus was responsible not only for the personal safety of Drusus but also members of his *consilium*, especially one who was a close *amicus* of Tiberius. It was decided to remove Lentulus from the menacing situation and send him to the legionary headquarters, which no doubt was still held by soldiers who remained loyal. The number of Praetorians inside the camp were far outnumbered by the rebellious legionaries, so the party hoped to act quickly, without summoning the guard and perhaps provoking the confrontation that Drusus had hoped to avoid. Instead, it was planned to take the legionary guards by surprise and reach the gates before the alarm could be raised. The elderly Lentulus probably slowed them down. The imperial party quickly began to attract large numbers of soldiers, who demanded to know where they were going. The presence of Drusus alongside Lentulus would have been interpreted as an escape attempt. Sejanus would have been at their side. The group was probably further delayed at the camp gates as they were ordered to be opened but remained firmly shut. Questions would have been asked, commands barked out, and all the while the passage of time reduced the likelihood of success. Soon they were surrounded by an angry mob. Lentulus was now exposed in the eye of the storm. The angry words directed at Lentulus were now replaced by projectiles: 'Simultaneously they closed in and began to stone him. He was bleeding already from a cut with a missile and had made up his mind that the end had come.' Drusus and Sejanus would have attempted to protect him. Their lives were in as much danger as his. However, the intervention of 'Drusus' numerous escort' saved all. Tacitus later mentions the gates were still held by the legionaries, so this must have been the Praetorians who had managed to enter the camp before the gates were barred.[41]

The situation, however, remained perilous. Drusus found himself a virtual prisoner as a guard of rebellious soldiers was placed around the *Praetoria* and *Principia* as darkness fell. Some of the soldiers started rioting, and perhaps the grain stores were sacked.[42] However, the night brought unexpected salvation. Around 3 am an eclipse of the moon sent most of the soldiers into a state of panic. As the lunar brightness faded, horns and trumpets were sounded to aid the moon in its struggle against the darkness. However, it drifted behind the clouds and then its flickering light faded and died. A deep silence descended upon the camp as the soldiers gazed upwards in terror. Most saw it as a sign of divine disfavour, the evil and chaos caused by their revolt against the natural order mirrored in the night sky above them. Others feared that the face of heaven had been averted from the crimes they had committed on earth. Drusus, ignoring the religious implications, was decisive in turning this event to his advantage.

Clemens, the centurion who was still held by the legionaries in high regard, and other junior officers who remained loyal but popular, were sent around the soldiers' tents to sow the seeds of discord. They passed between the huddled groups of men trembling in their tents, to the sentries at the gates, to the watches and patrols on the ramparts. They suggested that if they continued to abuse the son of the emperor, then imperial retribution was sure to follow. They asked how could they receive their discharges unless they found favour with Tiberius? It was suggested that those soldiers who first returned to the colours would receive a lesser punishment than those who continued to disobey their commanders. They played on the fears of those veterans who worried over their grant of land at discharge. Grizzled, battle-scarred veterans were divided from young recent recruits. The stratagem worked, and division took the place of unity. Legion split from legion, soldier from soldier. Dawn revealed the gates abandoned as the legionaries reluctantly returned to their standards.[43]

The Praetorians locked outside would now have entered the camp. Drusus summoned the legions on the parade ground and addressed them from the tribunal. Behind him would have stood his staff and advisors, including Sejanus. Drusus castigated the assembled ranks. He boasted that he would never be intimidated, but if they acted as supplicants and returned to order he would ask his father to find favour with their demands, now reincarnated as 'prayers'. Considering the supernatural message of the eclipse, his religious language would have resonated with his audience. He was met with a roar of approval. As before, Junius Blaesus' son was selected as a messenger, along with Lucius Aponius, an *eques* on Drusus' staff, and a centurion. Drusus then returned to his tent and met with his advisors. Sejanus as Praetorian Prefect would have been part of this *consilium*, but we do not know what his role was in the ensuing discussion. Some suggested waiting for the return of the messengers, while others recommended acting with ruthless force to add fresh terror to those already cowed by the previous signs of divine anger. Drusus, a man of forceful character, no doubt still smarted from his treatment at the tribunal on his arrival and at the gates. He wanted revenge and felt his position was now strong enough to act without restraint. Furthermore, a violent storm had descended upon the camp. The legionaries interpreted this as further proof of the condemnation of the gods. The rain lashed at all who ventured outside. Most found some form of temporary sanctuary inside their tents. Few hazarded the weather outside to witness the brutal and bloody end of many of their comrades. The leaders of the revolt,

Vibulenus and Percennius, were taken to Drusus' pavilion and there executed. Most reports read by Tacitus record their bodies being buried inside his tent.[44]

In the driving wind and rain, the ringleaders were now hunted down by the Praetorians and those loyal centurions who remained. Some were dispatched in their tents; others fled, only to be butchered outside the ramparts by men stationed there. To prove their loyalty some mutineers were handed over to their units, who were ordered to execute them. The end was savage and brutal. The spirit of resistance broken, the legions departed for their winter camps. First, the VIII Augusta headed for Poetovio, then the XV Apollinaris for Emona. The IX Hispana legion remained for a while, waiting with hope for the return of the messengers. However, isolated by the departure of the other legions, they also broke camp and returned to Siscia. Around the beginning of October, Drusus, Sejanus and the Praetorian escort returned to Rome, their mission successfully accomplished and their status greatly enhanced.[45]

On 12 October, the unrest Tiberius had feared broke out in the capital. The *Augustalia* had been refounded to honour the deified Augustus, who was honoured with the establishment of a new college of twenty-one priests drawn from the aristocracy. Tiberius, Drusus, Germanicus and his brother and future emperor Claudius were numbered amongst them. The festivities took place in the circus officiated by the tribunes. However, the games 'were marred by a disturbance due to the rivalry of the actors'. One of the actors apparently felt that their pay did not adequately reflect their elevated stature above the other performers and refused to perform. The crowd then rioted in a demonstration of their support. Sejanus and Drusus would not have arrived in Rome. It would have been Seius Strabo who dealt with the situation, using the remaining Praetorian cohorts and the urban cohorts. The situation was only restored when the tribunes called an emergency meeting of the Senate requesting permission to increase the legal monetary limit allocated to the games. Presumably, the Senate granted their request and the actor, and the populace, were placated.[46]

Tiberius would have welcomed the news from Pannonia, but the situation on the Rhine continued to cause concern. The news of Augustus' death had sparked a mutiny amongst the XXI Rapax and V Alaudae, who were encamped in the territory of the Ubii on the lower Rhine. The revolt soon spread to the other legions in the province, the XX Valeria and I Germanica, and then to those in Upper Germany, the II Augusta, XIII Gemina, XIV Gemina and XVI Gallica. These legions and their governors, A. Caecina

Severus and C. Silius respectively, were under the command of Tiberius'
adopted son Germanicus, who was absent at the time organizing a census
of the Three Gauls, which was also included in his province. Tiberius could
take some comfort in the distance between these rebellious legions and
Rome, but the potential threat of eight legions would have greatly concerned
him. Furthermore, there existed a political threat as many saw Germanicus
as the rightful heir to Augustus, as his maternal grandmother Octavia was
the sister of the deceased emperor. In addition, he was accompanied by his
wife Agrippina, the daughter of Augustus' daughter Julia the Elder. She had
numerous reasons to hate Tiberius. Her mother had been exiled in 2 BC for
adultery and probable conspiracy, leaving her effectively orphaned by the
age of 12, as her father Agrippa had died in 12 BC. Julia the Elder despised
Tiberius as an inferior, an attitude that is reflected in Gaius' treatment of
his stepfather and in many of Agrippina's words and actions. Her mother
remained in the town of Rhegium and would soon be placed under close
house arrest by her ex-husband Tiberius and die before the end of the
year, probably of starvation.[47] Her older brothers Gaius and Lucius were
already dead, but her elder sister, Julia the Younger, remained alive, although
since AD 8 she had been in exile on the island of Tremirus, charged with
adultery and treason. There she remained to rot under Tiberius until death
released her in AD 29. Another brother, Agrippa Postumus, she would soon
learn, had been executed on his island exile at the accession of Tiberius, and,
many contemporaries asserted, on his orders.

Both Agrippina and Germanicus were immensely popular, both in Rome
and with the army. Should the eight Rhine legions acclaim Germanicus
emperor, a civil war would ensue whose outcome was by no means certain.
He was potentially the greatest single threat to Tiberius. The initial demands
of the Rhine legions were similar to those made by their comrades in
Pannonia. The arrival of Germanicus changed the dynamic. The legionaries,
sensing a greater reward from supporting the claims of Tiberius' potential
rival, offered him the throne. Germanicus, however, remained loyal, and
drawing his sword threatened to kill himself rather than betray his adopted
father. The mutinous legionaries were then shocked when one of their
number offered Germanicus his sword, claiming that it was sharper. The
public insult stunned the mob, allowing Germanicus' staff to hurry him
away to his tent.[48]

Germanicus was far more conciliatory than Drusus in dealing with the
rebellious legions. He forged a document purporting to be from Tiberius
agreeing to their demands on pay and conditions and the discharging of

veterans. He also failed to adequately sanction those soldiers who had insulted and threatened a senatorial delegation which came with the news of the senatorial decree conferring *proconsular imperium* on Germanicus. Instead he sought to humiliate the rebellious soldiers by sending his wife and son Caligula to the protection of the Treviri. Agrippina, with the little Caligula at her side, performed the role of a frightened and humiliated Roman matron and mother to perfection. Effectively she put down the mutiny.[49] The sight of the granddaughter of Augustus and daughter of Agrippa leaving in supposed fear for her life brought many back to their senses. As an act of self-purification, Germanicus allowed the soldiers to murder their comrades whom they considered ringleaders of the rebellion. The centurions were then presented to the assembled legions and those charged with bribery, corruption or excessive brutality were dismissed. A demand was then sent to the camp of the V and XXI legions who remained steadfast in their refusal to return to the colours: the soldiers should either execute the leaders of the revolt or both legions would face destruction at the hands of their former comrades. A massacre ensued, with men dragged from their tents, and both innocent and guilty were slain as grievances were settled. Others managed to gather their weapons and form some kind of order to defend themselves from their attackers. There were no officers to restrain their madness or call a halt to the bloodshed. The sight that greeted Germanicus as he entered the camp caused him to burst into tears. The revolt had been crushed, but at great cost. To restore the esprit de corps of the Rhine legions, Germanicus would campaign beyond the Rhine for two further years and would only return to Rome to celebrate his German triumph in AD 17.

The contrast between the stratagems used in the successful suppression of the revolts on the Rhine and in Pannonia could not have been more stark. Tiberius continued to view Germanicus with suspicion. His loyalty had been proven, but his ability to deal with crisis situations was now doubted. Drusus and Sejanus had both proven their worth. Both would have become close advisors to the emperor; Drusus as he was a member of the imperial family and Sejanus as joint commander of his guards alongside his father. At this early stage in his career, Sejanus' influence would have been overshadowed by others. Augustus had effectively established a hereditary monarchy where power and influence primarily lay with members of the *domus* or *familia Caesaris*. The close relatives of the emperor, his wife and children, possessed unrestricted access to him, and they would play a central role in imperial politics.[50] Livia, now honoured with the title Augusta, had been posthumously adopted by her husband in his will to reinforce Tiberius' claim to the throne. She had been a powerful influence during the reign of her husband, especially as illness and age affected her husband's ability to govern.[51] Her position in AD 14 had been further strengthened by the immense wealth she had inherited. In his will, Augustus passed a third of his estate to his wife, while the remainder went to Tiberius. Her continued access to Tiberius and the political debt he owed her allowed her patronal influence to stretch far and wide:

> For she occupied a very exalted station, far above all women of former days, so that she could at any time receive the Senate and such people as wished to greet her in her house; and this fact was entered in the public records. The letters of Tiberius bore for a time her name, also, and communications were addressed to both alike. Except that she never ventured to enter the Senate-chamber or the camps or the public assemblies, she undertook to manage everything as if she were sole ruler. For in the time of Augustus she had possessed the greatest influence and she always declared that it was she who had made Tiberius emperor; consequently, she was not satisfied to rule on equal terms with him but wished to take precedence over him.

Inscriptions from Spain dating from around AD 20 praise the Augusta for 'her many great favours to men of every rank', and add that 'she could rightly and deservedly have supreme influence in what she asked for from the Senate, though she used that influence sparingly.'[52]

Over time, the influence of Livia would diminish as her relationship with Tiberius became ever more strained. However, Sejanus' star could only rise to its zenith once hers waned. One thing that both Livia and Tiberius shared was their suspicion of Agrippina; her arrogance and her motives.[53] Agrippina took great pride in being the granddaughter of Augustus, a fact that undermined the position of Tiberius, whose position as head of state was based primarily on his adoption by the late emperor. Agrippina was the very antithesis of both Livia and Tiberius. Just as they were reserved, conservative and restrained, she was excitable, passionate, headstrong and impulsive. This was exemplified by her actions in saving a Roman army from destruction in AD 16. Rumours had reached the deplete Rhine garrison that Germanicus' deputy, Caecina, and his army that was campaigning beyond the river had been surrounded and slaughtered. The soldiers guarding the bridge at Vetera panicked and prepared to demolish it. This would have trapped in hostile territory their comrades, many of whom had been wounded and their supplies had been lost. However Agrippina saved this army by preventing the destruction of the bridge, for 'it was this great hearted woman who assumed the duties of a general throughout those days; who, if a soldier was in need, clothed him, and, if he was wounded, gave him dressings.' Pliny, the historian of the German Wars, asserts that she stood at the head of the bridge, offering her praises and thanks to the returning legions. The action sank deep into the soul of Tiberius.[54]

Livia, ever the traditionalist, like her son, worked behind the scenes and avoided a significant public profile. In Rome's patriarchal society, women were expected to be dutiful and demure. This did not inhibit Livia's influence, and she would have expected Agrippina to conform to these expectations. Tiberius saw Agrippina's actions as the usurpation of the role of officers and commanders. Furthermore, the emperor opposed on principle any role for women in public life, even his mother. He admonished the Senate in AD 14 for voting what he considered excessive honours for Livia, 'declaring that official compliments to women must be kept within bounds'. Tacitus adds somewhat as an aside that Tiberius 'regarded the elevation of women as a degradation of himself'.[55] Although this is probably an exaggeration, Tiberius did not comprehend the implications of Augustus' foundation of a hereditary monarchy in the form of what modern historians call the Principate. The creation of an imperial family elevated the role, influence and power of all women related to the emperor. This attitude undermined his relationship with his second wife, Julia the Elder, the daughter of Augustus, and then his mother and Agrippina. It is perhaps unsurprising that he retained an undying love for the dutiful and obedient Vipsania, whom Augustus forced him to divorce for Julia.[56]

Sejanus' influence with the emperor had grown by AD 16. The Praetorian Prefect had made an accurate assessment of Tiberius' character and attitudes, in particular towards his prejudiced role of females on the political stage, to 'inflame and exacerbate his jealousies; and with his expert knowledge of the character of Tiberius, kept sowing the seed of future hatreds – grievances for the emperor to store away and produce someday with increase'.[57] It is difficult to understand what these jealousies were, as Germanicus was Tiberius' adopted son and designated heir, and Agrippina would inevitably be empress. Therefore Sejanus must have exploited Tiberius' attitudes towards the role of women in public life. This stratagem would also allow him to indirectly undermine the emperor's relationship with Livia. This was dangerous, but Sejanus is described even by his enemies as both brave and ambitious.

Chapter 3

His Rise: AD 15–20

'Fathers, think not of the last day of Sejanus, but of the sixteen years of Sejanus.'
(Marcus Terentius, an equestrian client of Sejanus, addressing the Senate in AD 31, in Tacitus, *Annals* 6.8)

The year AD 15 opened with the inauguration of the two ordinary consuls, Gaius Norbanus and Drusus, Tiberius' son. Their appointment had probably been agreed earlier in AD 14 by Augustus, Tiberius and no doubt Livia. This was a great honour for Norbanus, whose probable father, C. Norbanus Flaccus, had shared the consulship of 24 BC with Augustus.[1] Tiberius, the scion of the great noble houses of the Drusii and Claudii, ensured that throughout his reign the aristocracy received the honours and status that they felt was their due, the greatest of these being the two annual ordinary consulships as the year was named after the holders of these offices. To extend this honour, the ordinary consuls were often asked to resign their posts after a few months, so the emperor could appoint *suffect* consuls. Tiberius had transferred the election of the various magistracies from the popular assemblies to the Senate. The appointment of consuls was entirely under his control, as he had simply to nominate his choices with the Senate merely required to ratify them. The elections of the twelve annual praetors was more of a contest. Tiberius limited himself to recommending only four candidates, who as *candidatii Caesaris* were guaranteed appointment to office.[2] The remaining candidates were elected by an open vote in the Senate, and so had to press their *amici* and clients for their support. An *amicus* or client who had received a favour was expected to return it at the appropriate time. Reciprocity was embedded in Roman society and formed the foundation of religious, social, political and economic relationships. The ultimate patron was the emperor himself, who through granting offices, priesthoods, estates, governorships and money bound the recipients to him through the bonds of *amicitiae*. Those with access to Tiberius, either through friendship or their office, possessed the greatest power and influence as brokers of imperial *beneficia*. These *amici Caesaris* were able through their proximity to the emperor to build their own nexus of patronal and client relationships.[3]

Tiberius dissolved the senatorial *consilium* set up in AD 13 by Augustus and relied for most of his reign on an informal advisory body whose membership was more ad hoc and dependent upon the issues being discussed. However, perhaps reflecting the initial weakness of his political position, the new emperor, to curry favour with the nobility, had asked the Senate to select twenty leading senators to offer advice when required, to which he added 'certain old friends and intimates'. Suetonius comments that only one or two of these men were to die natural deaths, as the rest, including Sejanus, he killed. Strabo was certainly a member of the imperial *consilium* and he was destined to number amongst the few of its members to die from natural causes.[4] Another was a former close *amicus* of Augustus, the prominent *eques* C. Sallustius Crispus, who would also die of old age in AD 20. The emperor relied upon some advisors whom he had inherited from Augustus and others who were his *amici* before he became emperor. The great-nephew of the historian Sallust, C. Sallustius Crispus had inherited his relative's great wealth and upon the fall of Maecenas became Augustus and Livia's 'partner in imperial secrets'. Upon hearing the news that Tiberius threatened to refer the death of Agrippa Postumus to the Senate, it was he who went to Livia to advise her 'not to publish the mysteries of the palace, the counsels of her friends, the services of the soldiery; and also to watch that Tiberius did not weaken the powers of the throne by referring everything and all things to the Senate'. The advice was accepted. His power and influence had not weakened by AD 16. Clemens, the former slave of Agrippa Postumus, had grown his beard, and using his similarity to his former master in appearance, developed a considerable following. Rumours were circulated that Agrippa survived through the direct intervention of the gods. The threat appears to be underplayed in Tacitus, who focuses instead on his arrest. According to Dio, Clemens' conspiracy extended 'to Gaul and won many to his cause there and many later in Italy, and finally, he marched upon Rome with the avowed intention of recovering the dominion of his grandfather. The population of the city became excited at this, and not a few joined his cause.' It was to Sallustius Crispus that Tiberius turned rather than Sejanus. Two soldiers, who were clients of Sallustius, managed to gain the confidence of Clemens, who was arrested and taken to the palace. There he was tortured but he refused to divulge the names of his fellow conspirators, many of whom were suspected to be members of the imperial household, equites and senators. Despite the implicit threat that these conspirators posed, no further investigations were carried out. Clemens was executed in the palace and the whole affair was quietly forgotten.[5]

The pivotal role of Sallustius Crispus is surprising on several levels. Clearly, Praetorians were used in the arrest of the imposter and were involved in his torture and execution that took place in the palace. Sejanus and Strabo, the Praetorian Prefects and members of Tiberius' *consilium*, would have had knowledge of the operation. Furthermore, their primary role was to ensure the safety of the emperor, a role that appears, in this instance, to have been supplanted by Sallustius Crispus. The fact Sallustius used his clients to infiltrate the followers of Clemens might suggest that their loyalty was entirely trusted; the inference being that the loyalty of some of the guard was not. Furthermore, Tacitus, by employing the phrase 'at last', might suggest that Tiberius gave the task to Sallustius after the crisis had been known to be developing over time and known to the emperor. Had Strabo and Sejanus tried unsuccessfully to capture Clemens, and in frustration the emperor delegated the task to a man he felt had the requisite experience to bring it to a successful conclusion? A man who had been heavily involved in the termination of another threat, that of Agrippa Postumus.

Strabo, rather than Sejanus, appears to have taken responsibility for the failure to capture Clemens in AD 14 or 15. Strabo was made the Prefect of Egypt around AD 15. This was not a demotion, as a set equestrian career structure had yet to be established and the Praetorian Prefecture was not recognized as the most prestigious office. The Prefecture of Egypt was the more illustrious post at this time and the promotion of Strabo was recognition of years of loyal service to Augustus and then Tiberius. The fact Tiberius did not appoint another prefect to work in conjunction with Sejanus suggests the emperor felt confident in the new sole prefect's abilities. Strabo would not survive long to enjoy his new role based in the old Ptolemaic palace in Alexandria. He was replaced at some point in AD 16 or 17 by C. Galerius, presumably due to his death.[6] Sejanus would have inherited his natural father's bonds of *amicitiae*, clients, wealth and estates. These would have been extensive.

The position of Sallustius Crispus as one of Tiberius' main advisors posed a problem to Sejanus. Tacitus provides a detailed epitaph for this great statesman on his death in AD 20:

> Crispus, a knight by extraction, was the grandson of a sister of Gaius Sallustius, the brilliant Roman historian, who adopted him into his family and provided his name. Thus, for him the avenue to the great offices of state lay clear; but, choosing to emulate Maecenas, without holding senatorial rank he outstripped in influence many who had won a triumph or the consulate; while by his elegance and refinements he was sundered from the old Roman school, and in the ample and generous scale of his establishment approached extravagance. Yet under it all lay a mental energy, equal to gigantic tasks, hidden from view by his display of somnolence and apathy. Hence, next to Maecenas, while Maecenas lived, and later next to none, he it was who sustained the burden of the secrets of emperors. He was privy to the killing of Agrippa Postumus, but with advancing years he retained more the semblance than the reality of his sovereign's friendship.[7]

His fall from favour must have been sudden, as he clearly held the reality of influence and power in AD 16 and died in AD 20. Age may have wearied him, but we should see the corresponding rise in the influence of Sejanus as another reason for his loss of the emperor's ear. After all, Sejanus, as sole Praetorian Prefect, could manage and monitor access to the emperor. No doubt Sallustius Crispus was the first casualty of Sejanus' rise.

Under Sejanus, the role of the Praetorian Prefect rapidly evolved. Initially, the post was seen to be entirely military, its primary function to command the guard and guarantee the safety of the emperor. The otherwise unknown *eques* Marcus Terentius makes this clear in his own defence before the Senate on the fall of his patron: 'I had seen him the colleague of his father in command of the Praetorian cohorts; and later, discharging civil duties as well as military.'[8] The Praetorian Prefect had access to the bedchamber of the emperor, which provided the opportunity to ask for favours on behalf of his own *amici* and clients as well as become his main confidant. His very position at the side of the emperor implied imperial favour.[9]

The Stoic philosopher Epictetus explains the power of the Praetorian Prefect, who could greatly influence the distribution of imperial *beneficia* to those who became his own *amici*:

> But when I hear any man called fortunate because he is honoured by Caesar, I say, what does he happen to get? A province [the government of a province]. Does he also obtain an opinion such as he ought? The office of a Prefect. Does he also obtain the power of using his office well? Why do I still strive to enter [Caesar's chamber]? A man scatters dried figs and nuts: the children seize them, and fight with one another; men do not, for they think them to be a small matter. But if a man should throw about shells, even the children do not seize them. Provinces are distributed: let children look to that. Money is distributed: let children look to that. Praetorships, consulships are distributed: let children scramble for them, let them be shut out, beaten, kiss the hands of the giver, of the slaves: but to me these are only dried figs and nuts. What then? If you fail to get them, while Caesar is scattering them about, do not be troubled: if a dried fig come into your lap, take it and eat it; for so far you may value even a fig. But if I shall stoop down and turn another over, or be turned over by another, and shall flatter those who have got into [Caesar's] chamber, neither is a dried fig worth the trouble, nor anything else of the things which are not good, which the philosophers have persuaded me not to think good.[10]

The earliest account of how an emperor organized his day comes from the reign of Vespasian. However, Egyptian papyri show early imperial officials followed a similar pattern, so it is probable that Tiberius at the start of his reign had a comparable arrangement. The emperor would rise early before dawn, and in his bedchamber read letters and reports (*breviaria*) passed to him by his imperial freedmen. He would then admit his close *amici*, who would greet him whilst he got dressed. This would be the time to gain the emperor's ear and make requests or gain his confidence. After this, the emperor made his way to the palace's vast *atrium* for the morning *salutatio*.[11] Here the numbers were so large that the reception was divided into three groups in order of status. Firstly, senators would be admitted, Tiberius allowing them to enter together, and he greeted each with a kiss.

Pliny the Elder reports that for a time this practice was banned due to the outbreak of a facial disease that was passed on to the emperor. The *equites* were then admitted in small groups, followed by the third tier who entered en masse. There would be few opportunities for individuals in these last two groups to individually petition the emperor. All the while, the Praetorian Prefect would stand close to the emperor, listening to conversations, as well as acting as a physical manifestation of his station at the centre of power. Another opportunity to access the imperial favour existed with an invitation to an imperial banquet. Members of the imperial family and those who were counted as *amici Caesaris* possessing the highest status were sat closest to the emperor, allowing them to engage him in private conversations. Tiberius was also of the habit at the end of the evening of individually addressing each guest as they departed whilst standing in the middle of the banqueting hall.[12]

Conversely, any patrons who failed to gain the *amicitiae* of such powerful figures were unable to access magistracies, priesthoods, governorships or other honours and wealth, either for themselves or for their own *amici* and clients. This would have adversely affected their own influence and status in society and undermined their ability to repay their obligations of reciprocity or attract powerful *amici*. Almost all appointments were made through patronal influences.[13]

Members of the imperial family and the *amici Caesaris* had the greatest access to the emperor. Livia's influence is testament to this. Germanicus and his wife Agrippina remained on the Rhine and did not return to Rome until late AD 16 or early AD 17, and then in AD 18 he was sent to the East on a wide-ranging mission including the incorporation of the territories of Cappadocia and Commagene into the Empire. There he would die. Drusus was sent to Illyricum from AD 17 to 20 with proconsular *imperium maius*, accompanied by his wife Livilla, the daughter of Tiberius' deceased brother Nero Claudius Drusus and Antonia the Younger.[14] Their absence from Rome and the decline in influence of Sallustius Crispus coincides with the increased power of Sejanus.

Livia remained in the capital to act as a counterpoint to Sejanus, as did others. Marcus Aemilius Lepidus remained a powerful figure until his death in AD 33. The eminent senator Aurelius Cotta Messallinus complained of both his and L. Arruntius' *potentia* in AD 32, a pejorative synonym for *auctoritas*. Lepidus had held Hispania Tarraconensis at Tiberius' accession, and possibly from AD 26 to 28 he was granted the honour of holding the senatorial province of Asia.[15] L. Arruntius' *auctoritas* lay in his great wealth and the respect in which he was held by his fellow senators. However, although honoured by Tiberius with the governorship of Hispania Tarraconensis, he was retained in Rome. Tiberius was clearly unsure of his loyalty. He could not be counted amongst the *amici Caesaris*, but he could be numbered amongst a small group of others who 'reached the summits of their profession without a stain upon their life or their eloquence'. He managed to survive the hatred and antipathy of Sejanus but fell to his successor in the prefecture, Macro.[16]

Death removed some prominent senators who were close *amici* of the emperor. In AD 21 P. Sulpicius Quirinius, who had served as Gaius Caesar's advisor in the East after the disgrace of Marcus Lollius, was honoured by the emperor with a panegyric he personally delivered to the Senate. Then in AD 23 Lucilius Longus passed away and was given a state funeral with a statue erected to him, on a vote of the Senate, which stood in the Forum of Augustus. He had been the only senator to accompany Tiberius into his exile on Rhodes and is described by Tacitus as 'his comrade in evil days and good'. The aged Cn. Cornelius Lentulus the Augur, who had been Drusus' advisor in dealing with rebellious legions in Pannonia, would die in AD 25, but another close friend and confidant remained, the jurist Cocceius Nerva, described as 'the inseparable friend of the emperor'. He was the sole senator to accompany Tiberius to his second voluntary exile on Capri and would outlive Sejanus, choosing to end his life in AD 33. Another close *amicus* of both Augustus and Tiberius was L. Calpurnius Piso the Pontifex, who shared Tiberius' fondness for strong drink and classical literature. He was appointed City Prefect in AD 13 in anticipation of Augustus' death and held it until his own death in AD 32, aged 80, reflecting the trust in which Tiberius held him. Seneca echoes this salacious portrait of him, asserting that Piso was drunk every day that he held this office but, despite this, he was twice given *secreta mandata* by the emperor. M. Junius Silanus, the *suffect* consul of AD 15, having replaced Norbanus in June, shared the consulate for the remainder of the year with Drusus. He was able to employ his friendship with the emperor to successfully plea for the return from exile of his brother Decimus, who had been charged with adultery with Julia the Younger. This great aristocrat was descended from both the noble Silani and Claudii Pulchri, and was so esteemed that he had the honour of casting his vote first in the Senate. Tiberius, it is said, had such a great opinion of his intelligence and ability that he refused to hear an appeal from any case that had first been heard by M. Silanus. The emperor married Germanicus' son Caligula, his joint heir, to Junia, Silanus' daughter, in AD 33. Some historians suggested the increasingly old and isolated emperor was forced by circumstance and fate to turn to Sejanus, but despite the loss of some of his *amici* and his son Drusus in AD 23, many other close friends and advisors remained until the twilight of his life. These were Sejanus' competitors for power. All were members of the great noble houses who vied with each other for status and honours, but they were united in their disapproval of new men and equestrians of lesser rank who aspired for position above their rank in society.[17]

Another colourful character who had a long association with the emperor was the astrologer Thrasyllus of Alexandria. He was his close companion on Rhodes, where the exile found solace in both his Stoic beliefs but also his mastery of astrology. At this time his life appeared to be in great danger, but Thrasyllus' predictions appeared to reassure him that the future was far brighter than his present condition indicated. Tiberius became a firm believer in the powers of astrology, and under the tutorage of Thrasyllus became adept himself. Tiberius returned to Rome in AD 2 with his friend, who remained at his side until he died on Capri in AD 36. Tiberius appears to have rewarded him with Roman citizenship and made him a permanent member of his household, with whom he regularly shared his innermost concerns and secrets. Thrasyllus had accompanied Tiberius and Augustus to Capri in AD 14, enjoying the imperial hospitality in the palace on the island.[18] In his account of the year AD 16, Dio records that 'Tiberius, moreover, was forever in the company of Thrasyllus, and made some use of the art of divination every day.'[19] Personal access to the emperor made the astrologer a very powerful figure at court, and he handled Tiberius adeptly to the very end. In AD 36 the astrologer saved the lives of several eminent Romans who were suspected of plotting against the emperor by predicting that Tiberius would live for another ten years.[20] His granddaughter Ennia Thrasylla married Q. Naevius Sutorious Macro, one-time Prefect of the Vigiles and future Praetorian Prefect. Her father is likely to have been the *eques* Q. Ennius, whom Tiberius saved from prosecution for *maiestas*, treason, in AD 22. Ennius had melted down a statue of Tiberius to make silver plate. The emperor rarely intervened in such matters, so as not to undermine the integrity of the Senate. In this case, however, Tiberius forbade the case to be presented. The emperor then reaffirmed his veto, despite the protests of the eminent jurist Ateius Capito, who was left humiliated. Here we see the influence of Thrasyllus in broad daylight, which he used to protect his son-in-law.[21]

Throughout his rise, Sejanus was one of many competitors for the emperor's favour. Furthermore, Germanicus returned to Rome in AD 17 before setting off for the East in the following year, while Drusus would return to Rome in December of AD 19 and was again present in the capital in March AD 20, journeying between Rome and Illyria. He returned permanently as consul from January AD 21 and remained there until his death two years later. Tiberius was clearly not isolated during this period, and Sejanus had a significant number of rivals. Drusus, Germanicus and Thrasyllus would enjoy the same access to the private apartments of the emperor as the Praetorian Prefect. What gave Sejanus an advantage were the opportunities provided by his role as Praetorian Prefect to prove his worth in securing the safety of the emperor and relieving him of many of the administrative tasks that maddened and bored him.

After supporting Drusus in the suppression of the revolt of the Pannonia legions, another outbreak of rioting in the theatre in AD 15 demonstrated Sejanus' value to Tiberius whilst diminishing the emperor's trust in the judgement of his son Drusus. The rioting was precipitated by the emperor's attempt to reduce the costs of public entertainments by cutting the pay of actors and limiting the number of gladiatorial contests provided at the games. The rioting that ensued is described by Tacitus as being far worse than that which occurred in the previous year. The magistrates presiding over the festivities were abused by the crowd, and the soldiers were directed to restore order. These were probably Praetorians, as a Praetorian tribune was wounded as well as several soldiers and a centurion. Gradually, under Sejanus, the various roles of the Praetorians were extended in his attempt to make himself indispensable to Tiberius. The riot was discussed in the next meeting of the Senate, where the praetors proposed that the actors be lashed as punishment. However, the praetors were frustrated by the veto of the plebeian tribune, Decimus Haterius Agrippa, who reminded his audience that the divine Augustus had forbidden such punishment for actors. Tiberius was present in the *curia* but he did not speak. Tacitus implies that the emperor did want to interfere in this flickering of genuine debate and old republican liberty by indicating his own preferences, which would have dictated how the senators should vote. Furthermore, Tiberius was always deferential to the words, decrees and actions of his adopted father. Yet the consul Drusus had indicated his disfavour with the suggestions of the praetors: 'He was so friendly with the actors, that this class raised a tumult and could not be brought to order even by the laws that Tiberius had introduced regulating them.' Additionally, the surprising actions of

Haterius Agrippa can be understood by Drusus' and Germanicus' support for his candidacy for a praetorship in AD 17 when an officeholder had died in post. The *lex Papia Poppaea* stated that in these circumstances the vacancy should be filled by the candidate with the greatest number of children, which was not Haterius Agrippa. Despite significant opposition, the law was ignored. The support of Germanicus and Drusus for Haterius Agrippa, it can be conjectured, was the repaying of their debt owed from the veto deployed in AD 15. Tiberius' silence can also be readily understood. Clearly, he would have wanted to punish any form of public disorder and support his own proposals in reducing expenditure on games, but he could not be seen publicly disputing a resolution supported by his sons Germanicus and Drusus. A compromise was agreed upon whereby any further outbreaks of rioting were to be punished with exile, whilst senators were barred from entering the houses of actors, nor were equites to escort them.[22] Sejanus stayed aloof from the division between father and son, and merely presented himself as an efficient and effective administrator.

Further events of AD 15 additionally tested the relationship between Tiberius and Drusus. The young Caesar had rapidly gained a reputation for drinking coupled with a violent temper, the two probably related. His open pleasure at the slaughter of the games had been criticized by his father, who rarely attended these spectacles. Drusus' link with the games was publicly celebrated in his nickname 'Castor', who was a celebrated gladiator. This name was reaffirmed when Drusus, still consul, violently attacked and beat a prominent *eques*. Drusus appears to have relished his reputation for drinking. A fire broke out, which was a regular occurrence in the crowded tenements of the capital, and as the flames spread there was a call by the desperate property owners for more water, to which Drusus gave the order to the Praetorians who were assisting, to 'Serve it to them hot'. The Romans diluted their wine with hot water flavoured with herbs and spices. The phrase he used was a familiar cry at drinking sessions. In the meantime, the Praetorians, probably commanded by Sejanus if Drusus was present at the fire, continued in their extended role as firefighters.[23]

Sejanus may have used the popular unrest and the fire to persuade Tiberius to move all the Praetorian cohorts inside the boundary of the city to be housed amongst the local population. This would account for a disparity in our sources over their location. Suetonius, writing of the situation under Augustus, remarks that whilst three were kept on duty at any one time in the capital, the others were stationed in nearby towns. However, Tacitus records that prior to AD 23 all the Praetorian cohorts were lodged within Rome itself. The time delay in sending messages to the Praetorians stationed beyond the city, their mustering and the march to Rome would have been unacceptable in a time of crisis. The start of a fire or mob unrest was the optimum time to act, but an adequate force was needed at the inception of these emergencies. There can have been nothing seen as sinister on the part of Sejanus in this move, as none of our sources mention it.[24]

Over a short period of time, the role and responsibilities of the Praetorians had rapidly evolved from the reign of Augustus to Tiberius. Praetorians had been used by Augustus at the games, and had been used as guards around the city after the destruction of three legions under Varus in Germany led to the fear of unrest.[25] The execution of Agrippa Postumus at the accession of Tiberius had probably been carried out by a Praetorian tribune and centurion. Their use as imperial agents can be seen in the capture of Clemens and his secret execution in the palace. These more clandestine activities were carried out by the *speculatores*, who probably formed a unit of their own within the guard. Mark Antony formed a unit of these soldiers and Augustus honoured one with an invitation to an imperial banquet. Originally, these elite soldiers would have been mounted scouts, but their roles gradually evolved. They were, however, held in great esteem, being listed first on a military diploma of Praetorians from the reign of Augustus, and on inscriptions they take pride in their close association with the emperor, referring to themselves as *speculatores Caesaris* or *speculatores Augusti*. As mounted soldiers they were used as the imperial messenger service, enabling their commander, Sejanus, to monitor imperial correspondence. As an extension of their role they were no doubt used as imperial spies, a duty well established by the reign of Tiberius' successor, Caligula. To intimidate the Senate, Caligula had a message passed to the consuls in front of the gathered senators by a member of the *speculatores*. The function of the *speculatores* was clearly well known to the audience, the threat to all present implicit but terrifying. Such a role was probably established by Sejanus, as the sources frequently refer to his use of spies against members of the imperial family, who were after all surrounded by members of the guard in the palace which acted as an armed escort. Dio, in a fictional speech delivered by Maecenas to Augustus, describes the need for such soldiers, 'since it is necessary ... that there be some men who both listen covertly and watch closely with respect to everything that pertains to your rule, you must have such agents in order that you might not be ignorant of anything that needs scrutiny or modification'. Dio is commenting on the *frumentarii* who by the late first century carried out a similar role to the *speculatores*. These men would report directly to their Praetorian Prefect, who would then pass on concerns to the emperor. This provided another opportunity for Sejanus to prove his worth to the emperor as well as gather information for his own use in the deadly arena of courtly politics.[26]

Praetorians had long been used as bodyguards, accompanying both Augustus and Tiberius on all their journeys in the capital and beyond its confines. The act of providing the password to the Praetorians on the death of Augustus was, in Tacitus' eyes, tantamount to being emperor in all but name. They escorted him to the Forum and the doors of the *Curia*. The presence of these soldiers outside as the senators debated inside was a constant visual reminder of where real power resided.[27] Praetorians also guarded members of the imperial house. Drusus had used two augmented Praetorian cohorts in the suppression of the mutinous legionaries on the Danube, whilst Germanicus had two Praetorian cohorts on the Rhine which proved to be highly effective in his campaigns in Germany. It would appear to be the norm that members of the imperial family were always accompanied by two cohorts of guards as a public demonstration of their status. Tiberius' concern over popular unrest in AD 14 becomes ever more understandable with only five Praetorian cohorts remaining in Rome during the Pannonian mutiny.[28] Augustus had created three urban cohorts of 500 men each, recruited from Italians, to deal with popular disorder. These were numbered consecutively after the nine Praetorian cohorts, so were probably originally formed from Praetorian cohorts. In addition to these forces, in AD 6 seven cohorts of *vigiles* were recruited from non-citizens who acted as nightwatchmen and firefighters. However, both the urban cohorts and *vigiles* appeared to be considered inadequate to the tasks they faced. The Praetorians under Sejanus were increasingly used to deal with any threat to imperial order or property.[29]

The growing role of the Praetorians as agents of the state was demonstrated by their deployment in the confinement of the noble senator M. Scribonius Libo Drusus during his treason trial. In AD 16 Tiberius, convinced of the power of astrology and magic, was concerned with its potential use by his enemies. He was not alone in this. Augustus had passed a law in AD 11 forbidding seers from prophesising to any person alone or exploring any issue concerning death.[30] Libo's distinguished ancestry made him a potential rival to the position of Tiberius as Princeps. He was a cousin of the emperor and the great-grandson of Pompey the Great.

However, he is described as a foolish and impressionable young man whose enemies, under the cloak of friendship, put impossible dreams into his head. The senator Firmius Catus, described by Tacitus as 'his closest friend', pointed to 'his mansion crowded with ancestral portraits' and encouraged him in his luxurious lifestyle as he increasingly descended into debt. His access to Libo's house enabled him to suborn his slaves and other household staff to act as witnesses to the aristocrat's designs. In a strategy all too familiar in imperial politics, so armed, Catus in late AD 14 requested an audience with the emperor through Vescularius Flaccus, an *eques* and *amicus* of Tiberius who had accompanied him in his exiles in Rhodes and then later on Capri. The emperor declined to meet Catus, but continued to use the services of Vescularius Flaccus as an intermediary. It is clear the accusations were not entirely believed by Tiberius, but the kernel of doubt had been placed in his mind. Sejanus was to use a similar approach to his advantage in manipulating the complex yet flawed psychology of the emperor. No doubt Tiberius felt uncomfortable in the use of slaves and probably freedmen as witnesses against a man of such breeding. As his distinguished heritage demanded, Tiberius continued to invite Libo to imperial banquets and commended him for a praetorship for AD 15, yet the seeds of doubt grew and took hold for 'when Libo took part in a sacrifice among the priests, Tiberius, who was with him, had substituted a leaden knife that Libo would use; and later refused his plea for a private audience unless Drusus the Younger was present, and even then pretended to need the support of Libo's arm as they walked up and down together, and clung tightly to it.'[31] Sejanus, with the responsibility for the emperor's safety, would have been close by, armed, as was the Praetorian Prefect's privilege, with a sword in the imperial presence.

The Roman elite were ever-watchful of even the smallest signs of imperial disfavour. Libo, however, continued in his disastrous behaviours, oblivious to the fact he was being played. He continued to act and behave as though the privileges and freedoms that existed for the noble senatorial elite still applied under the Empire. Catus, probably aware of the emperor's suspicions of anyone who consulted astrologers and the legal implications of Augustan legislation, encouraged Libo to place himself in even greater danger by attempting to raise the spirits of the dead. The astrologer who had been employed by Libo then approached the senator Fulcinius Trio, a man who would be closely associated with Sejanus. He was a man slandered in Tacitus as a professional informer, a *delator*, who 'hungered after notoriety'. These were often new men, *novi homines*, who possessed immense oratorical ability and ambition but lacked the wealth and aristocratic background to attain the pinnacle of the *cursus honourum*, the consulship. The emperor had the sole monopoly on the choice of both the ordinary and *suffect* consulships, possession of which ennobled the officeholder and his descendants forever. The Senate had been filled with many wealthy provincials whose families had been rewarded for support of Julius Caesar and Octavian, as Augustus was then called, during the many civil wars. Now their children and grandchildren looked for more than a quaestorship, an aedileship or a praetorship, which were the less prestigious magistracies, but found their careers blocked after holding these posts by the aristocratic dominance of the consulship.[32]

To attain the consulship these men looked to gain imperial favour. Tiberius' steadfast adherence to Augustus' advice to keep Rome's frontiers at their present extent removed the path of gaining advancement through military glory. Instead, the only route available to these ambitious politicians was the courts. Senators were at this time tried by their peers on charges of treason or *maiestas*. Trio brought his accusations to the consuls demanding Libo be brought before the Senate. Ironically, one of the consuls was the accused's brother L. Scribonius Libo. The evidence against him was overwhelming and a date was set for the trial. The charges are preserved in an inscription found at Amiternum on which is inscribed the calendar of Roman holidays, and on 13 September it records: 'A holiday by decree of the Senate because on this day the wicked plots formed by M. Libo against Ti. Caesar and his sons and other principal men of the state and against the commonwealth itself were exposed in the Senate.' There was no 'revolutionary' and 'nefarious' conspiracy to assassinate the emperor and his family, as suggested in Velleius Paterculus, Dio and Suetonius. This interpretation was based purely on the imperial propaganda issued after the conclusion of the case. There was no great and grand conspiracy with revolutionary designs. Libo's sister Scribonia, married to the noble M. Licinius Crassus Frugi, survived, and even his brother L. Scribonius Libo was not charged with any crime. However, perhaps to prove his own loyalty, Lucius and his fellow consul decapitated a man accused of being an astrologer outside the Esquiline Gate in accordance with a senatorial resolution. Another man was thrown from the Capitoline Rock, whilst all astrologers and magicians were expelled from Italy. Tiberius considered the threat to his life supernatural rather than physical, based on the treasonous use of magic.[33]

Successful prosecutors of *maiestas* were often rewarded with a share of the estate of those convicted. Despite his debts, Libo would hold an immense amount of land. The problem for all emperors was the lack in Imperial Rome of any state prosecutors; therefore prosecutions had to rely on men willing to take the risk of attempting a prosecution in anticipation of their future reward, as failure often brought its own punishment in the confiscation of their own estate, exile or, on occasion, death. Many of the richest men in the state after the emperor were members of the nobility. Hence their hatred of the *delatores*, despite the fact that members of the aristocracy were adept at making their own accusations of *maiestas* for their own political purposes or to gain revenge, *inimicitia*, or to support a patron or an *amicus* or curry favour with the emperor. Indeed, the courts had long been used in the time of the Republic for political purposes. Libo went from mansion to mansion escorted by aristocratic female relatives, pleading for help in his defence. None volunteered. The prosecution, however, was augmented by Gaius Fonteius Agrippa and Gaius Vibius Serenus, who joined Catus and Trio: all were new men eager for imperial favour and the accused's wealth.[34]

Several frivolous and desultory charges were introduced, but the main charge was one of treasonously consulting astrologers and use of magic to bring about the end of the imperial family. Such a charge was regularly brought as it deprived the plaintiff of any effective support. None wished to be associated with allegations of treason against the emperor. Libo was already a dead man walking. He knew his conviction was inevitable, and so in desperation he appealed to the pity of Tiberius, a quality the emperor lacked. Libo, dressed in the garb of mourning, was carried into the Senate chamber in a litter, 'exhausted by fear and distress – unless, as some accounts have it, he counterfeited illness'. He was aided by his brother, and leaning on him for support, the desperate senator extended his hands to the emperor, who sat on the dais presiding over the case. Tiberius was unmoved by the appeals. Ignoring the gestures of Libo, he read over the charges against him and the names of his prosecutors with official solemnity. This very act of imperial impartiality had condemned Libo. No senator would risk a breach of *amicitiae* with the emperor in these circumstances.[35]

The denouement of the case against Libo was the production of papers listing the names of the imperial family and prominent senators. Against each name were strange and mysterious markings. Libo denied the writing was his. Senators demanded that Libo's slaves be put to torture to ascertain the truth; however, there existed a law which prohibited the use of a slave's testimony against his master. Tiberius, in his eagerness to know the truth and meaning behind these magical symbols, ordered Libo's slaves to be bought by the Treasury, allowing their evidence derived from torture to be admissible. Forgery or not, Libo's last hours had come.[36]

Libo was permitted an adjournment. He was escorted back to his mansion by Praetorians and placed under a strict guard. This was not to ensure that he did not escape. Where could he go? Relatives and friends all shunned him. It was clear to all that he contemplated suicide. He petitioned his relative and the emperor's *amicus* P. Quirinius to plead on his behalf, but to no avail. The reply came that he should direct all such requests to the Senate. The Praetorians must have received notice that Libo's last chance of salvation had gone. Their role was to use their intrusive presence to strike fear into his heart and pressurize him into committing suicide. Sejanus wished to extricate Tiberius from the position of failing to intervene in the interests of a member of the aristocratic elite by substituting the inevitable death sentence for that of exile. Libo would remain a threat even if he were left to rot on some desolate island. His final hours are described in pitiful detail by Tacitus:

> His house was picketed by soldiers; they were trampling in the portico itself, within eye shot and earshot, when Libo, thus tortured at the very feast which he had arranged to be his last delight on earth, called out for a slayer, clutched at the hands of a slave, stove to force his sword upon them. They, as they shrank back in confusion, overturned lamp and table together; and he in what was now for him the darkness of death, struck two blows into his vitals. He collapsed with a moan, and his freedmen ran up: the soldiers had witnessed the bloody scene and retired.

Despite the suicide of the defendant, Tiberius ordered the case to continue through the following day until the sentence of death was pronounced, to which, without any hint of irony, Tiberius announced that had Libo lived he would have granted him his life.[37]

The prosecution of M. Scriboinus Libo is significant for a number of reasons. It was not, however, the first trial for *maiestas*. Such a charge had already become established under Augustus. Tiberius had acted as prosecutor on behalf of Augustus in the *maiestas* trials of Terentius Varro Murena and Fannius Caepio: both were sentenced to death *in absentia*. What the outcome of the trial did was illustrate to the ambitious *novus homo* how they could gain the emperor's gratitude, as well as increase their own wealth. Libo's estate was divided up amongst the prosecution, and as he was of praetorian status, that rank was also was conferred on those prosecutors who were senators. Many now made to disassociate themselves from the fallen Libo and gain imperial gratitude by making ever more preposterous suggestions as the emperor presided over the vote on sentencing.[38] These scenes would reoccur time and again over the decades, reaching a tragic conclusion in the purges and terror that accompanied Sejanus' fall. The events also suggest that Sejanus' influence up to AD 16 remained in its infancy. Neither Catus nor Trio approached or involved Sejanus in these events; indeed, in his time of need it was Drusus whom Tiberius turned to. Tacitus says as much when commenting on the events of AD 23. The historian states that the 'power of the prefectship ... had hitherto been moderate', but by AD 23 Sejanus was ascendant.[39] The fall of Libo had been an opportunity for Sejanus, who had made himself useful in ensuring Tiberius could claim that he would have granted mercy if he had not been thwarted by the suicide of the defendant. The emperor could avoid the stigma attached to the execution of a member of the aristocracy, and for that he would have had Sejanus to thank. Tiberius was in no doubt of Libo's guilt and his use of magic and astrology to conspire against the imperial family. Subsequent penalties attached to astrologers prove that. Tiberius' overriding fear of assassination by physical or supernatural means make it highly unlikely that he would have spared Libo, despite his posthumous claims. Sejanus had again proved himself the consummate politician and advisor.

The case had also demonstrated to Sejanus the power of these ambitious *delatores* in political intrigues. He regularly employed these men in the destruction of his own opponents. These prosecutors would also be bound to him for protection, as powerful nobles such as Libo had many powerful relatives, *amici* and clients. The role of prosecutor was always a dangerous and risky business. Acting for the defence was relatively risk-free and readily undertaken by the defendants' relatives and those *amici* wishing to gain a patronal bond through *amicitiae*. However, prosecution would result in *inimicitia*, a virtual public declaration of enmity with the accused's *amici* and relatives. Many years later, in AD 32, Vescularius Flaccus, one of the agents of Libo's destruction, was executed by Tiberius, 'whence the greater joy, when it was learned that the precedents had recoiled upon their contrivers'. Catus fared little better. In AD 24 this rather unsavoury character prosecuted his sister for *maiestas*. However, the majority of the Senate supported his sister and convicted Catus of *calumnia*, making a false charge, and he was sentenced to exile with the loss of his senatorial status. Tiberius, however, no doubt remembering his past services, intervened and saved Catus from banishment, but not his removal from the Senate. Fonteius Agrippa appears to have attained no further offices after the praetorship. He did offer his daughter as a Vestal Virgin, but she was rejected by Tiberius on the religious grounds that her father was a divorcee but in compensation gave her a million sesterces as a dowry. Vibius Serenus was probably already a praetor in AD 16, and so in his mind he felt he had gone unrewarded despite gaining a share of Libo's estate. He wrote to Tiberius requesting a greater reward and subsequently became governor of Further Spain. However, his lack of tact had offended the emperor, and this left him vulnerable to prosecution. Upon his return to Rome in AD 23, he was charged and convicted with public violence, probably against a Roman citizen, and was exiled to the island of Amorgos. His own son, perhaps to escape the ignominy of his father and gain imperial favour – for it was well known that Tiberius hated his father – charged him with treasonous involvement in the revolt of Sacrovir in Gaul. Vibius Serenus the Elder was recalled and made to stand in rags and chains before his son. Despite the torture of his old slaves, a lack of evidence resulted in the charges being rejected, upon which Vibius Serenus the Younger fled, fearing the vengeance of the mob. However, Tiberius had him brought back to court to prolong the humiliation of his father and ensure 'justice' was seen to be done. The Senate knew the sentence the emperor desired and Vibius Serenus the Elder was found guilty. Those currying imperial favours suggested he should be decapitated or exiled to a waterless island. Tiberius vetoed these motions and he was returned to Amorgos to live out his days. The son, despite being universally despised, continued to operate as a *delatores*, even surviving a failed charge against the eminent and widely admired Fonteius Capito as he had become 'quasi-sacrosanct' under imperial protection.[40]

Only one of the four prosecutors of Scribonius Libo was associated with Sejanus: Lucius Fulcinius Trio. It is perhaps no coincidence that his career prospered after AD 16 until it was brought to an ignominious end in AD 35 through his close connection with the fallen Praetorian Prefect. Our sources fail to indicate when the two established a bond of *amicitiae*, but there is no hint of any involvement in the trial of Libo. However, from the fate of most of those involved, it was clear that the emperor might find favour for services rendered in a successful prosecution; future imperial protection under the guise of *amicitiae* was negligible once Tiberius felt his debt had been paid. In most circumstances, once Tiberius demonstrated his gratitude with a reward of an office, magistracy or wealth, the relationship of *amicitiae* was ended.[41] Many new men, especially those who took the risky course of accelerating their career through prosecutions, required a powerful figure who could act as their long-term protector in a client-patron relationship. The emperor of course, with his access to imperial *beneficia*, was the ultimate patron, but Tiberius would not wish to associate himself too closely with the infamous *delatores*. The emperor saw himself as a member of the aristocracy and strove to uphold the *auctoritas* of this class in the form of the Senate. Emperors who did associate themselves with the *delatores* were branded as tyrannical or mad. The fates of Caligula, Domitian or Commodus and their condemnation by the senatorial historians are testament to the aristocratic antagonism towards this threat to their security and status. Tiberius himself is criticized by Tacitus for his implicit encouragement of accusations and charges through the rewards offered on a successful prosecution. When it was suggested that these rewards be removed, the emperor rejected the proposal on the understandable grounds that his safety, synonymous with the safety of the state, depended upon these men. Even those emperors who, like Tiberius, initially attempted to legally restrict the force of the *maiestas* law, and impose restrictions on the role of *delatores*, soon rescinded the legislation. In the eyes of the emperors, the *delatores* were not forces of destruction but instead, as Tiberius argued, ensured the enforcement of the law and provided a valuable service to the emperor. Furthermore, an emperor could deflect criticism of himself by blaming a *delator*. To the aristocracy, however, they threatened the stability of society, as the status and position of the nobility was threatened by social inferiors whose use of informers and witnesses in prosecutions undermined the *fides*, trust, upon which the system of *amicitiae* was based. Note the shock of Tacitus when the noble Aemilius Scaurus prosecuted his fellow aristocrat Junius Silanus in AD 22, or when in AD 27 the equally illustrious P Cornelius Dolabella prosecuted Quintillius Varus. These were men who betrayed their own class.[42]

The philosopher Epictetus compares the choices facing a politician considering the dangers they might encounter as they journeyed along the *cursus honorum* to that of a traveller anticipating the threats posed on a notoriously dangerous road:

> This is the way circumspect travellers act. Word reaches them that the road is beset with highwaymen. A solitary traveller does not like the odds, he waits in order to attach himself to an ambassador, quaestor or provincial governor and only travels securely once he is part of their entourage. Which is how a prudent person proceeds

along life's road. He thinks, 'There are countless thieves and bandits, many storms, and many chances to get lost or relieved of one's belongings. How are we to evade them and come through without being attacked? What party should we wait to join, with whom should we enlist, to ensure safe passage? With this man perhaps – the person who is rich and influential? No, not much to be gained there; he's liable to lose his position, break down and prove of no use to me at all. And suppose my travel companion himself betrays and robs me? Well, then, I'll become a friend of Caesar – no one will try to take advantage of me as long as I am Caesar's friend. But in the first place, what will I need to suffer or sacrifice in order to get close to him? How much money will I have to spend, on how many people? And if I do manage it – well after all the emperor is mortal too. Add to which by some mischance he becomes my enemy, I suppose I will have no recourse except to flee and take refuge in the wilderness.'[43]

To the ambitious *novus homo* hoping to attain the consulship, Tiberius appeared to be an unpredictable and reluctant travelling companion, and due to his advancing years, he might possibly leave them to journey on alone. Sejanus, aged around 36 in AD 16 and, although related to the nobility, not counted amongst them, had established himself at the side of the emperor. He presented a more reliable long-term companion. His patronage was sought by the ambitious senators who lacked a noble name and equites, including Fulcinius Trio. The prosecutor of Libo had even before this date gained renown as an oratorical genius but a sullied reputation as a 'professional informer'. After receiving his share of Libo's estates and his rank as praetor, Trio made a greater name for himself as a prosecutor of Gnaeus Caplurnius Piso in AD 20. Piso had been charged on three counts. In the first count he stood accused by Trio of extortion when governor in Spain, the other more serious charges being of inciting a civil war by illegally raising troops to force his reinstatement as governor of Syria and poisoning Germanicus, Tiberius' adopted son. After the trial, Tiberius rewarded the other prosecutors with priesthoods, but to Trio the emperor 'promised his preferment but warned him not to let impetuosity become the downfall of his eloquence'. In AD 22 he became the governor of Lusitania, and then on 1 July AD 31 became *suffect* consul, replacing the emperor and Sejanus who resigned their tenure as ordinary consuls.[44] Tiberius would have appointed him to the consulship, perhaps as a fulfilment of the promise he made after the trial of Piso. It was evident to all, however, that he was an *amicus* of Sejanus. In narrating the events of AD 35, Dio explains that Fulcinius Trio 'had been a friend of Sejanus but had stood high in the favour of Tiberius on account of his services as an informer'. Trio had managed to survive the fall of Sejanus in AD 31 despite being threatened with prosecution, but the hatred of Macro made further accusations inevitable and he committed suicide in AD 35.[45]

A number of former *amici* of Germanicus later appear as *amici* of Sejanus. These aspiring politicians had fulfilled their promise to avenge his death by bringing his supposed poisoner to justice. Some continued to patronise his wife Agrippina, but others looked to Sejanus as someone in a better position to support their quest for future offices and honours. Quintus Servaeus, an ex-praetor, was appointed to govern Commagene in Armenia by Germanicus in AD 17, but upon his death returned to Rome to prosecute Piso and was rewarded with a priesthood by Tiberius. He next reappears to history in AD 32 as a former *amicus* of Sejanus who elicited some sympathy during his trial for the fact he had not abused his *amicitiae* with the former Praetorian Prefect. This did him little good as he was found guilty, and only managed to save his life by turning informer.[46]

Another prosecutor of Piso was Germanicus' *amicus* Publius Vitellius, who had served as a legate of Germanicus in the campaigns in Germany and the East. The Vitelli were an equestrian family from Nuceria; his father was a procurator of Augustus whose successful career enabled his four sons to enter the Senate. The fates of Publius and his three brothers, all new men, are an embodiment of the vicissitudes of courtly politics. Quintus lost his status in a purge of undesirable senators initiated by Tiberius in AD 17, supposedly impoverished by his vices, whilst Aulus gained the reputation of an epicure, holding sumptuous banquets. He was honoured with a *suffect* consulship in AD 32 during the terror following the purges of Sejanus' supporters, indicating that there was no link between them. His brother Publius appears to have courted the patronage of Sejanus after the death of Germanicus, and at some point before AD 31 he attained a praetorship, but the demise of his patron led to a series of accusations against him. He was first placed into the custody of his brother Aulus, whose attempts to save him ultimately failed as he died in prison. The youngest brother Lucius, described by Suetonius as a man of integrity and industry, as well as being a skilful flatterer, looked to the patronage of Antonia the Younger, the widow of Tiberius' dead brother Nero Claudius Drusus. He gained his first consulship in AD 34, and his services to Claudius were rewarded with further consulships in AD 43 and 47. The political connections of Aulus and Lucius shielded them from any accusations linked to the fall of Publius, despite their attempts to save him. It was probably Antonia's influence with Tiberius that protected them.[47]

It must be more than coincidence that three of the four prosecutors of Piso later became known associates of Sejanus. The fourth, Q. Veranius, disappears from the pages of history. The Praetorian Prefect was rumoured to be involved in the background, operating beyond public scrutiny. Tacitus states that as a young man he remembered 'hearing my elders speak of a document seen more than once in Piso's hands. The purport he himself never disclosed, but his friends always asserted that it contained a letter from Tiberius with his instructions about Germanicus; and that, if he had not been tricked by the empty promises of Sejanus, he was resolved to produce it before the Senate and to put the emperor upon his defence. His death, they believed, was not self-inflicted: an assassin had been let loose to do the work.' The historian appears to doubt the authenticity of this oral account, yet it reappears in a slightly different form in Suetonius: 'It is even believed that he [Tiberius] arranged for Gnaeus Piso, the Governor of Syria, to poison Germanicus; and that Piso, when tried on this charge, would have produced his instructions had they not been taken from him when he confronted Tiberius with them.' According to Tacitus, before the case was heard before the Senate, Tiberius had held a private review of the case in the palace, where accompanied by 'a few intimate friends for assessors, he heard the threats of the accusers, the prayers of the accused; and remitted the case in its integrity to the Senate'. This was possibly the occasion for Sejanus, accompanied by members of the guard and the four prosecutors, to pressurize the isolated Piso into handing over any incriminating documentation. Despite the accusations of the prosecutors, and the cries of the mob baying for Piso's blood, Tiberius is extremely unlikely to have sanctioned the murder of his adopted son, despite his doubts regarding his capabilities. The emperor was punctilious in following the wishes and guidance of Augustus. However, Tacitus refers to a 'belief' that Piso had received 'private instructions' from Tiberius to monitor and restrain the actions of Germanicus, with Piso's wife Plancina receiving a similar directive from her friend Livia, directed in this case towards Agrippina.[48]

Piso faced daily threats and abuse from the mob as he was carried in a litter from his house to the Senate-house escorted by Praetorians, and then in the Senate itself he faced a sea of invective as the emperor sat presiding, imperious and coldly impartial. Support came only from his sons, who had disowned their mother as she abandoned her husband and sought sanctuary in the protection of Livia. Upon his arrival home after each harrowing day in court, a Praetorian tribune with his soldiers stood sentinel around his mansion, until one morning Piso was found in his bedroom with his throat cut. The intimidating presence of the Praetorians that had worked so effectively in undermining the will of Libo had again played a part in this suicide. His death, though, did not save the emperor from further embarrassment. Livia demanded that Tiberius plead for Plancina, an act he resented but felt it was his matriarchal duty to acquiesce to. The emperor stood before the Senate asking for mercy for the wife when he had failed to intervene on behalf of her husband. The Senate dutifully complied. The emperor was not one to forgive or forget. His mother's death in AD 29 released him from his promise, and Plancina was charged once more. She committed suicide to avoid an inevitable conviction.[49]

The actions and attitude of Tiberius in both the cases brought against Libo and Piso are remarkably similar. There was a studied impartiality and rectitude in his public persona, and yet behind the scenes there are glimpses of his Praetorian Prefect acting to manage events to the emperor's advantage. The Praetorians, an extension of Tiberius'authority, were used to strike fear and terror into the hearts of the accused; their very presence an indication that the emperor's clemency was denied. The bonds that were clearly established between Sejanus and at least three of the prosecutors of Piso suggest, but by no means prove, that some form of deal was struck at this time.

The death of Germanicus changed the dynamics of imperial politics. Sejanus appears to have kept out of the factions that had coalesced around the two possible heirs to the throne, even though 'the court was split and torn by unspoken preferences for Germanicus or for Drusus', yet despite this, the two men 'maintained a singular unanimity'. Sejanus could not later accuse Germanicus' widow, Agrippina, of creating factions and divisions within the imperial family if he himself had done so.[50] Furthermore, Germanicus' *amici* could hardly have sought the patronage of Sejanus if it were publicly known that he was attempting to undermine Germanicus, and later Agrippina. Drusus had returned from Illyricum in March AD 20 to receive the ashes of Germanicus in Rome and attend his funeral. He must have returned to his province soon after, but was back in Rome again to appear at the trial of Piso and receive his ovation for his campaign beyond the Danube that nullified the threat of the Marcomanni. Drusus continued to cast a benevolent eye over his adopted brother's children despite the fact he had twins of his own, born to Livilla in AD 19, of whom only Tiberius Gemellus would survive childhood.[51] Germanicus' own children were in AD 20 too young to be considered as immediate heirs to the ageing Tiberius. The eldest, Nero, born *c*. AD 6/7, was officially recognized as an adult when he assumed the *toga virilis* on 7 June, with Tiberius requesting that the Senate allow him to stand for the quaestorship five years before the legal age. Nero was also honoured with a priesthood and a donative was given to the people. However, his youth precluded his ability to become emperor should the emperor die. Nero had two younger brothers, Drusus, aged 12, and Caligula, nearly 8. Tiberius' intentions became clear when his own son Drusus was nominated as consul for AD 21, the office to be shared with his father, whilst Nero was betrothed to Julia Livilla, Drusus' daughter. Augustus had planned for Germanicus to succeed Tiberius, but that design had been destroyed by the intervention of fate. Tiberius now saw that a regency was needed in the figure of his son who would be succeeded, as Augustus had wished, by an emperor of his own bloodline, Germanicus' son Nero. This arrangement was cemented by an imperial marriage, just as Julia had been married to Tiberius.[52]

The announcement of the marriage of Nero and Julia Livilla was well received; however, the proclamation included a surprise that stunned many. Sejanus' young daughter Junilla was betrothed to the son of Germanicus' brother Claudius and Urgulanilla. Claudius was an often-forgotten member of the imperial house, whose slight physical impediment meant that he was frequently overlooked and ignored by contemporaries and members of his own family. He was the grandson of Octavia, Augustus' older sister, and was Tiberius' nephew. Members of the aristocracy resented the link between a municipal equestrian and the house of the emperor. The betrothal can only have been an informal arrangement, as both parties were too young, with a formal engagement to follow at a later date. The arrangement, however, only lasted a few days due to the tragic death of Junilla's betrothed, who choked to death when the boy threw up a pear and caught it in his upturned mouth.[53]

Another indication of Tiberius' favour towards Sejanus came in the form of the *ornamenta praetoria*. This honorary status of a senator with praetorian rank derived from the Republican tradition of honouring a man who had provided distinguished service with the insignia, privileges and appropriate dress of a senator of this office without conferring senatorial service. Augustus had given the decoration to members of his own family, but the award to Sejanus was the first occasion that the honour was bestowed on anyone outside this group. It became established custom later for *ornamenta consularia* to be given to Praetorian Prefects, although Macro, Sejanus' successor, turned down the senatorial offer of *ornamenta praetoria*, no doubt because Sejanus had been criticized for accepting too many honours.[54]

According to Dio, AD 20 marks the point when Sejanus' power and influence were ascendant, as Tiberius 'had made him his advisor and assistant in all matters'. Both Tacitus and Dio link his consolidation of power to the establishment of the Praetorian camp. Sejanus brought 'together into a single camp the various cohorts which had been separate and distinct from one another like those of the night watch. In this way, the entire force could receive its orders promptly, and would inspire everybody with fear because all were together in one camp.' Tacitus also acknowledges the power of the Praetorian Prefect in the creation of the Praetorian fortress, but places this in his account of the year AD 23: 'The power of the prefectship, which had hitherto been moderate, he increased by massing the cohorts, dispersed throughout the capital, in order that commands should reach them simultaneously, and that their numbers, their strength, and the sight of one another, might in themselves breed confidence and in others awe.'[55] The difference in dates is probably to be accounted for in the length of time it took to construct the camp, with building beginning in AD 20 and completed in AD 23. Tacitus opens book four with an assessment of Sejanus, who would dominate the following pages, and this allowed him to link the two together as a literary symbol denoting the rise of the prefect. The Romans were fixated on status symbols; this ranged from the grandeur of houses and the luxurious nature of banquets, with food served on gold and silver plates, to the seating arrangements in the theatre or the order a man gave his *sententia* or opinion in a senatorial debate. Sumptuary laws tried to limit the ostentatious display of wealth, but they were often ignored. The ultimate symbol of power was control over life and death, and that came in the presence of the imperial guard, forever at the side of the emperor, his immediate family and at the command of Sejanus.[56]

Despite the insinuations of both Dio and Tacitus, the relocation of the Praetorians would be Tiberius' decision. Suetonius refers only to the emperor when explaining the reasons for the relocation of the cohorts. There was no sinister motivation behind the creation of the Praetorian camp. Both our sources note that one of the reasons was purely administrative, to coordinate the communication of commands and orders. Tacitus also adds that before the relocation of the troops from the surrounding towns to the capital, discipline had become lax. The Praetorians would have taken full advantages of the bars, inns and brothels that populated the streets of Rome, as well as the baths, which did not just supply services dedicated to hygiene but offered, in many instances, other opportunities for relaxation and pleasure. Furthermore, the ancient sources are replete with numerous examples of altercations between the civilian population and off-duty soldiers acting with the arrogance that comes with the point of a sword. A greater concern was the potential delay that would occur, as 'when a sudden emergency called, help was more effective if the helpers were compact'. Unrest in the theatre probably precipitated the relocation of most of the Praetorians from the surrounding towns, and in AD 20 there was a further outbreak of popular unrest when 'the commons protested against the appalling dearness of corn'. A delay in the deployment of the Praetorians around the palace, in the theatre or on the streets of Rome might have served as the reason for the creation of a central barracks.[57]

The Praetorian fortress was built in the north-east corner of the city on the Viminal Hill. This brooding physical edifice was a constant reminder of the power of Tiberius and his Praetorian Prefect. The design was unique, planned around the practicalities of housing many soldiers within the limited confines of an urban metropolis. The walls were 5m in height, composed of brick faced with concrete, topped with a wall walk and interspersed with sixteen towers that did not project beyond the wall. There were four gates, one on each wall, but no defensive ditch. The purpose was to impress and intimidate. The fortress protected the vulnerable north-east approach to the city, but in the opposite direction, a road ran straight to the imperial forum and the palace above it. The fortress covered nearly 17 hectares, with every available space used to the maximum. Barrack blocks built back-to-back were found running along the entire length of the interior, divided by a narrow strip of more opulent buildings which consisted of rooms arranged around a small courtyard with *impluvia* and basins. These were probably the houses of the centurions and other officers. Excavation of the barrack blocks has found the base of stairs, indicating that the blocks were two storeys high. Inside the inner-facing walls of the fortress were built a series of concrete vaults with mosaic floors and plastered ceilings, which have been interpreted as communal living quarters for the *contubernia*, the smallest unit of the army which was originally linked to the group of men who shared a tent. At the intersection of the four roads that entered the camp, there was a large apsidal building within which were discovered many votive offerings. This building clearly had a religious function and was one of many shrines that catered for the different religious persuasions of the soldiers. A large underground chamber in the south-east corner was likely to be the armoury, although a prison did exist as well. Other structures normally associated with a military camp were lacking, including baths and hospitals, as the facilities of the capital were expected to provide these. There was also no headquarters building, so we can assume this remained within the imperial palace. Sejanus would want every excuse to remain as close to the emperor as possible, and much of his time would have been spent in the palace so, for practical reasons, it made sense to retain the *principium* there. There were no living quarters for the prefect, so again, Sejanus would have owned a large townhouse, probably situated on the Palatine Hill near to the emperor.[58]

The fortress had room for around 15,000 men. There were nine Praetorian cohorts of a 1,000 men each, and three of the urban cohorts were also housed in the Praetorian camp. These urban cohorts were numbered ten to twelve, indicating that they had originally been formed from guard units. This was a clever rouse by Sejanus, as the urban cohorts were technically under the command of the City Prefect, the ageing Lucius Calpurnius Piso the Pontifex. He was a close confidant of both Augustus and Tiberius, whose trust in him is demonstrated from his tenure of the post from AD 13 until his death in AD 32. He was 68 years old in AD 20 and probably more than willing to acquiesce to the practical and logical arguments of relocating his cohorts in the new Praetorian fortress. This would enable Sejanus to effectively control these three cohorts as well. In AD 31 Tiberius questioned the loyalty of the Praetorians and the urban cohorts, and instead had to rely on the *vigiles* in his plan to remove Sejanus.[59] There was though room for an additional three cohorts, which appears strange considering the plan maximizes the use of space. It is possible that Sejanus used the popular unrest in Rome and the need to send Praetorians to accompany members of the imperial family on campaigns to argue for an expansion of the number of cohorts. Germanicus had two Praetorian cohorts on the Rhine, and probably two when he toured the East. Two Praetorian cohorts were sent to accompany his ashes on their return to Rome from Brundisium. Drusus no doubt had two Praetorian cohorts in his campaigns in Illyria and beyond the Danube. Soldiers were also sent to crush disturbances at Pollentia in northern Italy. There were twelve Praetorian cohorts by the reign of Caligula. The expansion does appear to have occurred under Tiberius, as an inscription discovered in Lecce Dei Marsi records the unusual career of an Aulus Virgius Marsus. It says he had served as the elite centurion, the *primus pilius*, in the legions before being promoted to serve as tribune in the 'IIII' [sic] Praetorian cohort around AD 14. He then returned to the post of *primus pilius* for a second time, followed by promotion to two senior offices as *praefectus castrorum* in Egypt and the *praefectus fabrum*, but then he returned to the guard as a tribune of the XI cohort around AD 23. This epigraphical evidence suggests that the move to the Praetorian fortress was used as an opportunity by Sejanus to create three new cohorts which required the need for more experienced officers.[60]

The move to the Praetorian camp and the possible expansion of the cohorts probably accounts for the scorpion insignia which was adopted by the guard, which is seen on their shields. The scorpion was the birth sign of Tiberius. The emperor thereby claimed that he had refounded the guard. His close advisors were no doubt involved in the decision, Sejanus included.[61] The Praetorian Prefect worked to ensure the officers of the guard remained bound to him as their patron. All appointments throughout the Empire were made based on patronage. Tacitus implies a sinister motive in Sejanus' actions as 'he began little by little to insinuate himself into the affections of the private soldiers, approaching them and addressing them by name, while at the same time he selected personally their centurions and tribunes.'[62] This appears to be the behaviour of a good commander, and as the Praetorian Prefect he would have appointed his own officers, probably passing the list for the approval of the emperor. A legate in command of a legion appointed his own tribunes and was responsible for the appointment of centurions and other officers, reviewing their record and letters of recommendation. During the reign of Augustus, the Praetorians were mainly recruited from Umbria, Etruria and the oldest Roman colonies, although increasingly this extended to northern Italy. Strabo and Sejanus were major landholders and patrons in Etruria, so it would be expected that some appointments would be their clients. Praetorian tribunes had often served as elite centurions in the legions, the *primus pilius*, and then as tribunes in the *vigiles* and urban cohorts to the guard, although as yet there was no established career path. The ambitious officer looking to progress from a tribunate in the lesser military units in the capital to the elite guard cohorts would look to the favour and patronage of the Praetorian Prefect, which would help to extend Sejanus' influence. Furthermore, many Praetorian soldiers joined the legions as centurions. This was not part of a sinister plan, as suggested in the sources, but a natural effect of the system of *amicitiae* that formed the foundation of Roman society.[63]

Tiberius' trust and increasing reliance on Sejanus' advice is not only demonstrated by the construction of the Praetorian fortress and inclusion of the urban cohorts within the ramparts, but also the Praetorian Prefect's accumulation of great estates and wealth. In AD 32 Tiberius transferred Sejanus' estates that had been confiscated on his *damnatio memoriae* from the state treasury to the imperial, probably as it was he who had granted the majority of them to him as a public sign of his imperial favour. Juvenal comments on the illusion of power and questions the misplaced desire of those who looked to the 'prestige and prosperity' of the emperor's once great counsellor: 'Do you wish to be greeted like Sejanus? To be as rich? To dispense the seats of highest office to some, and to appoint others to army commands?'[64] Sejanus competed with his rivals in demonstrating his political influence by the pursuit of the exotic and the extravagance of his luxurious lifestyle. One of Sejanus' eunuchs named Paezon, meaning 'toy boy', was purchased for 50 million sesterces by the noted equestrian poet Clutorius Priscus. The price apparently reflected the beauty of the slave rather than the desires of the purchaser. This wealth, and his access to the emperor, allowed Sejanus to extend his own network of *amici* and clients. The senator Junius Otho was said to have owed his entry to the Senate to the influence of Sejanus. Tacitus asserts he had previously been a schoolmaster. There can be little doubt that Sejanus provided the 1 million sesterces that was the minimum entry requirement to enter the Senate. He was a praetor in AD 22, so must have entered the Senate at the start of Sejanus' career. Otho would not have been the only one of Sejanus' monetary *beneficia*; members of the equestrian class were also recipients. The knight Geminius appears to have been beset by debts incurred through his 'prodigal expenditure and effeminacy of life', but was drawn into Sejanus' *amicitiae* through a gift of money. Vast amounts of wealth granted to Sejanus through imperial favour enabled him to extend his influence. In AD 31 Tiberius was so worried that the Senate would not vote for the execution of Sejanus that the consul Regulus was instructed to only ask one senator, who had probably been previously suborned, whether the former imperial favourite should be imprisoned. There were so many relatives and friends of Sejanus in the Senate that Tiberius feared significant opposition to his demands. This extensive and formidable network of *amicitiae* would have taken many years to build.[65]

Chapter 4

The Right Hand of Caesar: AD 21–23

'Tiberius, far from demurring, was complaisant enough to celebrate "the partner of his labours" not only in conversation but before the Fathers and the people.'

(Tiberius, commenting on his reliance upon Sejanus, in Tacitus, *Annals* 4.2)

It is not difficult to imagine Drusus' reaction to Tiberius' lauding of the Praetorian Prefect, a man who he now appeared to compete with in the affections of the emperor. Drusus was positioned as the chosen heir of the ageing Tiberius, with both opening the year AD 21 as joint consuls. After the necessary ceremonies had been completed, Tiberius left Rome for Campania and Capri on the grounds of poor health. Tiberius had rarely left the environs of the city since the commencement of his rule, and then only as far as Antium, a coastal town about 30 miles south of Rome. He now felt that his son could be relied upon to take charge of the administration of the Empire and his absence from the capital would publicly indicate to the world he was the chosen successor. Sejanus almost certainly accompanied Tiberius on his sojourn away from Rome. This was no abandoning of his son, but a public announcement that Drusus stood at the helm of the ship of state. At 61 years of age, Tiberius was preparing the world for his death as well as anticipating the retirement he earnestly desired.[1] The situation was a threat to the position of Sejanus. Clearly, he was Tiberius' appointment and there was little certainty that his son would warm to his counsel or indeed retain him in post. The 'promotion' of Strabo to the prefecture of Egypt was a reminder that office was at the gift of the emperor. Limited access to imperial *beneficia* and patronage would inevitably loosen the bonds that secured Sejanus' own *amici* and clients to him. However, fortune appeared to be on his side.

Early in the year Drusus fell dangerously ill and appeared on the point of death. The records of the *Arval Brethren* in a fragmentary inscription state that 'Caesar' was too ill to attend the celebrations in May AD 21 and his place had to be taken by a substitute. Clearly, this must refer to Drusus as Tiberius was absent. The same inscription records that sacrifices had been offered for the recovery of some important personage. It is surprising that the emperor did not return to Rome to tend to his ailing successor as he did return the following year upon receiving news that his mother Livia was seriously ill. Tacitus explicitly states that he received news of the Gallic revolt of Sacrovir whilst in Campania and that he did not return to Rome until AD 22, which is confirmed by the *Fasti Praenestini*. Dio's account, which is preserved and summarized in the *epitome* of Xiphilinus, is less specific, describing how Tiberius returned to Rome 'when his consulship had expired'. Tiberius resigned his consulship after three months, allowing Drusus to continue as consul until the end of the year alongside a number of *suffect* consuls. This might suggest the emperor returned in April, as suggested by Bellemore; however, Dio places Tiberius' return after the trial of Clutorius Priscus, which is dated with certainty to the end of AD 21.[2]

The failure of Tiberius to travel to Rome is surprising, perhaps suggesting that Drusus' illness was not as serious as first thought. However, the prosecution of Clutorius Priscus would suggest otherwise. The renowned poet, who had bought the eunuch Paezon from Sejanus for an exorbitant price, perhaps hoping to gain the Praetorian Prefect's favour, had, upon the death of Germanicus, composed a panegyric for the deceased Caesar for which he was handsomely rewarded by Tiberius. He now made a serious mistake of anticipating the death of Drusus by composing a second panegyric, which he intended to publish upon news of the Caesar's imminent demise. Instead of shelving this work when Drusus recovered, he erred in giving a public reading of it in the house of Publius Petronius. He was denounced by an informer and charged, possibly with *maiestas*.[3] Drusus as consul would preside over the case, whilst the senior prosecutor was Haterius Agrippa, the consul designate whom Drusus had personally supported for the post of praetor in AD 17 along with Germanicus. Marcus Lepidus and the ex-consul Rubellius Blandus alone came to Clutorius Priscus' defence to urge clemency. The anger of Drusus would have ensured the inevitability of a guilty verdict and the imposition of the maximum penalty. The poet was immediately dragged from the Senate to his execution. A few days later the Senate received an angry letter from Tiberius, who, whilst commending its members for their diligence and loyalty, reprimanded the senators for 'such a hurried punishment for a verbal offence'. The Senate then issued a *senatus consultum* that in future nine days had to elapse between sentencing and execution.[4]

The moderate demand of the emperor is understandable. The time delay would allow messages to reach him in Campania and a reply to be returned. This might suggest that Tiberius was considering a protracted stay in Campania in the future. Furthermore, the emperor wished to reassert his right to review all capital sentences upon persons of note. This law was ignored in the execution of Sejanus.[5] It could be that in the frenzy and lust for revenge that accompanied his fall this legal requirement was conveniently forgotten. None but a brave or foolish man would have drawn the attention of the Senate to this at this moment of political turmoil. However, none of our contemporary sources refer to his execution as an illegal act. Perhaps it was known that Sejanus' influence was behind Tiberius' objections in AD 21 to the hurried execution of Clutorius Priscus as the absent Praetorian Prefect would have been unable to use his influence to defend his own clients and *amici* if this judicial action remained unchallenged.

A surprising number of Sejanus' network of clients and *amici* were noted for their literary pursuits and oratorical talents. The equestrian poet Clutorius Priscus was clearly such a regular visitor to the house of Sejanus that he came to appreciate the 'qualities' of the eunuch Paezon. Another client was Junius Otho, who had kept a school and was made a senator through Sejanus' influence. Otho was, according to Seneca the Elder, a rhetorician of great repute who used humour and wit to gain the favour of his audience. He also wrote four books of *colores*. He was elected praetor in AD 22 and so was nominated the previous year, gaining Tiberius' approval whilst he was accompanied by Sejanus in Campania. Otho practised declamations with another of Sejanus' clients, Bruttedius Niger,[6] who was an aedile in AD 22 and had no doubt benefited from Sejanus' influence in attaining this minor office. He was destined through his eloquence for greater things. He had trained under the rhetor Apollodorus of Pergamum, to the extent that he was 'amply provided with liberal accomplishments, and bound, if he kept the straight road, to attain all distinctions, was goaded by a spirit of haste, which impelled him to outpace first his equals, then his superiors, and finally his own ambitions: an infirmity fatal to many, even of the good, who disdaining the sure and slow, force a premature success, though destruction may accompany the prize'. Tacitus clearly admired the man for his abilities but condemned him for choosing as his patron a man whose ambitions echoed his own. Niger paid the penalty of looking beyond a place in the Senate sat alongside former praetors, and instead let his gaze rest upon the highest offices of state. He was not only a gifted rhetor but also an accomplished historian, writing a work on the fall of Cicero.

He was clearly a man admired for his wide-ranging accomplishments, lacking only the advantage of a noble name. Ironically, Tacitus identifies Bruttedius Niger as a 'man abounding in noble talents' whilst criticizing him for an ambition that was unsuited to his status.[7] Another senatorial poet identified as a client of Sejanus was Sextius Paconianus. Described by Tacitus as a *delator* who was 'bold, wicked, prying into everyone's secrets', he was possibly praetor *peregrinus* in AD 26 and praetor in AD 32. Attempting to save himself after the execution of Sejanus, he turned informer and prosecuted another of Sejanus' clients, but was still imprisoned. He continued to write verses slandering the emperor from the cell in which he was strangled.[8]

Otho, Niger and Paconianus were new men who through necessity would look for the patronage of a powerful figure at court for their social, political and literary advancement. Such men, lacking the *dignitas* of a great name or the inherited wealth and connections through the bounds of *amicitiae*, could at most aspire to the lower offices of state, the aedileship, perhaps a praetorship or a minor priesthood. A consulship would be for most beyond their aspirations.[9] Sejanus had nurtured their careers, no doubt acting initially as a patron of the arts. Sejanus also appears to have developed connections to members of the aristocracy with interests in literary pursuits. Mamercus Aemilius Scaurus came from an ancient family and was destined for the consulship from birth. Praetor in AD 14, during the senatorial debate he attempted to cajole Tiberius into accepting imperial powers without delay but succeeded in merely arousing the emperor's anger and suspicions.[10] His name carried him to a *suffect* consulship in June/July AD 21 and he was a member of the *frates Arvales*, so his friendship with Sejanus cannot be interpreted as an attempt to further his career. In AD 22 he joined with both Bruttedius Niger and Junius Otho in the prosecution of C. Junius Silanus for *repetundae* or corruption whilst governor of Asia and *maiestas*. This was an astute move by Scaurus, who feared the hatred of the emperor and looked to either placate him through involvement in prosecuting a crime that Tiberius despised, or to gain the favour of the Praetorian Prefect through cooperating openly with his clients. The prosecution for *repetundae* was successful, but Tiberius remained implacable in his hatred of Scaurus. However, he did gain the *amicitiae* of Sejanus. Scaurus was also a writer of tragedies, which would be the instrument of his eventual demise rather than the fatal friendship of Sejanus. He was accused of *maiestas* in AD 32, but the case was postponed as Tiberius wished to preside over it himself. In AD 34 he was again accused, but this time at the instigation of Sejanus' successor Macro. The charges were criticizing the emperor in his play *Atreus*, as well as adultery with Drusus' widow Livilla and use of magic. Scaurus committed suicide. His reputation suffered through his association with Sejanus, but despite this he is described by Tacitus as 'the most fluent orator of that generation'. Seneca, however, praises his great talent but criticizes him for being too lazy to develop his abilities as his speeches lacked planning and were considered too aggressive, striving to antagonize his opponents and draw them into an altercation.[11]

Another distinguished senator whose early career appears linked to the family of Sejanus was Publius Pomponius Secundus. He is described by Tacitus as 'a man of great refinement of character and shining talents'. His father was possibly Gaius Pomponius Graecinus, the *suffect* consul of AD 16, or his brother the ordinary consul of AD 17, Lucius Pomponius Flaccus. A tragic poet of great repute, he was the subject of a now lost biography by Pliny. Pomponius also appears to be a man of integrity and bravery as he attempted to hide Sejanus' son in his gardens after the arrest and execution of his father. P Pomponius Secundus was sentenced before the Senate but his life was saved by his brother Quintus Pomponius Secundus; however, he was kept under house arrest for seven years. Freed by Caligula, his career then flourished, holding a governorship of Crete with Cyrenaica, then Germania Superior, and a *suffect* consulship in AD 44.[12] Interestingly, Sejanus betrothed his son to a daughter of Lentulus Gaetulicus, a match suggested to the consul of AD 26 and governor of Germania Superior by the emperor himself. The aristocratic Gaetulicus was one of the most powerful men in the state, but also a writer of Greek and Latin poetry on erotic themes and a prose work, possibly his memoirs.[13]

Throughout his life Tiberius sought out the company of great men of learning. Suetonius describes him as being 'deeply devoted to Greek and Latin literature', and he wrote eulogies and Greek verse.[14] Tiberius had studied rhetoric under Theodore of Gadara, and there lay the attraction of Rhodes as his tutor had set up a school on the island and whilst in semi self-imposed exile he attended the lectures of Diogenes, another Greek rhetor and philosopher. He took on his travels a retinue of academics skilled in Greek and Latin rhetoric, philosophy and the classics, whose knowledge he liked to test. He built an extensive library on his island retreat of Capri and discoursed with the intellectuals who accompanied him, including Seleucus, described as a professor of literature.[15] Just as Strabo had been able to involve Augustus in a discussion of the classics, so Tiberius would have expected the same degree of classical education in his son. Sejanus, like Tiberius, a patron of Greek philosophers and literary men, could use this as an opportunity to deepen his relationship with the emperor, earning his admiration.[16] Furthermore, the Roman elite were in many ways defined by their shared knowledge derived from an extensive education in literary classics, philosophy and the practical skills of rhetoric and oratory. The Roman concept of *paideia*, or a classical education, was demonstrated in conversations at banquets, speeches in the Senate or before magistrates, and the creation of extensive libraries so loved by the elite and, for those with the ability, the writing of verses or speeches, and for those lacking these skills, the patronage of poets, philosophers and orators. These qualities were regularly exhibited in the public domain and so elevated their social status.[17]

One of the greatest teachers of Latin oratory under the early Principate was Cassius Severus. He employed a new aggressive style which, although highly successful, served to create a long-lasting enmity from those on the receiving end of his skills. He was eventually exiled and lived out the remainder of his life on the barren island of Seriphos, to die in AD 32. An imitator of his style was another *amicus* of Sejanus, L. Fulcinius Trio, the prosecutor of Libo in AD 16 and Piso in AD 20. He had been advised by Tiberius to tone down his antagonistic oratorical delivery but received the promise of future imperial favour. In AD 22 he became the governor of Lusitania, whilst C. Fulcinius Trio, probably his brother, became praetor *peregrinus* in AD 24. L. Fulcinius Trio became *suffect* consul in July of AD 31, replacing Sejanus in this office and, according to Dio, owing his predecessor for this honour. However, he had made many enemies through his successful prosecutions of members of the aristocracy. Marcus Scribonius Libo and Gnaeus Calpurnius Piso came from ancient noble families who traced their ancestors back to the early Republic. Libo's niece was married into the Calpurnii Pisones. Two members of this family were close friends with Tiberius; Lucius Calpurnius Piso the Pontifex was Prefect of Rome until his death in AD 32, but he had been unable to save his son Gnaeus, and his other son Lucius Calpurnius Piso the Augur would also suffer. Lucius Calpurnius Piso the Augur was himself accused of *maiestas* in AD 24, but death saved him the ordeal of an inevitable conviction. Piso the Pontifex also adopted a son of M. Licinius Crassus, the consul of 14 BC, who became M. Licinius Crassus Frugi and the husband of Scribonia, Libo's niece. He was chosen by Tiberius as consul in AD 27. The great families of Rome were unified by blood as well as by education and status. L. Fulcinius Trio had chosen to prosecute Gneaus Piso for his own personal gain, unlike many of the other prosecutors in this trial who did so out of a sense of duty to avenge the death of their *amicus*, Germanicus. They could be forgiven in part, but not Trio, who needed protection and Sejanus provided it. He would, however, only temporarily survive his patron's fall and be dragged down by his association with the Praetorian Prefect, committing suicide to avoid a worse fate.[18]

The use of delation was a risk that was worth taking for many aspiring and ambitious politicians. Standing for the defence brought the gratitude and bonds of obligation that glued Roman society together in the form of *amicitiae*.[19] Prosecution was a hostile act which invited *inimicitia*, which often led to a counter-prosecution by the defendant's family, *amici* or clients. A failed prosecution could lead to exile, expulsion from the Senate or confiscation of the estates of the *delatores* or *accusatores*, who were often charged with committing *calumnia*, an unwarranted prosecution based on fabricated evidence.[20] The *amicitiae* of Sejanus would minimize the risk of such a prosecution. Both Julius Caesar and Augustus had filled the Senate with new men from Italy and the provinces as a reward for their loyal service during the civil wars. It was often their children who now desired a greater political influence and status through the holding of the prestigious magistracies and governorships which were seen by the aristocracy as their preserve. The prosecution of rivals or those who had fallen from imperial favour were a means of attracting the emperor's attention and goodwill. There were no state prosecutors, so the emperor relied on such men to ensure that those who acted with treasonable intent were punished. Added to this was the custom of awarding a proportion of the estate of the guilty to the prosecutors and, at times, the witnesses as well. This encouraged charges of *maiestas* to be attached to any charges of corruption or adultery in anticipation of financial reward, but it also served to deter *amici* or clients of the defendant from coming to the aid of the accused through the fear that they too would be associated with the treason charge.[21]

Under the system of patronage that formed the bedrock of Roman society, the *delatores* established their loyalty and *fides* through defending the interests of their patron, and the ultimate patron was Tiberius himself. The prosecution of Libo and then Piso are cases in point, with Trio being awarded a share of the defendants' estates but also gaining imperial favour. *Delatores* were not forces of destruction, as portrayed in the senatorial sources, but essential guardians of the state who enforced the law through service to Tiberius or his instrument, Sejanus.[22] Increasingly, the instructions and actions of the Praetorian Prefect were seen to be synonymous with the wishes of the emperor, as Sejanus 'bound Tiberius fast: so much so that a man inscrutable to others became to Sejanus alone unguarded and unreserved', to the extent that 'Tiberius, far from demurring, was complaisant enough to celebrate "the partner of his toils" not only in conversation but before the Fathers and the people.'²³ It is hardly surprising then that, in the words of the equestrian Terentius, who when charged before the assembled senators with the crime of *maiestas* through his friendship with Sejanus in AD 32, challenged their hypocrisy, for:

> [W]e courted, not Sejanus of Vulsinii, but ... the partner of your consulate; the agent who discharged your functions in the state. It is not ours to ask whom you exalt above his fellows, or why; you the gods have made the sovereign arbiter of things; to us has been left the glory of obedience. Moreover, we see only what is laid before our eyes – the person who holds wealth and dignities from you – those who have the greatest power to help or injure – and that Sejanus had all, no man will deny.²⁴

Tiberius had made Sejanus a broker of imperial patronage alongside his son Drusus, and to a lesser extent his mother Livia.²⁵ However, through most of AD 21 Tiberius remained in Campania, isolated to a large degree from the aristocracy and the influence of his son. Sejanus as Praetorian Prefect could control access to the emperor. The letters that passed between the capital and the emperor would have been carried by the *speculatores*. This would have provided Sejanus with the opportunity to review their contents, which the correspondent, governor, magistrate, officer or petitioner would have known, further isolating the emperor. The absence of the emperor at the bedside of his son might be explained through Tiberius' Stoicism or perhaps Sejanus' understating the severity of Drusus' illness. Sejanus must have used the remaining officers of the guard retained in the palace and his *amici* and clients in Rome to keep informed of developments and extend his influence. Terentius refers to the veneration awarded to Sejanus' *amici*, Satrius and Pomponius, no doubt to be identified with Satrius Secundus and Pomponius Secundus. Both must have been close confidants of the Praetorian Prefect and regular visitors to his house, as it was to Pomponius that Sejanus' son Aelius Gallus fled upon the arrest of his father, no doubt trusting his loyalty. Satrius Secundus occupied a position that allowed him to be a credible witness to the alleged plot by Sejanus to overthrow Tiberius.²⁶

Even when absent from Rome the influence and *auctoritas* of the Prae-torian Prefect dominated the political landscape. The senatorial province of Africa was suffering from attacks by a Numidian Berber deserter from the Roman Army named Tacfarinas. A defeat had taught the former Roman auxiliary to employ the superb mobility of his forces in guerrilla tactics, which he used to devastating effect, accumulating a huge amount of booty from attacks on the coastal cities extending between Cirta and Lepcis Magna. The governor of the province, L. Apronius, had managed to capture his camp in AD 20, but Tacfarinas merely retreated into the desert to renew his attacks the following year. The situation required an experienced commander to replace Apronius at the end of his term in office of the senatorial province.[27] Tiberius consistently worked throughout his reign to reinforce the authority and dignity of the Senate, but the situation required a senator with the necessary ability and proven military knowledge to take command of the war. Tiberius sent a letter from his Campanian retreat advising the Senate on this matter. The lack of specific guidance on the names of possible candidates led to indecision and uncertainty. The leading senators feared causing offence to the emperor by supporting a man who lacked imperial support, and instead referred the choice back to Tiberius.[28]

Another letter arrived from a now angry and frustrated emperor whose attempt to thrust some degree of governmental responsibility upon the august body had been met with dithering indecisiveness. The letter was read out. It started with a criticism of the Senate, 'who transferred the whole of their responsibilities to the sovereign'. Tiberius was determined to force the Senate to take some responsibility, so he nominated the names of two suitable contenders for the Senate to vote upon. Sejanus' influence in the imperial *consilium* that decided on the nominees is evident in the choice of one of the candidates; the honour falling upon Marcus Aemilius Lepidus and Junius Blaesus. The *novus homo* Blaesus was Sejanus' uncle and had been governor of Pannonia during the mutiny in AD 14. Lepidus was the descendant of one of the oldest patrician families in Rome. Added to this, the blood of the Scipios ran in his veins and, through his mother, that of Sulla and Pompey the Great. His consulship in AD 6 was followed by a command in the Illyrian War, where he distinguished himself by fighting his way from Siscia to join the main army under Tiberius. The following year saw his army involved in the subduing of Dalmatia, marching from the north in a pincer move as Tiberius invaded from the south. For this Lepidus was awarded an *ornamenta triumphalia*. As his loyalty was beyond doubt, he was made governor of Hispania Tarraconensis with its three legions in preparation for the succession of Tiberius in AD 14. Tiberius rewarded his *amicus* in AD 17 by insisting that the vast estates of Aemilia Musa, who had died without issue, should be passed on to Marcus Aemilius Lepidus on the extremely tenuous grounds that they must be related. Lepidus had the necessary *auctoritas* and confidence in the friendship of the emperor to be able to defend Gnaeus Piso, to whom he was related, without fear of recriminations, just as in late AD 21 he urged the commuting of the poet Clutorius' sentence to exile rather than death, despite the wrath of Drusus. Velleius Paterculus, writing in AD 30, describes him as 'closest to the name and station of the Caesars'. His integrity and nobility were held in great esteem, both by Tiberius, who betrothed Lepidus' daughter to Germanicus' son Drusus, but also by most of the Senate. In AD 32 the well-connected senator M. Aurelius Cotta Messallinus, who was involved in a monetary dispute with Marcus Lepidus, complained of the *potentia* or power that he held over the senators. There can be little doubt that M. Lepidus was the logical choice.[29]

Faced with a simple choice between Blaesus and M. Lepidus, the senatorial vote for the province of Africa should have gone to Lepidus, based on imperial favour and the splendour of his ancestry, his military experience and the nobility of his character. Lepidus was an astute and skilful politician, as evidenced by the fact he was able to die a natural death in AD 33. However, rather than offending Sejanus, Lepidus declined the nomination, 'excusing himself with particular earnestness, pleaded the state of his health, the age of his children, and his now marriageable daughter; while it was also understood, though not said, that Blaesus was Sejanus' uncle, and therefore too powerful a competitor'. This event allows the *potentia* of Sejanus to be drawn from the shadows and revealed to its full extent. M. Lepidus did well to keep clear of any conflict with the Praetorian Prefect. His reward came in the form of the proconsular governorship of Asia, probably from AD 22–23.[30] Blaesus, for appearance's sake, now stood before the *curia* to decline the post, but he was easily persuaded to forego his initial reluctance.

The war against Tacfarinas was pursued by Blaesus with a high degree of strategic acumen. The IX Hispania had been transferred from Pannonia in AD 20 to support the Roman forces already in Africa. Three columns were used to pin down the elusive enemy: one, under the command of P. Cornelius Lentulus Scipio, was based at Lepcis Minor in the east and threatened the Garamantes, a Berber tribe allied to Tacfarinas, whilst Blaesus' son commanded another army in the west centred on Cirta and Blaesus himself took charge of the central column. As the columns advanced they were further divided to counter the guerrilla tactics of their enemy. Finally, in the winter of AD 22, Tacfarinas' brother was captured and Blaesus withdrew, with Tiberius declaring victory. This is surprising from a man of Tiberius' military experience. Tacfarinas was still at large and his forces had not been decisively defeated in battle. Blaesus' own correspondence would have clearly overplayed the military significance of his campaign, but perhaps Sejanus' advice could have been the deciding factor in Tiberius' decision. An *ornamenta triumphalia* was granted to Blaesus, and Tiberius allowed his troops to hail him as *imperator*, the last time this honour was granted to a commander who was not a member of the imperial house.[31] However, Tacfarinas was not finished and used the recall of the IX Hispania to again ravage the province. The war continued through AD 23 and into the following year, when P. Cornelius Dolabella, with reduced forces, but employing Blaesus' strategy, was able to bring Tacfarinas to battle and he was killed. Rightfully the honours for the defeat of Tacfarinas were Dolabella's, but his request for an *ornamenta triumphalia* in AD 24 was refused as it would serve to humiliate Blaesus, but more importantly Sejanus. This denial only helped to heighten Dolabella's reputation and dim that of Blaesus.[32]

The opening of AD 22 saw the continued absence of Tiberius from Rome. Drusus, after the fulfilment of his consular year, had probably joined him in Campania. Tiberius now sent a letter to the Senate making a formal request for tribunician power for his son. This was a public confirmation that Drusus was to be his successor, receiving equal magisterial authority to that of Tiberius. The emperor had 'placed Drusus on the threshold of the empire'. Tacitus appears to actually quote from Tiberius' letter of commendation: 'He had a wife and three children; and he had reached the age at which, formerly, he himself had been called by the deified Augustus to undertake the same charge. Nor was it in haste, but only after eight years of trial, after mutinies repressed, wars composed, one triumph, and two consulates, that he was now admitted to share a task already familiar.'[33] The Senate readily granted the emperor's request, but Drusus caused offence by remaining in Campania rather than returning to thank the Senate in person. Instead, the Senate had to be content with a letter of thanks from Drusus that 'was read, which, though tuned to a modest key, left an impression of extreme arrogance. "So the world," men said, "had come to this, that a mere boy, invested with such honour, would not approach the divinities of Rome, set foot within the Senate, or, at least, take the auspices on his native soil. War, they must assume, or some remote quarter of the world detain him; though that instant he was perambulating the lakes and beaches of Campania!"[34] The anger resonates from the pages of the *Annals*. This was a political mistake from the 'boy' of 35 years of age. Tiberius, always at pains to acknowledge and support the dignity of the Senate, as well as pay homage to custom and religious formalities, would no doubt have advised his son to return to the capital. Something more pressing must have occupied the joint rulers of the Empire. We can speculate on a recurrence of Drusus' illness, although if this was the case it would be doubtful the co-ruler of the Empire would be taking the air along Campania's fine coastal scenery, unless this was merely a turn of phrase employed by Tacitus. Perhaps the antagonistic relationship between Drusus and Sejanus had its origins at this time with the new joint head of state unwilling to allow the Praetorian Prefect free rein at the imperial *consilium* in Campania. Whatever the reason, Tiberius, no doubt accompanied by his prefect and son, was soon urgently summoned back to Rome.

The 80-year old Livia had fallen dangerously ill and Tiberius hurried to be at her bedside, putting into stark contrast the decision of the emperor not to be with his son when he had fallen ill the previous year. A little before her illness, the aged Augusta had made a dedication to her husband Augustus near the Theatre of Marcellus, where she placed her own name above that of Tiberius. This caused offence to her absent but fastidious son, who felt this act insulted the imperial dignity. The relationship between mother and son remained for the most part dutiful and cordial. The dedication is dated 23 April AD 22, as recorded on the Fasti Praenestini, so Tiberius must have hurried to Rome soon after this. The Senate decreed various supplications to presage the intervention of the gods on behalf of Livia, while the equites made an offering to Fortuna Equestris. Livia recovered and was to live for another seven years.[35] Coins were struck celebrating her recovery late in AD 22, carrying the legend Salus Augusta beneath her portrait. Salus was the goddess of health and well-being. Other coins carrying the inscription SPQR Iuliae Augustae show a *carpentum*, a two-wheeled covered carriage which only the Vestal Virgins were permitted to use. Livia had clearly not made a full recovery, and the Senate, with a care for her welfare, had granted the elderly and weak lady the use of this carriage as she moved around the capital.[36]

It is likely that as her health declined so did her influence, which is reflected in her gradual fading from the pages of our sources. Tiberius had already moved to reduce her role in imperial politics. His attitude to Agrippina is consistently reflected in his frustrations with Livia. Dio gives an overview of Tiberius' interventions in curtailing his mother's ability to act as a patron:

> [For] instance, she had once dedicated in her house an image to Augustus, and in honour of the event wished to give a banquet to the Senate and the equites together with their wives, but he would not permit her to carry out any part of this programme until the Senate had so voted, and not even then to receive the men at dinner; instead, he entertained the men and she the woman. Finally, he removed her entirely from public affairs, but allowed her to direct matters at home; then, as she was troublesome in that capacity, he proceeded to absent himself from the city and to avoid her in every way possible; indeed, it was chiefly on her account that he removed to Capri.

Her last recorded petition to Tiberius in AD 26 was refused, which lead to a final fracture in the relationship between mother and son. The great patrons, finding Livia unable to provide imperial *beneficia* for their own *amici* and clients, would look to others who could, namely Drusus and Sejanus.[37]

Tiberius, once ensconced in the capital again, took a greater role in the political landscape. As his mother made a gradual recovery, the emperor attended senatorial meetings and judicial hearings. One case, previously mentioned, tried before the Senate was used by Tacitus as a prime example of the corruption and sycophancy of the times. Gaius Silanus had just returned to Rome from his governorship of Asia (AD 20–21) and he stood accused of extortion and, for good measure, *maiestas*. The charge of treason was purely the customary attempt to ward off potential supporters of the accused and gain a financial reward. However, even Tacitus admits there could be no doubt as to his guilt 'on the counts of cruelty and maladministration'. Two of his own staff provided evidence for the prosecution, which was ably pursued by three men closely associated with Sejanus: Mamercus Scaurus, the praetor of AD 22, Junius Otho and the aedile Bruttidius Niger. The case had been brought by the provincials themselves and was heard by 'an array of hostile senators' and a clearly angry emperor. Tiberius despised corruption in the governance of the provinces; he said to an overly enthusiastic governor of Egypt who raised an excessive amount of revenue from taxes that 'he wanted his sheep shorn not shaven'. The emperor warned the accused's potential supporters not to come to his aid, and also took an active part in cross-examining the defendant and assisted the prosecution by taking the proactive step of ordering the state to buy Silanus' slaves so they could be examined under torture, as it was illegal for a slave to testify against their owner. Tacitus sees this case as evidence of the growing influence of Sejanus, but it is difficult to see what the Praetorian Prefect could gain from a successful prosecution, apart from the goodwill of the emperor. The *delatores* and *accusatores* would also gain the favour of the emperor, which in the case of Mamercus Scaurus was vitally important as it was widely believed that the emperor despised him. Furthermore, the prosecutors would gain the patronage of the prosperous cities of Asia through acting on their behalf. Silanus, surrounded by adversaries on all sides, abandoned his defence and instead wrote a letter to the emperor placing himself at his mercy. The emperor ignored the request and asked the Senate to decide his punishment: he was exiled, but some of Silanus' property was retained by his son.[38]

A chance but recurring event allowed Sejanus to rise further in the emperor's estimation. Fires were a regular occurrence in the capital, due to the overcrowded buildings and the use of oil lamps and fires for cooking. In AD 16 both Tiberius and Livia gave monetary assistance to those whose properties and wealth had been destroyed in a fire, and in AD 27 he paid for the rebuilding of blocks of housing on Caelian Hill destroyed in a further conflagration. The rapidity with which fires could spread caused consternation amongst both rich and poor alike. The Theatre of Pompey in the Campus Martius was destroyed in a blaze that threatened the surrounding area. Originally built in 55 BC to celebrate his victories, Pompey the Great had envisioned a monumental complex of buildings to symbolize his status and conquests. The great general also built his home nearby, so it was said that the *domus* and theatre looked 'like a small boat towed behind a ship'. The theatre incorporated five temples into its structure, including one to Venus Victrix, as well as porticos enclosing a huge garden that linked the theatre to a large *curia* in which Julius Caesar had been murdered at a meeting of the Senate. The whole complex was adorned by many statues of satyrs, the Muses, Apollo and of Pompey himself, which Augustus had placed in an arch behind the theatre. Nearby stood the Theatre of Balbus, the Circus Flaminius and the Baths of Agrippa, all central to the entertainment of the masses. Prompt action by Sejanus limited damage to the theatre itself, but the building required extensive repairs, which were not completed until after the emperor's death. Tiberius, though, publicly recognised the role of the Praetorian Prefect, to whom 'he gave high praise', for it was, in what looks a direct quote from the senatorial records, 'through [Sejanus'] energy and watchfulness so grave an outbreak had stopped at one catastrophe'.[39]

Prominent senators, in order to curry favour with both the emperor and Sejanus, then proposed that a bronze statue of Sejanus be erected in the restored theatre. In private, some senators were shocked that a statue of Sejanus would stand at the side of one of the greatest of all Roman politicians and generals.[40] A precedent had been set, so the elite rushed to demonstrate their loyalty to Sejanus in the form of public praise before the Senate and people, and 'numerous images of Sejanus were made by many different persons'. Dio continues to describe how the 'leading citizens, including the consuls themselves, regularly resorted to his house at dawn, and communicated to him not only all private requests that any of them wished to make of Tiberius, but also the public business which required to be taken up. In a word, no business of this sort was transacted henceforth without his knowledge.'[41]

One of the most important roles of an emperor was to provide *beneficium*, or gifts, in the form of favours, wealth, offices, estates, legateships, citizenship and so on. Access to the emperor was vital in order for Rome's elite to grant *beneficia* for their own *amici* and clients, extending the bonds of *amicitiae*. Nerva later wrote that he became emperor 'in order that I might confer new *beneficia* and preserve those already granted by my predecessors'. Tacitus records that all appointments were made through patronal influences. Those with the greatest access to the imperial person had the greatest influence in the form of *auctoritas* and *potentia*. Invariably this primarily consisted of members of the imperial family, then those *amici Caesaris* who were close friends of the emperor and then court officials. Livia had fallen from favour, but Drusus would remain a key member of the emperor's *consilium*. Sejanus was both an *amicus Caesaris* and a court official whose role as Praetorian Prefect would bring him into daily contact with the emperor, often in his private apartments where personal and intimate conversations could take place. Those without such access had to rely on the patronage of a member of the emperor's inner circle, or on approaching the emperor himself through an invitation to a banquet at the palace, at the morning *salutatio* or as he moved around the capital or countryside. The elite, including the emperor, who could expect a large gathering of *amici* and clients at their *salutatio*, had since the Republic tried to make the whole affair more manageable by dividing the petitioners into different categories. Sejanus would have employed this arrangement in his own morning *salutatio*.[42]

Tiberius at first ensured he was accessible to all. In his account of AD 14, Dio records that he was 'extremely easy to approach and easy to address'. He regularly invited the magistrates to dinner, where 'he would both receive them at the door when they entered and escorted them on their way when they departed', allowing them the opportunity of a private conversation. As he moved around the capital in a litter he refused an escort of senators and equites, who might otherwise restrict access to him, and stayed in the house of an imperial freedman, *amicus* or client before a public event to enable people gathered there to approach. 'His purpose in doing this was, that the people might meet him with as little difficulty as possible.' However Dio, in his earlier eulogy to the demise of Augustus, comments that 'real grief was not in the hearts of many at the time, but later was felt by all. For Augustus had been accessible to all alike and was accustomed to aid many persons in the matter of money.' This appears to be in pointed contrast to Tiberius' accessibility for the majority of his reign, as he initially followed the customs and habits of his predecessor but then gradually resorted to splendid isolation.[43]

Over time, Tiberius removed himself from the social customs of the elite of Roman society and thus deprived the aristocracy of opportunities to elicit petitions and favours that they believed came with their social status. Dio suggests this change took place in AD 20 with the death of Germanicus.[44] Tiberius had remained in the capital or its environs from AD 14 until early AD 21. After this he remained in Campania until the illness of his mother brought him temporarily back around May AD 22. Tacitus notes the change in the emperor's behaviour to AD 23, which he appears to link stylistically with the rise of Sejanus, symbolized by the completion of the Praetorian fortress. Writing of events in AD 25, Tacitus mentions that 'it was a convention of the period to address him [Tiberius] in writing even when he was in the capital'.[45] No source mentions that Tiberius no longer employed the *salutatio*, and it would be a breach with convention and custom if he did. However, it appears that the emperor demanded all appeals and petitions be communicated to him in writing. This meant that he was no longer required to listen to time-consuming oral requests, which were often accompanied by cringing sycophancy. Such written communication would have to be read and reviewed by members of the imperial bureaucracy, as sheer numbers would preclude the emperor himself fulfilling this task. Sejanus, as Praetorian Prefect, would have the opportunity to appraise, restrict and review these communications, and so control imperial access. He was Tiberius' 'advisor and assistant in all matters',[46] his gatekeeper, and so he had to be petitioned first to ensure written requests reached the emperor and met with a favourable decision. Even as Tiberius moved around the city, 'he refused to let senators approach his litter, whether in greeting or on business'.[47] Later, in AD 26, as he left the capital for good, 'the Caesar, after dedicating temples in Campania; though he had warned the public by edict not to invade his privacy, and the crowds from the country-towns were being kept at distance by troops appropriately disposed'[48] he refused to be formally greeted by the local magistrates and populace of the towns the imperial entourage passed through. Tiberius had made himself an island long before he made his journey to Capri.

Dio provides an account of the morning *salutatio* at the mansion of Sejanus. At dawn a slave, opening the doors to his atrium, was greeted by a 'rivalry and jostling about the great man's doors, the people fearing not merely that they might not be seen by their patron, but also that they might be among the last to appear before him; for every word and every look, especially in the case of most prominent men, was carefully observed'. The historian goes on to describe the scene on New Year's Day of AD 31 as 'all' gathered at Sejanus' house in order to attend on him on the day he was inaugurated as ordinary consul, recording that 'the couch that stood in the reception room utterly collapsed under the weight of the throng seated upon it'.[49]

By AD 23, the power and influence of the Praetorian Prefect rivalled that of Drusus, only recently acknowledged as co-emperor alongside his father. An argument took place between Drusus and Sejanus whose origins lay in the elevated status and political power of the Praetorian Prefect. Dio suggests Drusus was angered by the arrogance of 'Sejanus, puffed up by his power and rank, in addition to his overweening behaviour'. Tacitus describes him as being 'cringing at once and insolent; orderly and modest to outward view, at heart possessed by a towering ambition, which impelled him at whiles to lavishness and luxury, but oftener to industry and vigilance'. It would seem a man of such courtly wiles would avoid any pretext for a confrontation. Indeed, Sejanus appears to have studiously avoided taking sides when others gravitated towards either Germanicus or Drusus when both were still alive, despite the amicable relationship that existed between the two. Tacitus appears to place the blame for the clash on Drusus, who was 'impatient of a rival'. Certainly, the throngs that attended the Praetorian Prefect's daily *salutatio* would be ample reason for suspicion and distrust.[50]

However, an event must have precipitated this sudden open hostility. Perhaps this was the banishment of the actors from Rome as 'they kept debauching women and stirring up tumults'. Suetonius appears to allude to this event when referring to the billeting of the guard in the Praetorian fortress; the biographer praises their role as they 'discountenanced city riots, and if they broke out, crushed them without mercy. The theatre audience had formed factions in support of rival actors, and once when their quarrels ended in bloodshed, Tiberius exiled not only the faction leaders but the actors who had been the occasion of the riot; nor would he ever give way to popular entreaties by recalling them.'[51] There had been rioting caused by factions associated with the actors in AD 14 and 15, so it is not surprising that Tiberius would have finally taken decisive action, despite Drusus' association with this group. The issue would have been discussed in the imperial *consilium*. If Sejanus had taken a pivotal role in Tiberius' ultimate decision, it is easy to understand Drusus' anger, which would have been deflected from his father to focus instead upon the man whom he already saw as his opponent.

Drusus, renowned for his fiery temper, confronted Sejanus and, according to Tacitus, 'in a casual altercation raised his hand against the favourite, and upon a counter demonstration, had struck him in the face'. According to Dio, it was Sejanus who was the aggressor, hitting Drusus 'a blow with his fist', which perhaps was the 'counter demonstration' referred to by Tacitus.[52] Soon after, on 14 September AD 23, Drusus was dead. There was no hint of foul play at the time. Perhaps his death was a recurrence of the ailment that nearly cost him his life in AD 21. Suetonius suggests Tiberius felt his son's death was due to his 'debauched habits', as he was infamous for his drinking. Tiberius, adhering to his stoical beliefs, remained to outward show without remorse, leading to a rumour that he himself had murdered his own son. This piece of idle gossip was quickly dismissed by Dio, who noted the similarity in Tiberius' response to adversity and misfortune in that 'this was his regular practice, as a matter of principle, in every case alike, and besides he was greatly attached to Drusus, the only legitimate son he had'.[53] However, both Tacitus and Dio accuse Sejanus of poisoning Drusus. According to Dio, Sejanus feared Drusus but felt he could control Tiberius once his son had been removed. Tacitus provides one motive and then appears to dismiss it. The historian suggests that Sejanus aspired to be emperor himself, and removing Drusus was one step in the fulfilment of that ambition. Tacitus regularly repeats the assertion that Sejanus had 'designs upon the throne', leading him to plot against Agrippina and her children. However, he then pointed to the fact the imperial house had a 'plentitude of Caesars' who would have a greater claim to the throne than the Praetorian Prefect. There were the sons of Germanicus, Nero and Drusus, now aged 17 and 15 respectively, and their younger brother Caligula, aged 11. Drusus and his wife Livilla (also known as Livia) had twins born in October AD 19, Tiberius Gemellus and Germanicus. At the start of AD 23, the younger Drusus had just received the *toga virilis*, formalizing his entry into adult life. Beyond these there were the female members of the imperial family, foremost being Agrippina and Livilla. Then there came the powerful members of the senatorial nobility, some related to the imperial family, who could assert their claim. Furthermore, in a letter sent in AD 25 by the emperor to Sejanus, Tiberius makes the point that as a member of the equestrian class, any role he sought within the imperial family would be unacceptable to the aristocracy as a whole. This had previously been made abundantly clear to the Praetorian Prefect by the hostile public reaction in AD 20 to the news of the betrothal of Sejanus' daughter to a son of Claudius, the brother of Germanicus and future emperor.[54]

Sejanus was a realist. He would have known he could never be emperor. The fight with Drusus would have made it abundantly clear to him that once the aged Tiberius died and his son became emperor, his tenure of the Praetorian Prefecture would end abruptly. Such a fall would undoubtedly be followed by prosecution, exile or death. It certainly was in the interests of Sejanus that Drusus should die. As Dio asserts, there can be little doubt that Sejanus feared the prospect of Drusus as emperor. If Sejanus did murder Drusus, poison would be the logical means with which to do it, as his previous illness in AD 21 would provide the credible context for the Caesar's death. Administering the poison, though, would be the problem.

According to Tacitus, Suetonius and Dio, it was Drusus' wife who joined Sejanus in murdering the heir to the throne.[55] Sejanus' motive for murder is plain to see, but the supposed involvement of Livilla is difficult to understand. She would be the future Augusta, her husband would be emperor and her children would inherit the throne. The death of Drusus meant that her sister Agrippina's children, Drusus and Nero, being older than her twins, would become the recognized heirs. Conversely, Sejanus was an equestrian with no right to the throne with children of his own. Marsh suggests that she murdered her husband for her children. It is extremely difficult to see how the murder of the imperial heir would strengthen the position of her children. This view has been discredited by a number of historians.[56] They had a more certain future if their father lived. Perhaps love was the reason for their joint complicity. Drusus, although brave and courageous, was often to be found in his cups, quick to anger, and a streak of cruelty ran through his character, often to the dismay of his father. Despite this, as he was about to embark on his journey to the Danubian provinces just a few years earlier in AD 21, Drusus made a public declaration of his devotion for his wife, demanding that she have the right to accompany him to his province.[57] Livilla herself was said to be 'in her early days a harsh-favoured girl, later a sovereign beauty'.[58] Sejanus was certainly in love with Livilla and hoped to marry her, 'for whom he entertained a passion'.[59] The two had started an affair, and at the urging of Livilla, Sejanus had divorced his wife Apicata. Some historians suggest that the divorce appears to have taken place in AD 23, possibly before the death of Drusus. Tacitus seems to imply as much in his remark that Sejanus 'seduced her to adultery', which he places in his account after Sejanus' confrontation with Livilla's husband. The Praetorian Prefect then 'moved her to dream of marriage'. The passage appears to place events chronologically, as the historian then goes on to describe the death of Drusus. The historian appears to imply that the divorce of Apicata took place before the death of Drusus, but he might be telescoping events back in time, based on the fact that Sejanus did divorce his wife after the death of Drusus combined with the infamous marriage proposal made by the Praetorian Prefect two years after the Caesar's death.[60] In AD 25 Livilla, driven by 'feminine passion', pressed Sejanus to ask Tiberius for her hand in marriage.[61] The divorce between Apicata and Sejanus can only be placed with any certainty to the latter half of AD 23. If it had taken place before the death of Drusus, it would make sense for Tacitus, who was keen to blacken the name of Sejanus, to explicitly state this.

There can be little doubt that Sejanus and Livilla formed a liaison, and from events, this desire was mutual. However, Apicata placed the blame for her divorce firmly at the feet of Livilla, whom she considered was the 'cause of a quarrel between herself and her husband, resulting in their separation'.[62] That quarrel must have been the affair between the two. Apicata would have burned with resentment, but for the sake of her children she accepted the situation. However, her world was turned upside down over a few days in October AD 31. Her ex-husband fell dramatically from power, his body exposed on the Germoniae Steps. This elicited no response from Apicata.

Two days later her eldest son was executed at the command of the emperor, guilty of being the son of the deposed Praetorian Prefect. His siblings would suffer a similar fate in November. On 26 October Apicata sent a letter to the emperor detailing the murder of his son at the hands of the now dead Sejanus and the still living Livilla. Apicata then committed suicide. The aged emperor was sent into a frenzy, ordering the torture of members of his son's household. Torture extracted a number of 'confessions'.[63] Livilla was named, as was her doctor and *amicus* Eudemus, who stood accused of using regular consultations to administer the poison to the unsuspecting Drusus. However, Pliny contradicts Tacitus in embellishing the account by asserting that Eudemus was, in fact, Livilla's lover. A very complex situation is portrayed by the ancient sources, with Livilla involved in two affairs which she apparently kept secret from both her husband and, no doubt, her household. The fact Drusus was regularly seeing a doctor does also confirm that he was seriously ill before he died. Tacitus then adds that a poison was chosen that was 'so gradual in its inroads as to counterfeit progress of a natural ailment'. Clearly, Drusus' physicians had no suspicions that his condition might be due to a slow-release poison. Tiberius also attended senatorial meetings during his son's illness, implying this was a protracted complaint. Another conspirator enters the scene in the person of Lygdus, whose confession to administering the poison, like that of Eudemus, was extracted under torture. Tacitus, after referring to this evidence based on 'the most numerous and trustworthy authorities', now includes information based on 'contemporary rumour' in that Sejanus seduced Lygdus, echoing the gossip that Sejanus was seduced by his father-in-law Apicius. If Eudemus and Lygdus were involved in this plot, Sejanus would surely not have allowed possible witnesses to survive. On this point alone Seager finds the authenticity of the plot dubious. Tacitus goes on to relate 'the commonly repeated account' of a story that the Praetorian Prefect was audacious enough to warn Tiberius that the first cup passed to him at a banquet would be poisoned, which the emperor accepted and then knowingly passed on to his son. Although discounting the 'falsities of the oral tradition', by mentioning it, Tacitus cleverly further stains the name of the Praetorian Prefect.[64]

Some historians feel there is little reason to doubt Apicata's assertions, as Livilla would have expected Sejanus to ascend the throne.[65] The poisonous letter was clearly sent with revenge in mind. On receipt of the letter, Tiberius shut himself away in his island hideaway for six months, his hours spent obsessively investigating the last days of his son's life, ably assisted by Macro, his new Praetorian Prefect, who let his master's fixation run unhindered. The emperor even came to suspect that his grandson Tiberius Gemellus might be illegitimate, a belief no doubt fostered by Macro, who supported the claims of Agrippina's son Caligula. If Macro could establish that the affair between Sejanus and Livilla started before the death of Drusus, then the claims of Tiberius Gemellus and his supporters to the throne would be irreparably damaged.[66] Livilla herself, thanks to Apicata's letter, was, according to some accounts, executed, while others assert that she was handed over to her mother Antonia, who starved her to death.[67] It is difficult to understand how Apicata would have come by this secret information. Sejanus is unlikely to have confided in his estranged wife, whom he planned to separate from or had already divorced. Credence is further stretched in the implicit contention that she is then supposed to have kept this knowledge a secret for seven years. Apicata's actions, followed by her suicide, appear to be an act of vengeance. It would appear that this letter and the statements extracted by torture formed the basis of the poisoning of Drusus we find in Tacitus, Dio and Suetonius. The later request by Sejanus for the hand of Livilla in AD 25 would add a degree of credibility to the assertion that both were having an affair before the death of Drusus. Who would dare question this account as the terror unleashed by the fall of Sejanus and the poisonous letter from Apicata devoured Rome's political classes after AD 31?

That Sejanus and Livilla conducted an affair is beyond doubt; however, when it started is based on fragile supposition, relying on Tacitus' own flawed account. Most modern historians have balanced the probabilities and concluded that Drusus died of natural causes.[68] If we also move the commencement of Livilla's affair to late AD 23, after the death of Drusus, we find her actions understandable. With the death of her husband, the Empire would pass on to her sister Agrippina's children, Drusus and Nero. They were much older and had a stronger claim to the throne through their father, the lauded idol of the early Imperial age, Germanicus, who was himself related to Augustus. Tiberius was also an old man who was not expected to live much longer. Who would now protect her and advance the interests of her children in the ruthless environment of courtly politics? Sejanus.

Chapter 5

The Inventor of all Villainies: AD 24–26

'Sejanus was held the inventor of all villainies: therefore, as the Caesar loved him over-well and the rest of the world hated both, the most fabulous horrors found credence.'
(Tacitus, *Annals* 4.11)

Fortune appeared to have smiled on Sejanus, if, as appears likely, Drusus died of natural causes. The Praetorian Prefect acquired at some point before AD 31 'a statue of Fortune, which had belonged, they say, to Tullius, one of the former kings of Rome, but was kept by Sejanus at his house and was a source of great pride to him'.[1] Fortuna was the goddess of luck, but also fate, and fate had favoured Sejanus. The goddess was also closely linked to the Roman concept of *virtus*, or strength of character. This connection would have held great appeal to the man who stood at the side of the emperor. Perhaps it was Drusus' death that stirred the Praetorian Prefect to acquire the ancient cult figure, no doubt removed from the Temple of Fortuna in the Forum Boarium, which had been built by Servius Tullius. The statue was covered in the regal regalia worn by the legendary sixth king of Rome. This association would have added a further attraction to Sejanus. According to tradition, Tullius was the son of a noblewoman captured during the siege of Corniculum who was brought to Rome to serve in the royal household. Tullius proved himself both loyal and reliable, and married into the royal family. As the king lay ill he was made regent of the city, and following the king's death, became his successor.[2] This link with the sixth king of Rome would later be used by Sejanus' enemies to cast the seeds of doubt into the mind of Tiberius, leading the emperor to question the ambitions and loyalty of his Praetorian Prefect.

Rogers believes that Tiberius had a regency in mind when he entered the Senate upon the death of Drusus to commend Germanicus' children Nero and Drusus to the assembled curia.[3] Upon entering the Senate, Tiberius found the two consuls had abandoned their normal seats as presiding magistrates as an act of mourning. The emperor ordered them to return so as not to undermine the dignity of their office. After receiving the senators' offers of condolence, he then gave a formal speech. He told the assembly that for the sake of the state, he put aside his personal grief to openly worry for the commonwealth as the death of his son had serious consequences for the issue of the succession. Tiberius was 65 years old, whilst his mother was 80. He continued after 'deploring the extreme old age of his august mother, the still tender years of his grandsons, and his own declining days, he asked for Germanicus' sons, their sole comfort in the present affliction to be introduced. The consuls went out, and, after reassuring the boys, brought them in and set them before the emperor.' Tiberius then commended the youths to the Senate, who were to act as their guides: 'These are the great-grandchildren of Augustus, scions of a glorious ancestry; adopt them, train them, do your part – and do mine!'[4] The emperor had returned to his desire for the Senate to take a greater responsibility for the management of the Empire, but the suggestion was met with scepticism and sycophancy. Tiberius had been on the point of retirement from the seat of power, but the death of his son had denied him the opportunity to live out the last years of his life in leisure. In his double anguish, with frustration and pain, 'he wished that the consuls or others would take the reins of government'.[5]

Who did he have in mind when referring to these 'others'? The consuls were the representatives of the Senate, so it would be unusual to refer to them twice in the same sentence. Perhaps the appeal was to the aristocracy and nobles assembled before him. Rogers, however, considers this phrase as the emperor introducing to the senators the idea of a regency in the form of Sejanus should he die before his successors had gained enough experience to rule Rome. To support this assertion, Rogers refers to a passage in Velleius Paterculus that alludes to events 'that impelled Caesar to put Sejanus to the test, and Sejanus to lighten the burdens of the princeps; and it also led the Senate and people of Rome to the point of willingly calling upon what they understood to be their best practical asset to take charge of their security'.[6] However, Velleius Paterculus was more likely to have in mind the political situation in AD 30, when he completed his work, rather than that in AD 23. Furthermore, in a letter to Sejanus in AD 25, the emperor mentions the opposition to the aristocracy, who complain that the Praetorian Prefect has 'long since transcended the heights of the equestrian order and left the *amicitiae* of my father behind; and in their envy of you they censure myself as well'.[7] In these political circumstances, there can be little doubt that Tiberius was not contemplating solving the problem of the succession using Sejanus as a regent at this time.

Tiberius retired to the palace and there grieved for his son in private, accompanied by Sejanus and members of his immediate family. The public funeral took place some days later. Tacitus describes the 'most arresting feature of the funeral was the parade of ancestral images, while Aeneas, author of the Julian line, with the whole dynasty of Alban kings, and Romulus, the founder of the city, followed by the Sabine nobles, by Attus Clausus, and by the rest of the Claudian effigies, filed in long procession past the spectator.'[8] Nothing could have brought home the prestige of the imperial house more than this parade of gods and illustrious heroes from Rome's past that accompanied the body of Drusus to the Rostra in the Forum. Sejanus could never compete nor claim a throne, hindered by his own insipid claims of *nobilitas*. Behind the body of Drusus would have walked Agrippina and her two sons. The images of the illustrious dead was a physical manifestation of their claim to power. In their veins ran the blood of Augustus, not through adoption, but imperial inheritance. Nero, Germanicus' son, gave a eulogy from the Rostra, and then he was followed by the emperor, standing next to the body of his son. Seneca, who was possibly in the crowd to witness these events, gives a description of the emperor's stoical dignity as he delivered his eulogy:

> Tiberius Caesar lost both the son whom he begot and the son whom he adopted, yet he himself pronounced a panegyric upon his son from the Rostra, and stood in full view of the corpse, which merely had a curtain on one side to prevent the eyes of the high priest resting upon the dead body, and did not change his countenance, though all the Romans wept: he gave Sejanus, who stood by his side, a proof of how patiently he could endure the loss of his relatives.[9]

Sejanus outwardly supported his emperor in his hour of need, yet there could be no doubting that he would have privately rejoiced at the emperor's misfortune. Tiberius had lost his brother Nero Claudius Drusus in 9 BC; he was returning with his army from the Elbe in Germania when his horse fell, crushing him. Tiberius, upon hearing the news whilst at Ticinum, rode day and night to reach his brother just before he died. Devastated, but showing familiar public restraint, he escorted the body on foot from the Rhine to Rome. There is an echo of these future tragedies in the eulogy he then gave from the Rostra.[10] His adopted son Germanicus had, it was believed, been poisoned in AD 19, whilst his former wife Vipsania had died the next year, then in AD 21 his close *amicus* P. Sulpicius Quirinius and in AD 23 another close friend who had accompanied him to Rhodes, Lucilius Longus, perished. Soon after the death of his son, his grandson, the twin of Tiberius Gemellus, also joined the spirits of the departed.[11] Tiberius, beset by tragedy, had fewer people to turn to. Livia's influence had been curtailed by age, infirmity and the prejudices of the emperor. It was to Sejanus that the emperor increasingly turned for support and succour, yet others still had access to the emperor. The astrologer Thrasyllus was consulted daily and Piso the Pontifex was a regular drinking companion, along with L. Aelius Lamia. Piso remained in Rome as Urban Prefect and, upon his death in AD 32, L. Aelius Lamia, was appointed as his successor.

Although the succession of Nero and Drusus now appeared inevitable, the palace was divided between imperial women struggling for dominance. Livia still attempted to exert her influence, which only served to further irritate her son. Antonia was held in higher regard by the emperor. She was the widow of his brother Nero Claudius Drusus and the daughter of Augustus' sister Octavia and the Triumvir, Mark Antony. Her children Germanicus, Livilla and the future emperor Claudius, played a prominent role in courtly politics. Unlike the far more assertive Agrippina and Livia, Antonia used her influence in the background, earning the respect of Tiberius. Her influence was such that her patronage was sought by the great and good. The careers of both new men D. Valerius Asiaticus and L. Vitellius benefitted from her support, the former attaining the consulship in AD 35 whilst Vitellius became a consul for the first time in AD 34.[12] The question of the succession put Antonia in a very difficult position, as the rivalry between her daughter Livilla and daughter-in-law Agrippina divided the imperial house. Agrippina was the clear beneficiary with the passing of Drusus. Antonia's grandchildren Nero and Drusus were now the undisputed successors of Tiberius. No source mentions Antonia's relationship with Agrippina, but she was bound to look to protect the interests of her grandchildren. Livia, however, despised Agrippina, a hatred no doubt exacerbated by the knowledge that her own surviving grandchild, Tiberius Gemellus, now had little prospect of attaining the throne. Antonia's daughter Livilla would also have feared for the future of her son. During the lifetime of her husband, the court had been 'split and torn by unspoken preferences for Germanicus or for Drusus', but now it was to the women that people looked in anticipation of the aged emperor's death. Whilst Agrippina had the emperor's commendation of her two eldest children made before the Senate, Livilla had Sejanus to act on her behalf. She had no need to push the claims of Tiberius Gemellus and so risk the patience of the emperor, for the Praetorian Prefect would act as her mouthpiece and his protector.[13]

Fate had opened doors to Sejanus that before the death of Drusus had remained firmly shut. The idea of a regency on behalf of the young Tiberius Gemellus, perhaps cemented by marriage to Livilla, now presented itself. For this future to occur, Agrippina and her children would need to be removed. The villainies of Sejanus lay in his Machiavellian campaign to destroy Agrippina, Nero, Drusus and Caligula.[14] The Praetorian Prefect could never be directly implicated in this scheme: he was a man 'fearless by temperament; skilled to conceal himself and to incriminate his neighbour'.[15] Instead, Sejanus worked in the shadows utilizing the ambitions of his *amici* and clients to undermine each in turn. Sejanus exploited his position at the side of the emperor as he 'inflamed and exacerbated his jealousies; and with his expert knowledge of the character of Tiberius, kept sowing the seed of future hatreds'.[16] The strategy he employed relied on Tiberius' traditional conservative attitude towards the role of women in politics, but also the flaws in the personality of Agrippina herself, whom he sought to provoke into rash and emotional actions that would only serve to inflame the emperor's prejudices and dislike of his daughter-in-law. Agrippina should have taken to heart the wise words of Germanicus, who, as he lay dying, begged her 'by the memory of himself, and for the sake of their common children, to strip herself of pride, to stoop her spirit before the rage of fortune, and never – if she returned to the capital – to irritate those stronger than herself by a competition for power'.[17] Agrippina was as much an agent of her own destruction as Sejanus was. Tacitus, writing of events in AD 24, describes her as unheeding of the wise advice, as her 'failure to hide her maternal hopes'[18] hastened her destruction.

A consummate judge of character, Sejanus drew on the flaws of those around him to achieve his aims:

> He proceeded, therefore to declaim against her [Agrippina's] contumacity, and by playing upon Augusta's [Livia's] old animosity and Livilla's recent sense of guilt, induced them to carry information to the Caesar that, proud of her fruitfulness and confident in the favour of the populace, she was turning a covetous eye to the throne. In addition, Livilla, with the help of skilled calumniators – one of the chosen being Julius Postumus, intimate

with her grandmother owing to his adulterous connection with Mutilia Prisca, and admirably suited to her own designs through Prisca's influence over the Augusta – kept working for the total estrangement from her grandson's wife of an old woman, by nature anxious to maintain her power.[19]

As always, Sejanus was pushing against an open door, playing on Livia's resentment at the rise of Agrippina as her own influence declined. Tiberius still invited his mother to imperial banquets, with her couch placed in the position of honour next to that of the emperor. There were plenty of opportunities for Livia to vent, even though Agrippina was positioned close by. Mutilia Prisca's husband C. Fufius Geminus, the ordinary consul of AD 29, was said to have owed his appointment to this high office to the influence of Livia. It is just as likely Sejanus urged the emperor to elevate him to the consulship, eager to return his debt for further poisoning the mind of the aged Augusta against Agrippina. Tiberius hated Fufius as he was 'accustomed to ridicule Tiberius with those bitter jests the powerful remember so long'. Upon the death of Livia in AD 29, Fufius was charged with *impietas* towards Tiberius, and forsaken by Sejanus, he and his wife were forced to commit suicide. The unforgiving and vindictive nature of the emperor is demonstrated by his failure to intervene when Fufius' own mother was charged in AD 32 with mourning the death of her own son. She was put to death for her humanity.[20]

Sejanus probably used his morning *salutatio* and contacts with the nobility to pass on fictitious 'information' regarding the emperor's attitude to the succession to Agrippina's *amici*, knowing that these would be communicated to her in due course. These were unwittingly doing the Praetorian Prefect's bidding by further inducing impolitic reactions from the imperial princess, for: 'Even Agrippina's nearest friends were suborned to infuriate her haughty temper by pernicious gossip.'[21] Events appeared to support the perception that the succession of Nero and Drusus was not a certainty. After commending the two boys to the Senate, Tiberius had failed completely to advance their careers, honours and experience of public office. In 5 BC Augustus marked out his chosen successors Gaius and Lucius by allowing the equestrian order to honour them with the title *principes iuventutis*, whilst Gaius was designated consul five years in advance, and in 2 BC Lucius received the same honour at the age of 15. Agrippina's eldest, Nero, would not even become a quaestor until 5 December AD 25, and so could not expect a consulship until AD 34. The treatment of both appears to be without Augustan precedent, which is highly unusual for Tiberius, who based his rule upon those models set by his predecessor. Here surely the influence of Sejanus was at play, almost goading the excitable and overly passionate Agrippina into a reaction. The frustrations of their mother are almost audible. Inevitably, she must have pressed the emperor to accelerate the honours and offices to be granted to her children. We can only imagine Tiberius' response.[22]

It came on 3 January AD 24. The pontiffs and other priests had offered their traditional New Year vows and sacrifices for the safety of the emperor, when they also added the names of Nero and Drusus in their prayers. No doubt they based their additional vows on the basis of the emperor's commendation of the two young boys in the Senate in the previous September, and it was meant in honour of the emperor. Excessively ambitious Roman women, as perceived by Roman men, deprived as they were from an active role in politics, pursued their aspirations through the careers of their children. Seneca commends his own mother, who, in stark contrast to other women, was 'an example to those mothers who exercise their influence over their children with a woman's lack of restraint. Women may not hold office, so they gratify their ambition through their sons; they take over their sons' inheritance, exhaust their sons' eloquence in their own interest.'[23]

The emperor was a staunch advocate of these views:

> [Tiberius] was now stung beyond endurance to find a pair of striplings placed on a level with his own declining years. He summoned the pontiffs and asked if they had made this concession to the entreaties – or should he say the threats? – of Agrippina. The pontiffs, despite their denial, received only a slight reprimand (for a large number were either relatives of his own or prominent figures in the state); but in the Senate, he gave warning that for the future no one was to excite to arrogance the impressionable minds of the youths by such precocious distinctions.

From the emperor's comments, it is clear how the Praetorian Prefect had started to poison the mind of the emperor towards the family of Germanicus. The character of Nero and Drusus had been questioned, with the added implication that further honours would only increase the arrogance of the two young princes. The second prong of Sejanus' whispering campaign was to increase the emperor's dislike of Agrippina by imputing her active interference in the politics of the state. Tiberius had spent the early years of his reign in weakening the influence of his mother, and now in his eyes he was faced with a similar threat in the form of an overly ambitious woman who, unlike Livia, had none of his interests at heart. Sejanus would have provided a drip feed of insinuations and rumour to feed the fires in Tiberius' mind. At the same time, he ensured gossip and rumours came to the ears of the imperial princess to feed her frustrations and encourage her into actions that would only confirm Sejanus' warnings to Tiberius. The over-reaction of the emperor to the traditional New Year prayers can only be understood if Agrippina had been demanding more honours and opportunities be granted her children. Sejanus had also suggested that overly ambitious senators and equites were attempting to gain favour with Agrippina and her sons in anticipation of their future ascent to the throne: 'the truth was that Sejanus was pressing him hard: – "the state", so ran his indictment, "was split into two halves, as if by civil war. There were men who proclaimed them of Agrippina's party: unless a stand was taken, there would be more; and the only care for the growing disunion was to strike down one or two of the most active malcontents."'[24]

It was only to be expected that many would seek the *amicitiae* of Agrippina in the expectation that the aged emperor was likely to die sooner rather than later. Many had previously attempted to gain the friendship of either Tiberius' son Drusus or Germanicus, despite both being close.[25] The sources do not record any concern with these solicitous approaches to his two sons in the mind of the emperor. Now, in similar circumstances, Tiberius reacts. Sejanus was not accusing Agrippina of actively seeking to form a faction; indeed it was highly unlikely Agrippina would have, as the future was hers and her children's. For this reason, there was little need for the imperial princess to initiate a conspiracy against the emperor.[26] She merely did little to contain the expectations of the elite. No doubt this is what Sejanus used against her. However, Tiberius only saw division fermented within the imperial house by an overly ambitious woman, rather than accepting the situation as a necessary step in securing the succession. Sejanus now gained a free hand to move against some of Agrippina's *amici* as a warning to the political classes not to actively seek the *amicitiae* of the princess in anticipation of the emperor's death.[27]

The axe fell upon Gaius Silius and his wife Sosia Galla, both devoted *amici* of Agrippina, a friendship formed during her stay on the Rhine with Germanicus. Silius had been governor of Upper Germany (AD 14–21) during the revolt of the Rhine legions and Germanicus' subsequent campaigns in Germany, and he had then helped suppress the Gallic rebellion of Sacrovir in AD 21. Tacitus also couples the prosecution with that of Titius Sabinus four years later, but this has to be doubted due to the duration of the delay between the two cases. Sejanus chose his agent and the victims wisely. Silius had already angered the emperor by boasting that Tiberius owed his throne to him as he had kept his legions loyal in AD 14: 'Such claims, the Caesar thought, were destructive of his position.'[28] Silius and his wife was charged with both *repetundae* and *maiestas*. As to their guilt on the former charge of extortion, there was, according to Tacitus, no doubt. Tiberius hated any form of corruption in the governing of the provinces, and it was said he despised Sosia due to her friendship with Agrippina.[29] The accusation that her husband had been complicit in the revolt of Sacrovir was completely baseless, but the animosities of the emperor made any defence futile. The *delator* was also cleverly chosen. L. Visellius Varro, the consul of the year, held a grudge against Silius as his father's claims to command the army that defeated Sacrovir were, in his eyes, usurped. The prosecution would demonstrate his *pietas*, his loyalty to his father, a widely admired, noble virtue.[30] Varro was not necessarily an *amicus* of Sejanus, he merely awaited an opportunity to repay the grievance his father had felt in a case of *inamicitiae*. His father, a *novus homo*, was probably forced to acquiesce to the greater nobility of Silius, whose probable father was Publius Silius Nerva, the consul of AD 13 and *amicus* of Augustus. Sejanus could merely have implied to the consul that the emperor would have looked favourably on a prosecution of Silius. As the *amicus* of Sejanus, Terentius, stated in his defence in AD 32, 'the closer a man's intimacy with Sejanus, the stronger his claim to the emperor's friendship.' Varro had already attained the consulship of the year, and consequently Silius sought to delay the trial on the grounds that it was not customary for a serving consul to prosecute a private citizen. He proposed the case be delayed until the term of Varro's consulship had ended.[31]

The emperor's role in the prosecution now became evident to all. Tiberius made a decisive intervention in the Senate, opposing the request as it was 'quite usual for magistrates to take legal action against private citizens, nor must there be any infraction of the prerogatives of the consul, on whose vigilance it depended "that the commonwealth should take no harm"'. Despite the emperor's assertions, such prosecutions were rare and were made to defend the state against rebellion or at a moment of constitutional crisis. In these circumstances the Senate had issued a *senatus consultum ultimum* during the Republic to invest the consuls with enhanced dictatorial powers to deal with the perceived threats from the tribune C. Sempronius Gracchus, and later the conspiracy of Catiline. The language used by Tiberius appears to echo these proclamations putting the state under martial law. The situation in AD 24 presented no threat to the state, but this imperial intervention made a guilty verdict inevitable. The charges were made in the Senate, 'with the defendant either holding his peace, or, if he essayed a defence, making no secret of the person under whose resentment he was sinking'; bowing to the fates, Silius took his own life. Sosia was exiled on the motion of Asinius Gallus, whilst M. Aemilius Lepidus demonstrated his humanity by successfully proposing that three-quarters of her estate be preserved for her children, the remainder being awarded to the successful prosecutors.[32]

Agrippina understood the prosecution as an attack on her: a warning shot to those who had sought her *amicitiae*. AD 24 saw an increase in the number of prosecutions for *maiestas*. Lucius Piso, the brother of Gnaeus Piso who had been charged with poisoning Germanicus in AD 20, was prosecuted by Q. Veranius, an *amicus* of the dead prince. The case should probably be seen as a further act of vengeance on the Pisones. He was charged, amongst other indictments, with using treasonable language in private. Previously, the emperor had rejected out of hand proposed accusations based on insults to himself as *maiestas*. Tiberius' attitude now appears to have changed and L. Piso was entered for trial, but death saved him further suffering. This conviction acted as a precedent for charges laid against Cremutius Cordus in AD 25, the indictment based on insults to the *maiestas* of the emperor. There can be no doubt that Sejanus was the force behind this action. Perhaps the influence of the Praetorian Prefect can be discerned behind the hardening of Tiberius' attitude towards what constituted *maiestas*. This broadening of the legal definition of this crime certainly served his purpose, but others took advantage of it as well. AD 24 saw C. Cominius condemned for producing a 'poetical lampoon' at the emperor's expense, but his life was spared 'as a concession to the prayers of his brother, a member of the Senate'. Clearly, he had already been found guilty. Tiberius had always encouraged the severest punishments for bribery, corruption and extortion, and so it was not surprising that P. Sullius, a former quaestor of Germanicus, was found guilty of accepting bribes whilst serving on a jury and had his place of exile selected by the emperor. He was exiled to a barren island rather than the initial suggestion of mere banishment from Italy. Conversely, the emperor rescinded the exile of Firmius Catus, who had been found guilty of bringing a false charge of *maiestas* against his sister, to merely expulsion from the Senate. The emperor was repaying his debt of gratitude to Catus, who had entrapped M. Scribonius Libo in AD 16.[33]

The most striking case of AD 24 came in the prosecution of Vibius Serenus the Elder, who had previously been exiled to the barren island of Amorgus under the *lex Julia de Vi Publica*, which prohibited the torture, imprisonment or execution of a Roman citizen, which he transgressed as governor of Further Spain. Like Firmius Catus, he had helped to prosecute Scribonius Libo. He was indicted for *maiestas* by his own son, and so the 'father, hauled back from exile, a mass of filth and rags, and now in irons, stood pitted against the invective of his own son: the youth, a highly elegant figure with cheerful countenance, informer at once and witness, told his tale of treason plotted against the sovereign and missionaries sent over to Gaul; adding that the funds had been supplied by the ex-praetor, Caecilius Cornutus'.[34] By attempting to associate his father with acting with Sacrovir during his governorship in Spain, Vibius Serenus the Younger appears to have been attempting to both shed the political ignominy associated with his father's condemnation and also gain imperial favour, as Tiberius loathed his father. Cornutus, anticipating conviction, committed suicide.[35] However, the resilient Vibius Serenus the Elder girdled his courage and defended himself before the Senate. He demanded from his son a list of fellow conspirators, as he stated that he could hardly have plotted revolution on his own. Surprisingly, Vibius Serenus the Younger accused 'Gnaeus Lentulus and Seius Tubero, greatly to the discomfiture of the Caesar, who found two most prominent nobles, close amici of his own, the former far advanced in years, the latter in failing health, charged with armed rebellion and conspiracy against the peace of the realm'.[36] Lentulus had been chosen by Tiberius to accompany his son Drusus and Sejanus as an advisor during the mutiny in Pannonia, whilst Seius Tubero was possibly the adopted son of Sejanus' father L. Seius Strabo. Tiberius immediately dismissed the allegations and ordered the ex-slaves of Vibius Serenus the Elder to be put to torture. The son's nerve now broke, his fears inflamed by the mob who demanded he be flung from the Tarpeian Rock, imprisoned or punished for parricide by being sown into a bag with a dog, a cock, a snake and an ape and then thrown into the sea. He fled to Ravenna.

The accusations made by Vibius Serenus the Younger against men so well connected appear to have been a moment of madness. He did have imperial protection, and perhaps he consequently felt safe even from the power of Sejanus. Tiberius ordered Vibius Serenus the Younger to return, and the case continued with 'Tiberius making no effort to disguise his old rancour against the exile. For, after the condemnation of Libo, Serenus had written to the emperor, complaining that his zeal alone had gone without reward, and concluding with certain expressions too defiant to be safely addressed to that proud and lightly offended ear.'[37] The torture of the ex-slaves had, however, failed to provide the evidence needed to incriminate their former master, yet the Senate still favoured condemnation and execution. Instead, Serenus the Elder was returned to his place of exile whilst his son continued to prosper under Tiberius' favour. In the following year Vibius Serenus the Younger unsuccessfully prosecuted Fonteius Capito, who had governed Asia, but, despite public hatred, he survived accusations that the charges were fictitious as he had become 'quasi-sacrosanct'.[38]

It is difficult to see what Vibius Serenus the Younger stood to gain attempting to associate Seius Tubero and Gnaeus Lentulus in his accusations. The emperor had been severely embarrassed and had attempted to save face by declaring: 'I am no longer worthy to live, if Lentulus, too, hates me.'[39] Neither would Sejanus have taken the attack on his adoptive brother lightly. Yet Serenus the Younger survived. The prosecution also led to another forced intervention by Tiberius. The suicide of the ex-praetor Caecilius Cornutus led to a senatorial resolution that an accuser's reward should be forfeited whenever the defendant in a charge of *maiestas* had resorted to suicide before the completion of the trial. Suicide was often taken as an admission of guilt, so this proposal is surprising and possibly reflects the increasing fears of the aristocracy after the trial of Silius at the increased use of delation as a political tool by Sejanus and Tiberius. After all, charges of *maiestas* and resulting suicides had not brought similar senatorial proposals in the past. 'The resolution was on the point of being adopted, when the Caesar, with considerable asperity and unusual frankness, took the side of the *delatores*, complaining that the laws would be inoperative, the country on the edge of an abyss: they had better demolish the constitution than remove its custodians.'[40] The emperor had been forced to publicly acknowledge that these men, so hated by the senatorial aristocracy, played a vital role in protecting the security of the emperor.[41] The *delatores* were not the mechanical instruments of Sejanus, rather they were perceived by Tiberius, and no doubt by themselves, as the guardians of the state and his safety.

They were ambitious politicians who often lacked the *nobilitas* of a great name to secure the highest offices of state, and so looked to imperial favour in the person of Tiberius acting through Sejanus.

The added incentive of acquiring part of the accused's estates would act as a further inducement to many *delatores*, who were new men lacking the advantage of the huge fortunes inherited by the great nobility. Both Tiberius and Sejanus would have been severely hamstrung in their campaign to bring Agrippina's 'ambitions' into line if the proposal had been allowed to stand. The death of Tiberius would inevitably lead to the succession of her children, and those who had brought charges against her *amici* could expect a problematic and very uncertain future.[42]

As the repairs on sections of the Theatre of Pompey neared completion, the promised statue to Sejanus was raised alongside those of Pompey the Great. For some this was too much, but criticisms were kept private. However, the senatorial historian Cremutius Cordus made an impolitic public comment,

> because he was not able to keep his silence and see Sejanus climbing up to take his seat upon our necks, which would have been bad enough had he been placed there by his master. He was decreed the honour of a statue, to be set up in the theatre of Pompeius, which had been burned down and was being restored by Caesar. Cordus exclaimed that 'Now the theatre was really destroyed.' What then? Should he not burst with spite at a Sejanus being set up over the ashes of Gnaeus Pompeius, at a faithless soldier being commemorated within the memorial of a consummate commander?[43]

Sejanus would not allow such an affront to his *dignitas* to stand. An example needed to be made of this man who had the temerity and bravery to openly criticize the Praetorian Prefect, otherwise others would follow in his footsteps. The Senate, despite being stocked with *amici* and clients of Sejanus, still retained many who hated him with a passion, men 'who still remained unconquered when all other necks were broken in to receive the yoke of Sejanus'. Sejanus used two senatorial clients to indict Cordus, Satrius Secundus and Pinarius Natta. These were powerful individuals, who, along with Pomponius Secundus, were later 'venerated' as they became his closest advisors and controlled access to the prefect. Both Natta and Satrius were *municipalis*, like their patron, whilst Natta appears to have gained some renown as a social wit and was well-known to Seneca, who presents in his account this opportunity to prosecute Cordus as a 'present'. Satrius and Natta could make a name for themselves and be potentially rewarded with *beneficia* in the form of wealth or support for magistracies and offices. These 'keen-scented hounds' struggled to find evidence or witnesses that could form the basis of a charge of *maiestas*. Instead, the evidence was found in Cordus' work, whose history covered the fall of the Republic. Under an extension of the *maiestas* law, Cordus was charged with praising Cassius and Brutus, the assassins of Julius Caesar, despite the fact Augustus himself had read the work and the historian had not been indicted for treason. Augustus had banned the public display of statues of Cassius and Brutus, but this charge was a further broadening of the *maiestas* law, which must have had imperial support as the emperor 'bent his attention to the defence' as Cordus stood before his peers in the curia at the start of AD 25. The senator soon recognized the futility of his defence and retired to his house, determined to starve himself to death in one final act of defiance. Sejanus' opponents delighted in this final act of opposition; when Cordus'

> determination became known there was a general feeling of plea-sure at the prey being snatched out of the jaws of those ravening wolves. His prosecutors, at the instance of Sejanus, went to the judgement-seat of the consuls, complained that Cordus was dying, and begged the consuls to interpose to prevent his doing what they themselves had driven him to do; so true was it that Cordus appeared to them to be escaping: an important matter was at stake, namely, whether the accused should lose the right to die. While this point was being debated, and the prosecutors were going to attend court a second time, he set himself free from them.

The extended debate and the probability that his accusers were not awarded a share of Cordus' estates suggest considerable opposition to Sejanus in the Senate. A law was passed ordering copies of the offending history burned, but the work survived, secreted away and preserved as a reminder of courage in the face of oppression.[44]

The potential death of Tiberius left Sejanus and Livilla in an extremely vulnerable position. The emperor was unlikely to live long enough for Tiberius Gemellus to come of age, and Sejanus, even if he retained his position of Praetorian Prefect, would not have commanded the influence he now held with Tiberius under Agrippina or her sons. Livilla's room for manoeuvre was limited by the emperor's conventional and traditional views on the role of women in the affairs of state. Their solution was a marriage proposal communicated to the emperor by letter, made after a suitable period of mourning, in AD 25. This initially appears a little odd when Sejanus would have attended the emperor in his private chambers on a daily basis. Tacitus clarifies this situation as being a result of 'a convention of the period to address him in writing even when he was in the capital'.[45] The marriage appeal was supposedly made at the insistence of Livilla, as Sejanus could disavow the entreaty if it met with a negative response and instead blame his daughter-in-law's 'feminine passion', as Tacitus does. The historian appears to have read the letter which he then summarizes:

> The gist of the document was that owing to the benevolence of the prince's father Augustus, followed by so many expressions of approval from Tiberius, he had formed the habit of carrying his hopes and his vows to the imperial ears as readily as to the gods. He had never asked for the baubles of office: he would rather stand sentry and work like the humblest soldier for the security of the emperor. And yet he had reached the supreme goal – he had been counted worthy of an alliance with the Caesar. This had taught him to hope; and since he had heard that Augustus, when settling his daughter, had to some extent considered the claims even of equites, so, if a husband should be required for Livia, he begged that Tiberius would bear in mind a friend who would derive nothing from the connection but its glory. For he did not seek to divest himself of the duties laid on him: it was enough, in his estimation, if his family was strengthened against the unfounded animosities of Agrippina; and that simply for the sake of his children. As to himself, whatever the term of years he might complete under such a sovereign, it would be enough and to spare![46]

The authenticity of the letter has been doubted by Syme, who questioned how the senatorial historian could have seen a letter that would have been kept in the palace archives rather than documents retained by the Senate. Instead, he believes that Tacitus used the letter, as speeches were used by the ancient historians, to demonstrate his 'inventive art'. Some doubt has been cast on whether such an embarrassing letter would have been preserved at all. Yet Suetonius is able to cite letters sent by Augustus to Livia which refer to his wife's grandson and future emperor Claudius in unfaltering terms; they question whether he had 'full command of his senses' and label him as being 'physically and mentally deficient'. Tacitus had access to two lost works on the reign of Tiberius – one by the Epicurean Aufidius Bassus and that of the prominent senator Servilius Nonianus – whilst Seneca the Elder wrote a history of his times published by his son Seneca the Younger. Tacitus probably also used the brief account of his reign written by Tiberius himself, whilst he certainly utilized the work by Agrippina the Younger, the daughter of Agrippina the Elder, which gave an account of the history of her family. He also accessed the senatorial archives, including the *acta senatus* and possibly the *comntentarii prinicipum*, the private journals of the emperor. The correspondence could have been preserved in one of these records. Analysis of the language used in the letter containing the emperor's reply finds words and phrases that are characteristic of Tiberius. Speeches were understood at the time, through tradition and convention, to be literary inventions on the part of the writer, and Tacitus at no point claims these to be genuine. However, in the case of this letter, the historian infers that he had read it and provides an accurate summary of its contents.[47]

The letter, if we accept it as genuine,[48] provides a fascinating insight into courtly politics at this important juncture of Sejanus' ascent to an authority and power that rivalled even that of the emperor. Knowing the mind and character of Tiberius, Sejanus refers to Augustan precedent. Cleverly, after first reminding Tiberius that Claudius' son was, before his unfortunate death, betrothed to his daughter, Sejanus then refers to the rumour that Augustus had considered marrying his own daughter Julia to the eques C. Proculeius.[49] Not only was Proculeius a close friend of Augustus from his earliest days and ranked by Juvenal as equal in influence with Maecenas, and by Horace equal to Sallustius Crispus, but he was related to Sejanus, being the half-brother of Varro Murena and Terentia.[50] The mind of an incredibly clever and skilful politician was at work here. He presents himself as a hardworking and loyal soldier, which is reflected in his official propaganda as published by Velleius Paterculus, who describes the prefect as having 'a great capacity for hard work and loyal service' who 'claims nothing for himself'.[51] The letter also confirms Sejanus' ambition to become the guardian of Tiberius Gemellus, and so, in effect, the regency. What is also illuminating is the open attack on Agrippina, made with no fear or hesitancy, confident that he is writing to a man who thinks and feels the same towards the princess and the acknowledged successors, Nero, Drusus and Caligula. The letter appeals to Tiberius, claiming Sejanus, the potential husband to Livilla, could, as Praetorian Prefect in his role as guardian of the safety of the imperial family defined by their relationship to Tiberius and not Augustus, protect Tiberius' family from the 'animosities of Agrippina'. The claims of Agrippina's children are ignored in the letter. Finally, he appeals to the emperor 'for the sake of his children'. This, as Seager points out, is puzzling, as Drusus' surviving children were Tiberius Gemellus and Julia Livilla, who was betrothed to Nero, so it is unlikely Agrippina would be a threat to her daughter-in-law. This might imply that Sejanus was suggesting that he might have a son of his own with Livilla. This would appear to have been an extremely risky suggestion in the present circumstances. A more likely scenario was that Tiberius had been considering calling off the engagement between Julia Livilla and Nero.[52]

Tiberius, ever cautious, played for time to allow himself opportunity to draft a measured response as well as take advice on the potential reaction to the proposed marriage. He 'praised Sejanus' devotion, touched not too heavily on his own services to him'.[53] Clearly, the emperor had been surprised and now looked upon his Praetorian Prefect in a new light. Tiberius must have consulted widely. No doubt Thrasyllus was also involved. The letter Sejanus now received made clear the extent of opposition, both towards him and the marriage. Tiberius explained that 'the weightiest affairs had to be regulated with an eye upon public opinion'. This concern he returns to later in the narrative; when addressing Sejanus directly, he accuses the Praetorian Prefect of deluding himself:

> [D]o you suppose the position will be tolerated by those who had seen her brother, her father, and our ancestors, in the supreme offices of state? You wish, for your own part, to stop short at the station you hold: but those magistrates and men of distinction who take you by storm and consult you on any and every subject make no secret of their opinion that you have long since transcended the heights of the equestrian order and left the friendships of my father far behind; and in their envy of you they censure myself as well.[54]

Tiberius makes his points with barbs of steel. Sejanus' power had transcended that of Augustus' equestrian advisors Maecenas and Sallustius Crispus. Even Sejanus' allusion to C. Proculeius was then negated in the letter, as the emperor pointed out that he and other equestrians were 'remarkable for their quietude of life and implicated in none of the business of state'. A pointed comparison is made to Sejanus' involvement in state affairs. Then Tiberius addresses the elephant in the room, the marriage of Julia the Elder to the great equestrian general and imperial advisor Agrippa: 'But, if we are to be moved by the hesitancy of Augustus, how much more cogent the fact that he affianced her to Marcus Agrippa and later to myself.' No comparison is made between the positions, status and imperial marriage of Sejanus and Agrippa, despite the obvious existence of similarities. Velleius Paterculus, writing in *c*. AD 30, makes this very comparison in that 'the deified Augustus made use of Marcus Agrippa and of Statilius Taurus right after him', before comparing these 'new men' to Tiberius' 'peerless assistant'. The offence was meant. Sejanus had overreached.[55]

The emperor had also expressed his displeasure at the burgeoning size of Sejanus' morning *salutatio*, where the consuls, magistrates and aristocracy came to offer their greetings and make a formal show of friendship. This satellite court had partly come into existence due to the increasing withdrawal of the emperor from public life and his duties as emperor. Yet Tiberius viewed this assembly with suspicion. By drawing Sejanus' attention to the hypocrisy of those members of the aristocracy who had greeted him and sought his friendship, yet criticized him in private to the emperor, he aimed to undermine the Praetorian Prefect's bonds of friendship. The aristocracy hated Sejanus as a '*municipali adultero*'. The barriers that existed due to the Praetorian Prefect's equestrian status were also brought home to him when Tiberius asked if Livilla would be content to marry him if he retained his present rank; after all, would a woman who had 'been wedded successively to Gaius Caesar and to Drusus be complaisant enough to grow old at the side of a Roman *eques*?'

Almost as an aside, the emperor mentioned another reservation. Tiberius envisaged further division in the imperial house due to Agrippina's potential hostility to such a marriage, for 'as matters stood, there were outbreaks of feminine jealousy, and the feud was unsettling his grand-children. What if the strife was accentuated by the proposed union?' Tiberius foresaw that Agrippina would demand a husband if Livilla was granted her request. The husband of Agrippina would act as her advocate and considerably strengthen her position. Modern historians have focused on this objection and appear to underestimate the emperor's attack upon Sejanus, laced as it is by a scattering of praise and flattery.[56] This tactic was again used by Tiberius in his undermining of Sejanus' position in AD 31. Tiberius wrote of their friendship and laid before the Praetorian Prefect the tantalizing hope of 'further ties by which I propose to cement our union', adding that 'no station, however exalted, would be unearned by your qualities and your devotion to myself; and when the occasion comes, either in the Senate or before the public, I shall not be silent'. Sejanus, upon reading the letter, must have felt like a boxer on the ropes, who after receiving blow after blow, finds his assailant placing a comforting arm around him as he staggers to his corner.

Tacitus makes clear that Sejanus knew the marriage proposal was a grave error of judgement. The failure to gain the union both Sejanus and Livilla wanted was now a secondary consideration. Sejanus knew the emperor's trust and confidence in his loyalty was now questioned. His enemies were emboldened. The Praetorian Prefect, despite frequent contact with the emperor, had to follow protocol and communicate his reply in another letter. Tacitus (*Annals*, 4.41) says: 'Sejanus – now alarmed not for his marriage but on deeper grounds – urged him [Tiberius] to disregard the still voice of suspicion, the babble of the multitude, the attacks of his maligners.' Sejanus had miscalculated, and he was now vulnerable. He had provided ammunition for his enemies to use against him in their conversations with the emperor. These opponents were well known to Sejanus as he refused 'to give a handle to his detractors by receiving them', probably at his morning *salutatio*. The *amici Caesarii* must have been confident in the protection of Tiberius to stand so openly in opposition to the power of Sejanus. Their disdain at the prospect of a mere equestrian marrying into the imperial family might suggest that most were influential members of the aristocracy. Amongst their number may have been Lucius Arruntius, who had been retained in Rome despite holding the governorship of Hispania Citerior since AD 25. He had been long detested by Sejanus, and it may have been the influence of the Praetorian Prefect which deprived him of the opportunity to take up his post rather than the suspicions of the emperor. In AD 31 Sejanus had a charge brought against Arruntius, but the emperor quashed it.[57] The emperor's old *amici* were being thinned by death, and in AD 25 they were joined by Gnaeus Lentulus, the consul of 18 BC who had accompanied Drusus as an advisor during the Pannonian mutiny, and Lucius Domitius Ahenobarbus, the scion of a great aristocratic family who had married Antonia the Elder. Ahenobarbus is described by Suetonius as 'notorious for his arrogance, extravagance and cruelty'. His son Gnaeus Domitius Ahenobarbus attracted even greater notoriety from an early age: he had accompanied the Caesar Gaius to the East in 1 BC, along with Sejanus, but was dismissed from his staff for murdering 'one of his own freedmen for refusing to drink more as he was told'. He is later said to have deliberately run over a boy with his chariot, and being publicly criticized for this in the Forum, he attacked the individual, gouging out one of his eyes.[58] Perhaps the goddess of Fortune had favoured Sejanus again by removing possible adversaries, but other close *amici* of Tiberius remained, their tongues slowly poisoning the mind of the emperor towards the partner of his labours.

Another serious cause of contention in the imperial letter was the size and magnificence of Sejanus' *salutatio*. No source mentions the emperor ending this formalized greeting whilst in Rome, as they do when Augustus pleaded old age and infirmity to firstly dispense with it on the days the Senate met from 12 BC and then altogether.[59] In fact, it would have been surprising if Tiberius had done, as it would be a public statement indicating his retirement from public life, as Seneca indicated his retirement by refusing to receive the crowds who had formerly flocked to his *salutatio*. Tacitus suggests that one of the reasons for Tiberius' desire to retire to the 'quiet and solitude' of Campania was 'the endless stream of suitors' who brought requests and petitions for the attention of the emperor. Tiberius had probably withdrawn from opportunities for individuals to approach him at the imperial *salutatio*, and instead admitted the senators as a group. There were, therefore, few opportunities for private conversations with the emperor, and personal interviews rarely granted; instead, the imperial ear could only be realistically sought through his Praetorian Prefect. Yet at the same time, the emperor viewed the attendance of the great magistrates upon Sejanus with suspicion, despite the increasing delegation of civil functions upon him. Perhaps what added to Tiberius' doubts was the probable presence of one of the two ordinary consuls of AD 25 at Sejanus' *salutatio*, Marcus Asinius Agrippa, the son of Gaius Asinius Gallus and Vipsania. Tiberius saw threats and conspiracies everywhere.[60]

The *auctoritas* and influence of a member of the Roman elite was reflected in the numbers attending the *salutatio*, but also the status of those doing so. Tacitus, referring to the power and influence of Sejanus, makes reference to the 'great levées' that included 'magistrates and men of distinction who take you by storm and consult you on any and every subject'. This caused him to be viewed with envy by the great and the mighty, thus increasing his unpopularity. Pliny, describing the *salutatio* of the consul, writer and orator Silius Italicus, a man of minor influence compared to Sejanus, writes flatteringly that he was 'ranked as one of our leading citizens without exercising influence or incurring ill-will; he was waited on and sought after, and regularly spent many hours on his couch in a room thronged with callers who had come with no thought of rank'.[61] It is significant that Pliny refers to Italicus' *salutatio* as a reflection of his prestige, power and influence. This daily renewal of friendship and formal greeting by clients symbolized political success, social standing and utility to the state. For the aristocracy, the size and grandeur of the imperial *salutatio* was acceptable as the emperor was a Claudian adopted into the family of Julius Caesar and Augustus. However, Sejanus, whose *salutatio* mirrored that of the emperor, was a mere equestrian. The physical manifestation of his morning reception was a daily reminder of their subservient role in the Roman state. Personal contact with a patron was vital for the success of a request or petition, and, apart from banquets, the best occasion for this was admission to this cloistered audience. Sejanus' close *amici* Satrius Secundus and Pomponius Secundus acted as gatekeepers to this personal audience, and were 'venerated' for this reason. This would have caused only greater resentment amongst the nobility, who had to accept the humiliation of approaching social inferiors for access to a man whom they also considered of lesser status. In their opinion this was an inversion of the social order.[62]

Tacitus criticizes Sejanus for being 'unwilling to ... enfeeble his influence by prohibiting the throngs which besieged his doors', but this would have amounted to a rejection of his political influence, his bonds of *amicitiae* with his *amici* and clients and his social status. Sejanus was managing the aspirations of the aristocracy and the distribution of imperial *beneficia* which Tiberius, in his withdrawal from this aspect of political and social life, was denying them. The aristocracy did not envy the Praetorian Prefect's *salutatio* itself, but rather its size and membership that reflected the extent of his *potentia*, a power which came from his proximity to the emperor and his increasing role in the administration of the state. Ironically, it was Tiberius who created this situation and it was only in the emperor's power to remedy it. This would only have been achieved to the detriment of the status, power and probably life of the Praetorian Prefect. To Sejanus, the logical solution was to persuade Tiberius to realize his long-held ambition and retire in all but name to the comforts and pastoral cares of Campania.[63]

Unable to deal immediately with his opponents who were protected by the friendship of the emperor, Sejanus instead moved against more vulnerable targets. The Roman fabulist Phaedrus appears to preserve in his poems the criticisms of Sejanus that ran amongst the populace.

The allusions made in the verses are, by their very nature, open to interpretation, but the fact Phaedrus was prosecuted by *delatores* at the instigation of the Praetorian Prefect suggests that contemporaries were able to easily interpret the references and allusions made to the powerful figures of imperial politics. Sejanus, infamous for his pride and arrogance, is possibly the jackdaw who, 'swelling with empty pride, picked up some feathers fallen from a Peacock, and decked himself out therewith; upon which, despising his own kind, he mingled with a beauteous flock of Peacocks. They tore his feathers from the impudent bird, and put him to flight with their beaks.'[64] Another fable appears to make direct reference to the proposed marriage between Sejanus and Livilla, where Sejanus is represented by the sun, Tiberius by Jupiter and the Roman people by frogs:

> Once upon a time, when the Sun was thinking of taking a wife, the Frogs sent forth their clamour to the stars. Disturbed by their croakings, Jupiter asked the cause of their complaints. Then said one of the inhabitants of the pool: 'As it is, by himself he parches up all the standing waters, and compels us unfortunates to languish and die in our scorched abode. What is to become of us, if he beget children?'[65]

The meaning of the fables was perfectly clear to contemporaries, including Sejanus. Phaedrus was indicted and, lacking imperial support, his fate was sealed. He laments: 'I have made a road, and have invested more than it left, selecting some points to my misfortune. But if any other than Sejanus had been the informer, if any other the witness, if any other the judge, in fine, I should confess myself deserving of such woes; nor should I soothe my sorrows with these expeditions.'[66] The nature of his punishment Phaedrus leaves unsaid; however, his anger is reserved for Sejanus alone and the punishment that he would have accepted if it had come from an honest man.

Tacitus writes that there were 'so continuous a chain of impeachments that in the days of the Latin Festival, when Drusus [the son of Germanicus], as Urban Prefect, mounted the tribunal to inaugurate his office, he was approached by Calpurnius Salvianus with a suit against Sextus Marius: an action that drew a public reprimand from the Caesar and occasioned the banishment of Salvianus.'[67] Marius was a close *amicus* of Tiberius but not associated with Sejanus, as he survived his fall. Marius is not mentioned by Tacitus as accompanying Tiberius and Sejanus when they left Rome for Campania with a small circle of friends of the emperor, but he was on Capri before AD 33 as his execution in that year resulted from the unwelcome attentions of the aged emperor towards his beautiful daughter. Marius sent his daughter away, but he was then charged with incest and, upon being condemned, was thrown from the Tarpeian Rock. This might suggest his initial absence from the emperor's party in AD 26 was due to the intervention of the Praetorian Prefect, but upon Sejanus' fall he was brought back to the imperial court on Capri. Marius was so favoured by the emperor that he became the wealthiest man in Spain. His power is symbolized by a story told by Dio, who describes him as 'so powerful that once, when he was at odds with a neighbour, he invited him to be his guest for two days, on the first of which he razed the man's villa level with the ground and on the next rebuilt it on a larger and more elaborate scale; and then, when the other could not guess who had done it, Marius admitted his responsibility for both achievements and added significantly: "This shows you that I have both the knowledge and the power to repel attacks and also to requite kindness."' Perhaps the prosecution of Marius in AD 25 was an attack by Sejanus on one of his critics who had the imperial ear. If so, it failed thanks to Tiberius' intervention. The fate of Calpurnius Salvianus would then reflect the imperial suspicions directed towards the ambitions of the Praetorian Prefect.[68]

Another case heard before the emperor in the Senate certainly worked in Sejanus' favour, although the links to Sejanus are tenuous. The popular Narbonese orator Votienus Montanus was brought before the Senate charged with insulting Tiberius. He was indicted by P. Vinicius, the *suffect* consul of AD 2. Seneca implies that a feud existed between them, as P. Vinicius had prosecuted Votienus on behalf of the city of Narbo. His own son Marcus Vinicius was quaestor in AD 20, and in the following year was asked by Gnaeus Calpurnius Piso to act as part of his defence against the charge of poisoning Germanicus, a request he refused. He became consul in AD 30 during Sejanus' dominance of Roman politics, but in AD 33 married Julia Livilla, the youngest daughter of Germanicus and Agrippina. It is extremely doubtful the emperor would have made this match if he was connected in any way with his now deposed Praetorian Prefect. However, it was the witness called to testify against Votienus who caused the greatest upset. Aemilius is described by Tacitus as a simple military man, but, based on an inscription, it has been suggested that after serving under Germanicus, Aemilius was promoted to the rank of tribune in the Praetorian Guard, an appointment that would have been due to the patronage of Sejanus. Tacitus describes the scene in the Senate as Aemilius, in his role as a witness for the prosecution, described in graphic detail the slurs and rumours associated with the charge, to the obvious distress of the emperor and the horror of the senators:

> As chance would have it, this trial of the popular and talented Votienus Montanus forced Tiberius (who was already wavering) to the conviction that he must avoid the meetings of the Senate and the remarks, often equally true and mordant, which were there repeated to his face. For, during the indictment of Votienus for the use of language offensive to the emperor, the witness Aemilius, a military man, in his anxiety to prove the case, reported the expressions in full, and, disregarding the cries of protest, struggled on with his tale with great earnestness. Tiberius thus heard the scurrilities with which he was attached in private; and such was the shock that he kept crying out he would refute them, either on the spot or in the course of the trial; his equanimity being restored with difficulty by the entreaties of his friends and the adulation of all. Votienus himself suffered the full penalties of treason.[69]

P. Vinicius had clearly brought the case as part of his ongoing quarrel, but also to gain imperial favour, if not on his behalf, then for his son, the consul of AD 30. Was this at the suggestion of Sejanus, just as Visellius Varro was persuaded to prosecute Silius to further his grievance inherited from the treatment of his father? However, Tiberius had been utterly humiliated in front of the Senate, and despite his outcries, and those of the Senate, the 'military man' in his naivety had blindly continued in his testimony, despite clearly offending the emperor. It is difficult to believe that Aemilius was either that ignorant or lacking in emotional intelligence not to stop once he recognised the turmoil he had caused in the Senate. Aemilius must have moved in the circle of the senator and rhetor Votienus to act as a witness to his supposed crimes. This not only suggests he was a high-ranking military man, quite possibly a Praetorian tribune, but also educated and intelligent enough to socialize with this highly cultured senator. Furthermore, if Aemilius was a Praetorian tribune there can be little doubt that he would have reported Votienus' ill-advised comments to his superior. Aemilius must have known the effects of his testimony on his listeners, but possibly continued at the instructions of Sejanus. The consequences of this unfortunate incident were all in Sejanus' favour. Firstly, it acted as a further push towards Tiberius' decision to leave Rome, as the Praetorian Prefect understood the emperor would personalize the vindictive gossip and rumours so publicly aired. Secondly, the emperor's anger would have been directed firstly at Votienus, but also at the duplicitous Senate, which had acted as the audience of his humiliation, men whom Tiberius considered, in his infamous aside, fit only to be slaves.[70]

As a consequence of these events, Tiberius rarely attended Senate meetings, further isolating himself and allowing fewer opportunities for petitioners to approach him as he made his way to and from the curia. No doubt Sejanus offered a sympathetic audience to the anger of the emperor, and the emperor was persuaded to humiliate and intimidate the Senate in revenge. The Senate was summoned to watch 'an exhibition of the Praetorian Guard at drill, as if they were ignorant of the power of these troops; his purpose was to make them more afraid of him, when they saw his defenders to be so numerous and so strong'.[71]

The senatorial opponents of Sejanus would also have been reminded of the threat of his power, but this was also a clear indication that Tiberius' impasse with his Praetorian Prefect was now settled. The emperor would have stood on the tribunal alongside the commander of the guard, the armed and serried ranks assembled before them an implicit threat as to the fate of those who stood against Sejanus. Epictetus provides an indication of the fear and trepidation this exhibition would have affected when the philosopher reminds his audience of the emperor's power over life and death, symbolized by the weapons carried by the Praetorians, weapons which kill.[72]

Sejanus was slowly restoring Tiberius' faith and trust in him, whilst at the same time intimidating his enemies. Agrippina was now moved into making impolitic actions that would serve to further alienate her from the emperor and so threaten the succession of her children. Cn. Domitius Afer, the praetor of AD 25, came before the consuls the following year to accuse Agrippina's cousin and close friend Claudia Pulchra with adultery and *maiestas*. The charges also included the casting of spells and attempts to poison the emperor. The accusations were targeted at Tiberius' fears. There is little to link Domitius Afer with Sejanus, and that this notorious *delator* survived his fall suggests that this was, in fact, the case. Afer was a highly skilled orator from Nemausus in Gallia Narbonensis. Supremely talented, his ambitions were only matched by his ruthlessness.

As a *novus homo* he lacked the connections, *nobilitas* and money to attain a consulship under normal circumstances. Tacitus, whilst admiring his ability as an orator, criticizes the means by which he chose to accelerate his career, for he had 'a modest standing in the world, and hurrying towards a reputation by way of any crime', he indicted Claudia Pulchra. He gained a pre-eminent reputation through her conviction, but it is unlikely he would have risked charging such a well-connected member of the nobility unless it was indicated to him that such an action would be looked on favourably by the emperor. Agrippina was under no illusion as to whom she considered responsible, as 'fierce-tempered always and now inflamed by the danger of her kinswoman, [she] flew to Tiberius wearing the black of mourning to elicit public sympathy, and, as chance would have it, found him sacrificing to his father'. As a priest in the college *sodalium Augustalium*, Tiberius was taking part in a public sacrifice to Augustus, his father through adoption, in contrast to Agrippina, who was directly related to Rome's first emperor, a fact she was immensely proud of and which rankled with the ever-sensitive Tiberius. Ignoring the sound advice that her dying husband offered seven years previously, she exploded: 'It was not for the same man to offer victims to the deified Augustus and to persecute his posterity. Not into speechless stone had that divine spirit been transfused; she, his authentic effigy, the issue of his celestial blood, was aware of her peril and assumed the garb of mourning. It was idle to make a pretext of Pulchra, the only cause of whose destruction was that in utter folly she had chosen Agrippina as the object of her affection, forgetful of Sosia, who was struck down for the same offence.' Tiberius, anger now rising, grabbed hold of her 'and admonished her in a line of Greek that she was not necessarily "A woman injured, if she lacked a throne."' Agrippina had attacked the emperor's integrity, accusing him of hypocrisy in publicly respecting the settlement of Augustus whilst in private persecuting his one true descendant. These words were meant to hurt and should have been best left unsaid.[73]

Clearly, Agrippina only saw the vindictiveness of Tiberius behind the prosecution of Silius, Sosia and Claudia Pulchra. After her cousin's condemnation she 'met Domitius and perceived that out of embarrassment he stood aside from her path, called to him and said: "fear not, Domitius; it isn't you that I hold to blame, but Agamemnon."'[74] This was a reference to the legendary all-powerful conqueror of Troy who sacrificed his own daughter to calm the seas before embarking across the Aegean. Agrippina was the daughter of Tiberius through marriage to his adopted son Germanicus. Her analogy foresaw future events.

Not only did Agrippina's comments cut to the core of Tiberius' vulnerability, which had haunted him since his very succession, but his comments to Agrippina also reveal his suspicions and fear of her. She was the direct descendant of Augustus who wished to be Augusta, which was only possible if she married a future emperor or ruled through her children. Was this what Sejanus had been suggesting to Tiberius in the privacy of the imperial bedchamber?

These suspicions were, in the emperor's eyes, soon confirmed. Agrippina, overwhelmed by anger and loss at the condemnation of Claudia Pulchra, soon fell ill and took to her bed. Tiberius, dutiful to his familial obligations, visited her. The ensuing scene was taken by Tacitus from the history of her daughter Agrippina the Younger:

> Meanwhile Agrippina, obstinately nursing her anger, and attacked by physical illness, was visited by the emperor. For long her tears fell in silence; then she began with reproaches and entreaties: 'He must aid her loneliness and give her a husband; she had still the requisite youth, and the virtuous had no consolation but in marriage – the state had citizens who would stoop to receive the wife of Germanicus and his children.' The Caesar, however, though he saw all that was implied in the request, was reluctant to betray either fear or resentment, and therefore, in spite of her insistence, left without an answer.[75]

Tiberius, in his reply to Sejanus' request to marry Livilla, had reacted with suspicion and denied the appeal as it would increase the 'enmity' of Agrippina and further the divisions in the imperial house. The same suspicions would now have arisen at this request. There was little doubt in Tiberius' mind whom Agrippina had in mind, a man he hated and despised above all others: Asinius Gallus. One of his sons, Asinius Saloninus, had been betrothed to a daughter of Germanicus and Agrippina but had died in AD 22, whilst his two surviving sons had recently been consuls, C. Asinius Pollio in AD 23 and Marcus Asinius Agrippa in AD 25, but he died in the following year. The man's arrogance knew no bounds. He claimed to Asconius Pedianus that he, Gallus, was the 'Messiah' of Virgil's Fourth Eclogue. It was Asinius Gallus who had married Tiberius' beloved Vipsania, whom he had been forced to divorce to fulfil the dynastic plans of Augustus. It was Asinius Gallus who had tried to adopt his own son Drusus. It was now, in the emperor's mind at least, Asinius Gallus who would make Agrippina empress and become the stepfather of his successors Nero and

Drusus. Augustus, in one of his last conversations with his successor, forewarned him on the ambitions of Asinius Gallus, a man who was eager for the throne but totally unfit. When Agrippina died of starvation in her island exile in AD 33, Tiberius let loose his invective in a letter to a shocked Senate in which he accused 'her of unchastity and adultery with Asinius Gallus, by whose death she had been driven to tire of life'. The fact her two eldest sons had recently died in prison appears to have escaped his mind.[76] As for Asinius Gallus, he had been held in solitary confinement since AD 30 and he too was starved to death.

Sejanus now decided to seize on the opportunity offered by this crisis in the relationship between the emperor and his daughter-in-law. His aim was her destruction, thus undermining the succession of her children. Agrippina was clearly completely unaware of Sejanus' toxic role in courtly politics. To her, he must have acted with deference and equanimity, and she trusted him. Sejanus knew he could rely on her to act impulsively. Tiberius, perhaps motivated by her tears and pleading, attempted a reconciliation and invited Agrippina to an imperial banquet. This was an opportunity for Sejanus to fatally destroy the relationship between them.

> [The Praetorian Prefect sent] agents to warn her, under the colour of *amicitiae*, that poison was ready for her: she would do well to avoid the dinners of her father-in-law. And she, a stranger to all pretence, as she reclined next to him at the table, relaxed neither her features nor her silence, and refused to touch her food; until at last, either by accident or from information received, Tiberius' attention was arrested, and, to apply a more searching test, he took some fruit as it had been set before him and with his own hand passed it to his daughter-in-law, with a word of praise. The act increased Agrippina's suspicions, and without tasting the dish she passed it over to the slaves. Even so, no overt remark followed from Tiberius: he turned, however, to his mother Livia, and observed that it was not strange if he had resolved on slightly rigorous measures against a lady who accused him of murder by poison.

Agrippina was never invited to an imperial banquet again, a public announcement of her fall from favour which required no formal renunciation of *amicitiae*. Rumours now circulated that the emperor planned her destruction. Her *amici* and clients, recognizing that her access to imperial gifts and other *beneficia* was now curtailed, would begin to desert her. Many would also fear being associated with her fall. By AD 28 Tacitus describes the loyal Titius Sabinus as Agrippina's 'one survivor of that multitude of clients'. In Tiberius' autobiography, read by Suetonius, the emperor pointedly blames Sejanus for the persecution of both Nero and Drusus, but not for the campaign against Agrippina. Indeed, Agrippina was to remain on her prison island of Pandateria after the fall of Sejanus, and there be starved to death. Tiberius took full responsibility for Agrippina's fall and recognized that the Praetorian Prefect was carrying out the imperial will.[77]

Fortune again smiled on Sejanus' ambitions as the increasingly isolated and disenchanted emperor finally broke with his mother. Livia had found her influence gradually eroded by the attitude of her son towards the role of women in public affairs. Age and infirmity had taken their toll, but the great patroness still attempted to provide *beneficia* for her *amici* and clients. Tiberius had been repeatedly asked by her to enrol as a juror a man who had just been granted Roman citizenship. Eventually Tiberius relented, on the proviso 'that the entry should be marked "forced upon the Emperor by his mother"'. This was too much for the elderly Livia, who 'lost her temper and produced from a strong box some of Augustus' old letters to her commenting on Tiberius' sour and stubborn character. Annoyance with her for hoarding these documents so long, and then spitefully confronting him with them, is said to have been his main reason for retirement to Capri.'[78]

Tiberius had always contemplated retiring from his role as emperor. His retreat to Rhodes in 6 BC and to Campania during the consulship of his son Drusus in AD 21 are clear signals as to the emperor's thought processes in AD 26. Publicly in 6 BC Tiberius gave the excuse of travelling to Rhodes as an opportunity to complete his education, yet in reality he was probably disgusted at his treatment in the political manoeuvrings involving the succession of Julia's children Gaius and Lucius at the expense of his own child Drusus. His relationship with his stepsons had also broken down, whilst marriage with Julia had long since been merely a political association made at the insistence of Augustus despite his love for Vipsania. Pride, anger and frustration directed towards Julia's own domineering ambitions for Gaius and Lucius led Tiberius to abandon his position of virtual impregnable political strength. Julia wished to have a meaningful role as the wife of the emperor, a role that was an anathema to Tiberius' view of the role of woman in the state. Julia's adultery had a political aim in securing the succession for her children, as much as for herself.[79] The situation was different in

AD 21. Tiberius removed himself from Rome to publicly recognize Drusus as future emperor whilst, without officially retiring from the administration of the state, making it clear that this was his future intent.

There were many factors in his final decision to leave Rome and never to return. Unlike Tiberius' retirement in AD 21, the situation in 6 BC and AD 26 are remarkably similar. Tiberius had never liked court life, nor the political intrigues of the female members of the imperial family. For Julia, there was now Agrippina. Both had constantly reminded Tiberius of their biological links to Augustus, and thus their right to command and advise. Their pointed comments on his adoption into the imperial family through the marriage and influence of his mother were meant to offend. Both worked to ensure the succession for their children and promote their offspring's rapid advancement. In 6 BC it was extremely unlikely that Tiberius' son Drusus would inherit the throne as the claims of both Gaius and Lucius stood before his. The likelihood of both these Caesars dying was minimal, and now in AD 26 the son he loved so dearly, Drusus, was gone. The emperor was surrounded by widows whose matrimonial ambitions, if granted, would only further their political ambitions. Just as Julia's adultery was an extension of this, so Tiberius could see echoes of this in the demands of Livilla and Agrippina. In Tiberius' mind, Agrippina's desire to remarry and her supposed adultery with Asinius Gallus was evidence of her imperial designs. Tiberius' thoughts must have returned to the quiet life of study he had pursued on Rhodes and perhaps in Campania. Sejanus only needed to offer reassurances to enhance these desires, as Tacitus recognizes, and the Praetorian Prefect certainly had the skills to exploit them. Convinced, Tiberius remained absent from Rome even after the death of Sejanus.[80]

Other facts may also have come into play, such as the infirmities of age which assaulted the pride of this once formidable soldier who now 'possessed a tall, round-shouldered, and abnormally slender figure, a head without a trace of hair, and an ulcerous face generally variegated with plasters'. The emperor's withdrawal from Rome comes soon after his public arguments with Agrippina and his mother. Tiberius visited Livia for one final time, probably to inform her of his intentions, and then mother and son never set eyes on each other again. Tiberius, when informed of Livia's illness and subsequent death in AD 29, 'neither paid her any visits during her illness nor did he himself lay out her body; in fact, he made no arrangements at all in her honour except for the public funeral and images and some other matters of no importance. As for her being deified, he forbade that absolutely.' Tiberius was never one to forgive once slighted. Sejanus, up until this point, had manipulated Tiberius' fears and suspicions for his own benefit. Now he was able to pursue his own agenda. Events, at times guided and influenced by Sejanus, had again played out to the benefit of the Praetorian Prefect.[81]

Chapter 6

Regent: AD 26–30

Sejanus 'was building a high rise multi-storey tower, and from there the fall would be the greater and the collapse of the toppled ruin more terrible'. (Juvenal, *Satire*, 10 15)

A small imperial party left Rome accompanying the 66-year-old Tiberius, whose departure was a symbolic embodiment of his failings as emperor. Sejanus was at the side of his emperor and in charge of the Praetorian cohorts. It appears to have been the norm for two Praetorian cohorts to accompany members of the imperial family: two marched with Drusus to crush the Pannonian mutiny, whilst two fought with Germanicus beyond the Rhine. Drusus also had with him most of the Praetorian cavalry and the German cavalry. As emperor, it is possible Tiberius' superior status meant that at least one more cohort marched with him, although significant numbers of guards and cavalry would have brought with it increased problems of provisioning and billeting, especially when confined to the small island of Capri and its environs. A significant force of Praetorians remained in Rome to enforce order and remind the recalcitrant and intractable of the power of the absent ruler and his prefect.

Only one senator accompanied Tiberius, M. Cocceius Nerva, a man with little administrative experience but an expert on Roman law. He is described as 'an inseparable friend of the emperor, versed in all law divine or secular'. Clearly, Tiberius anticipated hearing cases and petitions submitted to him and felt his judgements would benefit from the experience of the eminent jurist as part of his *consilium*. The only other equites to join the party, apart from Sejanus himself, was Curtius Atticus, a former *amicus* of the great poet Ovid.[1] Added to these individuals were 'men of letters, principally Greeks, in whose conversation he was to find amusement'. Suetonius appears to preserve the name of one of these academics who fell afoul of Tiberius, who was in the habit of 'testing his companions at dinner on the topics he had been studying that day when Seleucus, a professor of literature, had been finding out from the imperial servants what books he was reading and came prepared with all the right answers; hearing of this, Tiberius dismissed him from the company, and later forced him to commit suicide'. Another distinguished rhetor who was part of the academic circle on Capri was Vallius Syriacus, a renowned scholar who had been a pupil of Theodorus of Gadara, Tiberius' tutor on Rhodes. He is mentioned by Seneca and was, according to Dio, 'renowned for his culture'. He was fated to become another victim of Tiberius. Juvenal also refers to Tiberius' 'herd of Chaldaeans', a reference to the astrologers that populated the imperial palace on Capri. Certainly, Thrasyllus retained his position at the side of the emperor, continuing to exert his influence through his mastery of soothsaying. His granddaughter Ennia was also on Capri, playing a significant role in courtly politics.[2] Others certainly joined the emperor later on Capri, including Sextus Marius, whilst many members of Rome's elite took up residence in their villas on the Bay of Naples opposite, including Antonia the Younger.

Curiously, Tacitus in Book 6 refers to the 14-year-old Caligula departing Rome with Tiberius, yet fails to include him in his description of the emperor's companions who left Rome in Book 4. Caligula was in Rome in AD 27/28 when he went to live with Livia, and in AD 29 he gave the eulogy at the funeral of his great-grandmother. Upon Livia's death he was taken in by his grandmother Antonia the Younger, and then in AD 31 was summoned to Capri. It would have been surprising for Agrippina to allow Caligula, who would only turn 14 in August AD 26, to depart under the 'protection' of Tiberius, whom she suspected of plotting the destruction of her and her family. Tacitus might be referring to Caligula's attendance of the *profectio*, the formal ceremony of departure of a magistrate and emperor from Rome, and he then possibly accompanied the emperor on the initial stage of his journey in Campania.[3] Tacitus does refer to Tiberius meeting Caligula's brother Nero, with 'either gloomy brows or with a hypocritical smile on his countenance; whether the boy spoke or held his peace, there was guilt in silence, guilt in speech'. Perhaps the historian is referring to encounters before the emperor's withdrawal from Rome. They were not with the emperor in the near catastrophic collapse of the cavern at the imperial villa at Sperlonga. It appears unlikely that Nero and Caligula were members of the imperial entourage for long after the departure for Campania, if indeed they accompanied the emperor at all.[4]

Another group that receives no mention but were certainly present were the imperial freedmen and slaves. Their lower social status meant they are often overlooked in contemporary accounts, yet their regular contact with the emperor provided them with an opportunity for influence and favours. Phaedrus mentions the 'true story' of an imperial slave who spied the emperor walking in the gardens of the sumptuous villa that had once been owned by Lucullus, perched on the cliffs overlooking the Bay of Naples and Capri. Seizing the opportunity of earning his freedom, the slave 'began with bustling officiousness to sprinkle the parched ground with a wooden watering-pot; but only got laughed at'. The account continues:

> Thence by short cuts well known to him, he runs before into another walk, laying the dust. Caesar takes notice of this fellow and discerns his object. Just as he is supposing that there is some extraordinary good fortune in store for him: 'Come hither,' says his master; on which he skips up to him, quickened by the joyous hope of sure reward. Then, in a jesting tone, thus spoke the mighty majesty of the prince: 'You have not profited much, your labour is all in vain; manumission stands at a much higher price with me.'[5]

The slave was an *atrienses* charged with responsibility for the *atrium* and escorting visitors around the villa, explaining to them the statues, images, pictures and murals around the building and the grounds. Such informal contacts with Tiberius were not a threat to Sejanus, but served to illustrate how personal contact with the emperor was vital.[6]

The imperial freedmen who constituted the imperial bureaucracy would have had regular contact with the emperor, and so potentially were in a position to counter the advice and influence of Sejanus. Their influence came to the fore in the reigns of Caligula and Claudius in the figures of Callistus, Tiberius Claudius, Helicon and Pallas. Tiberius Claudius originally entered the imperial household as a slave from Smyrna and received his freedom; he then served Caligula and was promoted by Claudius, perhaps to a procuratorship, and was then made a financial secretary (*a rationibus*) by Nero, finally being awarded equestrian status by Vespasian. He was able to moderate the behaviour of Caligula to such an extent that he was compared to an animal trainer controlling a savage beast. Another freedman, Callistus, engendered great fear and immense wealth from his position in Caligula's court, then becoming a secretary (*a libellis*) to Claudius. Helicon, a Greek from Alexandria, had entered Tiberius' service but his savage wit appears to have alienated his master, yet it was to serve him well under Caligula. Pallas started as a slave and then freedman of Caligula's grandmother

Antonia before entering the imperial household through Claudius. He would dominate Claudius' court, along with Narcissus, helping to engineer the fall of the emperor's wife Messalina, in favour of Agrippina's daughter Agrippina the Younger, the mother of the emperor Nero.[7] The careers of these important bureaucrats were to accelerate after the deaths of Sejanus and then Tiberius. Yet even under Tiberius their influence was recognized and sought after. At some point before AD 22, the young Marcus Julius Agrippa, an *amicus* of Drusus and future king of Judaea, wasted a huge fortune, not just in the pursuit of pleasure but also in the form of gifts to imperial freedmen to buy influence at court. His mother Bernice was a close friend of Antonia, who in return supported her son. However, saddled by debt, including owing a million sesterces to Antonia, Agrippa was forced to flee. After a series of adventures, he managed to borrow a million sesterces from a Samaritan freedman of Tiberius which he used to repay his debts to Antonia, and so returned to the heart of courtly politics on Capri. Pliny also records another freedman of Tiberius, a certain Nomius, who owned a citrus wood table that was finer than any owned by the emperor.[8]

Tiberius Claudius, Callistus and Helicon must have advanced their careers under Tiberius, but their influence was checked, probably by Sejanus, who had taken over a greater part of the administrative and civil affairs of government. The fall of the Praetorian Prefect appears to have precipitated a sudden increase in their power and influence. In AD 35 Fulcinius Trio, before taking his own life, wrote a will in which, as well as condemning Sejanus' successor in the Praetorian Prefecture, he launched into 'a long and appalling indictment of Macro and the chief imperial freedmen'.[9] It would appear that both parties worked together in denying Trio access to the emperor to respond to the charges of *maiestas* linked to his close association with Sejanus. It is likely that these powerful freedmen, resentful of the *potentia* of Sejanus, joined with Macro in undermining the emperor's confidence in the 'partner of his labours'. This might explain their sudden increase in influence in the later part of Tiberius' reign and that of his successors.

The fate of Curtius Atticus serves to illustrate Sejanus' desire to control those with direct access to the emperor. The emperor, no doubt at the suggestion of Sejanus, invited to Capri two of his companions from his time in Rhodes, Vescularius Flaccus and Julius Marinus. This was clearly a sign of great imperial favour, but it appears that Marinus was eager to support the position of Sejanus by advising him 'in the destruction of Curtius Atticus'. Flaccus does not appear to have been involved in this plot, but he was highly unpopular with his peers due to his role in the execution of Scribonius Libo in AD 16. Sejanus possibly offered him his protection in anticipation of the emperor's death. Levick suggests both may have been persuaded that they were acting in the interests of the emperor or furthering the interests of his son Tiberius Gemellus. This may well be the case; the same justification was used by Terentius in his defence before the Senate.[10] Both Flaccus and Marinus, however, would pay the ultimate price for their association with Sejanus. Atticus was too independent-minded for the comfort of Sejanus, who had him removed from the emperor's circle. He was replaced by men who were far more malleable.

The emperor's departure from Rome was met with predictions from astrologers that he would never return. Many believed that his end was near. He had another eleven years to live but, although at times coming close to the capital, he would not re-enter the city again.[11] Rumours of the imminent death of Tiberius only added to the volatile political situation, as many would look to the future. The city had been left in the hands of men loyal to both Tiberius and Sejanus. Tiberius' close *amicus* L. Calpurnius Piso the Pontifex remained Prefect of Rome and appears to have been invited to Capri to indulge in regular drinking bouts with the emperor, along with another close *amicus* and *novus homo*, L. Pomponius Flaccus, the ordinary consul of AD 17.[12]

The ordinary consuls of AD 26 were Cn. Cornelius Lentulus Gaetulicus and C. Calvisius Sabinus. Gaetulicus was the son of Tiberius' old friend and leading senator Cossus Cornelius Lentulus, who had been appointed as Drusus' advisor during the Pannonian mutiny. Cossus is described as outwardly a lazy and lethargic individual, but completely trusted by Tiberius. Gaetulicus' brother Cossus Cornelius Lentulus Lethegus had been appointed the ordinary consul of AD 25, whilst Gaetulicus himself was to be made governor of Germania Superior with its four legions in AD 29. C. Calvisius Sabinus appears to have been married to a Cornelia, perhaps the sister of his consular colleague. In AD 31 Sabinus, along with three other former consuls, was charged with *maiestas*, probably on the grounds of his links to Sejanus.[13] Probably around June, the two ordinary consuls were replaced. The *pontifex maximus* and *suffect* consul of AD 26, Lucius Antistius Vetus, was the brother of Gaius Antistius Vetus, consul in AD 23, both being the sons of the consul of 6 BC, Gaius Anitistius Vetus, whose priesthood Lucius inherited. His colleague for the remainder of the year was the son of Sejanus' uncle, Q. Junius Blaesus.[14] These men were trusted to do the bidding of Tiberius and Sejanus. The Praetorian Guard remained under the sole command of Sejanus, with the tribunes of each cohort remaining in the capital taking responsibility for administrative tasks. These men, along with the Praetorian centurions, owed their appointments to Sejanus and many were probably his clients.[15]

Sejanus was able to supervise and monitor access to the emperor whilst he was on Capri, but the Praetorian Prefect had to remain in Rome on occasions, leaving Tiberius unattended. The Praetorians on the island would act as Sejanus' eyes and ears in his absence, but Sejanus could also rely on the co-operation of members of the courtly circle. This he achieved to the extent that he 'made all the associates of Tiberius so completely his friends that they immediately reported to him absolutely everything the emperor either said or did, whereas no one informed Tiberius of what Sejanus did', to the extent that the emperor remained 'ignorant of anything that concerned his minister'. Curtius Atticus quite possibly felt he was not serving the interests of Tiberius in reporting private conversations with the emperor to Sejanus, and for this reason he became another victim of the Praetorian Prefect.[16]

Tiberius had left Rome officially to consecrate two temples; one at Capua to Jupiter and the other at Nola, built over the villa where his divine predecessor Augustus had died. However, in a rejection of custom, Tiberius ordered 'that he must not be disturbed throughout his journey' as he had passed an edict that his party should not be approached. Praetorians were posted along the route to ensure his orders were obeyed.[17] The emperor's desire to isolate himself and reject his duties as emperor only served to further Sejanus' cause. An imperial journey would have had an immense impact on the towns and cities it passed through. Vast numbers of wagons and carriages were chartered, and orders sent ahead for each municipality to stockpile huge quantities of food and drink. Crowds would empty from the surrounding countryside to witness the slow progress of the line of wagons, carriages, freedmen, soldiers and provisions. Upon the approach of the imperial convoy to a town, the local magistrates, the local elite and often the whole of the populace went out to formally greet their emperor, ritualized in the ceremony of *adventus*. It was expected that the emperor in return allowed the citizens access to him and heard their requests for favours. This refusal would clearly have caused great offence as well as publicly demonstrating that access to Tiberius was only achieved through the courting of his prefect.[18]

A few days into their journey, the goddess Fortuna again bestowed her favours on her devotee. Tiberius, Sejanus and the court were residing at the imperial villa of Spelunca, which has been identified with the remains of a palatial villa on the coast at Sperlonga, 75 miles south of Rome. A sea cave at the foot of the cliffs served as the villa's banqueting hall. It was decorated by a series of massive statues based around Odysseus' adventures from Homer's *Odyssey*, now found displayed in the local museum. The diners sat on a raised platform in the centre of the cave, which was indented with refuge areas where fish could gather from the surrounding circular pool. The guests and servants would probably use a retractable bridge or small boats to gain access to the *triclinium*. At the darkened rear of the grotto, behind the dining area, there could be found a huge statue of Odysseus blinding the drunken Polyphemus, whilst in front Scylla attacked Odysseus' ship and, on either side, statues showed the Rape of Palladion and the Pasquino group represented either Ajax carrying the body of Achilles or Menelaus holding that of Patroclus. By daylight, the view encompassed a panorama of heroes, monsters, sea and cliffs, where the diner played a role in Odysseus' exploits, whilst at night the torches and candles set in the cave walls backed by glass tesserae reflected light across the open water to merge myth and reality. Augmenting this evocative scene was the sound of the waves crashing onto the beach outside. However, brutal reality came crashing down upon the diners as the roof of the cave collapsed, killing guests and servants. The scene is described in detail: '[A] sudden fall of rock at the mouth buried a number of servants, the consequence being a general panic and the flight of guests present. Sejanus alone hung over the Caesar with knee, face and hands, and opposed himself to the falling stones – an attitude in which he was found by the soldiers who had come to their assistance.' The death of Tiberius would have brought the end of all Sejanus' and Livilla's dreams, and it is clear the prefect's actions were both spontaneous and courageous. Ever the consummate politician, Sejanus waited in his prone position, protecting the body of his emperor, until witnesses had arrived to confirm his devotion and loyalty at the side of Tiberius.[19]

Tacitus in his account makes it clear that this was the turning point in quashing the doubts that had grown in the mind of the emperor since the marriage proposal in AD 25. Sejanus' actions had provided 'the prince himself a reason for greater faith in the friendship and firmness of Sejanus', to the extent that it 'brought an accession of greatness, and, fatal though his advice might be, yet, as a man, whose thoughts were not for himself, he found a confiding listener'.[20] Although heavy with sarcasm, it is clear that Tacitus recognizes that Tiberius, now separated from almost any other independent advice, turned to Sejanus, and Sejanus, his position now fully restored, returned to his plans for a regency.

Tiberius, despite his suspicions concerning the ambitions of Agrippina, still saw her eldest son Nero as his successor. Nero had received the garb of manhood in AD 20 and married Julia Livilla, the daughter of Livilla and Drusus. Then in AD 23, upon the death of their father Germanicus, both brothers were commended to the Senate and the young Nero was given the opportunity to give a speech of thanks to the representatives of the cities of Asia for the construction of a temple to Augustus, Livia and the Senate. However, further public recognition was painfully slow and the pontiff's introduction of his name with that of his brother Drusus in the New Year vows resulted in a very public dressing down from Tiberius.[21]

Agrippina, along with Nero, Drusus and Gaius and their sisters Agrippina the Younger, Drusilla and Julia Livilla, remained in their residences in the imperial palace on the Palatine. Sejanus instructed the tribunes and guards to record all their comments as the soldiers 'dogged their steps, and recorded their messages, their interviews, their doings open and secret, with the exactitude of annalists'. These detailed records were even transcribed and sent to Tiberius for his appraisal. Nero's unguarded comments served to add fuel to the flames of the emperor's doubts. His heir felt he deserved greater recognition as Tiberius' successor and a significant role in the governance of the Empire in place of the absent ruler, and so, 'at intervals there fell from him defiant and unconsidered phrases; and these were seized upon and reported with enlargements by the watchers posted round his person, no chance of refutation being allowed him'. Furthermore, even Nero's most intimate thoughts spoken to his wife, Livilla's daughter, were reported to her mother: 'Even night itself was not secure, since his wakeful hours, his slumbers, his sighs, were communicated by his wife to her mother Livia [Livilla], and by Livia to Sejanus.' For this the daughter appears not to have been held responsible; perhaps it was perceived by contemporaries that she held a greater duty to her mother than her husband. Upon the death of Nero, Tiberius married her to an equestrian, Rubellius Blandus, a match made with 'contributory regret' as it was far beneath her status according to Tacitus. In the circumstances, she was lucky to escape with her life after the fall of Sejanus and then her mother.[22]

The naivety of Nero and Agrippina was reflected in the impolitic advice of their freedmen, *amici* and clients. The times demanded far greater circumspection from all concerned, but this was not in Agrippina's personality, nor that of her son, 'who stood next in line of succession, and, in spite of the modesty of his youth, too often forgot what the times demanded, while his freedmen and clients, bent on the rapid acquisition of power, urged him to a display of spirit and confidence; "It was this the nation desired and the armies yearned for, and Sejanus, who now trampled alike on the patience of an old man and the tameness of a young one, would not risk a counter stroke!"' The absence of Tiberius from Rome had enabled Sejanus to make public not only his own animosity towards Agrippina and Nero, but also the reservations that the emperor held towards his potential successor. Rumours had already been circulated that the emperor planned the destruction of Agrippina. Many questioned whether Nero was to share her fate? Tiberius, in his island seclusion, would have little access to objective information on the political situation in the capital. Sejanus even suborned some of the *amici* and clients of Nero to encourage his grievances and provide further evidence to add to Tiberius' fears. These could also act as witnesses to support the written documentation. However, time was not on Sejanus' side, as he had to engineer the fall of Agrippina, Nero, Drusus and Caligula before the death of Tiberius if Tiberius Gemellus was to be his imperial successor.[23]

In the meantime, Sejanus accompanied the aged emperor to his island tranquillity. Capri was not as isolated a position as our sources suggest, positioned on the southern side of the Bay of Naples, opposite the Sorrentine Peninsular. It was actually strategically situated, allowing both Tiberius and Sejanus efficient and quick communication with the capital using the *speculatores*. Facing the island on the north of the bay lay the massive imperial naval base at Misenum, 18 miles away. It would take around four to eight hours to travel by boat to the naval base, depending on the wind. A large lighthouse was built at the highest point of the island next to Tiberius' main palace, the Villa Jovis, to enable swift and efficient communications to and from Rome. The poet Statius describes the light of this lofty beacon as 'the rival of the moon'.[24] On the mainland promontory opposite Capri, overlooking the small town associated with the base at Misenum, was Lucullus' opulent villa that had been acquired by the imperial family, with its famous fish ponds. Nearby was the resort of Baiae, the playground of the elite. Its thermal springs and cool sea breezes made it immensely popular with the super-rich, who, since Republican times, had bought sumptuous villas along its coast to reflect their status and wealth. Money brought a licentious and luxurious lifestyle as the town became associated with hedonistic living and vice, many abandoning all restraint in the search of serious pleasure. The elderly Antonia owned a villa at Baiae, also famous for its well-stocked fish pools, which she had inherited from the Republican orator and politician Quintus Hortensius. Nestled in the shadow of Vesuvius, Agrippina owned a villa at Herculaneum, whilst 12 miles to the south-east of modern Naples lies the villa of Agrippa Postumus at Boscotreccase, whose preserved frescoes are masterpieces of the ancient world. This, and a further imperial villa at Surrentum, added to the allure of the area for the rich, attracted to the cache of abundant imperial property in the area, especially when Tiberius took up residence on Capri itself. From the Villa Jovis, the emperor could observe a series of major towns that nestled around the Bay of Naples, including Herculaneum and Pompeii, and the major port of Puteoli, which was the centre for the importation of grain and other commercial goods into Italy. To the southern end of the bay lay Stabiae and Surrentum, famous for its oranges and lemons. At the foot of Vesuvius stood the major city of Naples, which retained, like Capri and the surrounding area, its Hellenic culture. The city had just instituted Greek games in honour of Augustus and was the home to numerous Greek philosophers.[25]

The island of Capri itself was entirely Greek in its culture, language, customs and practices, which had appealed to Augustus, who in an agreement with Naples, received it in exchange for the imperial island of Ischia across the bay. Tiberius had regularly visited the island with his adopted father; no doubt it reminded him of his stay on Rhodes. The whole island was imperial property, with the small native population of subsistence farmers and fishermen now swamped by an inundation of imperial slaves, freedmen, guards and various officials. Suetonius preserves the story of one poor fisherman who accidentally stumbled upon the emperor who had only recently arrived on the island. The enterprising fisherman used this as an opportunity to present 'him with an enormous mullet which he had lugged up the trackless cliffs at the rear of the island. Tiberius was so scared that he ordered his guards to rub the fisherman's face with the mullet. The scales skinned it raw, and the poor fellow shouted out in his agony: "Thank Heaven, I did not bring Caesar that huge crab I also caught!" Tiberius sent for the crab and had it used in the same way.'[26]

This incident appears to have taken place close to the Villa Jovis, perched a thousand feet above the sea on the northern cliffs. This palace was the emperor's main residence, but eleven further imperial villas were available to him and members of his court, each probably named after a member of the Roman pantheon of gods. Some have been securely identified, including the Villa Damecuta, also located at the top of cliffs, giving views across the Bay of Naples. Close by is the famous Blue Grotto, a sea cave, illuminated by a shaft of sunlight that pierces an underwater cavity, creating an azure blue reflection through the water and into the depths of the cavern itself. Several statues dating from the first century have been found on the sandy floor of the pool, including images of the sea god Triton. According to the salacious stories in Suetonius, Tiberius trained 'little boys, whom he called his "minnows", to chase him while he went swimming and get between his legs to lick and nibble him'. Other sites dated to this era include those at Castiglione, Punto Tragara and Unghia Marina, and possibly the scattered remains at Capodimonte, Gradola and Gasto, where stone fragments provide glimpses of larger complexes which are awaiting excavation. Other possible villas have been located at Monte San Michele, Truglio, Ajano, Fontana, Mulo, Campo di Pisco, Camerelle, Matermania, Timberino and Monticello. Tiberius probably travelled between these properties, although some would have been residences of members of his court, including Cocceius Nerva and Sejanus. Each would have been staffed by a huge complement of slaves, including estate managers, secretaries, librarians, accountants, cooks, bakers, servants and gardeners. Capri has few natural resources and even water is scarce, so these numbers brought a logistical nightmare. Ships must have been plying to and from the mainland day and night to provision the emperor's court and his entourage. The island would have become an artificial state within a state. This dislocation from reality was also reflected in the surrounding countryside, which was transformed into a 'landscape of illusion' in which the fields, woods and streams were reformed to produce arbours, clearings and groves populated by statues and slaves recreating mythical scenes by posing as satyrs and nymphs. Such imaginings, the cultural chic of the time, appear to have been used as the basis for some of the sexual allegations made against the aged emperor; allegations and rumours stemming from his withdrawal from the world and isolation from frequent social interactions.[27]

The Villa Jovis, Tiberius' main residence, was reached by a steep and tortuous climb from the only port on the island. Rising above the harbour stood the vast edifice of the villa itself, covering some 5,400 square metres. A mural discovered at Baiae appears to show the Villa Jovis built in a series of storeys to dominate the island and its approaches. The main entrance to the complex faces west, alongside another door that gives access to the barracks of the Praetorian Guard. Little remains of the *atrium* apart from the basis of four marble columns. Off this reception area leads one corridor paved in white marble bordered by a black band which led to kitchens, servants' quarters and gave internal access to the barracks. At the end of the corridor a wide stairway opens, giving access to the floor above.

The massive kitchens had at least a dozen stoves and a huge oven, which stand testament to the numbers needed to be fed. A second *atrium* is to be found on the next storey up, which gave access on one side to a corridor that led to a massive cistern that collected the rainwater that fed the baths, latrines and fountains via hydraulic equipment, whilst through the opposite corridor the furnace room, cold, warm and hot rooms of the baths can be found. Further along another corridor is a series of rooms that have been interpreted as administrative, centred on a large chamber which is possibly the throne room. Either side of this large reception area are two smaller rooms. From here, Tiberius and Sejanus possibly met with the imperial freedmen and officials. The next storey appears to have contained the private quarters of the emperor, reached via a semi-circular corridor built to accommodate the location of the water cisterns below. The moist air rising upwards during the heat of the summer's day would have helped to cool this suite. Built into the walls of this corridor are three niches thought to have contained the emperor's household shrine. The corridor leads to a series of smaller rooms that are possibly the *cubicula* or bedrooms for guests and members of the court – for instance, Sejanus – whilst another door leads to the private rooms of the emperor. The most remarkable feature of this storey is the wide *ambulatio*, or promenade, running along the very edge of the cliffs that provided breathtaking views over the Bay of Naples to the islands of Pocida, Vivaria and Ischia, and to Misenum and across the wide expanse of the bay to Surrentum. On this promenade the main dining room is located, on either side of which are small *cubicula diurna* allowing for daytime siestas. Archaeologists have found indications of the luxury associated with this suite, including rare marbles, fragments of mural paintings and coloured alabaster. Here, it is quite possible, Tiberius and Sejanus dined, conversed and drowsed, enjoying an earthly paradise. However, intruding on Sejanus' thoughts of imperial control, adjacent to the promenade lay an exterior staircase leading to a *specularium*, or astronomical observatory, used by the emperor and his astronomer Thrasyllus to plot the stars and discern the future. The higher storeys to the palace have been lost, although Suetonius refers to a library which, if he is to be believed, contained erotic works and a 'number of small rooms were furnished with the most indecent pictures and statuary obtainable'.[28]

The choice of Capri was not only based on Tiberius' philhellene attitudes, but also on the emperor's insecurities and in particular his fear of plots, conspiracies and assassination. His overreaction to being caught by surprise by the Caprine fisherman points towards a volatile and anxious state of mind, exacerbated by Sejanus' warnings. Tacitus, whilst commending the island's mild climate, stresses the ease with which access was readily controlled:

> The solitude of the place I should suppose to have been its principal commendation, as it was surrounded by a harbourless sea, with a few makeshift roadsteads hardly adequate for small-sized vessels, which it is impossible to land unobserved by a sentry. In winter, the climate is gentle, owing to the mountain barrier which intercepts the cold sweep of the winds; its summers catch the western breeze and are made a delight by the circling expanse of open sea; while it overlooked the most beautiful of bays, until the activity of Vesuvius began to change the landscape.

Those wishing to land on the island in order to seek an audience with the emperor would presumably have had to follow the same procedures that Julius Agrippa used having paid off his debts to his creditors, including Antonia. He firstly landed at Puteoli, and then he sent a letter to Tiberius requesting an audience, which was then granted. Messengers would have been met by a sentry, and then the letter would have been sorted by the imperial freedmen and perhaps taken to Sejanus himself before being brought to the emperor's attention. In this way, Sejanus would always have controlled access to both the island and the imperial person.[29]

Tiberius, most likely accompanied by Sejanus, remained on Capri until early AD 27, when a sudden disaster required the imperial presence. With actors and games banished from Rome, an enterprising freedman built a temporary amphitheatre at Fidena, 5 miles outside the city. Thousands flocked to the show, but the badly built structure collapsed, killing between 20,000 and 50,000 people. Tiberius was forced to leave his island seclusion to deal with the tragedy and offer support to the survivors. He temporarily made himself available to accept petitions and requests before returning to Capri.[30] There soon followed another disaster, with a fire destroying most of the properties on the Caecilian Hill. Rumours circulated that these events were a result of the emperor's absence from the capital. The emperor failed to make an appearance, but he ordered a distribution of money to those affected and compensation was organized for those who had lost property. These actions checked discontent, but it would seem likely that at this point Sejanus returned to Rome.[31]

Sejanus had reason enough to return, despite the risk of temporarily leaving the side of the emperor. He needed to accelerate the campaign to undermine support for Agrippina and Nero whilst providing Tiberius with 'evidence' of their plotting. Sejanus, despite having the Praetorian Guards report on Agrippina and Nero, and even with Nero's wife passing on confidential information, had made little progress in finding evidence or witnesses that would convict either of *maiestas*. He now appears to have recruited Nero's brother Drusus as an agent of his family's destruction. Drusus was clearly envious of Nero, both in terms of his position as future emperor, but also as he was treated with great favouritism by Agrippina. Jealousy and frustrated ambition were emotions that Sejanus was able to manipulate, especially as Drusus should have been quaestor in AD 29 and there is no evidence he was. The arrangement with Drusus must have been made in a series of face-to-face conversations rather than through correspondence from Capri. Sejanus suggested to Drusus that the fall of Nero would lead to the throne; Nero, after all, was already in a precarious position. Drusus, according to Tacitus, was consumed by envy and hatred for his brother, which was coupled with a savage temper. The 19-year-old Drusus would have known that Sejanus wished to destroy his mother and brother, as this was already widespread public knowledge. However, Sejanus' affair with Livilla must have remained a secret, otherwise, despite being deceived by Sejanus' warm charm, he would have perceived the real purpose behind his approach. Nero's position was by now perilous:

> One man would avoid meeting him; some went through the formality
> of a formal salutation, then promptly turned away; many broke off
> any attempt at conversation; while, in contrast, any adherents of
> Sejanus who happened to be present stood their ground and jeered.

These actions were clearly attempts to earn Sejanus' favour by publicly rejecting Nero. This could only happen if it were widely believed that Sejanus' actions had the backing of the emperor, 'as if, foresooth, Tiberius himself had not been fond of him and thereby caused others to display such zeal on his behalf'.[32]

The campaign against the remaining *amici* and clients of Agrippina was also stepped up. Domitius Afer had developed a talent for oratory and rhetoric, but also for spending money. Having been richly rewarded for the successful prosecution of Agrippina's cousin Claudia Pulchra, he again found his wealth severely depleted. Returning to rich hunting grounds, and knowing Agrippina was in disfavour, he charged Claudia Pulchra's wealthy son Publius Quinctilius Varus, probably with *maiestas*. He was joined, to the disgust of Tacitus, by P. Cornelius Dolabela, the victorious conqueror of Tacfarinas and Varus's relative. Dolabella was ever keen to please Tiberius. Both survived the fall of Sejanus, which would suggest they were not closely associated with the Praetorian Prefect. Varus was betrothed to a daughter of Agrippina, probably Julia Livilla, and so the prosecution would suit Sejanus' plans. All that would possibly be needed was it to become publicly known that such a prosecution would meet with imperial favour. The case was heard before the Senate, who deferred it until Tiberius returned to Rome. Varus survived to pursue a highly successful legal career, although his marriage into the imperial family failed to materialize.[33]

The failure to convict Varus perhaps reflects a limit to Sejanus' power at this time. Varus was a powerful member of the aristocracy connected to the imperial family. Just as the absence of Tiberius from Rome allowed Sejanus a degree of freedom that he would otherwise not have possessed, so Sejanus' enemies in the Senate were able to use the emperor's absence as a tool to frustrate attacks on the house of Germanicus and Agrippina. Sejanus, as an equestrian, was not allowed to enter the Senate, but the debate would have been reported to him by his senatorial *amici* and relatives. His hatred of Arruntius might have been born from frustrations such as these.

One of the few remaining *amici* of Agrippina was now targeted: Titius Sabinus, a leading politician who had been assiduous in his duties towards Agrippina and her children, attending her morning *salutatio* and escorting them in public. He was entrapped into making injudicious comments under the guise of friendship. Four ex-praetors, knowing that a successful prosecution of Sabinus would gain imperial attention and earn the gratitude of Sejanus, and through him they hoped the consulship, plotted the downfall of Sabinus. Lucianus Latiaris (also named L. Latinius) was the principal prosecutor and the only one of the conspirators mentioned by Dio. He was possibly the son of Q. Lucanius, the proconsul of Crete under Augustus, and so the brother of Q. Lucianus Latinus, the praetor of the treasury of Saturn (*aerarium Saturni*) in AD 19. He was said to have received his 'just reward' in AD 32, and so in all likelihood was later executed for his actions in the prosecution of Sabinus. His fellow prosecutors, Marcus Opsius and Petilius Rufus, probably shared his fate in the reign of Caligula, but Tacitus, despite promising to describe their demise, fails to do so in the surviving books. Neither name appears on any consular list, but Petilius' son became consul in AD 74. The one man who appears to have attained some form of reward was Porcius Cato, who became a *suffect* consul in AD 36 and was *curator aquarum* two years later.

He may have been a descendant of the great noble house that boasted Cato the Elder and Caesar's indomitable foe Cato Uticensis. If so, his family had fallen into obscurity since then. The others were clearly *novus homo* who lacked the aristocrat name and heritage to attain the consulship by right. Latiaris, already an *amicus* of Sabinus, gradually encouraged him to speak freely of his views of Tiberius and his treatment of Agrippina. Then Latiaris invited his unsuspecting friend to his house after hiding the three other conspirators in the space between the ceiling and roof to act as witnesses. After praising Latiaris for his loyalty to the house of Germanicus and express horror at the treatment of Agrippina, Sabinus, with tears, broke into a diatribe where he denounced 'Sejanus, his cruelty, his arrogance, his ambition. Even Tiberius was not spared.' The evidence was sent to Tiberius on Capri, no doubt via Sejanus. Panic now set in. Many had made inappropriate and impolitic comments to clients and *amici* sequestered under the protection of the social conventions of *amicitiae*. Now such social constraints were under threat, conversations that were expected to remain private had the potential to send men to their deaths. Sejanus had created a state of fear, with all trust undermined.[34]

On 1 January AD 28 the emperor sent a letter to the Senate announcing the traditional prayers for the New Year before he launched into a denouncement of Sabinus, who was charged 'with the corruption of several of his freedmen, and with designs against himself; and demanded vengeance'.[35] The charges appear unrelated to the accusations made by Latiaris and his confederates. A subsequent letter sent in thanks by the emperor expressing gratitude for the swift execution of Sabinus further reveals Tiberius' suspicions, in that the Senate 'had punished a man who was a danger to his country. He added that his own life was full of alarms, and that he suspected treachery from his enemies. He mentioned none by name; but no doubt was felt that the words were levelled at Agrippina and Nero.' It would appear that Sabinus, after being denounced by Latiaris and his witnesses, appealed to the emperor for an opportunity to defend himself. Refused, he probably then approached some of the imperial freedmen to use their influence with the emperor to grant him an audience. Instead, keen to please Sejanus, they informed Tiberius of this approach, possibly elaborating on the nature of the communication. Pliny mentions that Sabinus was close to Nero and that his slaves were tortured, no doubt under the supervision of Sejanus. One slave was convicted, imprisoned and executed, his body exposed on the *Scalae Gemoniae* and finally thrown into the Tiber: a fate that echoed that of his master. Evidence could, therefore, have been forcibly procured

(*Above left*) Bust of the emperor Tiberius in Ny Carlsberg Glyptotek, Copenhagen. (*Wikimedia Commons*)

(*Above right*) Antonia the Younger. (*Rabax63, Wikimedia Commons*)

(*Left*) Marble portrait of Drusus ca. 21 AD in Louvre, Paris. (© *Marie-Lan Nguyen/Wikimedia Commons*)

(*Above left*) Greek marble bust of Agrippina the Elder. Portrait made in Athens under the reign of Caligula, between 37 and 41 AD, now in the Louvre, Paris. (*Wikimedia Commons*)

(*Above right*) Marble bust of Germanicus created on the occasion of the adoption of Germanicus by Tiberius in 4 AD from Córdoba, Spain. (*Wikimedia Commons*)

(*Below*) Bronze coin of Philadelphia, Lydia, possibly depicting Tiberius Gemellus. Struck in c 35–37 AD showing bare headed Tiberius Gemellus with winged thunderbolt on the obverse (RPC I 3017). (*CNG via Wikimedia Commons*)

(*Right*) Marble bust of Gaius (Caligula) in the Louvre, Paris. (*Wikimedia Commons*)

(*Below*) The Great Cameo of France is a sardonyx cameo created around 23 AD. It depicts the imperial family both living and deceased. (*Wikimedia Commons*)

(*Above*) Bronze As struck in 31 AD at Bilbilis. The name of Sejanus has been removed as he suffered damnatio memoriae. (*CNG via Wikimedia Commons*)

(*Below*) The grotto at the Villa of Tiberius, Sperlonga. (*Carole Raddato via Wikimedia Commons*)

(*Above*) Exterior of grotto from Villa of Tiberius, Sperlonga. (*Carole Raddato via Wikimedia Commons*)

(*Below*) Remains of the Villa of Tiberius, Sperlonga. (*Carole Raddato via Wikimedia Commons*)

(*Above*) Cast of the 'Binding of Polyphemus' which was part of a group of statues from the grotto of the Villa of Tiberius at Sperlonga. (*Carole Raddato via Wikimedia Commons*)

(*Below*) Copy of part of the Scylla Group from the grotto of the Villa of Tiberius, Sperlonga, depicting the right hand of Scylla catching one of Odysseus' companions. (*Wikimedia Commons*)

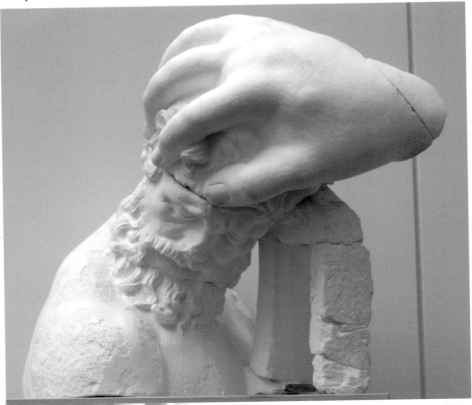

(*Above*) Villa Jovis, Capri. (*Wikimedia Commons*)

(*Below*) Tiberius' villa on Capri. (*Wikimedia Commons*)

(*Above*) Villa Jovis, Capri. (*Wikimedia Commons*)

(*Below*) View from Villa Jovis on Capri towards Sorrento on the mainland. (*Wikimedia Commons*)

(*Right*) Relief showing Praetorians. (*Jérémy Jähnick via Wikimedia Commons*)

(*Below*) The Roman Forum with the Arch of Septimius Severus in the centre. Behind and to the right of the arch is the building erected over the entrance to the Mamertinum Prison. It was here that Sejanus was held after his arrest and strangled to death. (*Jebulon via Wikimedia Commons*)

(*Above*) Interior of the Mamertinum Prison. The altar commemorates the many prisoners who suffered and were executed in its dark interior including Sejanus. (*Chris 73 via Wikimedia Commons*)

(*Below*) The view from Via di San Pietro in Carcere looking towards the forum. (*Patrick Nouhailler via Wikimedia Commons*)

(*Above*) The Porta Praetoriana in the Aurelian Walls of Rome. (*Wikimedia Commons*)

(*Below*) Northern wall of the Praetorian Fortress. (*Wikimedia Commons*)

(*Above*) Etruscan town of Vulsinii, modern Bolsena with views across the lake. Vulsinii was the birth place of Sejanus' father, Lucius Seius Strabo. (*Wikimedia Commons*)

(*Left*) A carving of a Praetorian guardsman from a triumphal arch for the emperor Trajan found at Pozzuoli, Italy, now located in the Pergamon Museum, Berlin. (*Magnus Manske via Wikimedia Commons*)

(*Above left*) Roman statue possibly depicting Drusus Caesar, the son of Germanicus and Agrippina the Elder. (*Sailko via Wikimedia Commons*)

(*Above right*) Bust of Gnaeus Domitius Ahenobarbus, the consul of 32 AD and married to Agrippina the Younger. (*Sailko via Wikimedia Commons*)

(*Right*) Nero Caesar, the son of Germanicus and Agrippina the Elder. (*National Archaeological Museum of Tarragona via Wikimedia Commons*)

Head of the goddess Fortuna dating to 101 BC now in the Capitoline Museum. (*Capitoline Museums via Wikimedia Commons*)

Portrait bust of Agrippa Postumus. He was the youngest son of Julia the Elder and Marcus Vipsanius Agrippa. (*Louvre Museum*)

Bronze bust of L. Calpunius Piso the Pontifex. He was a close and trusted *amicus* of Tiberius who shared the emperor's enthusiasm for classical literature and drink. (*Naples National Archaeological Museum*)

Bust of Tiberius Gemellus found at the Roman villa of Chiragan. He was the son of Livilla and Tiberius' son Drussus. (*Musée Saint-Raymond*)

Head of Odysseus from the Sperlonga Group. (*Jastrow via Wikimedia Commons*)

The House of Livia on the Palatine Hill, Rome. (*Carole Raddato via Wikimedia Commons*)

of a conspiracy to assassinate the emperor, although Agrippina and Nero escaped implication. Their fates lay in the future.[36]

There was no evidence that Agrippina and Nero were conspiring against the emperor, mainly because they weren't. Rogers believes that circumstantial evidence suggests that both were involved in a series of plots linked to the prosecutions against Silius and Sabinus. Tiberius, upon hearing of Agrippina's eventual death, wrote a letter to the Senate announcing that she was lucky that she was not strangled and thrown on the *Scalae Gemoniae*, the fate of all accused of treason. This is no evidence of a conspiracy, merely of a tortured and poisoned mind, a consequence of Sejanus' constant venom. It was Sejanus' agents who suggested that Agrippina 'take refuge with the armies of Germany, or, at the most crowded hour of the forum, to clasp the effigy of the deified Augustus and call the Senate and people to [her] aid'. Both proposals were calculated to strike at the very heart of the emperor's fears. The first was a reminder of the mutiny of the Rhine legions in AD 14 and Agrippina's heroic yet unwelcome intervention on the bridge, preventing the panicking legionaries from destroying it upon news of the false rumours that Germanicus' army had been destroyed. The second piece of advice cut to Tiberius' insecurities as he was merely adopted into the imperial family, a criticism made by Agrippina herself upon hearing news of Domitius Afer's charges against Claudia Pulchra. Here we see both the insecurities and flaws in Tiberius' character, and the intelligence and perceptiveness of his Praetorian Prefect. That Agrippina did neither surely counts against the possibility of a conspiracy.[37]

The brutal end of Sabinus' life was meant by Sejanus to be a very public threat to those who stood against him. The emperor's letter led to an immediate condemnation. There was no trial. Instead:

> [T]he doomed man was dragged to his death, crying with all the vigour allowed by the cloak muffling his head and the noose around his neck, that 'these were the ceremonies that inaugurated the year, these the victims that bled to propitiate Sejanus!' In whatever direction he turned his eyes, wherever his words reached an ear, the result was flight and desolation, an exodus from street and forum. Here and there a man traced his steps and showed himself again, pale at the very thought that he had manifested alarm.

The whole scene was made more pitiful by the presence of Sabinus' faithful dog, who lay with his master as he was thrown in the prison, was with him when he was strangled to death with a garrotte and then accompanied his body as it was thrown onto the *Scalae Gemoniae* and there exposed before being thrown into the river Tibur. The dog, ever loyal, leapt into the fast-flowing river to remain at Sabinus' side to the very end.[38]

Sabinus' final words were an invocation to Janus, a god closely associated with the inauguration of new consuls, the god of entrances, doorways and new beginnings to whom the new magistrates made a sacrifice in time-honoured fashion. Sabinus decried that now in this new Rome the consuls made a sacrifice of him to Sejanus who, like a god, oversaw the offices of state.[39] His body was exposed on the *Scalae Gemoniae*, a flight of stairs rising from the forum to the Capitoline and Temple of Juno Moneta, situated at the political heart of the Roman state. The stairs entered the Forum at the north-west corner near the Temple of Concord and the *Carcer*, the underground prison. During the violence associated with the trial of Calpurnius Piso, who stood accused of poisoning Germanicus in AD 20, the mob dragged his statues to these stairs and started to destroy them. This was probably in imitation of previous executions and exposures not mentioned in our sources. Sabinus was the first recorded aristocratic victim whose corpse was treated in this fashion. It was believed that the dead bore with them to the afterlife the wounds that were inflicted on them in the events surrounding their death. Sabinus would bear the marks of abuse that his corpse suffered on the steps for all eternity. There would be no monument or record of his deeds in life, so denying him contact with the living and deprived his family the opportunity to respect his memory.[40] The similar treatment of the corpse of Sabinus' slaves, which is ignored in the pages of Tacitus and Dio but preserved in Pliny, suggests that Sabinus was the first member of Rome's elite whose body was treated in this manner. Sejanus knew that the emperor's desire for vengeance meant he could make a public example of Sabinus in life and in death. This was a public demonstration by Sejanus of his power to inflict unconstrained violence against any individual.[41]

It now became imperative for many to make public their declarations of loyalty to Sejanus. Demonstrating a lack of courtesy and respect to Nero was one way. Another was attending the Praetorian Prefect's morning *salutatio*.'[42] The fall of Sabinus was not just another attack on the *amici* and clients of Agrippina and Nero, it was also key in establishing Sejanus' *auctoritas* as Tiberius' deputy in Rome.

Sabinus's downfall affected none more so than Asinius Gallus, who had most to fear from the vengeance of Tiberius. The prominent senator rose in the Senate and proposed that the emperor be requested to name those he felt were plotting against him in order that they might be charged and executed. Clearly, he was worried that he might be one of those accused and wished to demonstrate his loyalty by making this demand. This was a naïve and desperate attempt to curry favour, but many would fear a bloodbath if Tiberius was encouraged to make concrete his suspicions and terrors. Surprisingly, it was Sejanus who restrained the emperor. Why? According to Tacitus, it was not because Sejanus wished to protect Asinius Gallus, but instead he wanted the emperor's resentments to grow, knowing they would be unleashed with greater violence.[43] Anticipating Tiberius' future responses seems beyond the capacity of anyone, even a man of Sejanus' undoubted abilities. There did not yet exist the evidence that could be put before the Senate to charge Agrippina and Nero. Sejanus was yet again demonstrating to Rome's elite that he had the power to destroy or save, depending upon their acquiescence to his position alongside the emperor. 'Sejanus was so great a person by reason both of his excessive haughtiness and of his vast power, that, to put it briefly, he himself seemed to be emperor and Tiberius a kind of island potentate, inasmuch as the latter spent his time on the island of Capri.'[44]

By AD 30 Dio describes the Senate as under Sejanus' control, 'partly by the benefits he conferred, partly by the hopes he inspired, and partly by intimidation'.[45] When Nerva ascended the throne in AD 96, he announced that he became emperor that he might provide new *beneficia* or gifts and preserve those already granted by his predecessors. The emperor was the ultimate patron, conferring magistracies, money, priesthoods, estates, legateships and so on upon his *amici* in return for their *gratia* and loyalty. Imperial power was derived from the ability to distribute these resources. Sejanus had created a stranglehold on the network of imperial patronage that emanated from those who had access to the vast range of *beneficia* that was at the disposal of the emperor. These *amici Caesaris* who were favoured in this way were able to extend their own network of *amici* and clients in bonds of *amicitiae* that bound Roman society together. Emperors produced political and social cohesion through this mutual exchange relationship, where imperial *beneficia* secured the loyalty of his *amici*, allowing them to build their own network. With Tiberius' virtual isolation on Capri, Sejanus' position in Rome allowed him to become the major broker of imperial *beneficia*, creating enormous tensions in the aristocracy and instability in society. Terentius, when charged before the Senate with conspiring with Sejanus, explains this to the many senators who had approached the Praetorian Prefect for *beneficia*, as Sejanus was Tiberius' 'agent who discharged your functions in the state', who 'held the greatest power to help or to injure – and that Sejanus had all, no man will deny'. Tacitus himself describes how Sejanus 'did not fail to hold before the Senate the temptations of those offices and governorships with which he invested his satellites'. The aristocracy resented the humiliation of presenting requests and petitions to a mere equestrian, despite his illustrious links to many great families. He was to them the 'market town adulterer'. This attitude towards Sejanus is reflected in the annals of the senatorial historian Tacitus, who describes Sejanus' *amici* who prosecuted Cremutius Cordus in AD 25 as clients, men who have to go through the degradation of pandering to Sejanus. L. Pinarius Natta started his career as a military tribune in Egypt, where he was promoted to prefect of the district of Bericis. Upon his return to Rome he served as an aedile, then as one of the *duoviri*, before being awarded the post of quaestor. It was clearly not an illustrious career, but he was a powerful senator in his own right, with his son possibly attaining a consulship in AD 83. Despite their social prejudices, the aristocracy would have to suffer the perceived indignities of petitioning a social inferior.[46]

Clearly, Sejanus had immense power to distribute the great offices of state, but the consular lists suggest that appointments to this office that conferred nobility remained in the hands of Tiberius. The emperor chose the consuls for each year, submitting their names to the Senate for confirmation. The election for twelve annual praetors was more open, with the names of nominees submitted to the emperor, who was able to reject those whom he considered unsuitable. The list was then returned to the Senate, with Tiberius recommending a small number whose election was a mere formality. The remaining candidates were elected by open ballot in the Senate. There was far less competition for the numerous lesser magistracies, for example, the offices of quaestor or aedile. Members of the aristocracy could expect their name and ancestry to take them to the consulship, whether the more prestigious two ordinary consuls after whom the year was named or the lesser *suffect* consuls who replaced them. A *novus homo* might expect to reach a praetorship, but he would need the patronage of the emperor or a powerful *amicus Caesaris* to have a chance of attaining the honour of consular office. Sejanus would clearly be able to use his influence to ensure his *amici* reached the praetorship, but it would be Tiberius who appointed the ambitious senator to the ultimate rung on the *cursus honorum*.[47]

The ordinary consulship remained the preserve of the nobility and appears to be dominated by Cornelii Lentuli and Junii Silani at this time. The Cornelli Lentuli held five consulships in four years, with Ser. Cornelius Lentulus and P. Cornelius Lentulus Scipio in AD 24, Cossus Cornelius Lentulus in AD 25 and Cn. Cornelius Lentulus Gaetulicus in AD 26, who then became legate of Lower Germany from AD 29–39. The father of Cossus Cornelius Lentulus (consul in AD 25) and his brother Cornelius Gaetulicus (AD 26) was Cossus Cornelius Cn. Lentulus (1 BC), who was the close confidant of Tiberius, whom he sent with Drusus to Pannonia. Tiberius also made him City Prefect from AD 33–36. Gaetulicus' father-in-law L. Apronius was governor of Upper Germany from AD 28, whilst Gaetulicus' sister-in-law was married to Calvisius Sabinus, his fellow consul of AD 26. There can be little surprise that this family rose so high. They had no need of Sejanus, despite the fact Tiberius instructed Gaetulicus to betroth his daughter to a son of Sejanus to tie this family to his plans for the succession.[48]

The Junii Silani could boast an ancestry reaching back to the Hannibalic wars. M. Junius Silanus, the *suffect* consul of AD 15, was honoured with sharing the office with the emperor's son Drusus. He used his friendship with Tiberius to persuade him to recall his eldest brother D. Junius Silanus from voluntary exile in AD 20 after he had committed adultery with Julia the Younger. M. Silanus was so respected by Tiberius that the emperor refused to hear any appeal that had already been heard by him. An even greater indication of his favour with the emperor was the marriage of his daughter Junia Claudia to Caligula in AD 33. He later adopted a son of Gaetulicus. Another brother, C. Junius Silanus, the consul of AD 10, was prosecuted for maladministration during his governorship of Asia and committed suicide. His son C. Appius Junius Silanus was the ordinary consul of AD 28. He was charged with *maiestas* after the fall of Sejanus, along with three other pre-eminent *consulares*, but was freed on the evidence of a tribune of the Urban Cohorts. It would appear he had fallen foul of Caligula and Macro's plans for the succession. Another relation, L. Junius Silanus, replaced him as *suffect* consul. There were close connections between the Junii Silani and the great patrician family of Aemilii Lepidi. M. Junius Torquatus, ordinary consul of AD 19, was married to Aemilia Lepida, the daughter of Julia the Younger. Their five children suffered for their connection to Augustus. He became proconsular governor of Africa from AD 32–37 after the fall of Sejanus. Like his cousins, the consuls of AD 10 and 15, he had nothing to gain from any association with Sejanus, knowing they could rely on their nobility and friendship with the emperor.[49]

Tiberius clearly reserved the office of the ordinary consul for members of the old Republican aristocratic families like his own. As well as the Junii and Cornelii Lentulii, L. Calpurnius Piso, the son of Germanicus' alleged poisoner, was ordinary consul in AD 27. Even personal enmity did not hinder these appointments, with the sons of Asinius Gallus and Vipsania granted their birth-right, Gaius Asinius Polio being ordinary consul in AD 23 and his brother Marcus Asinius Agrippa in AD 25. Only four men of non-consular descent reached the consulship before AD 31, one being Sejanus himself and another, L. Pomponius Flaccus in AD 17, a close *amicus* of Tiberius, whilst Marcus Vinicius, consul in AD 30, was selected by Tiberius in AD 33 to wed Julia Livilla, the youngest daughter of Germanicus and Agrippina, so he would have no connections to Sejanus. Lastly, little is known of L. Rubellius Geminus, ordinary consul in AD 29.[50]

Sejanus was clearly unable to influence Tiberius' choices for the ordinary consulships. However, relatives in his extended family were consuls. His uncle Q. Junius Blaesus, a *novo homus*, was a *suffect* consul in AD 10, so probably owed his appointment to the influence of Sejanus' father Seius Strabo. His son of the same name was *suffect* consul in AD 26. His family had already been ennobled by his father's office, but Sejanus in all likelihood would have supported the appointment, especially as he had left Rome at this time to accompany Tiberius to Campania. Lucius Seius Tubero, *suffect* consul in AD 18, was probably Sejanus' adopted brother. He was a close *amicus* of the emperor and his appointment was likely too early in the rise of Sejanus to be attributable to him. Sejanus was related to the family of Q. Aelius Tubero's through his mother Junia's first marriage to him before marrying Seius Strabo. Q. Aelius Tubero was the consul of 11 BC, so would be unlikely to still be alive, but his brother Sex. Aelius Tubero, the consul in AD 4, might have been. Their possible sister Aelia married the noble L. Cassius Longinus, whose two children were both consuls in AD 30, his namesake the ordinary consul and his brother C. Cassius Longinus the *suffect* consul of that year. Furthermore, Claudius, the future emperor and Germanicus' brother, was married to Aelia Paetina at some date before AD 28. She was a Tubero and, as no source refers to her links to Sejanus, their connection must have been weak.[51] These familial links to Sejanus are so distant and tenuous that they can be discounted, especially in light of the fact that after his fall Lucius Cassius Longinus was married to Caligula's sister Julia Drusilla in AD 33, whilst his brother Gaius was governor of Asia under Caligula and then appointed to the militarily important province of Syria under Claudius. The members of this ancient and noble family would have attained the consulship without Sejanus.

What motivated the conspirators against Sabinus was the mere possibility of a consulship which could be gained through the favour of Sejanus. One, M. Porcius Cato, certainly achieved a *suffect* consulship in AD 36, suggesting his links to Sejanus were questionable as he survived his fall despite acting as a witness in the prosecution. The only other *suffect* consul that can be linked to Sejanus is Fulcinius Trio, the *delator* who helped to destroy L. Scribonius Libo in AD 16 AD and Gnaeus Calpurnius Piso in AD 20. He replaced Sejanus as *suffect* consul in AD 31 upon returning from the governorship of Lusitania. Even in this case, the influence of the prefect in securing the governorship and consulship for his *amicus* is not clear, as Tiberius stated that Trio's reward for successfully prosecuting Piso was the promise of future imperial support 'should he become a candidate for preferment'. The ordinary consulships were beyond the gift of Sejanus, being reserved for members of the ancient noble houses; however, he was able to use his influence with Tiberius to ensure a small number of the *suffect* consulships were awarded to some of his *amici*. Some of the known *suffect* consuls between AD 18 and 31 are mere names, but few, as far as we know, owed their appointment to the *amicitiae* of Sejanus. In fact, more new men attained the *suffect* consulship in the years after the fall of Sejanus than during his long years at the side of the emperor.[52]

According to our ancient sources, governorships were within the gift of Sejanus. The only concrete example of this was the appointment of Junius Blaesus to the senatorial province of Africa. According to Tacitus, the appointment was due to the influence of Sejanus after the withdrawal of the other candidate recommended by Tiberius, Aemilius Lepidus. Apart from this, there appear to be few tangible links between governors of both senatorial and imperial provinces to the Praetorian Prefect. C. Galerius, the Prefect of Egypt who succeeded Seius Strabo, may have been associated with Sejanus as he was quickly replaced by either the *eques* Vitrasius Pollio or, uniquely, by Hiberius, a freedman with links to Antonia, in AD 31. Hiberius was probably in the province at the time, managing Antonia's estates. Galerius' sudden replacement at the time of Sejanus' fall, after fifteen years in the post, does suggest an association, but this remains mere conjecture. Galerius was married to the aunt of the Roman philosopher and politician Seneca and died in a shipwreck on his return voyage to Rome.

Some historians also point to the conduct of Pontius Pilate as prefect of Judaea from AD 27–36 as evidence of an anti-Semitic policy pursued by Sejanus. This is based on the problematic account of the Alexandrian Jew Philo, who wished to contrast the supposedly favourable policies of Tiberius towards the Jews to that of his successor Caligula; consequently, he blamed Sejanus for the expulsion of the Jews from Rome in AD 19. According to Philo, Sejanus invented 'false slanders against the Jewish population of Rome ... because he wished to do away with the nation'. However, Tacitus, Dio and Suetonius link this action to Tiberius' concern for the growth of religions whose loyalty to the state was questioned, including the worshippers of the Egyptian goddess Isis. It was only five years after the execution of Sejanus that Pilate was recalled to Rome, which would have occurred far sooner if there was a connection.[53]

The effects of Tiberius' absence and Sejanus' dominance of politics in the capital can be seen by the Senate's abject response to a military defeat inflicted by the Frisians on L. Apronius, the governor of Lower Germany. Sejanus had probably left Rome to return to Capri, confident in his demonstration of strength at the expense of Sabinus. When news of the disaster reached Rome, the Senate failed to make any response as 'an internal panic had preoccupied their minds'. It was left to the emperor on Capri to bury the news and allow the Frisians to celebrate their new-found freedom. The Senate was impotent, with none willing to take a lead or risk making a proposal that would be disapproved of. Their only concern was gaining the favour of Sejanus and the emperor. The Senate did unite to vote an altar of Mercy and an altar to *amicitiae*, with statues of Tiberius and Sejanus on either side. A message was also sent to Capri requesting the presence of Tiberius and his prefect in Rome. Many continued to fear the consequences of impolitic comments made to *amici*, relatives and clients, naively trusting to their *fides*, loyalty, under the rubric of *amicitiae*: an assumption made moot by the entrapment and fate of Sabinus. The dread is described by Tacitus: 'In Rome, the anxiety and panic, the reticence of men towards their nearest and dearest, had never been greater: meetings and conversations, the ears of friend and stranger were alike avoided; even things mute and inanimate – the very walls and roofs – were eyed with circumspection.' Now they placed themselves at the mercy of the two rulers of the Roman world who stood side-by-side next to the newly consecrated altars.[54]

Tiberius refused to return to Rome. Instead, the emperor, with Sejanus at his side, returned to the mainland to receive their requests and petitions, probably staying at the imperial villa at Surrentum, which was the 'nearest shore of Campania'. The official reason for the gathering was for Tiberius to arrange the marriage of Agrippina the Younger, the daughter of Agrippina the Elder and Germanicus, to Gnaeus Domitius Ahenobarbus, who was the grandson of Mark Antony and Augustus' sister Octavia. He was 30 and she 13, but their issue would rule the Roman world in the figure of Nero. The marriage was to be celebrated in Rome without the emperor. Many had also come to the Campanian shores to request an audience with Sejanus. The rich could stay in their villas along the Bay of Naples, some could stay with *amici* or clients in the area, but the majority had to camp in the surrounding plain or on the beach. Tacitus describes how the senatorial and equestrian class journeyed from Rome to Campania, along with a large part of the populace. These were probably the *amici* and clients of the elite attending on their patron to add to their status. Access to Sejanus had become difficult and many found their requests for an audience turned down. Instead, they turned to his closest advisors, described by Tacitus as his janitors. Numbered amongst them were no doubt Satrius Secundus, P. Pomponius Secundus and Sejanus' uncle Junius Blaesus. Sejanus was deliberately increasing their standing and thereby their influence in the capital whilst he had to remain on Capri. The elite had sought to demonstrate their loyalty to Sejanus and seek reassurances, but many were left disappointed. Audiences were only granted to the few, those, no doubt, who had previously acted in the interests of the Praetorian Prefect.[55]

Sejanus wanted to be feared, his opponents to be divided by suspicions and concerns for their future and so more eager to support his designs or, at the very least, acquiesce to the political situation. Tacitus describes how:

[T]heir anxieties centred round Sejanus, access to whom had grown harder and had therefore to be procured by interest and by a partnership in his designs. It was evident enough that his arrogance was increased by the sight of this servility so openly exhibited. At Rome movement is the rule, and the extent of the city leaves it uncertain upon the errand the passer-by is bent: there, littering without distinction the plain or the beach, they suffered day and night, alike the patronage or the insolence of his janitors, until that privilege, too, was vetoed, and they retraced their steps to the capital – those whom he had honoured neither by word nor by look, in fear and trembling; a few, over whom hung the fatal issue of that infelicitous friendship, with misplaced cheerfulness of heart.[56]

Throughout AD 29 Sejanus received a significant increase in honours:

> It was voted that his birthday should be publicly observed, and the
> multitude of statues that the Senate and the equestrian order, the
> tribes and foremost citizens set up, would have passed anyone's
> power to count. Separate envoys were sent to him and to Tiberius
> by the Senate, by the knights, and by the people, who selected
> theirs from the tribunes and from the plebeian aediles. For both
> alike they offered prayers and sacrifices and they took oaths by
> their Fortunes.

Suetonius suggests the plethora of statues raised to Sejanus was a major
reason for Tiberius' loss of trust in his advisor; 'becoming aware that Sejanus'
birthday was being publicly celebrated, and that golden statues were being
raised to him everywhere, as a preliminary step to his usurpation of the
throne', the emperor decided to move against him. This seems doubtful
as Tiberius continued to honour Sejanus through the remainder of AD 29
and promoted him to the consulship alongside himself. This honour was
meant to reinforce Sejanus' status and position within the state. It is
extremely doubtful that the Senate would have voted honours for Sejanus
without imperial approval. The statues raised by individual senators and
equestrians may have raised the concerns of the emperor due to their
number and, if made of gold, appeared to rival the status of the imperial
cult.[57] Statues were also set up to Sejanus in the *principia* of the legionary
camps alongside those of Tiberius. This directly associated the Praetorian
Prefect in the imperial cult. One notable exception was the legions under the
command of L. Aelius Lamia, the absentee governor of Syria since AD 22.
He was a close *amicus* of the emperor and would become Prefect of Rome
in AD 33. Clearly, he opposed the influence of the Praetorian Prefect but
his close association with the emperor protected him.[58] Many left monies
to Sejanus, as they did to the emperor, in their wills. It was customary for
those who had benefited from imperial *beneficia* to express their gratitude
and loyalty by leaving part of their estate to the emperor. Clearly, Sejanus,
as a broker of imperial gifts, offices and honours, was now also revered in
this way. Such bequests were also a public announcement of their loyalty to
Sejanus as their patron.[59] The official state documents recorded the names
of both the emperor and Sejanus, whilst two gilded chairs to represent
the absent rulers were brought into the theatre at the commencement of
the games. Tiberius made it clear in his official communications with both

the Senate and the popular assemblies that Sejanus was his associate in power by repeatedly referring to him as 'My Sejanus'. It was evident to all that they were partners in power, but in the absence of the emperor, Sejanus was effectively regent.[60]

Dio records that official letters were sent to both Tiberius and Sejanus, which would suggest that Sejanus returned to Rome at some point in AD 29. In September the 86-year-old Livia died after a protracted illness. Tiberius had refused to visit his ailing mother or attend her funeral, even as her body laid in state for an extended time awaiting his arrival. None of her bequests in her will were honoured by her son, who also vetoed her deification. Her eulogy was read by the young Caligula. Whilst she lived, Livia had attempted to protect Agrippina and her children, despite the Augusta's hatred for the wife of her grandson Germanicus. This was probably to preserve the inheritance of her great-grandchildren in the form of Nero, Drusus and in particular Caligula. The fall of their mother would inevitably threaten their position as heirs. Caligula, upon his accession, would pay in full the bequests outstanding from Livia's will, and he called her a 'Ulysses in petticoats'. Clearly, both formed an affection for each other, probably during their residency in the various houses on the Palatine after the departure of Tiberius. Suetonius records that Caligula lived with Livia after the banishment of his mother, which contradicts the account of events in Tacitus. Agrippina and Nero had possibly been placed under house arrest, either in Rome or in her villa near Herculaneum. It would be surprising if this important development in Tacitus' portrayal of the persecution of the family of Germanicus escaped his narrative. It would be easier to assume that Suetonius' source was in error and Caligula merely shared the various imperial residences that populated the Palatine Hill with the members of the imperial family that remained in Rome. Another reason for Livia's protection of the children of Germanicus was the influence of Antonia, who had been Livia's companion since the death of her husband Drusus Claudius Nero, the son of Livia through a previous marriage and the brother of Tiberius. Germanicus was Antonia's son, alongside Claudius and Julia Livilla, and Caligula her grandson. So integrated were their households that Antonia's slaves and servants were also buried in the *Monumentum Liviae* alongside those from Livia's household. Both Livia and Antonia had raised the young children of various noble families orphaned by circumstance, as well as those of client kings, and they also provided dowries. Caligula gave Antonia the title of Augusta upon his accession, but she refused to use it.[61] Sejanus, despite being openly deferential to the elderly Augusta, would know from his regular visits to the palace, where the headquarters of the Praetorian Guard remained, that Livia was severely ill, and he merely needed to bide his time.[62]

Upon the death of Livia, a letter from the emperor arrived in the Senate denouncing Agrippina and Nero. So immediate was this that people felt the letter had been suppressed by the Augusta whilst she lived. The charges were not of conspiracy, but its 'wording was of studied asperity, but the offences imputed by the sovereign to his grandson were not rebellion under arms, not meditated revolution, but unnatural love and moral depravity. Against his daughter-in-law, he dared not fabricate even such a charge but arraigned her haughty language and refractory spirit.'[63] Despite Sejanus' network of spies and detailed recording of every interaction and conversation, the most that Nero could be charged with was homosexual relations, and Agrippina with arrogance. The problem for Sejanus was the simple fact that they were not involved in any conspiracy against Tiberius. A witness was found to support the charges in the imperial letter. The equestrian Avilius Flaccus, a close *amicus* of Tiberius, was later rewarded for his part in the attack upon Agrippina with the prefecture of Egypt in AD 32, only to be recalled to Rome in AD 37 by Caligula and later executed. Flaccus was acting as Tiberius' agent, the emperor being the driving force behind the accusations.[64]

The vagueness of the accusations stunned the Senate. There was no evidence of *maiestas*. Suetonius echoes Tiberius' fears that Agrippina could take sanctuary at the statue of Augustus in the Forum or with the armies, and these may have been the charges levelled by Avilius Flaccus. The senators sat in shocked silence. To add to their dilemma, a mob had gathered outside the meeting 'carrying effigies of Agrippina and Nero, surrounding the curia, and cheering for the Caesar (Nero), clamoured that the letter was spurious and that it was contrary to the Emperor's wish that destruction was plotted against his house'.[65] This would further inflame the emperor's suspicions. The demonstration was clearly organized by those who could remain in the shadows but remained loyal in their support of Agrippina. Sejanus no doubt used the Praetorians to ensure the safety of the senators, but as an equestrian, he would not have been allowed to enter the meeting. Cotta Messalinus, ever one to curry imperial favour, stood to demand condemnation of the accused, but other prominent senators, including the magistrates, looked to the future and their own possible denunciation at the hands of a guilt-ridden Tiberius or an imperial successor related to Agrippina. Instead, Junius Rusticus rose to address the consuls.

He articulated what many were thinking, that the consuls should hesitate before bringing a motion of condemnation before the Senate, a motion that the emperor might in the future regret. It was a brave act as many could now escape imperial anger by asserting that as Rusticus had been appointed by Tiberius to edit the *acta senatus*, or official records, of the Senate, they believed he would have a greater understanding of the emperor's feelings on this matter. Rusticus could be offered as their sacrificial scapegoat if imperial anger needed placating.[66]

In the days that followed, pamphlets attacking Sejanus were distributed containing fictitious speeches under the names of the consuls. The purpose was no doubt to stir up popular support for Agrippina and Nero as none were prepared to openly back them, fearing the consequences. The move merely provided Sejanus with ammunition to use against the heir and his mother to inflame the suspicions of Tiberius. He could suggest that both were planning to use the mob in their designs upon the throne. Tiberius, having received a report of these events, issued an imperial edict reprimanding the Roman populace for its actions, whilst a letter read to the Senate expressed the emperor's disappointment 'that by the dishonesty of a single member the imperial majesty should have been publicly turned to scorn', but demanded that the entire affair should be left in his own hands.[67] The implication was clear, in that *maiestas* charges were invited to be made against Junius Rusticus. His fate is unknown, as the majority of Book 6 of Tacitus' *Annals* has been lost whilst the summary of Dio's account is reduced to frustrating brevity. However, Rusticus' disappearance from the pages of history suggests he became the sacrificial offering in the senators' desire to demonstrate their loyalty to Sejanus and the emperor.

Tiberius, by dealing with Agrippina and Nero himself, employed his position as head of the family, the *paterfamilias*, to impose exile on both.[68] Agrippina was despatched to the island of Pandateria, 29 miles off the coast from Baiae and the Bay of Naples. Tiberius could look out across the sea from the Villa Jovis to contemplate the fate of his daughter-in-law on her island. In his own mind, he was convinced she was guilty of treasonous designs. Upon her death through starvation in AD 33, he wrote to the Senate that she had been treated with clemency as her crimes were deserving of strangulation and exposure on the *Scalae Germoniae* (Stairs of Mourning), the fate of those sentenced under *maiestas*. That she remained on her island prison after the death of Sejanus indicates that Tiberius was convinced of her guilt, and nor did he accuse his Praetorian Prefect of acting against his wishes. Agrippina suffered brutal treatment on Pandateria, where her continued protests led to Tiberius' order that she be flogged, which resulted in her losing an eye. Tiberius had chosen the island well, not for its two imperial villas commanding stunning views of the sea, but as the location for the exile of his hated ex-wife Julia the Elder, sent there by Augustus acting in his role as *paterfamilias*. Agrippina's own sister Julia the Younger had just died in AD 29 in her own island prison of Tremirus. Nero was exiled to the nearby island of Pontia. Both were moved in chains, hidden in a covered wagon, possibly via Herculaneum, to their separate exiles, apart yet within sight of each other. The emperor's decision was reinforced by a senatorial decree declaring both public enemies. Nero's siblings Caligula, Agrippina the Younger, Drusilla and Julia Livilla were now placed into the sole care of their grandmother Antonia, Tiberius' sister-in-law and Livia's old companion.[69]

Agrippina's pride always made it likely that she would fall foul of Tiberius, yet Sejanus' skill as the consummate intriguer is seen in his associating Nero with her fall. Those who had developed any association with them now looked to safeguard their positions, foremost amongst them Asinius Gallus. Tiberius' animosity towards him was deep-seated, originating with his marriage to Tiberius' ex-wife Vipsania and his attempted adoption of Drusus. Agrippina may have also considered him a future husband when making her marriage request to the emperor, and now her exile had revealed the vulnerability of his position. The leading senator no doubt feared a political rival laying a charge of *maiestas* against him, followed by a summary condemnation before a Senate eager to win Tiberius' approval. Asinius Gallus had already gained the friendship of the eminent Greek philosopher Syriacus, who may have been on Capri. To further strengthen his position, he now courted Sejanus. It was Gallus who proposed many of the honours granted to Sejanus by the Senate. However, it must be doubted, as some historians have suggested, that Gallus was already an *amicus* of Sejanus, as any association with Gallus was poison and could only serve to undermine the emperor's trust in his Praetorian Prefect. Dio hints at this when he states that one of the possible reasons for Gallus' approach was to 'make Sejanus irksome to the emperor himself and so cause his ruin'. It is extremely unlikely that Gallus would consciously sacrifice himself in this manner, but it is indicative of the emperor's hatred of the senator. Consequently, Sejanus informed Tiberius of Gallus' approach and the emperor rapidly destroyed him. The unsuspecting Gallus was honoured with an invitation to Capri, which he gladly accepted, but as he dined with the emperor, an imperial letter denouncing the imperial guest had been sent to the Senate which was read out, stating, 'among other things that this man was jealous of the emperor's friendship with Sejanus'. Tacitus makes clear what these 'other things' were, for on Agrippina's suicide from starvation, Tiberius wrote to the Senate accusing her of adultery with Gallus, who also died in AD 33 of slow starvation at the hands of his guards. Gallus suffered *damnatio memoriae*, with his name erased from inscriptions and documents. This suggests the official charge was *maiestas*. Tiberius was not willing to leave it there, as many others were condemned for their *amicitiae* with Gallus, including Syriacus, who was executed.[70]

Sejanus now turned his attention towards Agrippina's son and Tiberius' sole heir Drusus. He had already been duped into serving Sejanus' interests by spying on his brother Nero in the hope of securing the succession for himself. Here Sejanus' desire to be regent becomes ever clearer. The opportunity to remain the most important advisor to the 22-year-old Drusus, a man who would have been beholden to Sejanus, would have presented itself. If Sejanus had chosen to take this path, his history and that of Rome's would have been entirely different. Sejanus chose a more uncertain route in undermining Drusus, leaving Tiberius Gemellus and Caligula as successors. Caligula was approaching his nineteenth birthday, whilst Tiberius Gemellus was merely 10. The removal of Drusus would also necessitate the removal of Caligula if Tiberius Gemellus was to ascend the throne, but his young age would require Sejanus to act as regent, a position that would not be required if Drusus or Caligula were emperors. Furthermore, Caligula was likely to desire revenge for the treatment of his family, a revenge that he did enact.

Sejanus now elicited the support of Drusus' wife Aemilia Lepida, the daughter of Tiberius' close *amicus* Marcus Aemilius Lepidus. Her cooperation with Sejanus is surprising considering her future position as wife to an emperor. Dio suggests she was seduced by the Praetorian Prefect into providing evidence against her husband on the promise of marriage. Her evidence would have supported the information given by the Praetorian Guards in the palace. Aemilia Lepida would later pay a heavy price for this collusion. Her influential father managed to protect her until his death in AD 36, when she was immediately accused of adultery with a slave and, anticipating her fate, committed suicide. If Sejanus did form a relationship with Aemilia Lepida, it must have been with the tacit approval of Livilla. The charges brought before the emperor on Capri have been lost, Tacitus merely stating that Drusus was accused of 'a succession of calumnies'. The charges no doubt resembled those previously levelled against Nero. Drusus had already been summoned to Capri, probably after the first allegations were made in the Senate against Agrippina and her eldest son. The absence of both Tiberius and Nero enabled Sejanus to plot the ruin of Drusus by isolating Aemilia Lepida from her husband. To Sejanus' horror, however, Tiberius 'merely sent Drusus to Rome', the imperial displeasure being represented in his exclusion from the court. The evidence had clearly not been incriminating enough to warrant further sanction.

Sejanus managed to persuade a certain Cassius 'to propose some action against him'.[71] L. Cassius Longinus was an ordinary consul in AD 30, whilst his brother C. Cassius Longinus was a *suffect* consul, and these have been identified as the *delator*.[72] This appears to be highly unlikely, as Tiberius was to solely blame Sejanus for the fall of both Nero and Drusus. L. Cassius Longinus was married to Agrippina's daughter Drusilla in AD 33, and it would be remarkable if Tacitus failed to mention the prosecution of her sister if he was involved. Furthermore, C. Cassius Longinus was able to pursue a highly successful career under both Caligula and Claudius, giving his name to a school of law and drawing the admiration of Tacitus himself. This future success appears improbable if he had been closely associated with Sejanus and the death of Nero. These new and obviously manufactured charges were clearly believed, and led to Drusus being declared a public enemy by the Senate and imprisoned below the palace on the Palatine in Rome. There, under the close supervision of Sejanus' Praetorians, his every word and deed were recorded, to be used to further undermine the emperor's relationship with his former heir.[73]

Sejanus, concerned by the prospective death of the emperor, would have wished to permanently remove Drusus from the succession. A curious event took place in Achaea and the Cyclades, where a man claiming to be Drusus raised a large following. He claimed to have escaped his imprisonment and declared his intention of heading for the Syrian legions to gain their support. From there it was said he intended to take over Syria or Egypt. Dio dates this incident to AD 34, whilst Tacitus refers to it as 'towards the same time' as the executions of Sejanus' two young children. Historians have tended to reject Dio's date, pointing to previous errors where incidents are compressed into a kaleidoscope of events that pay little attention to their original chronology. Tacitus himself appears confused over the context of this incident or its outcome. If, as Tacitus suggests, this curious affair was finally concluded around December AD 31, it is quite possible that its initial stages stretched back to the previous year. The 'false' Drusus had been seen first in the Cyclades, and then he travelled to mainland Greece. There, imperial freedmen pretended to recognize him to add to his credibility. Dio describes his appearance in 'the regions of Greece and Ionia'. As soon as the governor of the province, Poppeaus Sabinus, heard of this imposter he determined to hunt him down. The journey took him 'from the bays of Torone and Termae, left behind him the Aegean island of Euboea, Piraeus on the Attic seaboard, then the Corinthian coast and the narrow neck of the isthmus and made his way by the Ionian Sea into the Roman colony of Nicopolis'. It was here that the adventurer declared that he was, in fact, the son of the great noble and *amicus* of Tiberius, Marcus Silanus, whereupon he set sail for Italy. The frustrated Poppeaus Sabinus, legally obliged to remain in his province, wrote a report to the emperor. These events could easily have commenced in the preceding year and been part of Sejanus' stratagem to persuade the emperor to order the execution of Drusus. A revolt in the name of Drusus would probably be the occasion of his death. The false Drusus made no attempt to reach the Syrian legions, which is understandable if he was following instructions from Sejanus, who did not want a military revolt. The Syrian legions had refused to place his images in their military shrines, whilst the German legions, which were usually linked in previous allegations of Agrippina's plotting, were under the command of Gaetulicus, to whom Sejanus would be attached through marriage. Furthermore, the Syrian legions would have been linked in Tiberius' mind to the chaos created by the disputes between Germanicus and Calpurnius Piso. When Poppeaus Sabinus suddenly appeared on the scene, the false Drusus made for Italy, a strange choice of refuge unless he headed for the security offered by Sejanus in Rome. The involvement of imperial freedmen also points to a person of immense influence who could persuade these officials to risk giving credence to a rebel. The sudden declaration by the imposter in Nicopolis that he was not the real Drusus can be explained by his receiving news that Sejanus had been executed. In desperation, the imposter now claimed to be the son of M. Silanus. He would in the circumstances have not made this claim if Silanus were seen to be an *amicus* of Sejanus; rather the opposite. By claiming to be the son of a great aristocrat with the ear of the emperor, he could convince the captain of a merchant ship to take him to Italy on the promise of a lavish reward. Although Tacitus was unable to find any information as to his fate, Dio states that he was recognized and taken to Tiberius. No doubt he would have been amongst the many victims of the emperor thrown from the cliff tops upon which the Villa Jovis stood.[74]

With Drusus now removed from the equation, Tiberius was once more faced with the problem of the succession. There were only two possible surviving heirs: one far too young to rule the empire, and the other lacking any experience in administration or governance, a state of affairs that Sejanus had manipulated. Another possibility was Claudius, the brother of Germanicus, but he was considered by Augustus, Livia, Tiberius, Caligula and clearly by Sejanus himself to be unacceptable due to a limp, stutter and a slight deafness, which in their minds reflected both a physical and mental unsuitability for ultimate power. According to Suetonius, his own mother, Antonia, called him 'a monster: a man whom nature had not finished but merely began', whilst his sister Livilla, being told of a prophecy that he would one day ascend the throne, 'prayed openly and aloud that the Roman people might be spared so cruel and undeserved a misfortune'. Neither mother nor sister were destined to see that day. Instead, Claudius avoided imperial politics. Dismissed and ridiculed, Claudius focused on academia, writing several books on Roman, Carthaginian and Etruscan history.[75]

The 71-year-old Tiberius would have realized that he was unlikely to live long enough to prepare Tiberius Gemellus or Caligula for the position of emperor, so he looked to Sejanus to act as their guide and advisor. Tiberius now raised the status of Sejanus by engaging him to 'Julia, the daughter of Drusus'. Dio or his epitomizer appears to have confused the official name of Livilla with that of her daughter Julia Livia. Livilla's full name was Claudia Livia Julia, but to avoid confusion with Tiberius' mother Livia, she is often referred to by the name Livilla. Tacitus twice refers to Sejanus as the emperor's son-in-law, firstly in Terentius' speech in the Senate, where the defendant states as such, and then in a speech by an unknown senator after the fall of Sejanus. Both preclude a marriage alliance with the emperor's granddaughter. Livilla's previous marriage to Drusus, Tiberius' son, and as sister to Germanicus, who was adopted by the emperor, made her in the eyes of contemporaries the emperor's daughter. The imprisonment of Agrippina removed one of the emperor's previous concerns at this union, whilst the urgent need to prepare for the succession changed the political necessities. Sejanus would be stepfather to Tiberius Gemellus, an heir to the throne and positioned to rule in his name. To consolidate his hold on the northern armies, Tiberius ordered Gnaeus Cornelius Lentulus Gaetulicus, the governor of Upper Germany, to engage his daughter to Sejanus' son, probably Aelius Gallus. The son of the governor of Lower Germany, L. Apronius, was an *amicus* of Sejanus. The armies were expected to remain loyal to Sejanus as he was acting on behalf of a member of the imperial family. Except for the Praetorian Guard, the legions exhibited no loyalty to him as a potential emperor. The army remained loyal to the dynasty itself.

A regency is further implied when Seneca refers to Sejanus' elevated status as 'consecrated too was his signature', indicating that he was able to sign imperial documents on behalf of the absent emperor.[76]

To publicly cement Sejanus' position, the emperor nominated Sejanus as ordinary consul for AD 31, an office he was to share with the emperor himself. Tiberius had held the consulship with his heirs in the past, Germanicus in AD 18 and his son Drusus in AD 21, to advertize his choice of successor. It is also clear that it was planned for the emperor to leave his island solitude and accompany Sejanus to Rome, a city he had not seen since AD 26. This was a singular honour to enhance the status of Sejanus, who held no constitutional position apart from that derived from the office of consul. It was probably agreed at this time that upon leaving office Sejanus would receive proconsular *imperium* and then *tribunicia potestas*, powers equal to those held by the emperor. As *suffect* consuls to replace them, the pair agreed on Faustus Cornelius Sulla Lucullus, the scion of great noble families, who was married Domitia Lepida the Younger, a great-niece of Augustus, and Sex. Tedius Valerius Catallus. The latter was possibly related to the great poet Catullus and adopted by him. Sex. Tedius Valerius Catullus was to be replaced by Sejanus' *amicus* L. Fulcinius Trio, and so be ennobled by his *suffect* consulship. The Senate responded enthusiastically to this news of the emperor's joint consulship with Sejanus and their planned return to the capital, with a vote granting them both the ordinary consulship every five years. A decree was also passed stating that Sejanus should be honoured with an *adventus*, the ceremonial greeting usually reserved for the emperor, whenever he entered Rome.[77]

To some degree, there were precedents to Sejanus' position, which Velleius Paterculus, writing around AD 30, refers to: 'Eminent men rarely fail to enlist the services of great assistants in the management of their fortunes … the deified Augustus made use of Marcus Agrippa, and of Statilius Taurus right after him. In these men's cases "newness of family" did not obstruct their elevation to multiple consulships, to triumphs, and to numerous priesthoods.' The populist historian goes on to commend the qualities of Sejanus to the reader. Tiberius constantly looked to Augustan precedent for his own decisions.[78] Marcus Vipsanius Agrippa was Augustus' great military strategist and close confidant, who was married to the emperor's daughter Julia the Elder before his death in 12 BC. Agrippa's marriage to Julia was to tie him closely to the imperial family upon the death of Augustus' designated heir Marcellus, leaving two young, inexperienced potential successors in Agrippa's children with Julia, Lucius and Gaius

Caesar. By 18 BC Agrippa had been granted proconsular imperium across both imperial and senatorial provinces, as well as *tribunicia potestas* to enable him to act as regent in the event of Augustus' death and during the minority of his young grandchildren whom he adopted. To cement the plans for the succession, Tiberius had been married in 16 BC to Vipsania, whom he would later be forced to divorce. Agrippa's role in Augustus' plans was passed to Tiberius and his elder brother Nero Claudius Drusus, who died in 9 BC, rather than Statilius Taurus, who remained a close and trusted *amicus* of Augustus, holding numerous consulship and the city prefecture.[79]

In many ways their positions were not comparable. Firstly, Agrippa, should the situation have arisen, would have acted as regent for his own children. Tiberius appears to have made no decision as to whether Tiberius Gemellus or Caligula would be his ultimate successor, but neither was related to Sejanus. Furthermore, Sejanus appears to have been *adlected* or promoted to the consulship whilst still retaining his equestrian status. He held *insignia praetoria*, which did not provide senatorial status, only the symbols associated with the rank. This created a major dysfunction between power and status, with an equestrian attaining an office that was the preserve of the senatorial class. This social inversion would have horrified the nobility, but to criticize the decision to appoint Sejanus as consul was to criticize the emperor. Such was the atmosphere of fear created by the condemnation of Titius Sabinus that no disapproval, either public or private, emerges from the pages of our sources. No source mentions Sejanus dispensing with his sole command over the Praetorian Guard, a post he was anxious to retain, in his marriage request to Tiberius in AD 25. Dio also records the Praetorians guarding both a senatorial meeting in October AD 31 and Sejanus himself. Sejanus had proconsular imperium at the time, but had resigned the consulship at the same time as Tiberius. The escort of Praetorians must indicate his continued tenure of the post of Praetorian Prefect; however, such a bodyguard was a symbol of imperial status, as Tiberius on Augustus' death 'did not hesitate to exercise imperial power immediately by calling on the Praetorians to provide him with a bodyguard; which was to be emperor in fact and appearance'.[80] Agrippa, although holding several consulships, did not command any soldiers in Rome. Nor did Augustus abdicate his powers and responsibilities as Tiberius did. By retiring to Capri, the elderly emperor allowed Sejanus to control access to the emperor as well as securing his own position. Augustus remained in Rome and Italy as Agrippa commanded Roman forces in the East and on the Danube as the relationship between the two became increasingly fractured. Sejanus remained at the centre of power, either at the side of his trusting emperor or in the capital itself. Sejanus, Praetorian Prefect, a future member of the imperial family and consul, the nemesis of his opponents with the Senate reduced to abject servility, was at the pinnacle of power.[81]

Chapter 7

His Fall: AD 31

'Whatever gift Fortune bestows upon a man, let him think while he enjoys it, that it will prove as fickle as the goddess from whom it came.'

(Seneca, *Consolation to Marcia* 10)

Preparations were made for the return of Sejanus and the emperor to Rome in the last weeks of AD 30 to take up their joint consulship at the start of the following year. They were to be greeted by the magistrates, Senate, equites, *collegia* and people of Rome in the formal ceremony of *adventus*.[1] However, at the last minute, Tiberius, 'feigning illness, sent Sejanus on to Rome with the assurance that he himself would follow. He declared that a part of his own body and soul was being wrenched away from him, and with tears he embraced and kissed him, so that Sejanus was still more elated.' Tiberius' emotional reaction to the departure of Sejanus appears genuine, and did so to his Praetorian Prefect. Suetonius implies that the emperor's suspicions were awakened before the departure from Capri, but their joint consulship and the later honours granted to Sejanus in the first part of the year suggest otherwise.[2] The breakdown in the emperor's trust must have come later, in AD 31. Tiberius' failure to return to Rome can be put down to his hatred of the city, the servility of its ruling classes and his overwhelming desire for the solitude and peace of Capri, which undermined his best intentions of accompanying the consul designate.

Sejanus entered Rome probably with little expectation that Tiberius would follow. The ordinary consuls entered office on the first day of the year. Before first light, Sejanus would have risen and taken the *auspices* for himself, looking for favourable signs from the gods, before returning home. He then attended his *salutatio*, where a large crowd of senators, equites and clients were admitted to his *atrium* and there they greeted the new consul with 'prayers, rejoicing, congratulations'. The numbers were so large that a couch collapsed from the weight of those sat upon it, whilst a weasel also darted through the throng, both being considered an ill omen. The magnitude of the crowd that escorted him to the Capitol reflected his power and status. The *sella curulis*, a chair decorated in ivory which was a symbol of his office, was carried before him along the crowded streets as the people flocked to gain a glimpse of their new consul. Sejanus made a sacrifice of a white bull to Jupiter Optimus Maximus and then changed from his civil dress, in the form of the *toga praetexta*, for the military clothing of the red *paludamentum*, symbolic of the primary responsibility of the consul in the Republic, which was to defend the *res publica*. His accompanying lictors who had also escorted him from his house did the same. To the sound of horns, he descended to the Forum, but the size of the crowd meant that his servants who were acting as his bodyguard became separated. Instead of following their master, they took a shortcut down the Germonian Stairs, where they slipped and fell. These and other bad auspices were ignored at the time due to the position of Sejanus, for 'not even if some god had plainly foretold that so great a change would take place in a short time, would anyone have believed it'. The Senate then met, where the consul and the remainder of the magistrates and senators swore to uphold the acts of Augustus and further auspices were taken. Sejanus was then expected to make a speech thanking the emperor and celebrate the festive atmosphere.[3]

However, it appears that Sejanus, already appointed consul by the emperor and having received the assent of the Senate, now strangely called a popular assembly to receive the vote of the people. The election of magistrates had been transferred from the people to the Senate in AD 14, although some form of ceremony may still have been played out where the popular assemblies recognized the choice of the senators. A large but fragmentary tablet was discovered on the Aventine which records an inscription that historians agree from its syntax preserves a letter from Tiberius read to the Roman people after the fall of Sejanus:

> But now, since the criminal incitement [or possibly 'demand'] of Sejanus has destroyed the peace of sixty years [?], and that irregular electoral assembly has taken place on the Aventine at which Sejanus was elected consul and I, the feeble companion of an unserviceable [or 'useless or 'harmful'] staff, was brought to become a supplicant, I ask you with all my might [?], my worthy fellow tribesmen, if I have always seemed to you to be a worthy and serviceable member of our tribe, if I have never deserted my duty nor...[4]

The letter was an attempt by the emperor to praise and placate the Roman mob who had rioted after the overthrow of Sejanus. The emperor's anger resonates throughout the surviving text. Tiberius sarcastically describes himself as a frail old man who is completely reliant upon his stick or staff, which he describes as 'harmful'. This physical support is clearly a reference to the role of Sejanus. Tiberius presents himself as a supplicant at the election of his consul, an office the emperor appointed him to. This popular election was a betrayal of the plan agreed on Capri and was seen by the emperor as an attempt to undermine imperial authority. Sejanus' actions had threatened the stability of Rome that had lasted since 30 BC, the end of the civil wars. Furthermore, in a further breach with tradition, the *Comitia Centuriata* that had elected the magistrates during the Republic and had met on the Campus Martius was convened by Sejanus on the Aventine Hill. The Aventine was associated with the Roman plebs, who in times of conflict with the aristocracy had resorted to occupying the hill in protest, most famously during the secession of the revolutionary tribune C. Gracchus. Also, King Servius Tullius, seen as the friend of the people, was linked to the Aventine. He had built there a temple to Diana of the Latins. This legendary ruler was not Roman but an Etruscan like Sejanus himself, born in Volsinii, which was famous for its temple to Nortia, the Etruscan goddess of Fortune. Sejanus himself kept a statue of the goddess Fortuna in his house, a statue that he had taken from the Temple of Fortuna founded by Servius Tullius in the Forum Boarium. Tiberius, a man of deep suspicions but formidable learning, possessed an expert knowledge of Rome's history and myths. He would have been fully aware of the connotations and implications of Sejanus' actions. The seeds of doubt were now growing in Tiberius' mind, doubts that were to take root and be watered by Sejanus' enemies who now had access to the emperor.[5]

Sejanus had made a serious error of judgement, but what were his motivations? There can be little doubt that he was presenting himself as a champion of the people. Sejanus' opponents would have had little difficulty in suggesting this was his first step to become emperor by instigating a civil war with the support of some of the senators, the Roman mob and the Praetorians. In time the emperor became convinced of this, which is reflected in the official pronouncements issued after Sejanus' fall and reproduced in contemporary sources. Tacitus refers to Sejanus' 'crime by which he strove to seize an empire', and his undoubted skills were bent on 'the winning of a throne'. Dio's account echoes this, in that Tiberius grew ever more concerned as the Senate and people 'looked up to him as if he were actually emperor and held Tiberius in slight esteem. When Tiberius learned of this, he did not treat the matter lightly or disregard it, since he feared they might declare his rival emperor outright.' The contemporary Valerius Maximus accuses Sejanus of parricide on two counts. Firstly, the emperor was the father of the nation, and secondly, as Tiberius was Sejanus' father-in-law through marriage to Livilla, who had been married to the emperor's son, Drusus. Parricide was considered one of the most heinous crimes that a Roman could commit. Interestingly, Suetonius believed it was Tiberius who used an unwitting Sejanus as a tool to destroy the family of Germanicus so that his grandson Tiberius Gemellus might ascend the throne. According to this theory, the emperor hoped to avoid any criticism for the destruction of his adopted son and his family, but this is hardly supported by events.[6] Most modern historians follow Syme by concluding that the only conspiracy we can be certain of is the one of Tiberius against Sejanus.[7] The consulship would have ennobled Sejanus in preparation for his proposed marriage to Livilla once he became convinced of his treachery. However, he could not hope for the throne himself as he was not a Julio-Claudian. The nobility, army and people remained wedded to the dynasty to Augustus, to which Sejanus was only linked by marriage. Furthermore, Sejanus would need to have removed Tiberius Gemellus, Caligula and Claudius. There also existed many other members of the aristocracy who were related to the imperial family, including Gnaeus Domitius Ahenobarbus (consul in AD 32), who had married Agrippina the Younger, or the young M. Junius Silanus (consul in AD 46), born in AD 14 to Aemilia Lepida, the daughter of Julia the Younger. Sejanus' own position was tied to the survival of Tiberius, so long as the emperor continued to trust him.

Sejanus' bid for popularity must be placed in the context of the impending regency. Sejanus must have believed that the continued absence of the emperor from Rome allowed him a degree of latitude and freedom to prepare for the succession. The choices of magistrates, especially the consuls, would become a major issue upon the death of Tiberius and a minority of Tiberius Gemellus. It could not be expected that the consuls be chosen by a 12-year old boy, nor would Sejanus possess the constitutional powers to perform this role. It is entirely possible that Sejanus was considering returning the elections to the popular assemblies, which would not only enhance his popularity with the pepole but also serve to divide the aristocracy, who would be faced with a return to the expensive and often humiliating business of canvassing for the vote. If this was the case it would explain why he did not discuss it with Tiberius, as the emperor would have pointed out that Caligula was of an age to take on the responsibilities of Princeps. However, Caligula did not figure in Sejanus' plans. The reintroduction of genuine elections would also be welcomed by those new men and senators lacking a noble name who had little chance of attaining consulships. The aristocracy would have been horrified by Sejanus' 'election' and what it implied. The recent protests in favour of Agrippina and Nero before their exile had served to reveal to Sejanus his unpopularity. He was now attempting to counter it by returning to genuine popular elections. His propaganda associated himself with Servius Tullius and the goddess Fortuna, all part of this strategy. Juvenal confirms the success of this approach: the tenth *Satire* in part derides the fickleness of the mob, who, ignorant of the political subtleties of Sejanus' position, considered him the heir apparent as they 'are followers of Fortune, as always, and hate those who are condemned. This same crowd, if Nortia had supported her Etruscan, if the aged emperor had been smothered off his guard, would be hailing Sejanus as Augustus within minutes.'[8] Sejanus, to outward appearance, was emperor in all but name. Dio records that people 'swore by his Fortune interminably and called him Tiberius' colleague, covertly referring to the supreme power rather than the consulship', until 'in the end they sacrificed to the images of Sejanus as they did to those of Tiberius'. Now, however, the emperor 'was no longer ignorant of anything that concerned his minister'.[9] This less than subtle flattery, that Sejanus did little to counter, was more tinder to feed the fires of imperial suspicion.

Sejanus, overly confident in his position, now moved against the remaining male heir of Germanicus. Agrippina, Nero and Drusus were imprisoned under the guard of Praetorians, their treatment designed to accelerate their demise. After the death of Livia, Caligula, along with his sisters Drusilla and Livilla, were in the care of Antonia, who had probably left Sejanus' Rome to live in her villa at Baiae. Sejanus employed the same strategy that had been so successful against Nero and Drusus in spreading rumours questioning Caligula's morals and sexuality. After Sejanus' fall, several senators were prosecuted for attempting to undermine the emperor's confidence in his heir, including Sextius Paconianus, M. Aurelius Cotta Messalinus and Sextus Vistilius. Paconianus is described by Tacitus as 'fearless, mischievous, a searcher into all men's secrets, and the chosen helper of Sejanus in the laying of his plot against Gaius Caesar [Caligula]'.[10] Paconianus may have been designated praetor for AD 32 for his services to Sejanus. He was an accomplished poet who was able to utilize his ability to write slanderous verses.[11] Cotta was a leading senator, an *amicus* of both Augustus and Tiberius, who was a renowned patron of writers and poets, including Ovid. Juvenal, in his *Satires*, wishes for a 'second Cotta'. However, he was despised by Tacitus:

> [T]he father of every barbarous proposal and therefore the object of inveterate dislike, found himself, on the first available occasion, indicted for hinting repeatedly that the sex of Gaius Caesar [Caligula] was open to question; for dining with priests on Augusta's birthday and describing the function as a wake; for adding, when he was complaining of the influence of M. Lepidus and Lucius Arruntius, his opponents in a money dispute: 'The Senate will side with them, but my pretty little Tiberius with me.'[12]

Cotta's caustic wit appears to have been used by his enemies. His remark directed at Livia's funeral rites appears to refer to the ritual meal that was laid on the deceased's tomb nine days after the burial and was likely directed at Tiberius' reluctance to deify her and so leave his mother a mere mortal.[13] Yet he was a man of generosity, as evidenced by an inscription found on the Appian Way outside Rome dedicated to Zosimus, one of his freedmen, and written by the deceased's wife:

> I admit that I was a freedman; but now my shadow has been ennobled by my patron Cotta. Several times he was willing to grant me an equestrian fortune, he ordered me to let my children live so that he could provide for their upkeep. He was always ready to grant me his own wealth. He also gave my daughters the dowries a father provides. He promoted my son Cottanus, to the rank of tribune in which he bravely served in Caesar's army. What did Cotta not give us? Now, sadly, he provided these verses which can be read on my tomb. Aurelia Saturnia [Zosimus' wife][14]

The hatred Cotta faced in the Senate and in the sources clearly emanated from his cooperation with Sejanus, as many others had made servile proposals in the curia but escaped prosecution. Cotta was found guilty 'by men of the highest position; and, as they pressed their case, he appealed to the emperor'. Luckily for him, Tiberius' letter dismissed the charges, commenting on the friendship between them and his services to the state. The question is what would such a prominent figure as Cotta, the consul of AD 20 and proconsul of Asia in AD 25/26,[15] *amicus* of the emperor, have to gain from working to destroy Caligula. The answer once again lies in Terentius' defence of his own actions before the Senate, in that Sejanus was seen as Tiberius' agent, whom he 'made the sovereign arbiter of things; to us has been left the glory of obedience'.[16] Cotta clearly believed he was acting in the interests of the emperor, and his defence, no doubt, was that he was deceived by Sejanus. It was a defence the emperor clearly accepted. Sextus Vistilius was not so lucky. The ex-praetor was also accused in AD 32 of 'either his authorship of certain attacks on the morals of Gaius Caesar [Caligula] or a false statement credited by the emperor'. The emperor officially withdrew his bonds of *amicitiae* and thereby invited a prosecution. Vistilius, accepting the inevitable, opened his veins, but then had second thoughts and, after binding his wounds, wrote a futile appeal to the emperor. The imperial reply robbed him of all hope, and he opened his wounds once more. The tense of a verb which Tiberius used in his autobiography, and is preserved in Suetonius, indicates that he felt Sejanus was a continuing and existential threat to Caligula.[17]

Vistilius had been an *amicus* of the emperor's brother Nero Claudius Drusus, and upon his death, Tiberius accepted him into his own network of *amicitiae*. Clearly, Sejanus was using the authority of those with known close connections with the emperor, in the figures of Cotta and Vistilius, to create the impression that the slanders directed at the morals of Caligula emanated from the emperor himself. The lack of imperial clemency towards Vistilius in comparison to that granted to Cotta was due to his close connection to another prominent agent of Sejanus. Vistilius was probably the brother of Vistilia, who was married six times, conceiving seven children. One of these was Quintus Pomponius Secundus, who gave shelter to Sejanus' son during the rioting following the execution of his father. Quintus Pomponius himself was convicted of *maiestas* in AD 31, but his life was saved by his brother Publius Pomponius Secundus and his sentence was commuted to house arrest.[18]

News of Sejanus' various transgressions was gradually drip-fed to Tiberius. The emperor was surrounded at court by adherents of the Praetorian Prefect, guarded by soldiers reporting to their commanding officer with messages transmitted by the *speculatores*. Any information regarding Sejanus' actions would have had to be transmitted in private and in secret by someone who had access to news from Rome. This person would also require unsupervised contact with the emperor, and so be trusted by Tiberius implicitly. Antonia the Younger, the guardian of grandson Caligula, had long enjoyed Tiberius' trust and respect. She had remained aloof from courtly politics, even declining to attend the public funeral of her son Germanicus, preferring to mourn her loss in private. She was seen as the ideal Roman matron, living in quiet dignity; qualities that drew the emperor's admiration. She stood in stark contrast to Livia and Agrippina.[19] However, Antonia now intervened, armed with information from Rome. Josephus, probably using the lost works of the historian Cluvius Rufus and the Judean court records of Agrippa the First, whose mother Bernice was a close friend of Antonia's, writes of Antonia's role in the fall of Sejanus:

> Now, Antonia was greatly esteemed by Tiberius on all accounts, from the dignity of her relation to him, who had been his brother Drusus' wife, and from her eminent charity; for though she was still a young woman, she continued in her widowhood, and refused all other matches, although Augustus had enjoined her to be married to someone else; yet did she all along preserve her reputation free from approach. She had also been the greatest benefactress to Tiberius, when there was a very dangerous plot laid against him by Sejanus, a man who had been her husband's friend, and who had the greatest authority, because he was the general of the army, and when many members of the Senate and many of the freedmen joined with him, and the soldiery corrupted, and the plot was come to a great height. Now Sejanus had certainly gained his point, had not Antonia's boldness been more wisely conducted than Sejanus' malice, for, when she had discovered his designs against Tiberius, she wrote to him an exact account of the whole, and gave the letter to Pallas, the most faithful of her servants, and sent him to Capri to Tiberius, who when he understood it, slew Sejanus and his confederates; so that Tiberius, who had her in great esteem before, now looked upon her with still greater respect, and depended upon her in all things.[20]

Antonia would not have been directly privy to Sejanus' designs. She probably received a visit from his enemies in Rome, who persuaded her of their interpretation of recent events, including his 'election' by the people, his tacit encouragement to be treated as Tiberius' joint ruler and his whispering campaign against Caligula. This, in many peoples' eyes, pointed to his imperial ambitions. The use of Antonia was a very clever move, as any direct communication with the emperor was likely to fall into the hands of Sejanus, whilst any information from her was more likely to have been believed by the emperor. Antonia would have been ideally placed to pass on evidence to the emperor if she was based in her villa on the Bay of Naples, and her status as a member of the imperial family would allow her letter to remain secure from prying eyes. Indeed, Tiberius continued to hold banquets on Capri, where Antonia would be expected to recline close to him. There were clearly a number of communications from Antonia; another is recorded by Dio by her slave Caenis, who was employed by 'her as a secretary in writing a secret letter to Tiberius about Sejanus, and had immediately ordered the message to be erased, in order that no trace of it might be left'.[21] Both were well rewarded for this service. Caenis would gain her freedom and became the mistress of the future emperor Vespasian, accumulating great wealth and exerting a considerable influence on the governing of the Empire. Pallas would also gain his freedom, thereby acquiring the name Marcus Antonius, and he is recorded as owning land in Egypt around this time. Upon Antonia's death, he became a client of her son Claudius, becoming one of the leading figures in the imperial court and helping to bring Agrippina the Younger and her son Nero to power.[22]

Antonia's sudden appearance on the political stage has to be motivated by her fears for her grandson Caligula. The fates of his brothers were illustrative of what his future entailed now that Sejanus was utilizing the same strategy in attacking her grandson's morals and sexuality to undermine the emperor's confidence in his heir. However, Antonia would have been aware that Sejanus was engaged to her daughter Livilla, but she was probably unaware that their liaison had probably begun after the death of Drusus. Ignorant of this, Antonia would have calculated that the fall of Sejanus would not threaten the safety of her daughter, whose prospective marriage was arranged by the emperor himself.

To safeguard Caligula's safety, Tiberius summoned him to Capri. Soon after his arrival, in the first few months of AD 31, the 18-year-old was formally granted the *toga virilise* that identified him as an adult, but without the ceremony that had been accorded his brothers. This was a clear indication that Tiberius saw him as his heir, and would have been reported to Sejanus. The dangers that Antonia had attempted to protect Caligula from were still present on the emperor's island: he had entered a nest of vipers. The court was populated by Sejanus' agents, who now attempted to entrap the young man into making impolitic comments that could be reported to the emperor:

> The courtiers tried every trick to lure or force him into making complaints against Tiberius; always, however, without success. He not

only failed to show any interest in the murder of his relatives, but affected an amazing indifference to his own ill-treatment, behaving so obsequiously to his adoptive grandfather and to the entire household, that someone said of him, very neatly: 'Never was there a better slave, or a worse monster.'

Clearly, he had been well drilled for court life, but he had an ally on the island,[23] being joined by Lucius Vitellius, who had been allowed to buy a villa on Capri, no doubt due to the influence of his close patron Antonia.[24] Tiberius' increasing doubts of Sejanus' loyalty are reflected in the nature of the letters he sent to the Senate:

> [At] one moment he would heartily praise Sejanus, and again would heartily denounce him; and, while honouring some of Sejanus' friends out of regard for him, he would be disgracing others. Thus Sejanus, filled in turn with extreme elation and extreme fear, was in constant suspense; for it never occurred to him, on the one hand, to be afraid and so attempt a revolution, inasmuch as he was still held in honour, nor, on the other hand, to be afraid, to be bold and attempt some desperate venture, inasmuch as he was frequently abased.[25]

Questions would have been raised in private by the senators, but none were so bold as to openly move against him. Sejanus started to suspect that his position was no longer secure, especially when Caligula was invited to Capri along with L. Vitellius. However, as consul, Sejanus had to fulfil his official responsibilities and remain in Rome. On 8 May, Tiberius and Sejanus lay down their consulships to be replaced by Faustus Cornelius Sulla and Sex. Tedius Valerius Catullus.[26] To allay any suspicions on the part of his former consular colleague, Tiberius awarded a priesthood to him and his son Strabo. The emperor also awarded a priesthood to Caligula at the same time, praising him in letters sent to the Senate and people. This was interpreted by contemporaries as a sure indication that Tiberius meant for Caligula to be his heir:

> Tiberius, after appointing Gaius [Caligula] priest, praised him and gave some indications that he intended to make him his successor to the throne. Sejanus would therefore have set on foot a rebellion, especially as the soldiers were ready to obey him in everything,

had he not perceived that the populace was immensely pleased at the compliments paid to Gaius, out of reverence for the memory of Germanicus, his father. For he had previously supposed that they, too, were on his side, and now, finding them earnest supporters of Gaius, he became dejected, and regretted that he had not begun a rebellion during his consulship.[27]

The promotion of Caligula was Tiberius' insurance policy, believing as he did that Sejanus' attack on his heir was also an attack on himself. The emperor clearly thought Sejanus wanted to be emperor and plotted his destruction. The public promotion of Caligula also undermined Sejanus' attempt to win popular approval through his earlier 'election' to the consulship and promotion of his association with Servius Tullius and the goddess Fortuna. There is, however, very little evidence to support the official line that Sejanus was indeed plotting a revolt. The only later prosecution that implies any attempt to tamper with the loyalty of the soldiers comes from the charges made against the eminent senators Annius Pollio (with his son Vinicianus), Appius Silanus, Mamercus Scaurus and Calvisius Sabinus, who were charged in AD 32 with *maiestas*, but a tribune of the urban cohorts exonerated Appius and Calvisius. The tribune was to be used to give evidence of the accuseds' criminal intent to suborn soldiers in these units. The nobles were, however, horrified by the charges, primarily because many were connected by marriage or descent from those charged. Furthermore, the reluctance of the Senate to convict implies that the evidence against them was tenuous, as the Senate would be unable and unwilling to dismiss any secure evidence of inciting a military revolt and would have sought a condemnation as an expression of their loyalty, especially in the dark days that followed the execution of Sejanus. Indeed, the emperor himself postponed the case until he was present in person to adjudicate. All would have known that he had no intention of doing so.[28]

Sejanus had received proconsular *imperium* after the end of his consulship, probably agreed with Tiberius before he left Capri. The Senate also voted that future consuls be instructed to conduct themselves in the manner that both Tiberius and Sejanus did during their tenure of the office. This was as much a compliment and honour to the emperor as it was to Sejanus.[29] However, he was not granted *tribunicia potestas*, that would have placed his constitutional powers on a par with those held by Tiberius. Sejanus clearly expected to have received these at the same time as his proconsular *imperium*. This was a further indication of imperial disfavour. Having been refused authorization to return to Capri, Sejanus requested permission to travel to Campania, where Livilla was reported to have been taken ill. Campania was but a short distance from Capri. A hint of desperation permeates his appeals, but he was again refused. Tiberius provided the excuse that he was immediately returning to Rome. His failure to arrive would have been a defining moment in Sejanus' mindset.[30]

Sejanus reacted to these setbacks by going on the offensive: Nero was to be Sejanus' final victim. He had suffered immense hardships in his prison island of Pontia at the hands of his Praetorian Guards. His death can be placed after May AD 31, 'when Sejanus was already an object of suspicion'.[31] According to Suetonius, it 'is believed that Nero was forced to commit suicide when an executioner, announcing that he had come with the Senate's warrant, displayed the noose for hanging him and the hooks for dragging his corpse to the Tiber'.[32] It is evident from Tiberius' subsequent reaction that the executioner was not acting on his orders, so these must have emanated from the Praetorian Prefect himself. The emperor's subsequent letter read to the Senate makes clear the break with Sejanus. If Nero was to die, it was to be the emperor's decision. Nero, after all, was a direct descendant of Augustus. Tiberius' suspicions appeared by this act to have been confirmed. The letter made clear that the emperor no longer considered Sejanus the partner of his labours:

> And in a letter to the Senate about the death of Nero he referred to Sejanus by that name simply, without the addition of customary titles. Moreover, because sacrifices were being offered to Sejanus, he forbade such offerings to be made to any human being; and because many honours were being voted to Sejanus, he forbade the consideration of any measures which proposed honours for himself.[33]

By refusing any honours for himself, the Senate could hardly vote honours to Sejanus.

Sejanus had also made a move to destroy L. Arruntius, who must be considered the focal point of opposition, which would explain Sejanus' hatred of him. Aruseius and Sanquinius brought a charge against him at some point between July and October AD 31, probably of *maiestas*. The timing of the charge was meant to undermine the candidacy of Arruntius' adopted son for consular office in AD 32. Arruntius' public disapproval of Sejanus was admired by many members of the aristocracy and by Tacitus himself, who describes him as a 'spotless character', a man 'impatient of villanies'.[34] Tiberius instructed Lentulus Cossus, his close *amicus*, to introduce a senatorial resolution granting immunity from prosecution for office-holders, and since Arruntius had been the absentee governor of Hispania Citerior since AD 25, the prosecution was defeated. Cossus would be made Prefect of Rome in AD 33 after the death of the aged L. Calpurnius Piso the Pontifex. As an additional token of imperial anger at the attack on Arruntius, his adopted son L. Arruntius Camillus Scribonianus was nominated by the emperor as one of the ordinary consuls of AD 32. Arruntius' accusers were now charged by his *amici* with malicious prosecution, or *calumnia*, and were convicted. They were probably deprived of their rank as senators, for Tacitus later records that Aruseius was awarded a pardon in AD 36.[35]

Until the death of Nero, the imperial actions against Sejanus had been indirect and clothed in an ambiguity of intent. The reason for this was, firstly, that the emperor was not entirely convinced of Sejanus' treachery until he received the message from Pontia. Secondly, Tiberius was surrounded by potential threats from adherents of Sejanus. His own personal safety was in the hands of guards whose officers had been appointed by the Praetorian Prefect. His fears are illustrated by two incidents recorded in Suetonius in which the old general overreacted to minor misdemeanours: 'A guardsman once stole a peacock from the imperial aviary and was sentenced to death. On another occasion, during a country jaunt, the bearers of his litter were held up by a bramble thicket; he had the senior centurion of the Praetorian Guard, whose task it was to choose the right path, stretched on the ground and flogged until he nearly died.' To a terrified old man, fearful of assassination, such laxness was either premeditated or, if not, it endangered his security. That it was Tiberius and not the guard's commander carrying out the sentence suggests Sejanus was in Rome at this time. Additionally, the emperor could not count on the loyalty of the Praetorians in Rome, nor the urban cohorts with whom they shared the Praetorian Fortress. Dio explicitly states that Tiberius was well aware the guard 'had been on the side of Sejanus'.[36]

Imperial security on Capri was also threatened by his own courtly entourage, most of whom were the *amici* of Sejanus. These courtiers were already attempting to entrap Caligula and would be in communication with Sejanus in Rome. It is also likely that the emperor felt he could not trust some of his imperial freedmen. Tiberius was also unsure of the extent of support Sejanus enjoyed amongst the Senate and people of Rome itself. His numerous dispatches to the capital announcing his looming arrival or impending demise were not only an attempt to confuse Sejanus, but to assess potential support.[37] The popular reaction to the presentation of Caligula as his heir reassured him. He now worked to undermine Sejanus' association with the goddess Fortuna. Rumours were spread that unfavourable omens indicated that Sejanus had incurred the displeasure of the gods. Sejanus presented himself as Fortuna's favourite, guided by the divine in his rise to power. A statue of Sejanus started to emit smoke, and when the head was removed, a snake was discovered in its hollow core. In order to placate the divine, Sejanus prepared to sacrifice before the offending image, only to discover a rope attached to its neck like a garrotte. The implications were clear: traitors were strangled in the infamous *carcer*, the prison that stood in the Forum near the Gemonian Steps. Finally, his own protecting deity appeared to turn on him. The ancient cult figure of Fortuna connected with Servius Tullius, which Sejanus kept in his house, was found with its back turned. News of these events were spread and exaggerated through the streets of Rome, to the extent that it was reported by Dio that the goddess turned her back on him whilst he was in the act of sacrificing. Observers of these events would pass on the information with their own interpretation to their own friends and clients, who in turn passed it to theirs with added embroidery. The news would be used to confirm the belief that Sejanus was facing his end.[38]

The imperial letters would have made it clear that the former consul had fallen from favour, especially after the death of Nero. Tiberius doubted the Senate's collective loyalty, as many were bound by the ties of *amicitiae* to Sejanus and others were related to him.[39] Many prominent senators amongst the nobility were opposed to Sejanus, but the ambiguity of imperial letters and honours meant that 'privately they kept a sharp eye to their own safety, but publicly they paid court to him' during his consulship. It was a position that seemed to be confirmed by his award of a priesthood.[40] Through the following months, the balance of the emperor's rewards and criticisms started to weigh heavily towards the latter. In July Sejanus' *amicus* L. Fulcinius Trio became consul in place of Tedius Valerius Catullus, but then came the letter that effectively blamed Sejanus for the death of Nero. The pointers were clear and many now made the attempt to disassociate themselves from Sejanus; people 'avoided meeting him or being left alone with him, and that in a manner too marked not to be noticed'.[41] Here are echoes of the treatment of Agrippina and Nero when it became clear that they had fallen from imperial favour. Politics in Rome was brutal, unforgiving and, in many instances, fatal. Sejanus' *salutatio* would have become populated by ghosts, his dinner invitations unanswered and his escort reduced to only his closest *amici* and clients, who would have known that they shared his fate. The great man could have anticipated his end. In his dire situation, he may have contemplated desperate measures.

In the purges that followed Sejanus' death, Publius Vitellius was accused by informers of conspiring to provide funds for a revolution from the military treasury, for which he was responsible as prefect of the *Aerarium Militare*. Whether there was any substance to the accusations is to be doubted. P. Vitellius was a close *amicus* of Germanicus, and upon his death was amongst the foremost prosecutors of his alleged poisoner Calpurnius Piso. He was praised by Tacitus for his eloquence in the presentation of the case. It has been suggested that he became an *amicus* of Sejanus, fearing prosecution by the family of the Calpurnii Pisones. His brother Lucius Vitellius was so influential with both Antonia and Tiberius that he was invited to stay on Capri. In those rabid times, any charge of *maiestas* linked to Sejanus would stick. However, his sentence was commuted thanks to the influence of his brothers Lucius who was both an *amicus* of Antonia and Caligula, and Aulus Vitellius, the *suffect* consul of AD 32. Aulus accepted custody of his brother, who attempted suicide by opening his veins with a penknife. His friends begged him to bandage up his wounds and he relented. Despite the influence of his brothers, Publius was later imprisoned, where he died. Aulus himself would die in the year of his consulship, but Lucius became the ordinary consul of AD 34 and was appointed governor of Syria from AD 35–39 as, according to Suetonius, a reward for allowing his son to acquiesce to the emperor's improper advances. He would continue to pursue an illustrious and brilliant career under Caligula and Claudius.[42] Perhaps Sejanus was hoping to use the money to bribe the Praetorians and urban cohorts; certainly that was the imputation of the allegations. However, it is difficult to understand why P. Vitellius would agree to this when it was evident to all that the days of the Praetorian Prefect were numbered. His two brothers were clearly loyal to Tiberius, with Lucius firmly allying himself to Caligula as the future heir. Publius' actions, if there is credence to them, were directly opposed to his brothers' interests. What can be said is that both Dio and Suetonius, our main sources for the period between late AD 28 and the end of October AD 31, and the vast majority of modern historians discount a plot by Sejanus to ascend the throne, and consider that if there was one, it was only in response to the emperor's obvious attempts to undermine his position.[43]

Once it was evident that Sejanus' support was melting away and his network of *amicitiae*, which he had spent sixteen years building, was on the point of collapse, Tiberius made his move to finally crush him.[44] The plan will have been constructed by a small clique of advisors on Capri whom the emperor trusted implicitly. These can be deduced from those whose power and influence grew after the fall of Sejanus. Caligula would have known that if Sejanus became regent, his own life would be quickly cut short. He did succeed Tiberius; however, his age, his lack of political experience and the continuing imprisonment of his mother and brother Drusus would have precluded him from these discussions. Antonia may have been involved, but Tiberius' prejudices against the active role of women in politics count against this. The emperor's regular and private consultations with the astrologer Thrasyllus in the observatory in the Villa Jovis point to his involvement in the emperor's *consilium*. Thrasyllus' granddaughter Ennia Thrasylla was married to Q. Naevius Cordus Sutorious Macro, who had been a Prefect of the Vigiles, Rome's firefighters and night watch. Sejanus and Macro clearly knew each other, as can be deduced from their meeting before the Temple of Apollo on Sejanus' final day. Furthermore, he had the confidence of the emperor, who delegated to Macro the most demanding role in the plan to destroy Sejanus. It is likely that he had been allowed to remain on Capri in consideration of his marriage to Thrasyllus' granddaughter. Nothing is known of the whereabouts of her parents, although we can surmise that the *eques* Lucius Ennius was her father. He was accused of treason in AD 22, but Tiberius forbade him to be put on trial despite the disapproval of the Senate. There can be little doubt that his father-in-law exerted influence on his behalf.[45]

Another possible member of this inner circle that plotted the demise of Sejanus was Lucius Vitellius. He was honoured with the ordinary consulship in AD 34, despite his lack of nobility, his father only attaining the office of quaestor under Augustus. In AD 35 he was appointed to the strategic governorship of Syria, a clear indication of the trust placed in him by Tiberius. He remained a close confidant of both Caligula and Claudius. His brother Aulus Vitellius was a *suffect* consul in AD 32, but it is not known whether he was on Capri the previous year. Another close and trusted *amicus* of the emperor present on the island at this time was the great jurist Marcus Cocceius Nerva. Tacitus describes him as the 'inseparable friend of the emperor', the 'nearest of his friends'. He would have formed part of this small group of imperial advisors.[46]

One other person brought into the plot was P. Graecinius Laco, the Prefect of the Vigiles in AD 31, perhaps Macro's successor in the post. As the loyalty of the Praetorians and the urban cohorts was suspect, the only other significant military units in the capital were the night watch. These, however, were not soldiers but freedmen who were responsible for patrolling the streets after dark. Their fourteen cohorts would have been no match for the Praetorians, but they would take a significant role in the plans. Laco was obviously trusted, but it is not likely the equestrian would have been known to Tiberius so he must have been commended by Macro. Laco was to become procurator Galliarum, and in AD 44 be honoured with *consular ornamenta* by Claudius.[47]

The other key role had to be played by the consuls. Here there was a problem. L. Fulcinius Trio was considered to be Sejanus' man and not to be trusted. The other, Faustus Cornellius Sulla Lucullus, the bearer of a noble name to match his illustrious heritage, was not considered capable enough. It was decided to replace him as *suffect* consul on 1 October with Publius Memmius Regulus, a new man who became governor of Macedonia and Achaea after his brief tenure of the consular office, later becoming governor of the prestigious province of Asia. It must have been calculated that the removal of Trio as consul would have alerted an already suspicious and nervy Sejanus and so he remained in post.[48]

Success depended upon surprise and the reaction of the Praetorian Guard. They were to be offered a donative of 1,000 denarii each in order to secure their loyalty, but even then it was imperative to ensure the Praetorian Prefect was unable to enter their fortress. Tiberius, from his communication with Rome, felt confident of the support of a large number of senators, but the reaction of the volatile Roman mob was also a concern. If the plan failed, Tiberius and his advisors had made a number of contingencies. Firstly, Agrippina's son Drusus, incarcerated in the prison under the palace, was to be freed and appointed commander-in-chief. His hatred of Sejanus and desire for revenge would serve Tiberius' short-term interests. The expectation was that the populace would rise to support him and, in conjunction with those forces that remained loyal to the name of Germanicus, he would battle Sejanus' Praetorians in the streets of the capital. His defeat would have been inevitable, which would not have overly concerned the emperor; however, the name of Sejanus would have been sullied forever and time could have been bought to bring in reinforcements. If this failed, the emperor had organized for ships from the nearby naval base at Misenum to take him to the legions, probably those in Syria which had refused to place the images of Sejanus in their shrines. These soldiers would later receive a donative of 1,000 denarii in recognition of their loyalty. Finally, a system of couriers was created to rapidly communicate news of events in the capital to Capri. These were unlikely to have been *speculatores*. If, for any reason, these couriers were delayed, a system of bonfires were built from Rome to Misenum, with prearranged signals issued. Tiberius, from his high perch in the Villa Jovis, now awaited his fate.[49]

Rumours had already been spread in Rome that Sejanus was about to be granted *tribunicia potestas*, to reassure him and to buy time for the foundations of the plan to be put in place. Macro must have already been made Praetorian Prefect of those troops stationed on Capri, but this news would have remained a secret beyond the island. The new Praetorian Prefect entered Rome on the night of 17 October, armed merely with a letter from Tiberius confirming his appointment to the position. The consul Regulus then called a Senate meeting for the following morning in the Temple of Apollo on the Palatine, whilst intimating to all that Sejanus was going to be awarded *tribunicia potestas*. This information would have reached Sejanus' ears. The location of the senatorial meeting was important, as the Temple of Apollo, an integral part of the palace, was close to the prison where Drusus was held and as far away as possible from the Praetorian Fortress. The Palatine was also more readily defended than other locations where the Senate often met in and around the Forum.[50]

As dawn broke, Macro made his way up the Palatine Hill to the Temple of Apollo. Dawn had already seen Sejanus greeted at his *salutatio* by the Senate, whose members had been privy to the rumours of his impending new powers circulated by Marco. Sejanus was escorted from his house to the temple. The senators entered, but doubt prevented Sejanus from doing so. He would have known Macro had entered the city and he waited for him. He sought reassurance after Tiberius' previous treatment of him and his *amici*. Macro approached and, in false confidence, disclosed that his proconsular powers were about to be supplemented with the powers that he had long awaited, tribunician powers that were in effect a public acknowledgement of his place as regent upon the death of the emperor. He would have shown him the sealed letter as evidence. Duped, Sejanus entered to the applause of the Senate, who anticipated the bestowal of further imperial honours. Sejanus sat in the privileged position surrounded by fellow former consuls, eager, confident and buoyant. In the meantime, Macro showed the imperial letter to the Praetorian tribune whose cohort guarded the meeting and the person of Sejanus himself. The officer accepted the promotion of Macro to the command of the guard. He had little choice, as to disobey an imperial order was an act of mutiny. The letter did not mention Sejanus' position, so he would have assumed there would be two Praetorian Prefects as there had been before Seius Strabo. Macro dismissed the guard, who were to return to the Praetorian Fortress. They obeyed. He then entered the Senate and gave the emperor's letter to Regulus, and left immediately. Time was important, as he had to get to the Praetorian Fortress before the guards who had been relieved. This was because Laco had brought up his Vigiles to the palace. This is the point where the returning Praetorians would have realized that something untoward was transpiring, but they did not react. Macro ordered Laco to post sentries around the Temple of Apollo. He will also have ordered the Vigiles to relieve the Praetorians in the palace itself and those guarding Drusus.[51]

Inside the temple, the letter was opened and read to the gathering. Deliberately, it was a long and rambling affair. It had to buy time for Macro to get from the Palatine to the fortress, perched above Rome to the north-east. Juvenal describes it as 'an enormous, wordy letter' whose contents 'contained no wholesale denunciation of Sejanus, but first some other matter, then a slight censure of his conduct, then something else, and after that some further objection to him; and at the close it said that two senators who were among his intimate associates must be punished and that he himself must be put under guard'. The letter also expressed the emperor's fear that he could not safely travel to Rome, and requested one of the consuls to travel to Capri to escort him back. As for Sejanus:

> As it was, he paid no great heed to the successive charges as they were read, thinking each one a slight matter which stood alone, and hoping that, at best, no further charge, or, in any event, none that could not be disposed of, was contained in the letter; so he let time slip by and remained in his seat.

As the letter was read, the senators who had at first been acclaiming Sejanus were initially confused, then as realization dawned those senators who sat near the Praetorian Prefect stood up and walked away. Others, his *amici*, whose fate was tied closely to that of their patron, would have been dejected. Soon the majority burst into a cacophony of cheering. His enemies rejoiced in his fall, whilst others wished to demonstrate their loyalty to the emperor. The praetors and tribunes moved to surround Sejanus to prevent his escape. They need not have worried. He sat there, alone, dazed by the disaster that had overtaken him at the very moment he believed fortune had granted him virtual supreme power.[52]

The consul Regulus then summoned the emperor's quarry to approach him. Sejanus sat there, unable to process what had happened. Again he was called, and the consul pointed directly at him, raising his voice a second and then a third time:

> 'Sejanus come here.' He merely asked him, 'Me? You are calling me?' At last, however, he stood up, and Laco, who had now returned, took his position beside him. When finally, the reading of the letter was finished, all with one voice denounced and threatened him, some because they had been wronged, others through fear, some to conceal their friendship for him, and still others out of joy at his downfall.

Regulus, despite the outward signs of hostility towards Sejanus, knew that many there were his past supporters, so he did not put the arrest to a vote. Instead, the consul asked one senator, probably previously primed, whether Sejanus should be imprisoned, and he agreed. Sejanus was then led out of the temple, escorted by Laco, the magistrates and the Vigiles.[53]

The hypocrisy of many of the senators emanated from either a desire for vengeance or survival or, for most, a combination of both. Caligula, no friend of Sejanus' memory, later stood before the Senate denouncing their hypocrisy. He had previously announced that he had destroyed Tiberius' papers, but these had been copies. The documents contained the evidence provided by witnesses and accusers who had worked with Sejanus in his campaigns against his mother and brothers. In AD 39 Caligula had narrowly avoided death in a conspiracy involving many prominent senators. He now reproduced these documents and abused 'the Senate as having been friends of Sejanus, or informers against his mother and brothers (at this point producing the papers which he was supposed to have burned!); and exclaimed that Tiberius' cruelty had been quite justified since, with so many accusers, he was bound to believe the charges'.[54] These same senators who had escorted Sejanus from his home with words of praise and congratulations now escorted him from the Temple of Apollo to the *carcer* and his death.[55] At their head were the two consuls, one being Fulcinius Trio, his close *amicus*, who would be joined by many who feared to share their patron's fall and so became the most conspicuous in the persecution of his former friends and clients.

The road they took led down from the Palatine to the Forum. Sejanus attempted to cover his head from brutal reality and the blows that now rained down on him, and seek some refuge from the humiliation he endured. Many hit him in his face and pulled his purple-bordered toga down so he could see the physical manifestation of his fall. A mob had gathered that now lined his route. They had clearly known in advance the plans for his arrest, as there was no bemused silence at the scene of their former master being dragged to prison. There was no confused delay. These were probably the clients of Sejanus' prominent opponents who had been organized to provide a public humiliation that would empower the mob to attack his most prominent supporters. The populace took full advantage, as there were no Praetorians to protect him or provide order. They jeered, swore and cursed as he was dragged past. The blows kept raining down, both physical and mental. As he approached the Forum, Sejanus saw his statues being thrown down and smashed in a parody of his own fate, echoing the *damnatio memoriae* that was inevitably to follow and the abuse of his own body on the Gemonian Steps.[56]

Sejanus was thrown into the *carcer*, which in medieval times came to be known as the Mamertine Prison. It was a temporary prison for those held before trial or execution. It faced the curia, the Senate house and the Temple of Peace next to the Gemonian Steps. Its construction took advantage of an ancient quarry that stretched back into the Capitoline Hill. Sejanus was placed into one of the cells. Below these lay the single death cell described in 40 BC by Sallust: '[I]n the prison there is a place called the Tullianum … about twelve feet deep, closed all round by strong walls and a stone vault. Its aspect is repugnant and fearsome from its neglect, darkness and stench.'[57] Tradition asserts that it was ironically named after Servius Tullius, but more likely due to the spring water, in Latin called *tullius*, that ran through it. The supporters of Gracchus and Catiline had died there, as had Julius Caesar's Gallic opponent Vercingetorix. A modern memorial marks the horrendous execution of these, and future, victims of Roman justice. Sejanus will have known and awaited his fate. Fortune had indeed deserted her most devoted supplicant.

The Senate now met in the Temple of Concord to pass sentence. The letter from Tiberius had merely ordered Sejanus' arrest, but Macro would have made clear what was expected of them. The emperor had clearly stated that his life was in danger by requesting a consular escort to accompany him to Rome. It has been suggested that Tiberius, as was his practice, was unclear as to which consul he meant, and he really envisaged that it would be Sejanus' *amicus* Trio who could then be removed from Rome. Whatever the case, charges of treason were anticipated by the emperor. The senators had waited to see the response of the mob and the Praetorians to these events. The mob had rejoiced in the opportunity to abuse and abase a member of Rome's elite, whilst the Praetorians were absent from the streets of the capital. Emboldened, the Senate passed the sentence of death and his memory suffered *damnatio memoriae*. Sejanus was taken down from his cell into the Tullianum, and there garrotted. His body was then thrown onto the Gemonian Steps, where it was mistreated and desecrated for three days. What was left of his mutilated corpse was then dragged by a hook through the streets and thrown into the Tiber. His shade was destined to bare these marks of shame for all eternity.[58]

Juvenal's tenth *Satire* was written to engender some form of sympathy for the fallen, whom ambition and vanity had led to their demise. The desire for wealth, power, longevity, fame, eloquence or beauty is mocked through examples taken from history. Sejanus' fall was for Juvenal illustrative of the vanity of human wishes. The poet provides a vivid picture of the hours and days following the execution of Rome's deposed principal. He describes the great bronze statues being melted down and his body lying prone for all to see:

Now the flames are hissing, now that head idolised by the people is glowing from the bellows and furnace: huge Sejanus is crackling. Then the face that was number two in the whole world is turned into little jugs, basins, frying pans, and chamber pots. Hang your homes with laurel, drag a huge bull, whitened with chalk, up to the Capitol! Sejanus is being dragged by the hook – a sight worth seeing. Everyone's celebrating. 'Look at his lips! Look at his face! Take it from me, I never liked the man.'[59]

The flames of retribution rapidly spread, and Sejanus' *amici* feared the bloodlust of the mob and the vengeance of Tiberius. Many were desperate to make a public declaration of loyalty to Tiberius by rushing to the altars to make a sacrifice of thanks for the safety of the emperor. The orator Bruttidius Niger, a well-known companion of the Praetorian Prefect, went to desecrate Sejanus' body to publicly disassociate himself from his previous *amici* and affirm his loyalty to Tiberius:

'I hear many are to die.' 'No doubt about it. The furnace is huge.' 'My friend Bruttidius looked rather pale when I met him at the altar of Mars. I am terribly frightened that "defeated Ajax" [Tiberius] will take reprisals for being badly defended. Let's get a move on and trample on Caesar's enemy while he's lying on the riverbank. But make sure our slaves see us, so they can't deny it and drag their terrified master to court with a noose around his neck.' Those were their remarks about Sejanus at that time, those were the secret whispers of the mob.[60]

The exposure of Sejanus' unguarded corpse unleashed a frenzy of rioting and murder, 'for the populace slew anyone it saw of those who had possessed great influence with Sejanus and had committed acts of insolence to please him'. Sejanus' son, knowing his life was in grave danger, escaped to the house of Sejanus' *amicus* P. Pomponius Secundus, who hid him in his garden. Secundus no doubt had armed his slaves and freedmen to fend off the avenging mob, and had the strength of character to hold fast to his obligations of friendship.[61] The rioters were joined by members of the Praetorian Guard, who, 'angered because they had been suspected of friendliness for Sejanus and because the night-watch had been preferred to them and their loyalty to the emperor questioned, proceeded to burn and plunder, despite the fact that all the officials were guarding the whole city in accordance with Tiberius' command'.[62] Order was impossible to enforce. The Vigiles, armed with picks, mattocks and axes for dealing with fires, and with little military training, would have been slaughtered if they had attempted to confront the Praetorians. Laco appears to have recognized the realities of the situation and waited for these particular flames to burn themselves out.

The actions of the Praetorians is puzzling. They made no attempt to save their commander, nor did they appear on the streets of Rome until after his death, and then they rioted despite imperial orders for discipline. The riot clearly took place after the Senate had condemned Sejanus and had ordered his immediate execution. The proximity of the senatorial meeting in the Temple of Peace to the *carcer* was pre-planned to ensure that the *senatus consulta* was carried out with the minimum of delay. Some historians have suggested that the use of the Temple of Peace represented a desire to avoid civil war by both the Senate and emperor alike. However, the location of the meeting was for a practical rather than symbolic purpose. Macro must have entered the Praetorian Fortress a short time before the arrival of the cohort that had been stationed around the Temple of Apollo and the soldiers stationed in the palace. The timing of events was vital. The Praetorians would have been mustered to be addressed by Macro, and were then joined by the returning cohort, who will have resented their replacement by the Vigiles but not have known of the arrest of Sejanus. If the Praetorians had already been assembled before the tribunal, the returning guardsmen would not have had any opportunity to speak to their comrades. As they entered, the gates to the fortress would then have been shut and guarded by loyal soldiers to prevent news from outside entering. News of the execution of Sejanus would have thereby been delayed. There can be little doubt that another rambling imperial letter will have been read out to the assembled ranks, informing them of Macro's appointment to the Praetorian Prefecture and the promised donative in recognition of their loyalty to Tiberius. No mention would have been made of Sejanus. It was only upon their dismissal that the soldiers who had been guarding the senatorial meeting would have been able to tell their comrades of what had happened. With the gates barred, it would have taken time for the soldiers to receive news of events outside.

Macro could not have relied on the Praetorian tribunes and centurions, as most had been appointed by Sejanus. Once trouble started in the fortress, he may have used the urban cohorts to protect himself, in a secure location. This may account for the absence of any reference to the urban cohorts in our surviving narrative. However, the loyalty of these units was probably compromised, and it must be doubted that Macro would have placed his safety into their hands. Instead, he probably left the camp to ensure that his predecessor had been dealt with. The Praetorians will have received news of the execution of Sejanus, perhaps after they had forced the gates. Sejanus' appointees will have made a minimal effort to ensure order and discipline. The official account preserved in our sources records that these elite soldiers resented the fact that their role and responsibilities been usurped by ex-slaves in the form of the Vigiles, and their loyalty besmirched by the dismissal of the cohort from the Temple of Apollo. At this time it would have been dangerous to suggest that the soldiers' anger stemmed from the execution of Sejanus. It was far better to claim that their actions resulted from the insult engendered by the implied questioning of their loyalty to Tiberius. Order was restored, as ultimately the Praetorians existed only so long as there was an emperor to guard and protect. None would have relished joining the ranks of the legions posted on the far-flung borders of the Empire. However, Macro and Tiberius would have purged Sejanus' appointees from its ranks, as inferred from a story told by Seneca. A Praetorian was off duty, enjoying a dinner party and drinking far too much. His presence at a banquet suggests he was an officer. The Praetorian, needing to relieve himself, picked up a chamber pot while still wearing a ring bearing Tiberius' image. An informer witnessed this and called on the other guests to witness this desecration, but the soldier's life was saved by his slave, who quickly removed his master's ring and placed it on his own hand.[63] These were not normal circumstances where civilians stood in fear of the soldiers. Members of the imperial guard could now find themselves accused of disloyalty, which reflected the culture of spying, informing, accusation and counter-accusation that infiltrated all aspects of Roman society in the wake of Sejanus' fall.

Tiberius waited for news at the cliff-tops next to the Villa Jovis, looking to the distant headland for the fire signals that would either announce his doom or that of Sejanus. Eventually, he received the message he had hoped for, but he remained ensconced in his villa perched high above the waves for a further nine months. He even refused to give an audience to the consul Regulus, whom he had requested to come to Capri to escort him to Rome. No thanks were forthcoming.[64] The once great and courageous general had become a scared, suspicious and vindictive old man. He was not satisfied with the death of the man whom he had once proudly announced to be his partner in his labours, but also desired the destruction of Sejanus' family and his extensive network of *amici* and clients; a desire that would lead to another knife being struck into his tortured and poisoned soul.

Chapter 8

The Terror: AD 31–37

'So peace stands, the laws are valid, the course of private and public duty remains unimpaired. But he who essayed to subvert all this, violating the bonds of friendship, was trampled down along with all his race by the might of the Roman people, and in the underworld too, that is if it takes him in, he suffers the punishment he deserves.'
(Valerius Maximus IX.11, Ext 4)

Peace was consumed in an orgy of political bloodletting, and the bonds of friendship, ruptured by the entrapment of Sabinus, were further fractured in an unrelenting purge of those connected to Sejanus' network of *amicitiae*. Seneca compares the months and years after the fall of Sejanus to a time of political conflict where there existed 'an almost universal culture of informing, which was more ruinous to Rome even than the civil wars'.[1] Many had worked closely with Sejanus as the de facto ruler of Rome on the unspoken understanding that he was the emperor's agent in all things. Others worked for his favour or were bound to him for *beneficia* he had granted. Now there was a desperate need for these senators and equestrians to prove their loyalty to the emperor and avoid prosecution on charges of *maiestas*. Senatorial resolutions were passed that forbade the mourning of Sejanus, who was declared *hostis*, an enemy of the state, and the memory of him was obliterated from history in the form of the *damnatio memoriae*. The ferocity of the response is reflected by the total absence of any surviving statues or inscriptions that mention his name. One inscription shows his name chiselled away from a list of consular *fasti*, whilst a coin from Bilbilis in Spain, struck to commemorate his joint consulship with the emperor, has his name obliterated. Further laws were passed enacting an annual religious festival attended by all the magistrates and priests that commemorated his death, and a statue to Liberty was erected in the Forum. It was also prohibited to award excessive honours to one man, whilst oaths could be sworn only in the name of Tiberius. Sejanus' estates and wealth were confiscated by the public treasury, but Tiberius ordered that these be returned to imperial possession as, no doubt, it was the emperor who had gifted them to Sejanus from his own estates. Honours were also voted to Macro and Laco, which in the circumstances they felt it politic to decline.[2]

The rioting had led to the murder of several men associated with Sejanus, including Bruttidius Niger and T. Ollius.[3] His family was also targeted, and their deaths documented on the *Fasti Ostienses* which records Sejanus being strangled on 18 October, a fate his eldest son Aelius Gallus Strabo shared on 24 October. The gap of six days between the executions of father and son was caused by the desperate attempt of Pomponius Secundus to hide the young man from the rampaging mob. Then on 26 October the *Fasti* records that a woman whose name has been lost committed suicide. This would have to be Apicata, as Livilla's death only occurred after Tiberius received the letter from Apicata accusing her of complicity in the murder of his son Drusus. Then in December 'Sejanus' Capito Aelianus and Junilla lay on the Gemonian Stairs'.[4] The delay between the execution of Sejanus' eldest son and youngest children is explained by the emperor's receipt of Apicata's letter and his ensuing desire for vengeance. Dio, however, is in error when he describes how all three of her children were executed together, as the *Fasto Ostiensis* records a delay in the execution of the youngest two, which is supported by Tacitus. Apicata's divorce from Sejanus had initially saved her from sharing her ex-husband's fate, but after her visit to the Gemonian Steps to view the desecrated corpses she welcomed death, for 'after seeing their bodies on the Stairway, she withdrew and composed a statement about the death of Drusus, directed against Livilla, his wife, who had been the cause of a quarrel between herself and her husband, resulting in their separation; then, after sending this document to Tiberius, she committed suicide'.[5]

The hunt for the Sejanii had started to abate at this time, but now the emperor's hopes for peace were destroyed by this one letter. His tortured and suspicious soul sought confirmation of its contents. He was unwilling to accept the logic of Apicata's motivation as a desire for revenge and dismiss its contents, instead he took the information at face value. Macro was empowered to seek the truth by leading an imperial inquiry, which he used to destroy his enemies whilst at the same time feeding Tiberius' fears. It would not have suited his purpose to disprove the accusation. Torture was freely used, with detailed evidence documented for the emperor to read. The prosecutors and defendants, in their desperation to prove or disprove links to Sejanus, often implicated or accused others, who then suffered a similar fate. Many who had suffered at the hands of their rivals now sought to gain revenge through charges of *maiestas*:

> For it happened not only that those who had accused others were brought to trial and those who had testified against others now found others testifying against them, but also those that had condemned others were convicted in their turn. So it was that neither Tiberius spared anyone, but employed all the citizens without exception against one another, nor could anyone rely upon the loyalty of any friend; but the guilty and the innocent, the timorous and the fearless, stood on the same footing when face to face with the inquiry into the charges involving the acts of Sejanus.

Delators were terrified that they could be blamed for acting in the interests of Sejanus rather than Tiberius. As there were open ballots in the Senate, all felt compelled to demonstrate their loyalty by voting for condemnation. Rome's political classes were devouring themselves. Accusations were made to curry favour with Tiberius and Macro; others placed charges through *inimicitia*, or enmity, on their own behalf or that of a relative or *amicus*. Political vendettas could now be settled. Quintus Pomponius Secundus brought charges against Considius Proculus and his sister Sancia. Considius had been celebrating his birthday before being dragged to the Senate-house, charged, convicted and executed. His sister was exiled. Quintus Pomponius' motive was to gain the favour of Tiberius on behalf of his brother Publius Pomponius Secundus, who was held under house arrest for his close links to Sejanus. The man who had laid charges against his brother was probably Considius. Many of those convicted turned informer, leading to the destruction of many more. In AD 32 Cestius Gallus wrote a letter to the distant emperor accusing the former praetor and *amicus* of Germanicus, Q. Servaeus and the equestrian Minucius Thermus, of links to Sejanus. Both of the charged elicited the sympathy of the Senate as they had not become arrogant once they had secured the *amicitiae* of Sejanus, unlike many of their peers. Cestius was instructed by the emperor to read the letter to the Senate. This is clear evidence that the emperor was taking a lead in the destruction of Sejanus' network of *amicitiae*. Both of the accused were condemned but turned informer, making allegations against Julius Africanus and Seius Quadratus. Cestius was rewarded with a consulship in AD 35. The praetor Sextius Paconianus, upon being convicted of plotting with Sejanus against Caligula, turned informer, frustrating for a while the satisfaction of 'long cherished hatreds'. The opportunities that now existed from the two inquiries marshalled by Macro were seized on by the ambitious and aspiring, just as Sejanus had exploited these cravings. The first inquiry was into the 'plot' by Sejanus to overthrow Tiberius and remove Caligula, and the second into the 'plot' of AD 23 that led to the alleged poisoning of Tiberius' son Drusus. Macro himself had the opportunity to remove supporters of Tiberius Gemellus, clearing the way for the succession of Caligula and constructing his own position of power and influence.[6]

Livilla was among the first victims of the investigation into Drusus' death. Dio confusingly records two accounts of her death; in one he describes her executed at the emperor's command, and the other account relates a temporary reprieve from this gruesome fate by her mother Antonia, who instead starved her daughter to death in her villa.[7] Apicata's and Sejanus' two remaining children were no longer spared. Perhaps Apicata, blinded by grief, thought their youth would protect them. She was wrong. Their horrendous deaths in the *carcer* shocked even the most hardened of Sejanus' enemies:

> They were therefore carried to the dungeon, the boy conscious of the fate in store for him, the girl so completely ignorant that she asked repeatedly what her offence had been and to what place they were dragging her; she would do wrong no more, and she could be cautioned with the usual childish beating. It is recorded by the authors of the period that, as it was considered an unheard thing for capital punishment to be inflicted on a virgin, she was violated by the executioner with the halter beside her; they were then strangled, and their young bodies thrown on the Gemonian Stairs.[8]

Apicata's father, the gourmet Apicius, is said to have killed himself at an unknown date when he realized his huge wealth had been consumed. Having spent a hundred million sesterces on his kitchen, and with only ten million left, dreading the approach of poverty he chose to commit suicide. Contextually, the loss of his daughter would fit the scenario of his suicide, wishing to join his daughter and grandchildren, knowing that the emperor's retribution would soon be descending upon him. He chose to face death stoically and in a manner that mirrored his life.[9]

The fates of most of Sejanus' other relatives are unknown. Sejanus' adopted brother Seius Tubero was already described as 'in failing health'[10] in AD 24. He is unlikely to have been still alive in AD 31. Another Tubero,

Aelia Paetina, who was married to Claudius, was divorced by her husband around this time 'for slight offences'. Perhaps these were her tenuous links to Sejanus. She survived, and in AD 48 she was again considered as a potential bride of her ex-husband, who was now emperor. Sejanus' uncle Q. Junius Blaesus committed suicide, the emperor sending a letter to the Senate upon the news of his death in which he 'laid many revolting charges' against him.[11] Blaesus' children Q. Blaesus, the *suffect* consul of AD 26, and his brother Lucius survived for a short time, but finding priesthoods that Tiberius had promised them given to others, they too chose to end their lives. Both knew that the public withdrawal of imperial favour invited prosecution and certain condemnation.[12]

The list of those condemned for their association with Sejanus is dominated by the members of the senatorial class, with a scattering of equites. The slaves and freedmen of his household, or those of Apicata, Livilla or Blaesus, would have suffered torture at the hands of Macro, who had been tasked with destroying all those members of Sejanus' 'conspiracy' against the emperor and his son Drusus. Macro was chosen 'to crush Sejanus and had tormented the state by crimes worse than his' and, in a comparison with his predecessor, he 'practised the same arts with superior secrecy'. The fall of Livilla was accompanied by another frenzy of accusations. A fragment of Tacitus' lost fifth book describes that 'forty-four speeches were delivered on this subject, a few because of fear, rather more simply out of routine'. The context of this probably relates to the arrest of Livilla. Allegations of adultery were now targeted against political opponents. As with those charged with conspiring with Sejanus, many nameless victims were brought to Capri for questioning before their broken bodies were thrown from the cliff-top next to the Villa Jovis. A party of marines was stationed below to dispatch with oars and boat hooks any victim who showed any sign of life.[13]

Incriminating evidence, if it can be named as such, was also provided by Satrius Secundus, who is described as 'the divulger of the plot'.[14] Along with Natta he had prosecuted Cremutius Cordus in AD 25 at Sejanus' bidding, and is subsequently described as controlling access to his patron, along with Pomponius Secundus.[15] He turned informer to save his own life, but his knowledge of Sejanus' network of *amicitiae* would have allowed Macro to destroy hundreds. His knowledge of Drusus' co-operation with Sejanus in the destruction of his brother Nero may account for the fact he was not released from his prison under the palace after the fall of Sejanus. Tiberius probably had no real intention of releasing him except if he had been forced to by a successful rising of the Praetorian Guard led by Sejanus.

Drusus, along with his mother Agrippina, would have rejoiced at the news of Sejanus' death and hoped for release. It was not to be. It was not in Macro's interests to press for their freedom, as he firmly attached himself to the future of Caligula. Agrippina would have been able to counter his influence over Caligula, whilst his elder brother would have been the heir to the throne. Drusus was starved to death, forced to eat the contents of his mattress, his every plea and curse recorded by his Praetorian Guards and relayed to the emperor. Tiberius ordered the account of Drusus' last days be read to the horrified Senate. Despite the emperor's hatred for Sejanus, he clearly believed the accusations made against Drusus, whom, even after his death, he charged 'with unnatural vice and with sentiments pernicious to his family and dangerous to the state'. Many had believed the fall of Sejanus would save Agrippina's offspring, but the emperor's reaction to his death reveals the depth of Tiberius' hatred for both mother and son.[16]

Shortly after this Agrippina, with nothing now to live for, refused all food and was allowed to die. She passed away on the same day as Sejanus, two years previously. Tiberius' letter to the Senate, informing them of her death, commented with pride that he had not had her strangled, nor had he ordered her body thrown on the Gemonian Stairs like that of Sejanus. The emperor clearly continued to believe that she had conspired against him. The Senate decreed that 18 October be consecrated to Jupiter forever. An issue of *dupondii* carrying the legend *clementia*, in recognition of the emperor's supposed mercy shown towards Agrippina, probably dates from this time.[17] The campaign against the family of Germanicus, orchestrated by Sejanus, clearly had Tiberius' full backing. He was obsessed by conspiracies, plots and treachery, which Sejanus used to his own advantage.

Armed with information provided by torture and Satrius Secundus' spurious evidence, Macro filled the prisons in Rome to capacity. Many, clearly not senators or prominent equestrians, were not tried before the Senate, but instead before the magistrates. Conviction led to strangulation or being thrown from the Tarpeian Rock, a steep cliff at the summit of the Capitoline Hill. The two consuls and tribunes supervised these proceedings, including L. Fulcinius Trio. Injustice must have burned the hearts of the condemned.[18] Suetonius provides a description of the atmosphere that existed in the days, weeks and months following 18 October AD 31:

> Not a day, however holy, passed without an execution; he [Tiberius] even desecrated New Year's Day. Many of his male victims were accused and punished with their children – some actually by

their children – and the relatives forbidden to go into mourning. Special awards were voted to informers who had denounced them, and, in certain circumstances, to the witnesses too. An informer's word was always believed.

The prohibition on mourning places these events to the purges following the execution of Sejanus and the numerous nameless individuals who were members of the lower strata of society who had looked to their patron for protection against the vicissitudes of life.[19] Despite the constant stream of death, the prisons remained full of those accused of being Sejanus' *amici* and clients. For nearly two years they had awaited their fate, until in August AD 33 Tiberius decided to empty the prisons in the only manner he knew:

[He] gave orders for all persons in custody on the charge of complicity with Sejanus to be killed. On the ground lay the huge hecatomb of victims: either sex, every age; the famous, the obscure; scattered or piled in mounds. Nor was it permitted to relatives or friends to stand near, to weep over them, or even to view them for too long; but a cordon of sentries, with eyes for each beholder's sorrow, escorted the rotting carcasses, as they were dragged to the Tiber, there to float with the current or drift to the bank, with none to commit them to the flames or touch them. The ties of our common humanity had been dissolved by the force of terror.

As many as twenty a day were executed in this way.[20]

Macro was a driving force behind this destruction, using his influence and proximity to the emperor to ensure all those associated with his predecessor were destroyed. Dio describes how many were destroyed 'by means of the papers of Tiberius and the statements obtained under torture by Macro'. These papers must be the accusations sent to the emperor by *delators* in Rome, along with the written evidence of so-called witnesses to support their accusations. Many, through fear of being accused themselves, became fervent prosecutors to prove their loyalty, whilst the convicted provided evidence against others in the desperate hope for a pardon. Sextius Paconianus had been granted a temporary stay by turning informer and denouncing Latinius Latiaris, the man who had led the entrapment of Agrippina's loyal *amicus* Titius Sabinus. The sight of the two attacking each other 'furnished the most grateful of spectacles'; for whom, Tacitus fails to say. For many former *amici* of Sejanus in the Senate chamber this would have been uncomfortable viewing, but by necessity, their active encouragement would have been forced upon them. By AD 35, however, Sextus Paconianus was to be found in prison. Suetonius records how life was treated with disdain in the vicious world of courtly politics:

> An ex-consul has recorded in his memoirs that he attended a banquet at which Tiberius was suddenly asked loudly by a jester near the table: 'What of Paconius [Paconianus]? Why is he still alive after being charged with treason?' Tiberius told him to hold his saucy tongue; but a few days later requested the Senate to make a decision about Paconius' execution.

Whilst the jester would have had no interest in Paconianus' fate, Macro certainly would. Paconianus had spent the time during his incarceration productively writing verses castigating Tiberius. He was strangled; there is no evidence of any trial or charge. It would appear that under the feral atmosphere associated with the purges, death was the penalty for libel as well as treason.[21]

Another prominent associate of Sejanus destroyed by Macro was Fulcinius Trio. As *suffect* consul in AD 31, he appears to have saved himself by taking a prominent role in the prosecution of Sejanus' *amici* and clients. He officiated at the executions of many who were thrown from the Tarpeian Rock, and attacked his fellow consul Regulus in the Senate 'for slowness in crushing the creatures of Sejanus'. Regulus accused his colleague of complicity in Sejanus' 'plot'. Members of the Senate now intervened, urging them to 'lay down an enmity bound to have a fatal issue'. A truce was called, but the following year the despised former consul of AD 22, Haterius Agrippa, ever the seeker of imperial favour, attempted to exploit the febrile atmosphere, reopening their conflict by accusing both of complicity with Sejanus, as evidenced by their failure to charge each other. The consular senator Sanquinius Maximus poured oil on stormy waters by urging the Senate not to disturb the tranquillity of the emperor, a suggestion heartily supported by the Senate. However, in AD 35 fate and Macro caught up with Trio, who took his own life, despised and surrounded as he was by his accusers. In his will, he wrote a condemnation of the emperor and 'an appalling indictment of Macro'. Charges of *maiestas* associated with the name of Sejanus were normally a certain recipe for condemnation. Gnaeus Cornelius Lentulus Gaetulicus, the governor of Germania Superior since AD 29, had been ordered by the emperor around AD 30 to betroth his daughter to the son of Sejanus. He would have known that this was now an opportunity for an ambitious senator to lay charges of treason against him, but he had an insurance policy: the legions under his command, whose loyalty to him was assured. Sure enough, in AD 34 a former aedile who had previously been legate of one of Gaetulicus' legions charged him with *maiestas*. Gaetulicus cashed in his insurance policy and wrote a letter to the emperor, reminding him that the marriage proposal was at his request and that his 'loyalty was inviolate, and if he was not treacherously attacked, would so remain'. The emperor, wanting to avoid a civil war, took him at his word and his accuser found himself condemned and exiled. No doubt one of the governor's aristocratic *amici* made a counter-charge of *calumnia*, false prosecution.[22]

Many of those charged with *maiestas*, such as Fulcinius Trio and P. Vitellius, committed suicide. This was partly due to the horror that awaited them in the *carcer*, but also because:

> [They hoped] that their children might inherit their property, since very few estates of such as voluntarily died before their trial were confiscated, Tiberius in this way inviting men to become their own murderers, so he might avoid the reputation of having killed them – just as if it were not more dreadful to compel a man to die by his own hand than to deliver him to the executioner. Most of the estates of those who failed to die in this manner were confiscated, only a little or even nothing at all being given to his accusers.

Suetonius, however, records that the Senate voted to award extraordinary rewards for prosecutors following the execution of Sejanus. Perhaps these were later reduced as the plague of accusations and counter-accusations spiralled out of control.[23] A prominent senator whose name has been lost due to a gap in the preserved text of Tacitus stood before the Senate shortly after the deaths of Sejanus and Q. Blaesus to denounce the hypocrisy of those who now condemned him:

> The tide has turned, and while he [Tiberius] who designated the fallen [Sejanus] as colleague [in his shared consulship] and son in law pronounces his own exculpation, the rest, who fawned upon him in their degradation, now persecute him in their villainy. Which is the more pitiful thing – to be arraigned for a friendship or to arraign the friend – I do not seek to determine. I shall experiment

with the cruelty of none, the mercy of none: a free man, approved by my own conscience, I shall anticipate my danger. I conjure you to preserve my memory not more with sorrow than in joy, and to add me, one name more, to the roll of those who by a notable ending found an escape from public calamity.[24]

The speech expresses a desire that his memory be preserved, his suicide pre-empting the passing of a *damnatio memoriae*. The accused then retired to his house, where he received visitors who expected him to resist the charges: an unrealistic proposition in light of the carnage all around. Instead, in front of his *salutatio*, he drew a sword that he had concealed in his toga and fell upon it. His bravery saved his memory, and no doubt his family, from a worse fate. Unfortunately, his name has been lost to posterity.[25]

The fall of this prominent senator was a rarity for those who held similar rank and status. Junius Blaesus shared his fate due to his close familial relationship with Sejanus. The nobility looked after their own. It was the junior members of the Senate, the equestrians and freedmen with links to Sejanus, who suffered and died. L. Fulcinius Trio was twice saved by the Senate, in AD 31 and 32, before Macro forced the issue. Publius Pomponius Secundus, although convicted of *maiestas*, was, due to his brother's influence, only placed under house arrest, and was then released by Caligula to serve as governor of Crete and Cyrenaica before attaining the consulship under Claudius and the governorship of the strategically important province of Germania Superior. Another well-connected noble who survived his close links to Sejanus was the former praetor L. Apronius Caesianus, who was charged with *maiestas* but was pardoned by the emperor and would attain the consulship in AD 39 under Caligula. There can be little doubt that his father's influence secured the safety of his son. L. Apronius was governor of Lower Germany, with command of its legions, and his son-in-law Cornelius Gaetulicus was governor of Upper Germany. Domitius Afer, the great orator and *delator* who had prosecuted Agrippina's cousin Claudia Pulchra and later her son, would survive the reign of Tiberius without charge and use his skills, augmented with fawning servility, to escape a prosecution of *maiestas* under Caligula.[26]

The aristocratically named M. Porcius Cato, who bore witness against Sabinus, was awarded a *suffect* consulship in AD 36. Another member of the nobility, Gaius Fufius Geminus, the ordinary consul of AD 29, was executed before AD 32; not for any association with Sejanus, but because he had made jokes to his patroness Livia that mocked Tiberius. His mother shared his fate for publicly mourning her son. The only other persons from the upper echelons of society to pay a significant cost for their links to Sejanus were possibly the equestrian governor of Egypt, Gaius Galerius, who was recalled and drowned on his journey to Rome, and M. Aurelius Cotta Maximus Messalinus. Cotta stood accused of questioning the sexuality of Caligula, but he was an exception in that he was despised by his fellow nobles as the 'father of every barbarous proposal and therefore the object of inveterate dislike', yet he had imperial protection and so escaped.[27] The nobility was predestined to hold the great senatorial magistracies, but they still had to court Sejanus as he was the primary broker of imperial patronage. The consuls and other members of the elite regularly attended his *salutatio*. The names of these nobles are absent from the lists of those sentenced and condemned. Instead, it was those who had held the office of praetor or more junior posts, and members of the equestrian class, who felt the full force of 'justice'. The equestrian Terentius only saved himself by the powerful truth of his speech that made a connection with the senators, who in recognition of his bravery acquitted him.

The nobles who died during these purges were not *amici* of Sejanus but those who fell foul of the rising power of Macro. Five prominent senators were attacked in AD 32, but they survived due to the intervention of the emperor. Many in the Senate were related in some way to one of these men and so felt the threat of potential prosecution. Appius Silanus and Calvisius Sabinus were exonerated by one of the prosecutors, Celsus, a tribune in the urban cohorts. The alibi he provided was the probable reason for his demise. The following year, Celsus himself was arrested and committed suicide by breaking his neck using the chains he had been bound with in the prison. His fate was shared by his fellow equestrian Geminus, who 'through his prodigal expenditure and effeminacy of life, was certainly a friend of Sejanus, but to no serious purpose'. He does not appear to have been associated with the charges made against Celsus, but had instead been counted amongst the *amici* of Sejanus as he had borrowed money from his patron to finance his lavish lifestyle. It is evident that those who lacked the powerful bonds of *amicitiae* that the nobility possessed were fair game. One member of the aristocracy accused of *maiestas*, Calvisius Sabinus, may have had family ties to Sejanus' close *amicus* P. Pomponius Secundus, as his name appears in a fragmentary inscription as '...isius Sabinus P. Pomponius Secundus'. Calvisius' status and connections enabled him to escape the charges. He would go on to govern the strategic province of Pannonia. Another noble, Gaius Annius Pollio, and his son Lucius Annius

Vinicianus, along with the distinguished orator Mam. Aemilius Scaurus, had their cases adjourned until the emperor could hear them in person before the Senate; an event that all recognized as highly unlikely. It would appear that the influence of M. Aemilius Lepidus, a close *amicus* of both Tiberius and Annius Vinicianus, was brought to bear. However, the fate of Scaurus was only delayed. In AD 34 he was charged with adultery with Livilla and the use of magic. Tacitus is clear that his 'fall was brought about, not by the friendship of Sejanus but by something equally potent for destruction, the hatred of Macro'. A charge of *maiestas* linked to Sejanus or Livilla was often more than enough to ensure the accused lost the *amicitiae* of the emperor, even if the charges were unfounded or they were proven innocent. However, those who had personal access to the emperor or could exert their influence through one of his close *amici* could expect a safer passage through the trials and tribulations of Roman political life. Scaurus was an exception. He had been viewed with suspicion by Tiberius since the very start of his reign, and for this reason looked to Sejanus. It would not have taken much for Macro to poison the aged emperor's perceptions of this noble. Tacitus describes him as 'a man of distinguished rank and ability as an advocate, but of infamous life'. In AD 21 he defended the young aristocrat Lucius Sulla, along with L. Arruntius, who also felt the enmity of Macro. Scaurus was persuaded by his wife Sextia to commit suicide rather than face condemnation and conviction. His wife chose to share his fate.[28]

L. Arruntius, the probable fulcrum of the opposition to Sejanus, was also destroyed by Macro. In AD 37 the Senate received a host of documents extracted by Macro using torture that implicated Arruntius in treason and adultery, along with the aristocrats Vibius Marsus, the *suffect* consul of AD 17, and Gnaeus Domitius Ahenobarbus, consul of AD 32 and husband of Agrippina the Younger. There was, however, no covering letter submitted by the emperor, who was laid low by illness and, it was believed, on the point of death. Clearly many believed that Macro could have been acting without imperial approval. The Senate took the risk of delaying the trial until the emperor could be consulted. However, Arruntius, wearied by his opposition to Sejanus, could only look to a future dominated by Macro and Caligula, and so took his own life.[29]

Yet again the aristocracy closed ranks to protect its own. Macro now identified Domitius Ahenobarbus as a threat to himself and Caligula, as this illustrious and unsavoury noble could claim an imperial heritage. He had also been accused of committing adultery with Albucilla, the ex-wife of Satrius Secundus. That Satrius Secundus survived is remarkable and points to the protection of an extremely powerful figure at court: Macro. He continued to serve a use after he helped to identify members of Sejanus' network of clients and friends. It would make sense for charges of adultery to be laid by an estranged ex-husband, who could claim intimate knowledge of his wife's indiscretions and also feel secure from counter-charges being made by the *amici* of Domitius Ahenobarbus. Others also stood accused of adultery with Albucilla: the ex-praetor Carsidius Sacredos, the junior senator Pontius Fregellanus and D. Lealius Balbus, a man of savage eloquence who was always 'ready against the innocent', a 'master of truculent eloquence – the ever ready foe of innocence'. Balbus, ennobled by the consulship held by his father, had made a significant number of enemies. His sister was married to Vibius Marsus and his daughter was married to the adopted son of L. Arruntius. Like the destruction of Sejanus' network of *amicitiae*, Macro now targeted that of his potential rivals in preparation for the accession of Caligula. Sacredos was banished to an island, whilst Fregellanus and Balbus were expelled from the Senate. Balbus' career would be resurrected and he attained a *suffect* consulship in AD 46. Albucilla's fate was gruesome in the extreme. She attempted suicide in the Senate by stabbing herself but she was 'saved', only to be strangled in the *carcer*. Justice had to be seen to be done, and her suicide would have deprived the prosecution of their reward. She was another victim of courtly politics. Those who lacked the connections or name could do little apart from hope for a different fate. Domitius Ahenobarbus remained free and died of natural causes in AD 41, although he was exiled in the last year of Tiberius' life, charged with incest with his sister Domitia Lepida. Vibius Marsus also escaped death, and in AD 47 he was appointed to the governorship of Syria. The names of those who attacked the *amici* of Sejanus are a roll call of the great nobility. They bear the cognomens Scipio, Cassius and Silanus. The emperor gave the nobility the freedom to attack their opponents and they were joined by other aspiring junior senators otherwise lacking the wealth and connections to advance their position but now hoping to gain the gratitude and favour of the emperor. According to Dio, so many senators 'and others' lost their lives in the purges that governorships had to be held for three years by ex-praetors and six by former consuls. However, the vast majority of individuals who are named in our sources are either equestrians or minor senators. It was Caligula who in AD 38 turned on those whose status and connections had preserved them from prosecution. Many were executed by him and 'punished because of the wrongs done to his parents or to his brothers or the others who had perished on their account'. There can be little doubt that these were members of the aristocracy, a class this emperor now despised, having found many to have been involved in conspiracies against him.[30]

Tiberius allowed this atmosphere of terror to develop not from a position of weakness but strength.[31] He would have been well aware of the proscriptions of 43 BC that were used by the Triumvirs – Mark Antony, M. Aemilius Lepidus and Octavian, as Augustus was then known – to eliminate their opponents. Their enemies were listed for death, with their condemnation and execution a matter of course. Tiberius, though, was unable to identify all those he suspected of working with Sejanus and Livilla, despite the inquiries led by Macro. The *delators* acted as both the investigative arm of the state and the prosecution in the absence of any such governmental mechanisms.[32] The political conflict that erupted in the form of accusation, counter-accusation and the culture of informing was impossible to control, yet it fulfilled Tiberius' purpose.

The need to prove their loyalty to the emperor, and so renounce Sejanus, was felt at all levels of Roman society. From the upper strata, the governor of Crete and Cyrenaica made a public demonstration of his loyalty in vows permanently preserved in his dedication: 'To the divinity and providence of Tiberius Caesar Augustus and the Senate, in memory of that day, which was 18th October. Publius Viriasius Naso, proconsul for a third year, consecrated this at his own expense.'[33] An inscription from the small town of Interamna in Umbria records the dedication of a priest of the imperial cult, Faustus Titius Liberalis, who no doubt felt compelled by his role to also give vows to the safety of the emperor. He had little to fear from the carnage engulfing the more illustrious figures. In his dedication, Sejanus is portrayed as a monster who threatened the very stability of the Roman state, which was preserved by the watchfulness of the emperor:

> To the perpetual Augustan safety and the public liberty of the Roman people. To the municipal genius in the 704th year from the foundation of Interamna to the consulship of Gnaeus Domitius Ahenobarbus and [Lucius Arruntius Camillus Scribonianus]. To the providence of Tiberius Caesar Augustus, born for the eternal endurance of the Roman name, upon the removal of the most pernicious enemy of the Roman people: Faustus Titius Liberalis servir Augustalis for a second time, had this made at his own expense.[34]

The motivation behind another inscription found on the Via Flaminia near Capena is self-evident:

> To Tiberius Caesar Augustus, son of the divine Augustus, pontifex maximus, consul five times, in his 34th year of tribunician power, best and most just princeps, saviour of his country, for his welfare and safety; Aulus Fabius Fortunatus, consular and Praetorian messenger, first *Augustalis*, erected this in fulfilment of a vow.[35]

Valerius Maximus, writing towards the end of Tiberius' reign, denounces Sejanus, who remains nameless in his work due to the *damnatio memoriae*. The writer denounces his unrestrained ambitions that threatened the stability of Rome's domain; a world that was saved by the vigilance of the emperor, a repeated motif that appears to have been promoted by Tiberius himself:

> But the eyes of the gods were awake, the stars retained their force, the altars, couches and temples were protected by a present divine power and nothing which ought to have kept watch over the head of Augustus and the fatherland allowed itself drowsiness, and above all the author and defender of our safety saw to it by divine wisdom that his own most excellent achievements would not be destroyed in the ruin of the whole world.

The repeated allusions to the divine *Providentia* now becomes a prevailing theme in imperial propaganda. Tiberius is portrayed as possessing a divine ability to foresee the conspiracy of Sejanus and make the necessary steps to crush it. Imperial propaganda sought to demonize Sejanus as the epitome of evil, in counterpoint to the emperor as the guardian of peace and order which was linked to the imperial cult.[36]

Despite this, there were some who were prepared to publicly demonstrate their loss of loved ones accused of *maiestas* through their links to Sejanus. They went into public mourning for those relatives, *amici*, clients and patrons who had died through their own hands or those of the state. Tiberius had initially banned the relatives of the deceased to go into mourning, but after a significant period of time 'he permitted all those who so desired to go into mourning for Sejanus' and others who had lost their lives. The men would have worn black, whilst under the Empire it became customary for women to wear white. The mourners would have let their hair grow and not worn any jewellery or other ornamentation.

Public grieving for those who had been condemned under *maiestas* could be interpreted as a political act, an open demonstration of sympathy for those who had been executed for treason, and implied criticism of the emperor. This amnesty was, however, rapidly rescinded, perhaps when the numbers of those wearing distinctive mourning dress became politically embarrassing. However, many of those who had been brave or foolish enough to trust the emperor's word found themselves accused 'on sundry lawless charges' as they were now vulnerable. The prisons were soon full again and the slaughter continued to the end of Tiberius' reign.[37]

Surprisingly, according to Tacitus, it was Sejanus who acted as a restraint on Tiberius' cruelty, for whilst the partner of his labours lived, the emperor was 'still an amalgam of good and evil; so long as he loved, or feared, Sejanus'.[38] This observation on the restraining influence of the Praetorian Prefect on his emperor is echoed in Suetonius, who, commenting on the behaviours of Tiberius, notes that with 'Sejanus out of the way his savageries increased; which proved that Sejanus had not, as some thought, been inciting him to commit them'.[39] The internecine strife that erupted under the direction of Tiberius and Macro appears to support this, although this was partly brought about by the emperor's desire for revenge on a man whom he had trusted implicitly and whom he believed had murdered his son. It was in Macro's interests, as previously it had been in Sejanus', to feed the imperial vengeance in the pursuit of a 'truth' that Macro ensured favoured himself.

Ironically, it was now in the twilight of his life that Tiberius, the reluctant emperor, once more took an active role in the dispensing of justice; his justice. A perpetual state of terror spurred him on, tormented by the ghost of Sejanus' 'treachery'. An imperial letter read to the Senate reveals to all a man surrounded by daily terrors: 'My lords, if I know what to tell you, or how to tell it, or what to leave altogether untold for the present, may all the gods and goddesses in Heaven bring me to an even worse damnation that I now daily suffer!'[40] By contrast, we remember how Sejanus met his end with dignity, killed by a letter.[41] Condemned without trial, he rose from his seat in the Senate, refusing to protest, to plead his case, devoid of self-pity but exhibiting a studied poise as the abuse and blows rained down upon him as he was marched to the *carcer* and a gruesome death. Even Tacitus, Sejanus' unrelenting critic, grudgingly admits that he was a man 'fearless by temperament'.[42] Tiberius, one of Rome's greatest generals at the dawn of the Empire, was, by contrast, diminished by his words and actions. The emperor was by nature distant, suspicious, vindictive and wary;

a flawed personality that was to a certain degree compensated by a powerful intellect and immense learning. He had become, in his old age, an island. Dio is mistaken in explaining that the emperor's trust in Sejanus was based on the similarity of their characters. Both shared a certain arrogance that permeated the whole of the Roman upper classes, but there the similarity ended. Sejanus was a counterpoint to the emperor's damaged personality and personal failings. He was the consummate politician, ever ready to build relationships, being 'orderly and modest to outward view', able to conceal and persuade. He was a supremely capable administrator who was 'efficient and cunning enough to do what was required of him' and, in doing so, demonstrate on a daily basis both 'industry and vigilance'.[43] Sejanus' position at the side of the emperor allowed him to demonstrate his abilities and gradually relieve Tiberius of those tasks and responsibilities from which he had grown tired. Fortune clearly favoured her devotee with the death of Drusus, but it was not to the goddess that he owed his greatest debt of gratitude but to Tiberius himself. It was the gradual withdrawal of the emperor from public life and many of his imperial duties that enabled Sejanus to fill the resulting political vacuum and rise to the very summit of power in Rome. To all he appeared to be emperor in all but name. Juvenal asks:

> Do you wish to be greeted like Sejanus? To be as rich? To dispense the seats of highest office to some, and to appoint others to army commands? To be seen as the emperor's guardian as he sits on the narrow rock of Capri with his herd of Chaldaeans [astrologers]? I'm sure you'd like his javelins and cohorts and excellent cavalry and personal barracks. Why wouldn't you? Even people with no desire to kill like the power to do so.[44]

Sejanus certainly sent many to gruesome deaths; a fate he shared. History has condemned him as a villainous monster driven by an all-consuming ambition that ultimately destroyed him. Maybe so, but was he any worse than the emperor himself, or his successor Macro, or indeed all those other Praetorian Prefects who aspired to the post that Sejanus established as the pre-eminent office in the equestrian career? An office that enabled future occupants to be the maker and breaker of emperors. However, Sejanus' power, status and influence transcended them all. As men came to hate or love Caesar because of his command over life and death, a man possessing the power to grant or deny the advantages that wealth, rank, praetorships and consulships brought, so they hated or loved Sejanus.[45]

Julio-ClXaudian Family Tree

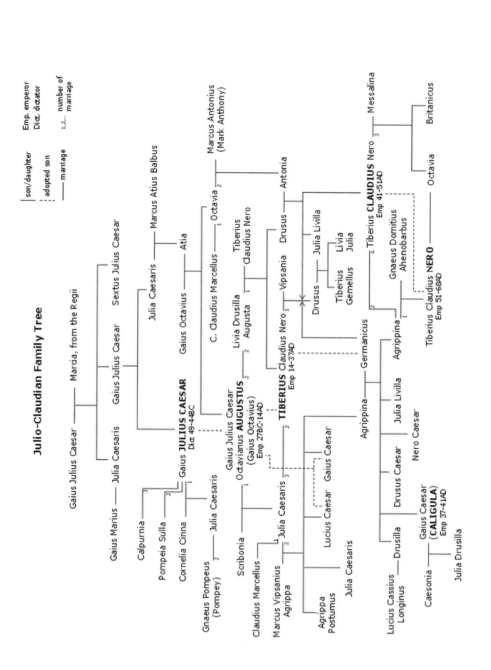

Emp. emperor
Dict. dictator

1,2... number of marriage

son/daughter
adopted son
marriage

Family Tree of L. Aelius Sejanus (Conjectured)

KEY
Genetic Relationship
Adopted
= Married

A. Terentius Varro

A. Terentius Varro Murena
Consul 23 BC

Maecenas

Terentia

M. Seius

Terentis. A.

[Junius]

Q. Junius Blaesus
Consul AD 10

?

L. Junius Blaesus
Consul 28 AD

Q. Junius Blaesus
Consul AD 26

Consconia Gallita 1.

L. Seius Strabo

2. Junia 1.

2. Q. Aelius Tubero

1. Sulpicia

Aelia

L. Cassius
Longinus
Consul AD 11

C. Cassius Longinus
Consul AD 30

L. Cassius Longinus
Consul AD 30

L. Seius Tubero
Consul AD 18

Q. Aelius Tubero
Consul 11 BC

Sex. Aelius Catus
Consul AD 4

Claudius

Aelia Paetina
(Divorced AD 31)

C. Propertius
Postumus

Aelia Gallia

L. Aelius Gallus
Prefect of Egypt 26–24 BC

M. Gabius Apicius

2. Livilla

1. L. Aelius Sejanus
Consul AD 5

Apicata

C. Ateius Capito
Consul AD 5

Aelius Gallus Strabo

Junilla

Capito Aelianus

Timeline

Key Events

27 BC: Octavian is called Augustus. He establishes the Principate, cloaking supreme power in the offices, powers and customs of the old Republic.

25 BC: Marriage of Marcellus and Julia the Elder.

23 BC: Death of Marcellus.

22 BC: Conspiracy of A. Terentius Varro Murena against Augustus. Tiberius prosecutes Fannius Caepio.

21 BC: Julia the Elder, the daughter of Augustus and Scribonia, marries Marcus Vipsanius Agrippa.

20 BC: Marriage of Tiberius and Vipsania, the daughter of M. Vipsanius Agrippa.

   c. 20 BC: Birth of Sejanus

18 BC: M. Vipsanius Agrippa granted tribunician power.

15 BC: Tiberius and his brother Drusus Nero campaign in Rhaetia and Vindelicia. Germanicus born on 24 May.

14 BC: Drusus probably born to Tiberius and Vipsania.

12 BC: Death of Augustus' deputy Marcus Vipsanius Agrippa in February. Birth of Agrippa Postumus. Tiberius forced to divorce Vipsania and engaged to Julia the Elder. Tiberius campaigns in Illyricum.

11 BC: Tiberius continues to campaign in Illyricum. Tiberius granted proconsular *imperium*. Tiberius marries Julia the Elder.

10 BC: Tiberius continues to campaign in Illyricum.

9 BC: Death of Tiberius' brother Drusus Nero whilst on campaign in Germany

8 BC: Death of Maecenas, Augustus' close *amicus*. Tiberius campaigns in Germany.

6 BC: Tiberius' tribunician power renewed but he chooses to go into voluntary exile in Rhodes.

5 BC: Gaius and Lucius Caesar raised to adulthood.

2 BC: Julia the Elder exiled for adultery and treason. Augustus annuls her marriage to Tiberius. Office of Praetorian Prefect created by Augustus and held by Q. Ostorius Scapula and Publius Salvius Aper.

1 BC: Sejanus accompanies Gaius Caesar to the East.

AD 1:   Gaius Caesar made consul.

AD 2:   Death of Lucius Caesar, brother of Gaius. Tiberius allowed to return to Rome but prohibited from entering public life.

AD 4:   Death of Gaius Caesar on 21 February. Tiberius adopted by Augustus and recognized as his successor by receiving tribunician power. Germanicus is adopted in turn by Tiberius despite having a son of his own. Agrippa Postumus also adopted by Augustus. Tiberius campaigns against the Marcomanni, who threatened Pannonia and Noricum.

AD 5:   Tiberius campaigns in Germany.

AD 6:   Tiberius campaigns in Illyricum and Pannonia after a widespread revolt that also encompasses Dalmatia. *Vigiles* created to serve as firefighters and night watchmen.

AD 7:   Agrippa Postumus, the youngest son of Julia the Elder, exiled. Tiberius campaigns in Illyricum.

AD 8:   Julia the Younger, eldest daughter of Julia the Elder, accused of adultery with Decimus Junius Silanus. Her husband, Lucius Aemilius Paullus, also executed around this time, probably for conspiracy. Julia the Younger and Silanus exiled and Paullus executed. Tiberius continues to campaign in Illyricum.

AD 9:   Illyrian and Pannonian Revolt ends. In September, three legions destroyed in Germany under the command of Publius Quinctilius Varus.

AD 10:   Tiberius campaigns in Germany in order to stabilize Rome's position on the Rhine.

AD 11:   Tiberius campaigns in Germany.

AD 12:   Tiberius campaigns in Germany and awarded a triumph. Germanicus consul. Birth of Caligula (31 August) to Agrippina the Elder and Germanicus.

AD 13:   Tiberius receives equal *imperium* to that of Augustus and his tribunician power renewed.

AD 14: 19 August Death of Augustus at Nola made public by Livia and Tiberius. Tiberius ascends the throne.

c. 21 August Agrippa Postumus executed.

3 September News of mutiny of the Pannonian legions reported to Tiberius. Reports of the mutiny on the Rhine soon follow. Germanicus travels to the Rhine from carrying out a census in Gaul to deal with the revolt in the two German provinces.

4 September Tiberius and Livia enter Rome escorting the body of Augustus. Sejanus probably appointed to Praetorian prefecture as colleague alongside his father, L. Seius Strabo, who had been made Praetorian Prefect late in the reign of Augustus. Sejanus takes command of a strong force of Praetorians who start to march north to counter the mutiny in Pannonia, accompanied by the aged Gneaus Cornelius Lentulus the Augur. Rome enters a period of official mourning for Augustus.

8 September Funeral of Augustus.

17 September Senatorial meeting addressed by Tiberius and his son Drusus grant Augustus divine honours and discuss Tiberius' constitutional position.

18 September Date Drusus probably sets out for Pannonia.

21 September Likely that Drusus reached Sejanus and the Praetorian force marching north.

27 September Arrival of Drusus in the camp of the Pannonian legions near Emona. Lunar eclipse allows Drusus the opportunity to undermine support for the mutiny amongst the soldiers.

12 October The mob in Rome riots after protests in the theatre.

Late AD 14: Julia the Elder dies. Germanicus ends the revolt amongst the legions on Rhine and campaigns beyond the Rhine until late AD 16.

AD 15: L. Seius Strabo appointed Prefect of Egypt, leaving his son as sole Praetorian Prefect. Riots again break out in the theatre. Tiberius' son Drusus made consul.

AD 16: Clemens, Agrippa Postumus' former slave who posed as his master, captured after trying to raise a revolt against Tiberius. Agrippina saves a retreating Roman army from destruction by preventing a bridge across the Rhine at Vetera from being demolished by panicking soldiers. On 13 September Marcus Scribonius Libo Drusus charged with treason and use of magic, and convicted by the Senate.

AD 17: Germanicus recalled to Rome and awarded a triumph. (May) Drusus campaigns in Illyricum and beyond the Danube until late AD 20, accompanied by his wife Livilla. Temporarily returns to Rome in December AD 19 and March AD 20. Germanicus sent on embassy to the East. Rebellion of Tacfarinas.

AD 18: Tiberius consul with Germanicus.

AD 19: 10 October, death of Germanicus in Syria. Birth of Tiberius Gemellus and his twin Tiberius Claudius Germanicus (died in AD 23).

AD 20: Construction starts on the Praetorian Fortress. Sejanus' daughter Junilla engaged to the young son of Claudius. The arrangement is short-lived due to the death of her betrothed. Trial and conviction of Gnaeus Calpurnius Piso on the charge of treason and poisoning Germanicus. Death of Tiberius' former wife Vipsania.

AD 21: Tiberius shares the ordinary consulship with his son Drusus. In March Tiberius, probably accompanied by Sejanus, retires to Campania. In May *Arval Brethren* offer sacrifices for the recovery of an important figure, interpreted as Drusus who was seriously ill. Revolt of Florus and Sacrovir in Gaul. Sejanus' uncle, Junius Blaesus, made proconsul of Africa and campaigns against Tacfarinas. Late AD 21, trial of Clutorius Priscus.

AD 22: Early in year Drusus joins his father in Campania and, in his absence, the Senate give him *tribunicia potestas*, granting him equal powers to Tiberius, effectively making him joint emperor. In May Tiberius returns to Rome as Livia is seriously ill. Drusus and Sejanus probably return at the same time. Fire destroys the Theatre of Pompey but further damage is prevented by the actions of Sejanus. Late AD 22, coins issued celebrating Livia's recovery. In the winter Junius Blaesus hailed imperator by his troops for victories over Tacfarinas in Africa, although the war continues.

AD 23: Completion of the Praetorian Fortress. The Praetorian guard probably expanded by three additional cohorts. In September, death of Drusus followed by his son Tiberius Claudius Germanicus. Sejanus divorces Apicata.

AD 24: In January, Tiberius disapproves of the public prayers offered to Germanicus' two eldest sons, Nero and Drusus. Trial of C. Silius and his wife Sosia for *repetundae* and *maiestas*. Silius commits suicide and his wife is exiled. Vibius Serenus the Elder prosecuted by his own son, Vibius Serenus the Younger. Death of Tacfarinas.

AD 25: At the start of the year, Sejanus' *amici* Satrius Secundus and Pinarius Natta prosecute Aulus Cremutius Cordus after he made disparaging remarks about the erection of a statue of Sejanus in the repaired Theatre of Pompey. Sejanus requests permission from Tiberius to marry Drusus' widow Livilla, but is denied.

AD 26: Cn. Domitius Afer prosecutes Claudia Pulchra, Agrippina's cousin. Agrippina confronts Tiberius as he was sacrificing to the divine Augustus, accusing him of persecution. During her subsequent illness Agrippina demands permission to remarry, a request ignored by the emperor. Tiberius leaves Rome for Campania and Capri, accompanied by a small party of intellectuals, philosophers, *amici* and Sejanus.

AD 27: Early in the year, Tiberius journeys to Capri but returns to the mainland to provide assistance after the collapse of the temporary amphitheatre at Fidena leaves thousands dead and injured. Sejanus and the Praetorians would have accompanied the emperor. A fire soon after on the Caelian Hill destroys a large number of properties. The unrest these events would have unleashed, and the continued absence of Tiberius, would have meant that Sejanus was likely to have returned to the capital at this time. Late in AD 27, prosecution of Agrippina's prominent *amicus* Titius Sabinus by Latiaris, Cato, Opsius and Petilius Rufus, all hoping to gain the favour of Sejanus.

AD 28: Tiberius accuses Sabinus of corrupting imperial freedmen and he is executed. Marriage of Germanicus' daughter Agrippina the Younger to Cn. Domitius Ahenobarbus.

AD 29: Death of Livia, Tiberius' mother, in September. In October Germanicus' widow Agrippina and her son Nero accused of immorality and exiled. Caligula and his brothers and sisters, Agrippina the Younger, Drusilla and Livilla, placed into the care of their grandmother Antonia.

AD 30: Asinius Gallus held under house arrest. Drusus, the son of Agrippina the Elder, accused of immorality and imprisoned in cells under the imperial palace in Rome. Sejanus betrothed to Livilla. In December, Sejanus departs from Capri for Rome to commence his consulship but Tiberius, his consular colleague, remains on the island.

AD 31: In January, Sejanus organizes a popular assembly on the Aventine Hill on the commencement of his consular office. In early AD 31 Caligula is summoned to Capri by Tiberius.

8 May AD 31: Tiberius and Sejanus lay down their consulships. Sejanus receives *proconsular imperium*.

Between June and September AD 31: Nero induced to commit suicide on the island of Pontia.

1 October AD 31: Faustus Cornelius Sulla replaced as a *suffect* consul by Publius Memmius Regulus.

17 October AD 31: Macro enters Rome during the night with letters and instructions from Tiberius.

18 October AD 31: After imperial letter read to the Senate by Regulus, Sejanus is denounced and taken to the *carcer*. A second Senate meeting in the Temple of Concordia orders the execution of Sejanus and his body is exposed on the Gemonian Steps. Praetorians and the mob riot, hunting down known *amici* and clients of Sejanus.

24 October AD 31: Sejanus' eldest son Aelius Gallus Strabo executed.

26 October AD 31: Apicata sends letter to Tiberius accusing Sejanus and Livilla of poisoning his son Drusus. She then commits suicide.

December AD 31: Execution of Sejanus' remaining young children, Capito Aelianus and Junilla.

AD 32: Death of Livilla.

AD 33: Death of Asinius Gallus. Death of Drusus and then his mother Agrippina the Elder (18 October) through starvation. In August Tiberius orders the execution of all those *amici* and clients of Sejanus still held in prison. Caligula marries Junia Claudilla, and his sisters Drusilla and Julia Livilla marry L. Cassius Longinus and M. Vinicius. Livilla and Drusus' daughter Julia marries C. Rubellius Blandus.

AD 34: Suicide of Mam. Scaurus.

AD 35: Suicide of Fulcinius Trio.

AD 37: Death of Tiberius on 16 March and accession of Caligula (Gaius).

Late AD 37/early AD 38: Tiberius Gemellus put to death by Caligula.

Consular List

AD 1
Ordinary consuls
Gaius Julius Caesar
L. Aemilius Paullus
Suffect consul
M. Herennius Picens

AD 2
Ordinary consuls
P. Vicinius
P. Alfenus Varus
Suffect consuls
P. Cornelius Lentulus Scipio
T. Quinctius Crispinus Valerianus

AD 3
Ordinary consuls
L. Aelius Lamia
M. Servilius
Suffect consuls
P. Silius
L. Volusius Saturninus

AD 4
Ordinary consuls
Sex. Aelius Catus
C. Sentius Saturninus
Suffect consuls
C. Clodius Licinius
Cn. Sentius Saturninus

AD 5
Ordinary consuls
L. Valerius Messalla Volesus
Cn. Cornelius Cinna Magnus
Suffect consuls
C. Vibius Postumus
C. Ateius Capito

AD 6
Ordinary consuls
M. Aemilius Lepidus
L. Arruntius
Suffect consul
L. Nonius Asprenas

AD 7
Ordinary consuls
Q. Caecilius Metellus Creticus Silanus
A. Licinius Nerva Silanus
Suffect consul
Lucilius Longus

AD 8
Ordinary consuls
M. Furius Camillus
Sex. Nonius Quinctilianus
Suffect consuls
L. Apronius
A. Vibius Habitus

AD 9
Ordinary consuls
C. Poppaeus Sabinus
Q. Sulpicius Camerinus
Suffect consuls
M. Papius Mutilus
Q. Poppaeus Secundus

AD 10
Ordinary consuls
P. Cornelius Dolabella
C. Junius Silanus
Suffect consuls
Q. Junius Blaesus
Ser. Cornelius Lentulus Maluginensis

AD 11
Ordinary consuls
M. Aemilius Lepidus
T. Statilius Taurus
Suffect consul
L. Cassius Longinus

AD 12
Ordinary consuls
Germanicus Julius Caesar
C. Fonteius Capito
Suffect consul
C. Visellius Varro

AD 13
Ordinary consuls
C. Silius A. Caecina Largus
L. Munatius Plancus Paulinus

AD 14
Ordinary consuls
Sex. Pompeius
Sex. Appuleius

AD 15
Ordinary consuls
Drusus Julius Caesar
C. Norbanus Flaccus
Suffect consul
M. Junius Silanus

AD 16
Ordinary consuls
T. Statilius Sisenna Taurus
L. Scibonius Libo Drusus
Suffect consuls
C. Vibius Rufus
P. Pomponius Graecinus

AD 17
Ordinary consuls
C. Caecilius Nepos Rufus
L. Pomponius Flaccus
Suffect consuls
C. Vibius Marsus
L. (?) Voluseius Proculus

AD 18
Ordinary consuls
Tiberius Caesar Augustus (III)
Germanicus Julius Caesar (II)
Suffect consuls
L. Seius Tubero
L. (?) Livineius Regulus
C. Rubellius Blandus

AD 19
Ordinary consuls
M. Junius Silanus
C. Norbanus Flaccus Balbus
Suffect consul
P. Petronius

AD 20
Ordinary consuls
M. Valerius Messalla
M. Aurelius Cotta Maximus Messallinus

AD 21
Ordinary consuls
Tiberius Caesar Augustus (IV)

Drusus Julius Caesar (II)
Suffect consuls
Mam. Aemilius Scaurus
Cn. Tremellius

AD 22
Ordinary consuls
Decimus Haterius Agrippa
C. Sulpicius Galba
Suffect consuls
C. Cocceius Nerva (or AD 21)
C. Vibius Rufinus (perhaps *suffect* consul of AD 16)

AD 23
Ordinary consuls
C. Asinius Pollio
C. Antistius Vetus
Suffect consul
C. Stertinius Maximus

AD 24
Ordinary consuls
Sergius Cornelius Cethegus
L. Visellius Varro
Suffect consuls
C. Calpurnius Aviola
P. Cornelius Lentulus Scipio

AD 25
Ordinary consuls
M. Asinius Agrippa
Cossus Cornelius Lentulus Lethegus
Suffect consul
C. Petronius

AD 26
Ordinary consuls
Cn. Cornelius Lentulus Gaetulicus
C. Calvisius Sabinus

Suffect consuls
Q. Junius Blaesus
L. Antistius Vetus

AD 27
Ordinary consuls
L. (formerly Cn.) Calpurnius Piso
M. Licinius Crassus Frugi
Suffect consuls
P. Cornelius Lentulus
C. Sallustius Passienus Crispinus

AD 28
Ordinary consuls
C. Appius Junius Silanus
P. Silius Nerva
Suffect consuls
L. Junius Silanus
L. Junius Blaesus

AD 29
Ordinary consuls
C. Fufius Geminus
L. Rubellius Geminus
Suffect consuls
A. Plautius
L. Nonius Asprenus

AD 30
Ordinary consuls
L. Cassius Longinus
M. Vinicius
Suffect consuls
C. Cassius Longinus
L. Naevius Surdinus

AD 31
Ordinary consuls
Tiberius Caesar Augustus (V)
L. Aelius Sejanus

Suffect consuls
Faustus Cornelius Sulla
Sex. Tedius Valerius Catullus
L. Fulcinius Trio
P. Memmius Regulus

AD 32
Ordinary consuls
Cn. Domitius Ahenobarbus
L. Arruntius (Furius) Camillus Scribonianus
Suffect consul
A. Vitellius

AD 33
Ordinary consuls
L. Livius Ocella Ser. Sulpicius Galba
L. Cornelius Sulla Felix
Suffect consuls
L. Salvius Otho
C. Octavius Laenus

AD 34
Ordinary consuls
Paullus Fabius Persicus
L. Vitellius
Suffect consuls
Q. Marcius Barea Soranus
T. Rustius Nummius Gallus (perhaps a *suffect* consul of AD 26)

AD 35
Ordinary consuls
C. Cestius Gallus
M. Servilius Nonianus (*suffect?*)
Suffect consuls
D. Valerius Asiaticus
A. Gabinius Secundus

AD 36
Ordinary consuls
Sex. Papinius Allenius

Q. Plautius
<u>*Suffect* consuls</u>
C. Vettius Rufus (?)
M. Porcius Cato

<u>AD 37</u>
<u>Ordinary consuls</u>
Cn. Acerronius Proculus
C. Petronius Pontius Nigrinus
<u>*Suffect* consuls</u>
Caligula
Claudius

A. Caecina Paetus

Appendix: The Family, *Amici* and Clients of Sejanus

Aelius Catus, Sextus

The consul of AD 4 was probably the son of Q. Aelius Tubero the jurist and his first wife Sulpicia. Tubero's subsequent marriage to Junia, Sejanus' mother, made them stepbrothers. Inscriptions record him as governor of Macedonia and Moesia in the early years of the first century. He may have been the Aelius Catus mentioned by Strabo who transplanted 50,000 Getae across the Danube. He was probably no longer alive at the time of Sejanus' fall. Aelia Paetina, who was possibly his daughter, was married in AD 28 to the future Emperor Claudius, but she was suddenly divorced in AD 31.[1]

Aelius Gallus, L.

The second Prefect of Egypt from 26–24 BC, who was replaced by Augustus after his failed expedition into Arabia Felix. Despite this he appears to have been considered a suitable adoptive father of Sejanus. The wealth Gallus must have accumulated as governor of Egypt would have been an incentive as the adoption would have made Sejanus his only son, although he did have a daughter, Aelia Gallia.[2]

Aelia

The daughter of Q. Aelius Tubero the jurist. She married L. Cassius Longinus, the consul of AD 11, and was the mother of L. Cassius Longinus and C. Cassius Longinus, both consuls in AD 30.[3]

Aelia Paetina

A member of the noble family of Aelii Tuberones, possibly the daughter of Q. Aelius Tubero, the consul of 11 BC, or his brother Sex. Aelius Catus, consul in AD 4. She married the future Emperor Claudius in AD 28, but was suddenly divorced in AD 31, the year of Sejanus' fall, 'for slight offences'. Possibly her distant connection with Sejanus through her grandmother Junia, who was the mother of Sejanus, may account for this decision. She survived, as Claudius later considered remarrying her, partly as they previously had a daughter together. Instead the emperor married Agrippina the Younger. Paetina's daughter Antonia was executed by Nero in AD 65 or 66.[4]

Aelius Gallus Strabo

The eldest son of Sejanus and Apicata. He fled to the house of P. Pomponius Secundus to escape the rioting mob upon Sejanus' execution on 18 October AD 31. However, he was soon captured and executed on 24 October. The exposure of his body on the Gemonian Steps led to his mother Apicata writing to Tiberius to allege that his son Drusus had been poisoned by her ex-husband and Livilla.[5]

Aelius Tubero, Q. (father)

A member of the noble Aelii Tuberones which was granted patrician status by Augustus. He was the son of L. Aelius Tubero, an *amicus* of Cicero. Born *c*. 80 BC, he had fought at the Battle of Pharsalus alongside his father, but was pardoned by Julius Caesar. He appears never to have attained the consulship. He had three sons and a daughter with his first wife Sulpicia, but upon her death he probably married Junia. Upon his death, Junia married L. Seius Strabo, who adopted Tubero's youngest son L. Seius Tubero, the consul of AD 18. He is likely to be the Tubero to whom Dionysius dedicated his treatise of Thucydides, as Dionysius was in Rome from 30–8 BC, although the work may have been dedicated to his son. He was an accomplished jurist and historian, writing a history of Rome.[6]

Aelius Tubero, Q. (son)

The consul in 11 BC is likely to be the son of the jurist and stepbrother of Sejanus.[7]

Aemilius Scaurus, Mam.

The consul of AD 21 was a noble, poet and orator. He was described by Tacitus as a man 'distinguished by birth and by his talent as an advocate, but in life a reprobate. His fall was brought about, not by the friendship of Sejanus but by something equally potent for destruction, the hatred of Macro.' According to Tacitus, Tiberius hated Scaurus, which might account for his links to Sejanus, to whom he looked for protection. He escaped charges of *maiestas* in AD 32 along with Annius Pollio, Appius Silanus, Calvisius Sabinus and L. Annius Vinicianus. They were probably accused of tampering with the urban cohorts in the supposed plot of Sejanus. Tiberius postponed the trial until he could appear in the Senate to hear it in person. However, in AD 34 he was prosecuted by Cornelius and Servilius at the bidding of the Praetorian Prefect, Macro. He was charged with criticizing the emperor in his work *Atreus*. Dio adds that another charge of adultery with Livilla was added, and the use of magic. Facing almost certain condemnation, he committed suicide along with his wife Sextia. He must have been linked to Sejanus and Livilla for the charges to have some credibility, although the adjournment of the case in AD 32 by the emperor might suggest the association was not close.[8]

Apronius Caesianus, L.

He was a well-connected noble who survived his close links to Sejanus. He served in the war against Tacfarinas under his father's command and brought the Numidian to battle, driving his army into the desert. At the age of 22 he was awarded membership of the priestly college of the *septemviri epulonum*, probably due to the influence of his father L. Apronius, who by then was governor of Germania Inferior with command of its legions. He was elected praetor but was then charged with *maiestas* due to his close relationship with Sejanus, but was pardoned by the emperor. Not only had Apronius Caesianus been a friend of Sejanus, but he had made a joke at the expense of the emperor during the festival of the Floralia, where he 'had seen to it that all the merry-making up to nightfall was done by bald headed men, in order to poke fun at the emperor, who was bald, and at night had furnished light to people as they left the theatre by torches in the hands of five thousand boys with shaved pates'. Many had been executed for less. There can be little doubt that his father's influence secured the safety of his son. Caesianus would attain the consulship in AD 39 under Caligula.[9]

Asinius Gallus Saloninus, C.

A noble whose desire to be ranked amongst the most prominent men in the Senate led to a series of impolitic choices that served to stoke the emperor's hatred of him. He had married Tiberius' first wife Vipsania after the future emperor had been forced by Augustus to divorce her in favour of Julia. Tiberius was heartbroken, but he appears to have directed his enmity towards Asinius Gallus rather than Augustus. Gallus then made the mistake of attempting to adopt Tiberius and Vipsania's son Drusus. The attempt failed, but Tiberius would not forgive, nor forget. Gallus was not trusted by Augustus, who, when discussing with Tiberius possible threats to his throne, warned him that Asinius Gallus was both 'eager and unfit'. This is reflected in his career. Upon Tiberius' accession Gallus made a number of impertinent comments that both offended and angered the new emperor. Tiberius also suspected that Agrippina the Younger planned to marry him, as he later accused him of adultery with her. By AD 30 Gallus 'was now paying court to Sejanus, either sincerely, because he believed this minister would become emperor, or out of fear of Tiberius'. Both motives were probably behind his approach. However, Sejanus knew any association with Asinius Gallus was poison to his relationship with Tiberius, and so he denounced him. Tiberius sent a message to the Senate 'declaring among other things that this man was jealous of the emperor's friendship with Sejanus'. Meanwhile, Gallus had been invited to Capri, where he was at first nobly entertained and then, after his condemnation in the Senate, was led away by a praetor sent to arrest him. He spent the rest of his life enduring a miserable existence in solitary confinement until he starved to death in AD 33.[10]

Ateius Capito, C.

Sejanus' youngest son Capito Aelianus appears from his name to have been adopted by a 'Capito', most likely this man, the consul of AD 5. He was renowned as a great jurist and prominent senator. In AD 11 he was appointed to the post of *curator aquarum* with responsibility for the water supply for the capital, and in AD 15, along with L. Arruntius, was tasked with dealing with the problem of flooding by examining the possibility of damming rivers and lakes that fed the Tiber. In AD 22 Capito criticized the emperor for refusing to accept the charges of *maiestas* made against L. Ennius, most likely the son-in-law of Tiberius' astrologer Thrasyllus. According to Sumner he died in AD 22. He appears to have had no descendants, which would support his adoption of Sejanus' son, who was executed in December AD 31.[11]

Apicata

From her name she is likely to be the daughter of the great gourmet and socialite Gavius Apicius. She was married to Sejanus, with whom she bore two sons and a daughter. Sejanus divorced her in AD 23 at the request of Livilla, for whom she developed an understandable hatred. The execution of her eldest son, and exposure of his body, led to her own suicide after writing a letter to the emperor alleging the involvement of her ex-husband and Livilla in the poisoning of Drusus. Postumus revenge was obtained with the execution of Livilla.[12]

Apicius (Gavius Apicius, M.)

A gourmet and lover of luxury, his banquets were sumptuous in the extreme and were attended by the elite of Roman society, including Maecenas and Tiberius' son Drusus. He is said to have committed suicide upon learning that his fortune had been reduced to 10 million sesterces, having spent a huge amount of money on improving his kitchens. He was alive in AD 28 as he entertained the consuls of that year, including L. Junius Blaesus, and the historian Asconius Pedianus. It is likely that the suicide of his daughter and execution of his grandchildren would have cast a dark shadow over his life and contributed to his decision to kill himself. Had he chosen a different course he would not have survived the vengeance of Tiberius, who believed his daughter Apicata had long kept secret the poisoning of his son Drusus by Sejanus and Livilla.[13]

Aruseius, L.

Along with Sanquininus he prosecuted L. Arruntius at some point between July and October AD 31, possibly for *maiestas*, upon the command of Sejanus. Tiberius intervened to quash the indictment. Aruseius and Sanquininus were then charged with *calumnia*, the making of a false accusation. Found guilty, he was deprived of his senatorial status. He was pardoned in AD 36 when others were being executed, which caused much indignation in the Senate.[14]

Avillius Flaccus, A.

An equestrian and close friend of Tiberius, he had laid charges against Agrippina the Elder that led to her exile. In AD 32 or 33 he was appointed Prefect of Egypt. This was probably his reward for the action against Agrippina. His survival after the fall of Sejanus points to few links with the fallen Praetorian Prefect. However, his fears over the rise of Agrippina's son Caligula would have made him a supporter of Tiberius Gemellus, so he possibly joined in common cause with Sejanus believing he was acting in the interests of the emperor. Emperor Caligula exacted his revenge on the man who contributed to the death of his mother: he was recalled and executed in AD 39.[15]

Bruttedius (Bruttidius) Niger

Juvenal calls him Bruttidius. An accomplished orator, he studied under rhetorician Apollodius of Pergamum. He was possibly related to the rhetor Bruttedius Brutus, mentioned by Seneca, but they may be the same man. Clearly a gifted and skilled senator and 'new man', he is described by Tacitus as being 'amply provided with liberal accomplishments and bound, if he kept the straight road, to attain all distinctions'. He wrote a history covering the death of Cicero. Described by Tacitus as a client of Sejanus, he prosecuted C. Silanus, the proconsul of Asia in AD 22, along with another of the prefect's clients, Junius Otho, and the noble Mamercus Aemilius Scaurus. Tacitus implies that Niger undertook the prosecution to increase his own political influence. He was aedile in AD 22 but appears to have held no further offices. This was possibly because he became infamous for prosecuting supposedly decent men. The only other known case that he undertook was against Vallius Syracus. He was too closely associated with Sejanus and so made a desperate attempt to disassociate himself on his patron's fall by kicking his corpse, which, from the inferences made by Juvenal, failed to save him.[16]

Capito Aeli(anus)

The youngest son of Sejanus, who was probably adopted by C. Ateius Capito. He was executed in December AD 31 and was old enough to realize the fate that awaited him as he walked to the *carcer* attempting to comfort his younger sister.[17]

Cassius Longinus, C.

Descendant of an ancient and noble family, his grandfather had been involved in the murder of Julius Caesar. Gaius was the son of Aelia and L. Cassius Longinus, the consul of AD 11, and so the grandson of Q. Aelius Tubero the jurist. He was the *suffect* consul in AD 30, an honour he shared with his brother in the same year, who was an ordinary consul. He was only distantly related to Sejanus, which enabled him to prosper after the Praetorian Prefect's fall. A Cassius was involved in the attack on Agrippina's son Drusus at the instigation of Sejanus. It is highly unlikely either Gaius or his brother Lucius are meant, as their marriages demonstrate continued imperial favour. He married Junia Lepida, who was descended from Augustus, and under Caligula he became proconsul of Asia in AD 40/41.[18]

Cassius Longinus, L.

Lucius, the brother of C. Cassius Longinus, was the ordinary consul of AD 30. In AD 33 Tiberius married him to Drusilla, the daughter of Agrippina the Younger and sister of the future emperor Caligula. Upon Caligula's accession to the throne he ordered Lucius to divorce Drusilla, so she could marry his close *amicus* Marcus Aemilius Lepidus. He was an affable character not made for imperial politics, as he would proudly and naively boast that his ancestor had murdered Julius Caesar. Despite this he was made governor of Syria, but was exiled by Nero.[19]

Cassius

Sejanus employed a Cassius as *delator* against Drusus Caesar, the son of Germanicus and Agrippina. He probably used information supplied by Drusus' wife Aemelia Lepida in his charges.[20]

Cornelius Lentulus Gaetulicus, Cn. (consul AD 26)

The scion of the powerful aristocratic family of the Corneli Lentulii. The ordinary consul of AD 26 was the son of Tiberius' close *amicus* Cossus Cornelius Cn. Lentulus whom he made City Prefect in AD 33 until his death in AD 36. At some point after his consulship Gaetulicus was made governor of Germania Superior, with its powerful legions, whilst his father-in-law Lucius Apronius commanded the legions of Germania Inferior. This made both of them secure from the repercussions associated with the fall of Sejanus. Tiberius had requested that Gaetulicus betroth his daughter to a son of Sejanus, probably Aelius Gallus Strabo. This left him vulnerable, and in AD 34 he was accused of *maiestas* by Abudius Ruso, an ex-legate of one of Gaetulicus' legions and a former aedile. Gaetulicus sent a letter to Tiberius, assuring the emperor of his loyalty so long as he 'was not treacherously attacked'. The charge was dropped and Ruso suffered the consequences of his risky venture. Tacitus remarks 'that, alone of all the family connections of Sejanus, Gaetulicus remained unscathed and high in favour'. That is until the reign of Caligula, when in AD 39 the emperor rushed north to the capital of Germania Superior at Moguntiacum to execute Gaetulicus, who appears to have conspired with Marcus Aemilius Lepidus, Agrippina the Younger and Livilla, Caligula's sisters, to murder the emperor. Gaetulicus was a man of culture and learning, writing poems in Greek, including some on erotic themes as well as a history, probably his memoirs. His elder brother was Cossus Lentulus, the consul of AD 25 AD, and his sister Cornelia married C. Calvisius Sabinus, his fellow consul in AD 26. Gaetulicus' father had in AD 31 frustrated the prosecution of Sejanus opponent L. Arruntius. Gaetulicus had little to gain from any association with Sejanus and it would appear, as his letter suggests, that the betrothal was purely to please Tiberius. The emperor was preparing for Sejanus' regency by securing the loyalty of the Rhine legions to a minority of Tiberius Gemellus or Caligula, guided by the Praetorian Prefect.[21]

Cosconia Gallitta

The first wife of Sejanus' father L. Seius Strabo, she was possibly a patrician and sister of Ser. Maluginensis, *suffect* consul of AD 10, and P. Lentulus Scipio, *suffect* consul of AD 2. However, it is unlikely she was Sejanus' mother, as Junius Blaesus is described as his uncle. Consequently, Cosconia Gallitta is likely to have died, as divorcing this well-connected Roman matron would have created too many powerful enemies for Seius Strabo. Strabo then married a Junia, the sister of Junius Blaesus and mother of Sejanus.[22]

Eudemus

He was the doctor and *amicus* of Livilla who was accused of poisoning her husband Drusus. Pliny embellishes the story, adding that Eudemus was Livilla's lover. Eudemus was tortured after Apicata accused Livilla and Sejanus of murdering the emperor's son. Most historians dismiss the allegations as a fabrication, but Eudemus fell victim to courtly politics.[23]

Fulcinius Trio, L.

A gifted orator and *delator* whose aggressive style of prosecution won him cases but made him many enemies. Tacitus describes him as a genius, who 'was famous among the professional informers'. After his successful prosecution for *maiestas* of the aristocratic Marcus Scribonius Libo, this new man was awarded a share of the condemned's estates. In AD 20 Trio was involved in the prosecution of C. Calpurnius Piso, who was charged with poisoning Germanicus, although Trio was delegated a minor role by charging the accused of corruption and cruelty in his governorship in Spain. Again successful, Tiberius 'promised his support, should he become a candidate for preferment, but warned him not to let impetuosity become the downfall of eloquence'. Surrounded by relatives and *amici* of Calpurnius Piso, he sought the protection of Sejanus. In AD 22 he became the governor of Lusitania, whilst C. Fulcinius Trio, probably his brother, became *praetor peregrinus* in AD 24. According to Dio, it was the influence of Sejanus that earned him a *suffect* consulship on 1 July AD 31. The fall of Sejanus precipitated his own demise, but he desperately clung to his position and his life. He took a lead in the executions of many accused of conspiring with Sejanus, despite the fact the emperor had not trusted him with any role in the overthrow of his patron. His consular colleague Regulus accused him of being an adherent of Sejanus, whilst, in a typically aggressive response, he accused Regulus of laxity in investigating Sejanus' supposed plot. Prominent senators intervened to put a halt to the conflict. In AD 32 Decimus Haterius Agrippa attempted to gain political influence by attacking both ex-consuls, but again the Senate put a stop to arguments. Luckily for Trio, Haterius Agrippa was hated almost as much as he was and, according to Dio, the emperor was still grateful for Trio's prosecution of Libo. However, his past caught up with him in AD 35 when Macro commended his prosecution. Trio, fully aware that his last days had come, wrote his will, in which he denounced the emperor, Macro and the imperial freedmen, and then he committed suicide.[24]

Galerius, C.

The governor of Egypt, Gaius Galerius, was recalled upon the fall of Sejanus and drowned on his journey to Rome. Galerius replaced Seius Strabo in c. AD 16, and unusually stayed in post for many years until suddenly being replaced in AD 31 by Vitrasius Pollio. Vitrasius' short tenure from AD 31–32 was a consequence of his death in office. Uniquely, Vitrasius was replaced not by an equestrian but by a freedman named Hiberus, who appears to have been present in the province administering the estates of Antonia. The removal of Galerius possibly suggests he was an *amicus* of Sejanus. Furthermore, the emergency appointment of Hiberus points to the influence exerted by Antonia after the fall of Sejanus. Hiberus was quickly replaced by Aulus Avillius Flaccus.[25]

Geminius

Put to death in AD 33 for conspiring against Tiberius. He is described by Tacitus as an equestrian, who 'through his prodigal expenditure and effeminacy of life, was certainly a friend of Sejanus, but to no serious purpose'. He no doubt shared with his patron a certain appreciation of the finer things in life and was lent money to attain them.[26]

Julius Africanus

A senator from the Gallic community of the Santones. He was found guilty of *maiestas* in AD 32 after being denounced by Quintus Servaeus and Minucius Thermus, former *amici* of Sejanus who had been condemned and then turned informer in an attempt to save themselves. Africanus shared this fate with Seius Quadratus, who joined the huge numbers of minor senators and equestrians purged after the fall of their patron. His son was a noted orator in the reign of Nero.[27]

Julius Marinus

An equestrian of Gallic or Syrian origin, this old friend of Tiberius had gone with him to Rhodes and Capri. He was executed on Capri in AD 32 for involvement with Sejanus. He appears to have been involved in fall of Curtius Atticus, a distinguished equestrian who had also accompanied Tiberius to the island along with Sejanus. Marinus is described as one of the Sejanus' 'advisers' in Atticus' fall. Levick suggests he may have done so in the belief that he was acting in the interests of Tiberius or Tiberius Gemellus. The Senate celebrated when it heard news of Marinus' death, probably because he had become closely aligned with Sejanus in the court circle that surrounded the emperor on his island.[28]

Julius Postumus

Suborned by Livilla to further poison Livia's mind against Agrippina and her children. Postumus had access to the Augusta through his adulterous relationship with Livia's close *amicus* Mutilia Prisca. According to Tacitus, Postumus was one of several courtiers who spread rumours that Agrippina hoped to become the power behind the throne on the accession of her children, as well as drawing on her popularity with the populace. These reports were meant to feed the Augusta's hatred considering her own fading influence and ignite the emperor's prejudices against the role of women in public life. The thinking of Sejanus was clearly behind these carefully crafted stories.[29]

Junia

The mother of Sejanus, as implied through the position of Q. Junius Blaesus, who is described as Sejanus' uncle. She was married to L. Seius Strabo after her first marriage to Q. Aelius Tubero, the writer and jurist, who had probably died.[30]

Junilla

The daughter of Sejanus and Apicata, executed in December AD 31 with her brother Capito Aelianus. Tacitus, horrified by her dreadful treatment, provides in shocking and poignant detail her last moments: 'They were therefore carried to the dungeon, the boy conscious of the fate in store for him, the girl so completely ignorant that she asked repeatedly what her offence had been and to what place they were dragging her: she would do no wrong no more, and she could be cautioned with the usual childish beating. It is recorded by the authors of the period that, as it was considered an unheard of thing for capital punishment to be inflicted on a virgin, she was violated by the executioner with the halter beside her: they were then strangled, and their young bodies thrown on the Gemonian Stairs.'[31]

Junius Blaesus, Q. (father)

The uncle of Sejanus through his mother. His consulship in AD 10 was too early to have been at the patronage of his nephew, nor his governorship of Pannonia. However, his brother-in-law L. Seius Strabo probably had a hand in the career of this new man, as his office of Praetorian Prefect gave him unrestricted access to Augustus. The revolt of the three Pannonian legions under his command in AD 14 does not appear to have had any negative impact on his career, despite his ineffective attempts to crush it. His slaves and bodyguard of gladiators were imprisoned by the mutinous legionaries and tortured. The influence of Sejanus was felt in Blaesus' appointment to the governorship of Africa and command of the war against Tacfarinas in AD 22. A victory over the insurgents led to an honorary triumph, the last awarded to a general outside the imperial family. This was despite the fact that Tacfarinas remained at large and was not defeated until P. Cornelius Dolabella's campaign. The latter was refused similar honours that had been granted Blaesus, as the emperor felt this would have offended Sejanus. He committed suicide in AD 31 upon the fall of Sejanus and was denounced by Tiberius, who 'laid many revolting charges against Blaesus'.[32]

Junius Blaesus, Q. (eldest son)

The eldest son of the consul of AD 10 was himself consul in AD 26. He had been a tribune in Pannonia in AD 14 and was used as a messenger between the mutinous legions and the emperor. Before Sejanus' fall he had been promised a priesthood, but in AD 36 Tiberius granted it to another. This was interpreted as a fall from imperial favour and, knowing the vultures would be circling, he committed suicide with his brother.[33]

Junius Blaesus, L. (younger son)

The younger son of the consul of AD 10 was probably a *suffect* consul in AD 28. He committed suicide with his brother after the priesthood that had long since been promised him was granted to another. He was well acquainted with Sejanus' ex-father-in-law Apicius, dining at his villa in AD 28 with the Roman historian Asconius Pedianus and sharing their host's interests in gastronomy.[34]

Junius Otho

According to Tacitus, Otho had once been the owner of a 'school', probably teaching rhetoric, who although 'created a senator by the influence of Sejanus, by his effrontery and audacity he brought further ignominy'. Sejanus probably financed the million sesterces qualification for his senatorial status. He was, according to Seneca the Elder, a highly skilled rhetorician and was widely admired. He wrote four books of *colores*. Otho was a praetor in AD 22 and so entered the Senate in the early years of Sejanus' Praetorian Prefecture. He used to practice declamations with Bruttedius Niger, but Seneca considered Otho the superior. Both prosecuted the proconsul of Asia C. Silanus for *maiestas* or *impietas*, Otho doing so to maintain the favour of Sejanus. It is difficult to understand what Sejanus could gain from this prosecution, although Otho would have looked to a share of the accused's estates upon attaining a conviction. He does not appear to have won any further offices, nor is his fate known. His son was a tribune in AD 37 who used his powers to veto a reward granted to D. Laelius Balbus upon the successful prosecution of Acutia, the wife of Sejanus' *amicus* Publius Vitellius. Soon after Lealius was expelled from the Senate and exiled to an island, having been charged with conspiracy along with Albucilla, the former wife of another of Sejanus' *amici*, Satrius Secundus. Levick suggested that all three cases were linked, with relatives of the condemned in each case seeking vengeance. The enmity between the tribune Otho and Laelius probably stemmed from Laelius' prosecution of his father as an *amicus* of Sejanus.[35]

Livilla (Claudia Livia Julia)

The daughter of Tiberius' brother Nero Claudius Drusus and Antonia, and so the sister of Germanicus and the future emperor Claudius. A certain bitter side to her nature is revealed in her arrogant and demeaning attitude towards Claudius, for, when 'his sister Livilla heard someone predict that one day he would succeed to the throne, she prayed openly and aloud that the Roman people might be spared so cruel and undeserved a misfortune'. She is described as being 'in her early days a harsh-favoured girl, later a sovereign beauty'. Her first husband was Augustus' chosen successor Gaius Caesar, and upon his death she was married to Tiberius' son Drusus Caesar. Upon Drusus' death in AD 23 she looked to Sejanus to protect her children, with the succession passing to Agrippina's offspring. There appears to have been a certain degree of discord between the two even whilst their respective husbands were alive, despite the fact both Drusus and

Germanicus exhibited 'a singular unanimity, unshaken by the contentions of their kith and kin'. Her actions also demonstrate that she possessed a burning ambition for herself and her surviving son Tiberius Gemellus. She undoubtedly had an affair with Sejanus, although it is uncertain when this started. She persuaded Sejanus to divorce his wife Apicata in AD 23, but his request to marry Livilla in AD 25 was firmly rejected by the emperor. Finally, as Tiberius looked to the succession, he appears to have relented and the match was agreed in AD 31. Upon the fall of Sejanus and execution of his eldest son, Apicata exacted revenge by sending a letter to Tiberius alleging that Livilla, along with Sejanus, had poisoned his son Drusus. Livilla was either executed or starved to death by her mother Antonia. Early in AD 32 she suffered *damnatio memoriae* when 'stern measures were advocated even against her statues and her memory'. Her name now became a useful tool in the prosecutions and accusations that rent apart the body politic. Her doctor Eudemus and the great noble and poet Mam. Aemilius Scaurus were accused of having had affairs with her.[36]

Lucanius(?) Latiaris, L.

There are some difficulties with his name. He was conceivably the son of the proconsul of Crete under Augustus, Q. Lucanius Proculus, and so possibly the brother of Q. Lucanius Latinus who was the praetor of the treasury of Saturn (*aerarium Saturni*) in AD 19. He was a former praetor who looked to further honours through currying the favour of Sejanus. In AD 27 he used his friendship with one of the few remaining *amici* of Agrippina, Titius Sabinus, to entrap him into making impolitic comments about Sejanus and the emperor. He gained the co-operation of other ambitious senators to act as witnesses: Porcius Cato, Petillius Rufus and M. Opsius. They were also former praetors who hoped through the influence of Sejanus and the favour of the emperor to attain a consulship. These men hid themselves in the ceiling of a room where Latiaris encouraged Sabinus to vent his anger and frustrations at the treatment of Agrippina. A letter and witness statements were then sent to Capri. There appears to have been no trial. An imperial letter read before the Senate denounced Sabinus and he was swiftly executed. In AD 32 Latiaris was denounced in the Senate by Sextius Paconianus, one of Sejanus' former clients, who accused him to save himself. The sight of two former *amici* of Sejanus clashing was enjoyed by those who felt safe from the accusations and counter-accusations that served as the new reality of political life in the Senate, as before them Paconianus laid charges against 'Latinius

Latiaris, accuser and accused – impartially detested as they were – furnished the most grateful of spectacles'. There can be little doubt that Latiaris was executed soon afterwards.[37]

Lygdus

A eunuch in the household of Drusus Caesar who was accused of poisoning his master as part of a plot organized by Sejanus and Livilla. He was doubtless a taster, 'whose years and looks had won him the affection of his master and a prominent place among his attendants'. He was arrested after Apicata's letter reached the emperor on Capri, and a confession was extracted under torture. He was probably one of those thrown from the cliff-tops upon which the Villa Jovis stood.[38]

Minucius Thermus

A prominent equestrian who was denounced, along with senator Quintus Servaeus, in a letter sent to Capri in AD 32 by Gaius Cestius Gallus. Minucius Thermus and his co-defendant were, however, widely admired, as each 'had refrained from abusing his friendship with Sejanus; a fact which gained then particular sympathy'. Tiberius had no such misgivings, and in his letter to the Senate accused them of being 'ringleaders in crime'. Both must have been prominent advisors to Sejanus. Cestius was directed by the emperor to read out the letter he had sent to Capri that included the charges against the two and take a lead in their prosecution. Tiberius clearly demanded a conviction, which was duly delivered. To save themselves, both Thermus and Quintus Servaeus turned informer, denouncing Julius Africanus and Seius Quadratus, and so Rome's elite continued to destroy themselves. The new man Cestius was well rewarded for his diligence in prosecuting the enemies of Tiberius, becoming an ordinary consul in AD 35.[39]

Ollius, T.

Ollius was murdered by the mob after the execution of Sejanus who hunted down known associates of the fallen Praetorian Prefect. He was of non senatorial ancestry but had married well, his wife being the daughter of C. Poppaeus Sabinus who had served as consul in AD 9 and served as governor of Moesia from AD 15 until his death in 35 AD. Ollius had only reached the quaestorship before his death in 31 AD. Despite his marriage Ollius' humble origins had clearly led him to look to the friendship of Sejanus to support his career. His daughter, Poppaea Sabina, was the second wife of the emperor Nero. She took her name from her maternal grandfather, no doubt to disassociate herself from the ignominy of her father's disgrace. Ollius' wife, Poppaea Sabina the Elder, managed to prosper after her husband's death, marrying into the aristocratic family of the Cornelii Scipiones.[40]

Opsius, M.

He acted as a witness in the trial of T. Sabinus in AD 27, wishing to earn the gratitude of Sejanus. He had already been a praetor, but lacked an aristocratic ancestry. By this act he hoped to be rewarded with the consulship, which he appears never to have attained. Along with M. Porcius Cato and Petilius Rufus, he hid in the space between the ceiling and roof to overhear Sabinus criticize both Sejanus and the emperor at the bidding of their fellow conspirator Latiaris. Tacitus promised to describe the fate of these prosecutors, but there is no further comment in surviving books, so this explanation was probably in a lost section, suggesting he fell in the reign of Caligula or immediately after the execution of Sejanus.[41]

Paconius, M.

A junior senator who was a legate of C. Silanus in Asia but then joined with Mam. Aemilius Scaurus and two other *amici* of Sejanus, Bruttedius Niger and Junius Otho, in prosecuting his former governor with *repetunae* and *maiestas* in AD 22. The fall of Sejanus promoted accusations of *maiestas* against him and he languished in prison until a dwarf, no doubt prompted by Macro, asked the emperor: "'What of Paconius? Why is he still alive after being charged with treason?" Tiberius told him to hold his saucy tongue; but a few days later requested the Senate to make a quick decision about Paconius' execution.'[42]

Petilius Rufus

An ex-praetor involved in the attack on Sabinus along with Latiaris, M. Porcius Cato and M. Opius in AD 28. His fate is not recorded, and was probably described in a lost section of the *Annals*. According to S. Rutledge, he later became a consul. His son was consul of AD 74 and governor of Roman Britain.[43]

Pinarius Natta, L.

Described by Tacitus as a client of Sejanus. He prosecuted the historian Cremutius Cordus in AD 25 along with Satrius Secundus. Cordus had angered Sejanus by publicly commenting that the Theatre of Pompey had not been destroyed by the fire that gutted it in AD 22, but when the statue of Sejanus was placed in it. Natta appears to have gained some renown as a social wit and to have been well known to Seneca, who describes the opportunity provided by Sejanus to prosecute Cordus as a 'present'. Struggling to find any evidence or witnesses to charge Cordus with *maiestas*, Natta and Satrius Secundus used Cordus' own work against him and he was charged with praising Cassius and Brutus, the assassins of Julius Caesar. Augustus had banned the public display of images of Cassius and Brutus, so a public reading of Cordus' work could have been legally interpreted as violating the spirit of the law. Seneca compares the two to 'ravening wolves' and 'keen scented hounds' let loose by their patron to hunt down their prey. Cordus realized the futility of attempting a defence and instead chose to slowly starve himself to death. Sejanus' opponents took delight in the frustration of the Praetorian Prefect's plans, so Natta and Satrius Secundus were sent to the consuls to demand Cordus be brought before the Senate and tried before death interceded. Cordus decided to accelerate the process and committed suicide. The protracted debate in the Senate suggests considerable opposition to Sejanus, and it is unlikely Natta received any reward for the prosecution. An inscription records that Natta was from a *municipium* and followed a traditional career path. He was a military tribune in Egypt with the third legion and was appointed praefect of the district of Bericis. He served thereafter as an aedile, then as one of the *duoviri* before attaining the office of quaestor. His fate is unknown.[44]

Pomponius Secundus, P.

An aristocrat with numerous connections to Rome's elite, his father was either Gaius Pomponius Graecinus, *suffect* consul in AD 16, or his brother Lucius Pomponius Flaccus, ordinary consul in the following year. They were new men appointed to the Senate by Augustus. Flaccus was a close *amicus* and drinking companion of Tiberius, and an able commander. He was governor of Moesia in AD 17, where he defeated the rebel King of Thrace, Rhescuporis. He was later appointed to the equally important governorship of Syria in place of Lamia. His tenure was brief, as he died in AD 33. Two fragmentary inscriptions from Germania Superior dated to the year of P. Pomponius Secundus' consulship in AD 44 preserves his full name as '...isius Sabinus P. Pomponius Secundus'. It was possible from this that he was adopted by a Calvisius Sabinus. The consul of AD 26 C. Calvius Sabinus is a possibility. He was a close *amicus* of Sejanus, whose friendship was cultivated by many senators when access to Sejanus became increasingly difficult after Tiberius' withdrawal from Rome. The equestrian Terentius defended his own friendship with Sejanus on the grounds that he did nothing more than those now sat judging him: 'We venerated even Satrius and Pomponius; it was accounted nobly done, if we grew known to his very freedmen and his janitors!' He was charged with *maiestas* after the fall of Sejanus. P. Pomponius Secundus was an accomplished poet and skilled political operator, about whom Pliny wrote a now lost biography. He also wrote tragedies that were performed during the reign of Claudius. Tacitus describes him as 'a man of great refinement of character and shining talents'. The mother of P. Pomponius Secundus and his brother Quintus was Vistilia, who through other marriages was the mother of Rome's great general and consul of AD 39 Gnaeus Domitius Corbulo, Publius Suillius Rufus – who was consul in AD 41 – as well as the last wife of Caligula, Milonia Caesonia. His uncle Sex. Vistilius lost the favour of Tiberius in AD 32, accused by him of spreading rumours that questioned the morals and sexuality of Caligula. Upon the fall of Sejanus in AD 31, P. Pomponius Secundus was accused by Considius Proculus of protecting Aelius Gallus, almost certainly the eldest son of Sejanus. P. Pomponius hid him in his garden, but the young man was soon found and dragged away to execution. Quintus interceded for his brother and stood as a guarantor in exchange for his life. Publius remained under house arrest but at some point he was transferred to prison, where he suffered poor treatment. There he remained for seven years until released by Caligula. A man of great talent, his career quickly blossomed, becoming governor of Crete with Cyrenaica, consul in AD 44 and then governor of Germania Superior.[45]

Pomponius Secundus, Q.

The brother of P. Pomponius Secundus. He was not closely linked to Sejanus, but was an active *delator* in the defence of his brother, exacting revenge on those who had attacked his family as well as attempting to gain the favour of Tiberius at the same time. Two years after Considius Proculus had laid charges against his brother, Quintus moved to exact retribution. Considius was celebrating his birthday when the party was interrupted by an escort to take him to the Senate house. There he was condemned and swiftly executed. His sister Sancia was also exiled. Tacitus describes Quintus as 'a restless character who pleaded that the object of his activity in this and similar cases was, by acquiring the favour of the emperor, to palliate the dangers of his brother Pomponius Secundus'. He was *suffect* consul in AD 41 under Caligula, but a year later he was accused of *maiestas* by his half-brother P. Suillius and he joined the Dalmatian revolt of Marcus Furius Camillus against Claudius. His name was erased from public monuments and the list of consuls, indicating he suffered *damnatio memoriae* and was executed. Surprisingly, the career of Publius does not appear to have been affected and he continued to retain the confidence of the emperor.[46]

Porcius Cato, M.

He had helped to entrap Sabinus in AD 27, hoping to attain the consulship through the favour of Sejanus. His hopes were fulfilled in AD 36, when he was granted a *suffect* consulship. He was possibly related to Cato the Younger and probably a member of the great Republican noble family, which would partly explain the award of consular office when some of the fellow prosecutors of Sabinus appear to have attained no reward. However, the granting of consular office to this known associate of Sejanus is surprising and suggests that the emperor was the driving force behind the persecution of Agrippina and her *amici*, with Sejanus merely adding fuel to the flames of Tiberius' fears and suspicions of his daughter-in-law. Cato had been a praetor at some point before AD 27, as well as a legate in Achaia and *curator aquarum*. Tacitus implies he was executed, probably in AD 38, but the account was in the lost sections of the *Annals*.[47]

Propertius Postumus, C.

Senator married to Aelia Gallia, the daughter of Sejanus' adopted father L. Aelius Gallus. He was probably related to the Umbrian poet Sex. Propertius.[48]

Sanquinius

At Sejanus' request, he brought charges against L. Arruntius between July and October AD 31, along with his fellow prosecutor L. Aruseius. According to Dio it was Tiberius who was responsible for the rejection of the accusations, on the grounds that an indictment could not be made against a serving magistrate. Arruntius had been serving as governor of Hispania Citerior since AD 25, a post he had served *in absentia* at the command of the emperor. A senatorial decree was then passed reinforcing this decision, the proposal being introduced by a Lentulus, probably Tiberius' close *amicus* Lentulus Cossus. Sanquinius and Aruseius were now charged with *calumnia*, or pursuing a malicious and unfounded prosecution, and were both found guilty. Sanquinius was expelled from the Senate. He may have been related to the Augustan financier M. Sanquinius or Q Sanquinius, who reached the praetorship. Another prominent member of the gens was Q. Sanquinius Maximus, who became City Prefect and reached a second consulship in AD 39, and then became governor of Germania Inferior in AD 45. His relationship with these other members of this senatorial house is uncertain.[49]

Satrius Secundus

Tacitus describes him as a client of Sejanus, but he was much more than that. Along with Pomponius Secundus, he controlled access to Sejanus and was clearly a close advisor. He was courted by the elite due to his access and influence with the Praetorian Prefect. He was from Italy's *municipia*, like his patron, and had links with Sulmo. In AD 25 Sejanus instructed him and L. Pinarius Natta to prosecute Cremutius Cordus, who had made derogatory and injudicious remarks after a statue to Sejanus was erected in the Theatre of Pompey. Tacitus describes him as the 'divulger of the plot', implying that it was he who had provided the supposed evidence to support the allegations that Sejanus and his supporters had conspired to murder the emperor. His survival after the fall of Sejanus would be explained by his turning informer in return for the protection of Macro. He was married to Albucilla, who, upon her divorce from Satrius Secundus, became notorious for having numerous lovers. It is probable that Satrius Secundus accused her of adultery with Vibius Marsus, Gn. Domitius Ahenobarbus and L. Arruntius in AD 37, as well as charging her with impiety towards the emperor. The machinations of Macro were behind these allegations. Albucilla attempted to commit suicide, but she failed. She was put on trial before the Senate and then dragged away to prison. L. Arruntius, despairing of the fate of Rome and fatigued by the hatred of first Sejanus, and then Macro, chose to end his life as well. The fate of Satrius Secundus is unknown.[50]

Seius Quadratus

He was possibly a dependant of Sejanus' father Seius Strabo or a member of his family. He was charged with *maiestas* in AD 32 by Q. Servaeus and Minucius Thermus, both of whom had turned informer.[51]

Seius Strabo, L. (Praetorian Prefect)

The father of Sejanus and sole Praetorian Prefect at the end of Augustus' reign. He was an equestrian from the Etruscan town of Vulsinii, modern Bolsena. His grandfather had defeated Pupius Piso in the elections for the curule aedileship in 74 BC, and his father was a wealthy landowner and *amicus* of Varro and Appius Claudius. His main claim to fame was the invention of fois gras. Tiberius appointed Strabo's son Sejanus to hold the post of Praetorian Prefect soon after his entrance into Rome as emperor in AD 14. Sejanus was sent north with Tiberius' son Drusus, whilst Strabo remained in Rome to deal with the potential threat of rioting that Tiberius feared would break out at the funeral of Augustus. In AD 15 or 16 Strabo was made Prefect of Egypt. This was probably seen as a promotion, as the established equestrian career structure of the Empire was still in a state of flux. It is likely he died soon after his arrival in Egypt. An inscription records his mother as 'Terrentis A.'. She has been conclusively identified as the sister of the wife of Gaius Maecenas, Augustus' equestrian *amicus*. It is likely Strabo married Cosconia Gallita before his marriage to Sejanus' mother Junia. This later marital bond provided the powerful equestrian with a link to the rising star of Q. Junius Blaesus, the consul of AD 10. At some point after the marriage to Junia, it is likely Strabo adopted her youngest son from her previous marriage, establishing ties with the noble family of Q. Aelius Tubero. From his nomenclature it is evident that Sejanus was also adopted by an Aelius, the most likely candidate being the former governor of Egypt, L. Aelius Gallus. Gallus had no surviving male children, so Sejanus could be expected to inherit the vast wealth that the disgraced Egyptian prefect had probably accumulated in his tenure of that affluent province.[52]

Seius Tubero, L.

In AD 16 he was a legate of Germanicus, fighting beyond the Rhine commanding the cavalry in one important battle. He must have served with distinction as he was a *suffect* consul in AD 18. In AD 24 Tacitus describes him as one of the 'most prominent nobles' and a 'close *amicus*' of the emperor, but he was suffering from 'failing health'. Both Sumner and Syme suggest he was the son of Q. Aelius Tubero, but he was adopted by Sejanus' father when he married Junia, who had previously been married to the renowned jurist. It is possible Seius Tubero was her son from this marriage, whilst Q. Aelius Tubero (consul in 11 BC) and Sex. Aelius Tubero (consul 4 BC) were the children of Q. Aelius Tubero's first marriage, probably to a Sulpicia. This would account both for the difference in their ages, as deduced from their consulships, and the adoption itself. If Seius Tubero had suffered from poor health in AD 24, it is unlikely he was still alive in AD 31 to witness the fall of Sejanus and suffer the consequences.[53]

Servaeus, Quintus

He served with Germanicus in the East and was appointed the first governor of Commagene upon the kingdom's incorporation into the Roman Empire. The revenues from this, and Cappadocia which was incorporated by Q. Veranius, enabled Tiberius to reduce the unpopular 1 per cent sales tax by half. Clearly, he was an able administrator. He assisted in the prosecution of Piso to avenge the death of Germanicus and fulfil his vow to the dying prince, but was censured by Tiberius, along with the other legates of Germanicus, P. Vitellius and Q. Veranius, for exposing the body of Germanicus to the public to prove that he had been poisoned. Upon the conviction of Piso he received priesthood from Tiberius as a reward. He now became an *amicus* of Sejanus, along with his fellow prosecutors P. Vitellius and Fulcinius Trio. All may have sought the protection of the Praetorian Prefect, as Piso had many powerful relatives and *amici* who would seek to avenge him. In AD 31 Gaius Cestius brought charges against him and Minucius Thermus. Both 'had refrained from abusing his friendship with Sejanus, a fact which gained them peculiar sympathy'. As a consequence Cestius hesitated, but the emperor wanted blood and told Cestius to read out the letter he had sent the emperor on Capri, as well as denouncing both as 'ring leaders'. Both were evidently closely associated with Sejanus. Following their inevitable conviction, they turned informer, accusing Julius Africanus and Seius Quadratus.[54]

Sextius Paconianus, (L.?)

A senator universally hated by the enemies of Sejanus. He was possibly *praetor pereginus* in AD 26 and praetor in AD 32. Tacitus describes him as 'fearless, mischievous, a searcher into all men's secrets, and the chosen helper of Sejanus in the laying of his plot against Gaius Caesar [Caligula]'. A charge came in an imperial letter read to the Senate in AD 32 which denounced Junius Gallio for suggesting in the Senate that Praetorians who had completed their service should be honoured with permission to sit in the first fourteen rows in the theatre, but the letter also accused Sextius Paconianus of plotting the destruction of Caligula on the instructions of Sejanus. Rumours had been circulated in AD 31 that questioned the sexuality of Caligula. The same stratagem that had been used against his brothers Drusus and Nero. M. Cotta Messallinus was also charged with, amongst other things, accusing Caligula of homosexuality. Cotta Messalinus could rely on the protection of Tiberius and escaped. Sextius Paconianus lacked connections and was convicted, but turned informer and accused the equally despised Latinius Latairis who had entrapped Sabinus. Others were to follow Paconianus' move and make accusations in a desperate attempt to save themselves. The Senate thoroughly enjoyed the spectacle of both Paconianus and Latairis sparring with each other in a deadly game of claim and counter-claim. Paconianus only managed to postpone his fate, and was soon imprisoned. He managed to survive the cull of Sejanus' *amici* and clients ordered by the emperor in August AD 33. He was left to rot in prison, but to alleviate his suffering Paconianus wrote lampoons against Tiberius. In AD 35 these poems came to the emperor's attention, so 'Paconianus was strangled in prison for the verses which he had there indicted against the sovereign'. Whether his crime fell under the charge of *maiestas* or libel is irrelevant, as imperial vengeance trumped the niceties of law. There was clearly no trial, and like Sejanus, no opportunity to defend himself.[55]

Sextus Vistilius

Served in Germany as a close *amicus* and legate under Drusus Claudius Nero, Tiberius' brother. Upon the death of Drusus Nero, Tiberius admitted Vistilius into his own network of *amicitiae*. He attained the office of praetor, but there his career ended. His sister was probably the Vistilia who was renowned for having six different husbands and seven children. He was uncle to Quintus and Publius Pomponius Secundus and Gneaus Domitius Corbulo. In AD 32 he was accused by the emperor of slandering the name of Caligula and questioning his sexual appetites: 'The ground of displeasure against Vistilius was either his authorship of certain attacks on the morals of Gaius Caesar or a false statement credited by the emperor.' Vistilius was extremely useful to Sejanus as he was a well-known *amicus* of the emperor, and criticism directed at Caligula would be assumed to have emanated from the emperor himself. Tiberius formally renounced his friendship with Vistilius in a letter to the Senate. Accusations and charges were sure to follow, so Vistilius decided to commit suicide. However, age and 'senile hands' meant that the wound he inflicted on himself was not immediately mortal, and instead he 'bound up his veins, then sent a written plea for pardon, and, on receiving a pitiless reply, opened them again'.[56]

Tiberius Gemellus

Born to Tiberius' son Drusus and Livilla on 10 October AD 19 on the same day Germanicus died in Syria. His twin was named Tiberius

Claudius Germanicus after his father. Tiberius also adopted Germanicus' children Nero and Drusus, indicating that they were his chosen successors. His twin died in AD 23, along with his father Drusus. Sejanus had in AD 23 divorced his wife Apicata and started an affair with Livilla. Sejanus' proposed marriage to Livilla was rejected by Tiberius in AD 25; however, the emperor's withdrawal to Capri in the following year allowed both a far greater degree of political latitude and independence. Sejanus orchestrated a campaign against Agrippina and Nero, no doubt with the tacit backing of Tiberius. Julia Livia, the sister of Tiberius Gemellus, who was married to Nero, provided information on her husband's conversations. In AD 29 Agrippina and Drusus were exiled on charges of immorality, whilst Nero was imprisoned below the palace in the following year. The elderly Tiberius now looked to Caligula and Tiberius Gemellus as his possible successors, but the fall of Sejanus and then the execution of Livilla left the position of young Tiberius Gemellus weak and vulnerable. Tiberius may even have suspected Tiberius Gemellus to be the illegitimate child of Sejanus and Livilla, such was the power of the campaign against him waged by Caligula and the Praetorian Prefect Macro. Despite this, the emperor had declared both Caligula and Tiberius Gemellus as his heirs in AD 35, declaring to Caligula: "'Thou wilt slay him,' he said, 'and another thee.'" The death of Tiberius removed Gemellus' sole protection. The Senate, on the command of Caligula and Macro, ignored Tiberius' will and made Caligula sole emperor. Caligula made a show of adopting Tiberius Gemellus and formally acknowledging his entry into manhood with the grant of the *toga virilis*. By late AD 37 or early AD 38 Tiberius Gemellus was dead, executed by an officer of the Praetorian Guard.[57]

Terentius, M.

An equestrian tried before the Senate for his bonds of friendship with Sejanus, his eloquent and brave speech persuaded the senators to acquit him. He acknowledged that Sejanus had plotted against the emperor, as to admit otherwise would have been both futile and suicidal in the circumstances. He admitted he had actively sought the *amicitiae* of Sejanus and rejoiced when he had gained it. However, he stressed the favour and honours showered on his patron was an indication of imperial favour and that it was not for any man to question the emperor's actions. Terentius stressed that his loyalty to Sejanus reflected his loyalty to the emperor. Every senator knew that he had spoken the truth and acknowledged his courage in doing so.[58]

Terrentis A.

The mother of L. Seius Strabo and grandmother of Sejanus. An inscription from Volsini honours an unnamed Prefect of Egypt, commonly identified as Seius Strabo, who was married to a 'Terrentis A.'. Her sister was married to Augustus' close *amicus* Maecenas and she was the sister of A. Terentius Varro Murena, who conspired against Augustus.[59]

Vescularius Flaccus

An old *amicus* of Tiberius who had accompanied him to Rhodes and then Capri. He was executed on Capri in AD 32, along with Julius Marinus. The latter was executed for his part in Sejanus' plot against Curtius Atticus. It is likely the Vescularius Flaccus was closely associated with Sejanus, as he remained a member of the courtly circle whilst Sejanus was based partly in Rome. Flaccus may have been his eyes and ears, sending regular reports to the capital in the belief he was acting in the interests of Tiberius Gemellus. Dio records that Sejanus 'had furthermore made all the associates of Tiberius so completely his friends that they immediately reported to him absolutely everything the emperor either said or did, whereas no one informed Tiberius of what Sejanus did'. The fall of Vescularius Flaccus was celebrated in the Senate, as many remembered his role in the suicide of Marcus Scribonius Libo Drusus in AD 16.[60]

Visellius Varro, L.

The consul of AD 24 was persuaded by Sejanus to prosecute C. Silius and his wife Sosia for conspiring with the rebel Sacrovir, along with corruption. Silius, the governor of Upper Germania under Germanicus, and Sosia Galla were close friends of Agrippina since her stay on the Rhine. Even Tacitus admits that there was no doubt as to their guilt of extortion. Their prosecutor Visellius Varro wished to avenge the humiliating treatment his father had suffered at the hands of Silius. As commanders of the legions of Upper and Lower Germania, they had both vied for command in the war against the Gallic rebels led by Sacrovir. Silius suggested the aged Varro lacked the resilience and health to successfully conduct the campaign, an argument that proved successful. Neither father nor son would forgive Silius. Furthermore, it had been reported to Tiberius that Silius had publicly boasted that the emperor owed his throne to him as he had kept his legions loyal during the mutiny of the other legions on the Rhine in AD 16. Varro would have needed little persuasion to avenge his father. Tiberius also despised Sosia because of her close association with Agrippina. Silius had attempted to delay the trial by objecting to a serving consul prosecuting the case. Tiberius quashed the objection, thus clearly indicating his own sentiments. Conviction was inevitable. Silius committed suicide and his estates were confiscated. Sosia was exiled, but L. Aemilius Lepidus intervened to preserve her estates for her children, apart from the quarter reserved as a reward for the prosecution. Hennig claims that Sejanus had little to do with this prosecution, which occurred due to *inamictia* in Varro's desire for revenge. However, Tacitus is clear that Sejanus, with the support of the emperor, suggested to Varro that charges against Silius and his wife would meet with imperial favour. That was all the persuasion Varro needed.[61]

Vitellius, Publius,

The son of the equestrian Publius Vitellius of Nuceria, described as a steward to Augustus. He had three brothers whose fates embraced all the extremes of Roman political life. Suetonius describes them in unflattering terms: 'Aulus, an epicure famous for his magnificent banquets died during his consulship, as partner to Nero's father Domitius. Quintus, the second brother, was degraded in a purge of undesirable senators proposed by Tiberius. Publius, the third, was an aide-de-camp to Germanicus, whose murderer, Gnaeus Piso, he arrested and brought to justice. He attained the praetorship but was himself arrested as an accomplice of Sejanus' conspiracy. When handed over to the custody of his own brother Aulus, he cut his wrists with a penknife; yet allowed them to be bandaged up, not through any fear of death, but because his friends begged him to stay with them. Later, he fell ill and died in prison. Lucius, the youngest son, became first consul and then Governor of Syria.' Despite the demotion of Quintus in AD 16, the Vitellii were a family on the rise in terms of wealth and political influence. Aulus was *suffect* consul in AD 32 and Lucius ordinary consul in AD 34. Whereas Lucius cultivated the patronage of Antonia and Caligula, Publius sought the friendship of Germanicus and, upon his death, Sejanus. He served as a legate to Germanicus in his campaigns beyond the Rhine. Publius was given command of the II and XIV Legions at the end of the campaigning season, with orders to march them back to the Rhine. A huge flood threatened to engulf both legions, and after losing many men, he managed to reach higher ground above the rising waters. His men were rescued by Germanicus' fleet. The following year he was sent to gather tribute from the Gallic provinces. He then accompanied Germanicus on his tour of the eastern provinces, witnessing the subordinate and arrogant actions of Gnaeus Calpurnius Piso, the governor of Syria. Like Quintus Servaeus, he fulfilled his vow to avenge Germanicus by prosecuting Piso in the Senate in a speech described by Tacitus as full of fervour and delivered 'with considerable eloquence'. Like his fellow prosecutor, he then probably feared the repercussions of his successful indictment and looked to the protection offered by Sejanus. In AD 31 Publius was a prefect responsible for the military treasury. He was accused by unknown *delators* of conspiring with Sejanus to use the money to fund a revolution. Tacitus records a truncated account similar to that in Suetonius. Aulus and Lucius Vitellius acted as guarantors of their brother's conduct, but Publius cut an artery using a penknife. The careers of Aulus and Lucius do not appear to have suffered because of Publius' conviction and suicide. In the deadly game of courtly politics, they had backed the winning cause in the figures of Caligula and Macro. Even Publius' wife was not safe. In AD 37 she was accused of *maiestas* by Laelius Balbus and condemned. However, the tribune Junius Otho, no doubt the son of Sejanus' *amicus*, vetoed the reward normally granted to the accuser. It is possible that Laelius Balbus had also been his father's prosecutor. This precipitated a feud between the two, which led ultimately to the destruction of Otho.[62]

Unnamed prominent senator

A fragment of Tacitus' lost Book V records a speech given by a leading member of the Senate. The speech appears to take place after forty-four speeches had been delivered on a subject likely to have been the condemnation of Livilla in late AD 31 or early AD 32. There then follows a gap in Tacitus' narrative, which commences again with a speech delivered by a close *amicus* of Sejanus who is addressing his own *amici* in a formal *salutatio*. He does not appear to have been a relative of Sejanus, as he criticizes those who 'fawned upon him in their degradation, now persecute him in their villainy. Which is the more pitiful thing – to be arraigned for a friendship or to arraign the friend – I do not seek to determine.' He also alludes to a choice that he had made in the past, which he 'considered likely to result in my own disgrace or the odium of Sejanus'. Clearly, he sought to retain the favour of the Praetorian Prefect, yet he does not appear to have been charged with *maiestas* at the time of his fall. However, if we consider the previous speeches made after the death of Livilla, this senator now found himself so imperilled by her fall that he publicly embraced making an end to his life in anticipation of the dangers he faced. He announced to the gathered throng that he would 'experiment with the cruelty of none, the mercy of none: a free man, approved by my own conscience'. This was clearly an oblique reference to the cruelty of the emperor in his persecution of the *amici* and clients of Sejanus, and a rejection of those who had turned informer to save themselves who then became enslaved to the caprice of Macro. Who was he? An *amicus* of Sejanus and possibly Livilla; a man so widely admired that many eminent men risked the anger of the emperor and his new Praetorian Prefect by attending his last *salutatio*. A man whom even the emperor so respected that his death brought forth 'no accusations or calumny from the Caesar who had laid many revolting charges against Blaesus'. His name is lost to history, but his actions cry out against the injustices and evils that befell the followers of Sejanus after their great patron's fall. The senator pleaded with the assembled company 'to preserve my memory not more with sorrow than in joy, and to add me, one name more, to the roll of those who by a notable ending found an escape from public calamity'. His final hours were spent in receiving his *amici* and clients, with many expecting some delay 'before the last act'. All had recognized that some unexpected event had sealed his fate. This must be the fall of Livilla. The senator summoned his nerve and withdrew a sword he had hidden in the folds of his toga, and, with all eyes fixed upon him, he fell upon it, ending his life with a dignity and valour that had eluded many others.[63]

Bibliography

Abbreviations

AE   L'Annee Epigraphique (Paris, 1888)

CIL   Corpus Inscriptionum Latinarum (Berlin, 1867)

ILS   Dessau, H., Inscriptiones Latinae Selectae (Berlin, 1892–1916)

PIR   Prosopographia Imperii Romani (Berlin and Leipzig, 1933)

Ancient Sources

Aelian, *Letters,* trans. Allen Rogers Benner and Francis H. Fobes in *The Letters: Alciphron, Aelian, and Philostratus,* Loeb Classical Library (Harvard University Press, 1989)

Athenaeus, *Deipnosophistae,* Book on Demand Pod (2011)

Braund, David, C. *Augustus to Nero: A Sourcebook on Roman History 31 BC–AD 68,* Croom Helm (1985)

Degrassi, A. *Inscriptiones Italiae* (Rome, 1947)

Dio Cassius, *Roman History,* translated by Earnest Cary, Loeb Classical Library (Harvard University Press, 1989)

Epictetus, *Discourses,* translated by W. A. Oldfather, Loeb Classical Library (Harvard University Press, 1989)

Eusebius, *The History of the Church,* trans. G. A. Williamson (Penguin Classics, 1989)

Frontinus, *Stratagems and Aqueducts of Rome,* Loeb Classical Library, 1989 trans. Bennett, C.E.

Horace, *Carmen Saeculare,* trans. John. Conington in *The Odes and Carmen Saeculare* (CreateSpace Independent Publishing Platform, 2018)

Josephus, *Jewish Antiquities,* (Wordsworth Classics of World Literature, 2006)

Justinian, *The Digest of Justinian,* (University of Pennsylvania Press, 2008)

Juvenal, *Satires,* in *Juvenal and Persius,* edited and translated by Susanna Morton Braund, Loeb Classical Library (Harvard University Press, 2004)

Macrobius, Forgotten Books 2018

Ovid, *Fasti,* trans. Roger Woodard (Penguin Classics, 2000)

Phaedrus, *The Fables of Phaedrus,* StreetLib Write

Philo, *Embassy to Gaius,* vol X translated by F H Colson and G H Whitaker, Loeb Classical Library (Harvard University Press, 1989)

Pliny, *Letters and Panegyricus,* translated by B Radice, Loeb Classical Library (Harvard University Press, 1969)

——, Natural History, trans. John Healey in *Natural History, A Selection* (Penguin Classics, 1991)

——, *Pliny's Natural History in Thirty Seven Books,* trans. Philemon Holland (Nabu Press, 2011 Kindle Edition)

Plutarch, Life of Pompey, trans. Rex Warner in *Fall of the Republic: Six Lives, Marius, Sula, Crassus, Pompey, Caesar, Cicero* (Penguin Classics, 1973)

Quintilian, *Institutes of Oratory,* trans. John Selby Watson (CreateSpace Independent Publishing Platform, Kindle Edition 2015)

Seneca the Elder, *Suasoriae,* trans. William A. Edward (Bloomsbury 3PL, 2013)

——, *Controversiae,* trans. Michael Winterbottom, Loeb Classical Library (Harvard University Press, 1990)

Seneca the Younger, Consolatione ad Helviam, in *Consolations From a Stoic: De Consolatione ad Marciam, De Consolatione ad Polybium and Consolatione ad Helviam* (CreateSpace Independent Publishing Platform, 5th April 2015)

——, Consolatione ad Marciam, in *Consolations From a Stoic: De Consolatione ad Marciam, De Consolatione ad Polybium and Consolatione ad Helviam* (CreateSpace Independent Publishing Platform, 5th April 2015)

——, De Beneficiis and De Clemetis, translated by John W. Blasore in *Moral Essays,* volume III Loeb Classical Library (Harvard University Press, 1935)

——, De Ira, trans. John W. Basore in Moral Essays: *De Providentia De Constantiade Ira De Clementia* v. 1, Loeb Classical Library (Harvard University Press, 1989)

——, De Tranquil, trans. Johnathan R. R. Owen in *The Secret to a Tranquil Mind* (Amazon Media EU. S.à.r.l. Kindle Edition)

——, Dialogues, trans. C Costa in *Dialogues and Letters* (Penguin Classics, 1997)

——, Letters, trans. Richard M. Gummere, in *Epistulae Morales,* v. 1–3, Loeb Classical Library (Harvard University Press, 1989)

————, Statius, *Silvae,* trans. D. R. Shackleton Bailey, Loeb Classical Library (Harvard University Press, 2015)

Suetonius, *The Twelve Caesars,* translated by Robert Graves (Penguin Classics, 2007)

Tacitus, *Annals,* Books 1–3 trans. Clifford H. Moore and John Jackson, Loeb Classical Library (Harvard University Press, 1931)

————, Books 4–6, 11–12 trans. John Jackson, Loeb Classical Library (Harvard University Press, 1937)

————, Dialogus, Trans. W. Hutton and W. Peterson in *Agricola, Germania, Dialogus,* Loeb Classical Library (Harvard University Library, 1989)

Valerius Maximus, *Memorable Deeds and Sayings,* trans. Henry John Walker (Hackett Publishing Company, 2004)

Varro, De Re Rustica, trans. W. D. Hooper and H. B. Ash in *Cato and Varro: On Agriculture,* Loeb Classical Library (Harvard University Press, 1989)

Velleius Paterculus, *The Roman History,* translated and notes by Yardley, J.C. and Barrett, Anthony, A. (Hackett Publishing Company, Inc. 2011)

Victor, Aurelius, *Epitome de Caesaribs* online translation found at De Imperatoribus Romanis: http://www.luc.edu/roman-emperors/epitome.htm

Modern Sources

Adams, Freeman, *The Consular Brothers of Sejanus,* The American Journal of Philology, Vol. 76, No.1 1955

Allen Jnr, Walter, *The Political Atmosphere in the Reign of Tiberius,* Transactions and Proceedings of the American Philological Association, Vol. 72, 1941

Balsdon, J.P.V.D. *The 'Murder' of Drusus, Son of Tiberius,* The Classical Review, New Series, Vol.1, No.2 (Jun., 1951)

Barrett, Anthony, A, *Agrippina: Sex, Power and Politics In the Early Empire* (Yale University Press, 1999)

————, *Caligula, The Corruption of Power* (B.T Batsford Ltd, 1990)

Barry, William, D. *Exposure, Mutilation, and Riot: Violence at the 'Scalae Gemoniae' in Early Imperial Rome,* Greece and Rome, Second Series, Vol. 55, No.2 (Oct. 2008)

Bauman, Richard A. *Lawyers and Politics in the Early Roman Empire: A Study of Relations Between Roman Jurists and Emperors From Augustus to Hadrian,* Issue 82, C.H. Beck 1989

Bédoyère, Guy de. Praetorian: *The Rise and Fall of Rome's Imperial Bodyguard* (Yale University Press, 2017)

Bellemore, Jane, *Cassius Dio and the Chronology of AD 21*, The Classical Quarterly, New Series, Vol.53, No.1 (May 2003)

———, *The Wife of Sejanus*, Zeitschrift für Papyrologie und Epigraphik, Bd. 109 (1995)

Bingham, Sandra. *The Praetorian Guard in the Political and Social Life of Julio-Claudian Rome,* PhD Thesis, University of Columbia

———, The Praetorian Guard: A History of Rome's Elite Special Forces (Taurus, 2013)

Bird H.W, *L Aelius Seianus and his Political Significance*, Latomus T.28, Fasc.1 (Janvier-Mars 1969)

———, *L Aelius Sejanus: Two Observations*, Latomus, T. 29, Fasc. 4 (October–December, 1970)

Birley, A. R., *Sejanus: His Fall* in N.Sekunda (ed) *Corolla Cosmo Rodewald* (Gdańsk, 2007)

Boddington, Ann, *Sejanus. Whose Conspiracy?* The American Journal of Philology, Vol.84, No.1 (Jan., 1963)

Booms, Dirk, *The Vernae Caprenses: Traces of Capri's Imperial History* after *Tiberius*, Papers of the British School at Rome, 78 (2010),

Bowen, Edwin, P., *Did Tacitus in the Annals Traduce the Character of Tiberius?* The Classical Weekly, Vol. 6, No. 21 (April 5, 1913)

Braund, Susanna Morton, *Juvenal and Persius*, Loeb Classical Library (Harvard University Press, 2004)

Brunt, P.A, *The Administrators of Roman Egypt*, The Journal of Roman Studies, Vol.65 (1975)

Carandini, Andrea, translated by Halavais, Andrew Campbell, *The Atlas of Ancient Rome* (Princeton University Press, 2012)

Champlin, Edward, *My Sejanus*, Humanities 31.5 (Sept/Oct 2010)

———, *Sex on Capri*, American Philological Association, (1974), Vol. 141, No.2 (Autumn 2011) p.315–332

Charlesworth, Martin, P. *The Banishment of the Elder Agrippina*, Classical Philology, Vol. 17, No. 3 (July 1922)

Chilton, C.W. *The Roman Law of Treason under the Early Empire*, The Journal of Roman Studies, Vol. 45, Parts 1 and 2 (1955)

Claridge, Amanda, *Rome, An Archaeological Guide* (Oxford University Press, 2011)

Clark, Gillian, *Roman Women*, downloaded from https://www.cambridge.org/core.

Cohen, Sarah, T., *Augustus, Julia and the Development of Exile "Ad Insulam"*, The Classical Quarterly, New Series, Vol. 58, No. 1 (May, 2008)

Cornell, T.J. *The Fragments of the Roman Historians*, (Oxford University Press, 2013)

Courtney, Edward, *The Fragmentary Latin Poets* (Oxford University Press, 2003)

Cowan, Eleanor, *Tacitus, Tiberius and Augustus*, Classical Antiquity, Vol.28, No.2 (October 2009)

Crook, J.A. *Political History, 30BC to AD 14*, Chapter 2. In A. Bowman, E. Champlin and A. Lintott (Eds.), *The Cambridge Ancient History, vol. X* (Cambridge University Press, 1996)

Dando-Collins, Stephen, *Legions of Rome: The Definitive History of Every Imperial Roman Legion*, (Quercus, 2010)

D'Arms, J. *Romans on the Bay of Naples: a Social and Cultural Study of the Villas and Their Owners from 150 B.C. to A.D. 400*, Cambridge (MA)

Decline, Tracy, *The Criminal Charges Against Agrippina the Elder in AD 27 and 29*, The Classical Quarterly 65 (2015)

Dennison, Matthew, *Empress of Rome: The Life of Livia* (Quercus, 2011) de Visscher, F. *Macropréfet des vigilers et ses cohortes contre la tyrannie de Séjan'* Mélanges A. Piganiol II (Paris 1966)

Drogula, Fred K. *Who was watching whom?: A Reassessment of the Conflict Between Germanicus and Piso*, American Journal of Philology, Vol. 139, number 1 (Whole number 541), Spring 2015

Eichholz, D. E. *The Art of Juvenal and His Tenth Satire*, https://www.cambridge.org/core

Eisenhut, Werner, *Der Tod des Tiberius-Sohnes Drusus*, Museum Helveticum, vii (1950)

Epstein, David, *Personal Enmity in Roman Politics 218–43 BC*, Routledge Revivals, (Oct. 2015)

Everitt, Anthony, *First Emperor: Caesar Augustus and the Triumph of Rome* (John Murray, 2006)

Feldherr, Andrew, *The Poisoned Chalice: Rumour and Historiography in Tacitus' Account of the Death of Drusus*, Materiali e discussioni per l'analisi dei testi classici, No. 61, Callida Musa: Papers on Latin Literature: In Honor of R. Elaine Fantham (2009)

Ferguson, John, *The Religions of the Roman Empire* (Thames and Hudson, 1982)

Fields, Nic, *The Walls of Rome* (Osprey Publishing, 2008)

Fishelov, David, *The Vanity of the Reader's Wishes: Rereading Juvenal's Satire 10*, The American Journal of Philology, Vol. 111, No. 3 (Autumn, 1990)

FitzPatrick, Mary, C. *Tiberius' Villa Jovis on the Isle of Capri*, The Classical Journal, Vol. 45, No. 2 (Nov., 1949)

Flint. W.W. *The Delatores in the Reign of Tiberius, as Described by Tacitus*, The Classical Journal, Vol. 8, No.1 (Oct., 1912)

Freisenbruch, Annelise, *The First Ladies of Rome* (Vintage, 2011)

Garner, Jane, F. and T. Wiedemann, *The Roman Household: A Sourcebook*, Routledge Source Books for the Ancient World (Routledge, 2013: Kindle edition)

Griffin, Miriam T., *Nero: The End of a Dynasty* (B.T. Batsford Ltd, 1984).

Hanson, Ann Ellis, *Publius Osterius Scapula: Augustan Prefect of Egypt*, Zeitschrift für Papyrologie und Epigraphik, Bd.47 (1982)

Hennig D. *L. Aelius Seianus. Untersuchungen zur Regierung des. Tiberius*, (Vestigia xxi) Munich: C. H. Beck 1975

Hölkeskamp, Karl-Joachim, *Consuls and Res Publica, Holding High Office in the Roman Republic*, Cambridge University Press (2011), edited by Hans Beck, Antonio Duplá, Martin Jehne, Fransisco Pina Polo

Holland, Richard, *Augustus, Godfather of Europe* (Sutton Publishing, 2004)

———, *Nero: The Man Behind the Myth* (Sutton Publishing, 2000).

Houston, George, W. *Tiberius on Capri*, Greece and Rome, Vol. XXXII No.2, October 1985

Jackson, John, *Tacitus Annals, Books 4–6, 11–12*, Loeb Classical Library (Harvard University Library, 1937)

Jameson, Shelagh, *Chronology of the Campaigns of Aelius Gallus and C. Petronius*, The Journal of Roman Studies, Vol. 58, Parts 1 and 2 (1968)

Jonson, Ben, *Sejanus, His Fall* (CreateSpace Independent Publishing Platform, 2017)

Koestermann, Erich, *Cornelius Taci* (Heidelberg 1965)

Laurence, Ray, *Rumour and Communication in Roman Politics*, Greece and Rome, Vol. LXI, No. 1 (April 1994)

Lawall, Gilbert, *Exempla and Theme in Juvenal's Tenth Satire*, Transactions and Proceedings of the American Philological Association, Vol. 89 (1958)

Levick, Barbara, *Claudius* (Routledge, 2001)

———, *Tiberius' Retirement to Rhodes in 6 BC*, Latomus, T. 31, Fasc. 3, (Octobre-Décembre, 1972)

———, *Tiberius, the Politician* (Routledge, 1999)

————, *The Politics of the Early Empire*, Chapter 4 in *Roman Political Life, 90 BC-69 AD*, edited by Wiseman (Exeter Studies in History,1985)

Lindsay, Hugh, *Who was Apicius?* Symbolae Osloenses 72:1, (July 2008)

Maier, Paul, L. *Sejanus, Pilate, and the Date of the Crucifixion*, Church History, Vol. 37, No. 1 (March 1968)

Marsh, Frank Burr, *Tacitus and the Aristocratic Tradition*, Classical Philology, Vol.21, No. 4 (Oct., 1926)

————, *The Reign of Tiberius* (Oxford University Press, 1931)

Meise, Eckhard, *Untersuchungen zur Geschichte derjulisch claudischen Dynastie*, Vestigia 10 (Munich 1969)

Mellor, R. *Tacitus* (London, 1933)

Mennen, Inge, *Power and Status in the Roman Empire, AD 193–284* (Brill, 2011)

Meyer, Reinhold, *Usurpation of Status and Status Symbols in the Roman Empire*, Historia: Zeitschrift für Alte Geschichte, Bd. 20, H. 2/3 (2nd Qtr., 1971)

Millar, Fergus, *A Study of Cassius Dio* (Oxford, 1964)

————, The Emperor in the Roman World (Duckworth, 1977)

Moore, Clifford, H. and Jackson, John, *Tacitus Histories Books 4–5, Annals, Books 1–3*, Loeb Classical Library (Harvard University Press, 1931)

Morgan, Llewelyn, *Tacitus, Annals 4.70: An Unappreciated Pun*, The Classical Quarterly, 1998, Vol. 48 (2)

Nicols, John, *Antonia and Sejanus*, Historia: Zeitschrift für Alte Geschichte, Bd. 24, H. 1 (1st Quarter, 1975)

Oost, S.V. *The Career of M Antonius Pallas*, American Journal of Philology 79 (1958)

Pappano, Albert Earl, *Agrippa Postumus*, Classical Philology, Vol.36, No.1 (Jan., 1941)

Platts, Hannah Frances Mary Landsbrough, *Art, Architecture and Landscape in 'Vila' Residences of Italy from c 1st century BC to 2nd century AD*, Ph.D dissertation, University of Bristol, 2006

Powell, Lindsey, *Eager for Glory, The Untold Story of Drusus the Elder, Conqueror of Germania*, Pen and Sword, 2011

Rankov, Boris, *The Praetorian Guard* (Osprey Publishing, 2008)

Rogers, Robert Samuel, *A Tacitean Pattern in Narrating Treason-Trials*, Transactions and Proceedings of the American Philological Association, Vol. 83 (1952)

————, *Criminal Trials and Criminal Legislation Under Tiberius*, American Philological Association, 1935

————, *Drusus Caesar's Tribunician Power*, The American Journal of Philology, Vol. 61, No. 4 (1940)

————, Lucius Arruntius, Classical Philology, Vol. 26, No. 1 (Jan., 1931)

————, Notes on the Gallic Revolt, AD *21*, The Classical Weekly, Vol. 36, No.7 (Nov. 30,, 1942)

————, Studies in the Reign of Tiberius (John Hopkins Press, 1943)

————, *Two Criminal Cases Tried Before Drusus Caesar*, Classical Philology, Vol.27, No.1 (Jan. 1932)

Rutland, L. *The Tacitean Germanicus*, Rhien.Mus.130 (1987)

Rutledge, Steven, H. *Delatores and the Tradition of Violence in Roman Oratory*, The American Journal of Philology, Vol. 120, No.4 (Winter, 1999),

————, Imperial Inquisitions (Routledge,2001 Kindle edition)

Saller, Richard P, *Personal Patronage under the Early Empire* (Cambridge University Press, 2010)

Schmitt, H.H. *Der panno nische Aufstand d. J. 14 und der Regierungsantritt des Tiberius*, Historia 7 (1958)

Seager, Robin. *Tiberius* (Blackwell, 2005)

Sealey, Raphael. *The Political Attachments of L. Aelius Seianus*, Phoenix, Vol. 15, No. 2 (Summer, 1961)

Shotter, D.C.A. *Agrippina the Elder: A Woman in a Man's World*, Historia: Zeitschrift für Alte Geschichte, Bd. 49, H. 3 (3rd Qtr., 2000)

————, Cneaus Calpurnius Piso, *Legate of Syria*, Historia: Zeitschrift für Alte Geschichte, Bd. 23, H. 2 (2nd Qtr., 1974)

————, *Elections under Tiberius*, The Classical Quarterly, Vol. 16, No. 2 (Nov., 1966)

————, *The Trial of C. Junius Silanus*, Classical Philology, Vol. 67, No. 2 (April, 1972)

————, The Trial of Clutorius Priscus, Greece and Rome, Vol.16. No. 1 (April 1969)

————, The Trial of M. Scribonius Libo Drusus, Historia Zeitschrift für Alte Geschichte, Bd. 21, H. 1 (1st Qtr., 1972)

————, *Tiberius and Asinius Gallus*, Historia; Zeitschrift für Alte Geschichte, Rd.20, H.4 (Third quarter, 1971)

————, *Tiberius and the Spirit of Augustus*, Greece and Rome 13 (1966)

————, *Tiberius Caesar* in the Lancaster Pamphlets series (Routledge, 1992)

Sinclair, Patrick, *Tacitus' Presentation of Livia Julia, Wife of Tiberius' son Drusus*, The American Journal of Philology, Vol. 111, No. 2, (Summer 1990)

Smallwood, Mary, E. *Some Notes on the Jews under Tiberius*, Latomus, XV (1956)

Smith, Charles Edward, *Tiberius and the Roman Empire* (Louisiana State University Press, 1942)

Sprenger, A. *The Campaign of Aelius Gallus in Arabia*, The Journal of the Royal Asiatic Society of Great Britain and Ireland, New Series, Vol. 6, No. 1 (1873)

Stewart, Zeph, *Sejanus, Gaetulicus, and Seneca*, The American Journal of Philology, Vol.74, No. 1 (1953)

Sumner, G.V. *The Family Connections of L Aelius Seianus*, Phoenix, Vol. 19, No.2 (Summer, 1965)

Syme, Ronald, *Antolica, Studies in Strabo*, (ed. A. R. Birley) Oxford: Clarendon Press

————, *Domitius Corbulo*, Journal of Roman Studies, 60 (1970),

————, *History or Biography: the Case of Tiberius Caesar*, Roman Papers 3, edited by Birley, Anthony, R. (Clarendon Press, Oxford, 1984)

————, *Marcus Lepidus, Capax Imperii*, Journal of Roman Studies, Vol. 45, Parts 1 and 2 (1955)

————, Tacitus (Clarendon Press, 1967)

————, The Augustan Aristocracy (Oxford University Press, 1986)

————, The Consuls of AD 13, Journal of Roman Studies, 56. 1966

————, *The Early Tiberian Consuls*, Historia Bd. 30, H. 2 (2nd quarter, 1981)

————, The Praetorian Guard in Roman Papers, Vol VI edited by Birley, Anthony, (Oxford University Press)

————, *The Roman Revolution* (Oxford University Press, 1979)

————, *Seianus on the Aventine*, Hermes, 84.Bd., H. 3 (1956)

Talbert, Richard J.A. *The Senate of Imperial Rome* (Princeton University Press, 1984)

Tuplin, Christopher, J. *The False Drusus of 31 AD and the Fall of Sejanus*, Latomus, T. 46, Fasc 4 (Octobre – Decembre 1987)

Vàrhelyi, Zsuzsanna, *The Religion of Senators of the Roman Empire*, (Cambridge University Press, 2010)

Walker, B. *The Annals of Tacitus* (Manchester, 1952)

Wallace-Hadrill, Andrew, *The Imperial Court*, Cambridge Ancient History, Chapter 7. In A. Bowman, E. Champlin and A. Lintott (Eds.), *The Cambridge Ancient History, vol. X* (Cambridge University Press, 1996)

Wardle, D. *Valerius Maximus on the Domus Augusta and Tiberius*, Classical Quarterly 50.2 (2000)

Wellesley, K. *The Dies Imperii of Tiberius*, The Journal of Roman Studies, Vol.57, No. 1/ 2 (1967)

Westermann, W.L. *Aelius Gallus and the Reorganization of the Irrigation System of Egypt under Augustus*, Classical Philology, Vol. 12, No. 3 (Jul., 1917)

Wiedemann, T.E.J. *Tiberius to Nero*, Cambridge Ancient History, Vol. 10, Chapter 5. In A. Bowman, E. Champlin and A. Lintott (Eds.), *The Cambridge Ancient History, vol. X* (Cambridge University Press, 1996)

Wilson, Emily, *Seneca, A Life* (Allen Lane, 2015)

Winterling, Aloys, *Caligula* (University of California Press, 2015)

————, *Politics and Society in Imperial Rome*, (Wiley-Blackwell, 2009)

Woodman, A.J. *Tacitus' Obituary of Tiberius: Tacitus Annals 6.51.1–3*, Classical Quarterly 39 (i) 1989

Notes

Chapter 1 His Rise: 20 BC–AD 14

1. Wallace-Hadrill, Andrew, *The Imperial Court*, Cambridge Ancient History, Chapter 7 (Cambridge University Press), pp.296–98.
2. Juvenal, *Tenth Satire* 110–13 in *Juvenal and Persius*, edited and translated by Susanna Morton Braund, Loeb Classical Library (Harvard University Press, 2004). The same fascination with the destructive power of ambition can be found in the presentation of Sejanus throughout literature. Ben Jonson in his play *Sejanus, his Fall* identifies him as a tragic character undermined by a fatal flaw in that: 'Ambition makes more trusty slaves than need' (Act 1 Sc1). The Sejanus of *I, Claudius* by Robert Graves closely follows the presentation in both Tacitus and Dio.
3. Syme, Ronald, *The Roman Revolution* (Oxford University Press, 1979), p.510; Hennig, D., *L. Aelius Seianus. Untersuchungen zur Regierung des. Tiberius,* (Vestigia xxi) (Munich: C.H. Beck, 1975), p.11.
4. Saller, Richard.P, *Personal Patronage under the Early Empire* (Cambridge University Press, 2010), pp.10, 59.
5. Levick, Barbara, *Tiberius, the Politician* (Routledge, 1999), pp.11–12.
6. Velleius Paterculus, *The Roman History*, translated and notes by Yardley, J.C. and Barrett, Anthony, A. (Hackett Publishing Company, Inc., 2011), 2.127.
7. Dio 55.10.17.
8. Bird H.W., 'L Aelius Seianus and his Political Significance', *Latomus* T.28, Fasc.1 (Janvier-Mars 1969), pp.61–98; Dio 57.19.5; Tacitus, *Annals* 1.24.
9. Tacitus, *Annals* 4.1; Adams, Freeman, 'The Consular Brothers of Sejanus', *The American Journal of Philology*, Vol. 76, No.1 (1955), pp.70–76; Pliny, *Natural History* 10.52, although Metellus Scipio, consul 52 BC, disputed this.
10. Juvenal, *Tenth Satire* 74–78 in *Juvenal and Persius*, edited and translated by Susanna Morton Braund, Loeb Classical Library (Harvard University Press, 2004).

11. Tacitus, *Annals*, 4.3.
12. Velleius Paterculus, *The Roman History*, 2.127.3
13. Brunt, P.A., 'The Administrators of Roman Egypt', *The Journal of Roman Studies*, Vol. 65 (1975), pp.124–47; Syme, R., 'The Praetorian Guard', in *Roman Papers*, Vol. VI, edited by Birley, Anthony (Oxford University Press), pp.25–36; Hanson, Ann Ellis, 'Publius Osterius Scapula: Augustan Prefect of Egypt', *Zeitschrift für Papyrologie und Epigraphik*, Bd.47 (1982), pp.243–53.
14. Bédoyère, Guy de, *Praetorian: The Rise and Fall of Rome's Imperial Bodyguard* (Yale University Press, 2017), p.28.
15. Bingham, Sandra, *The Praetorian Guard in the Political and Social Life of Julio-Claudian Rome* (PhD Thesis, University of Columbia), p.224.
16. Syme, R., 'The Praetorian Guard', *Roman Papers* Vol. VI, pp.25–36, considers the guard as not primarily designed for war despite being originally formed from veterans, as later recruits were drawn directly from civilian life rather than the legions; Bédoyère, Guy de, *Praetorian: The Rise and Fall of Rome's Imperial Bodyguard*, p.42, identifies a combination of functions including asserting Augustus' authority and imposing order.
17. Suetonius, *Augustus* 49.1; Bédoyère, Guy de, *Praetorian: The Rise and Fall of Rome's Imperial Bodyguard*, p.42.
18. Dio 68.16.12.
19. Millar, Fergus, *The Emperor in the Roman World* (Duckworth, 1977), p.123.
20. Bingham, Sandra, *The Praetorian Guard: A History of Rome's Elite Special Forces* (I.B. Taurus, 2013), pp.20, 51.
21. Syme, R. *The Augustan Aristocracy* (Oxford University Press, 1986), p.301; Bédoyère, Guy de, *Praetorian: The Rise and Fall of Rome's Imperial Bodyguard*, p.52; Hanson, Ann Ellis, 'Publius Osterius Scapula: Augustan Prefect of Egypt', pp.243–53, citing CIL 6.23601; Tacitus, *Annals* 3.30.
22. Saller, R.P., *Personal Patronage under the Early Empire*, p.62; Millar, Fergus, *The Emperor in the Roman World* (Duckworth, 1977), p.64.
23. Syme, R., *The Augustan Aristocracy*, p.301, citing ILS 4902.
24. Bédoyère, Guy de, *Praetorian: The Rise and Fall of Rome's Imperial Bodyguard*, pp.52, 293 n.58 base on ILS 4902. Also, ILS 171 (Alba Pompeia) PIR V 189.
25. Holland, Richard, *Augustus, Godfather of Europe* (Sutton Publishing, 2004), pp.260–62; Levick, Barbara, *Tiberius, the Politician*, p.41.

26. Crook, J.A., *Political History, 30 BC to AD 14*, Chapter 2, Cambridge Ancient History (Cambridge University Press), p.103, argues that as a pair of prefects were appointed of equestrian status we should not assume that the creation of the post was linked to the conspiracy of Julia and Iullus Antonius. However, these facts seem to suggest the very opposite; the emperor was extremely concerned about his security and the threat of assassination. Millar, Fergus, *A Study of Cassius Dio* (Oxford, 1964), p.115.
27. Tacitus, *Annals* 1.7.
28. Brunt, P.A., 'The Administrators of Roman Egypt', pp.124–47.
29. Macrobius (Forgotten Books, 2018), 2.4.18; Suetonius, *Augustus* 85.1; Syme, R., *The Roman Revolution*, pp.320, 506.
30. Velleius Paterculus, *The Roman History* 2.127.3; Dio 58.10.8.
31. Tacitus, *Annals* 3.35.
32. Velleius Paterculus, *The Roman History* 2.125.5.
33. Suetonius, *Augustus* 66; Syme, R., *The Augustan Aristocracy*, pp.301–08, conclusively argues that the inscription does relate to Strabo rather than Caecina Tuscus; Syme, R. *The Roman Revolution*, p.358 and stemma VI; Sumner, G.V., 'The Family Connections of L. Aelius Seianus', *Phoenix* Vol.19, No.2 (Summer, 1965), pp.134–45; Adams, Freeman, 'The Consular Brothers of Sejanus', pp.70–76; Hennig, D., *L Aelius Seianus. Untersuchungen zur Regierung des. Tiberius*, (Vestigia xxi), pp.5–12.
34. Dio 55.7.5.
35. Tacitus, *Annals* 4.40.
36. Syme, R., *The Roman Revolution*, p.358 and stemma VI; Sumner, G.V., 'The Family Connections of L Aelius Seianus', pp.134–45.
37. Tacitus, *Annals* 3.58.
38. Levick, Barbara, *Tiberius, the Politician*, p.310; Bird, H.W., 'L. Aelius Seianus and his Political Significance', pp.61–98; Sumner, G.V., 'The Family Connections of L. Aelius Seianus', pp.134–45.
39. Sumner, G.V., 'The Family Connections of L. Aelius Seianus', pp.134–45.
40. Adams, Freeman, 'The Consular Brothers of Sejanus', pp.70–76; Syme, R., *The Augustan Aristocracy*, p.301; Syme, R., *The Roman Revolution*, p.358 and stemma VI; Sumner, G., 'The Family Connections of L Aelius Seianus', pp.134–45; Levick, Barbara, *Tiberius, the Politician*, p.310; Bird, H.W., 'L. Aelius Seianus and his Political Significance', pp.61–98; Sealey, Raphael, 'The Political Attachments of L. Aelius Seianus', *Phoenix* Vol.15, No.2 (Summer, 1961), pp.97111; Cornell, T.J.,

The Fragments of the Roman Historians: L and Q Aelius Tubero (Oxford University Press, 2013), p.363.

41. Tacitus, *Annals* 2.20, 4.29.
42. Sumner, G.V., 'The Family Connections of L Aelius Seianus', pp. 134–45; Syme, R., *The Augustan Aristocracy*, p.301; Syme, R., *The Roman Revolution*, p.307.
43. Sealey, Raphael, 'The Political Attachments of L. Aelius Seianus', pp.97–111; Adams, Freeman, 'The Consular Brothers of Sejanus', pp.70–76; also suggested by Seager, Robin, *Tiberius* (Blackwell, 2005), p.227.
44. Tacitus *Annals* 5.8; Adams, Freeman, 'The Consular Brothers of Sejanus', pp.70–76, identifies the fugitive as the grandson of the prefect of Egypt but rejects the argument that he was Sejanus' son; Bird, H.W., 'L. Aelius Seianus and his Political Significance', pp.61–98.
45. Tacitus, *Annals* 4.3.
46. Syme, R., *The Augustan Aristocracy*, p.308.
47. Syme, R., *The Roman Revolution*, p.384 n.6 based on ILS 914.
48. Sprenger, A,. 'The Campaign of Aelius Gallus in Arabia', *The Journal of the Royal Asiatic Society of Great Britain and Ireland*, New Series, Vol.6, No.1 (1873), pp.121–41; Westermann, W.L., 'Aelius Gallus and the Reorganization of the Irrigation System of Egypt under Augustus', *Classical Philology* Vol.12, No.3 (July, 1917), pp.237–43; Jameson, Shelagh, 'Chronology of the Campaigns of Aelius Gallus and C. Petronius', *The Journal of Roman Studies* Vol.58, Parts 1 and 2 (1968), pp.71–84; Sumner, G.V., 'The Family Connections of L. Aelius Sejanus', pp.134–45.
49. Tacitus, *Annals* 4.1; Levick, Barbara, *Tiberius, the Politician*, p.159.
50. Dio 57.195; Tacitus, *Annals* 4.1.
51. Pliny, *Natural History* 9.30, 10.133.
52. Athenaeus, *Deipnosophistae* 1.7 a–c and repeated in garbled fashion in the Suda A 3207.
53. Saller, R.P., *Personal Patronage under the Early Empire*, p.62.
54. Seneca, *Letters* 95.42.
55. Pliny, *Natural History* 19.137.
56. Aelian, *Letters* Nos 113–14; Suda A 3213.
57. Syme, R. (ed. A.R. Birley), *Antolica, Studies in Strabo* (Oxford: Clarendon Press, 1995), p.322.
58. Lindsay, Hugh, 'Who was Apicius?', *Symbolae Osloenses* 72:1, (July 2008), pp.144–54.

59. Dio 55.10.17; Velleius Paterculus, *The Roman History* 1.101.1.
60. Syme, R., *The Roman Revolution*, pp.398–99, 429.
61. Velleius Paterculus, *The Roman History* 2.101.2.
62. Crook, J.A., 'Political History, 30 BC to AD 14', Chapter 2, p.104; Syme, R., *The Roman Revolution*, p.428; Dio 55.10.18.
63. Dio 55.10.19 states it was Chios, however Suetonius, *Tiberius* 12, refers to Samos.
64. Dio 55.10 19; Suetonius, *Tiberius* 12; Tacitus, *Annals* 3.48.
65. Suetonius, *Tiberius* 12–13.
66. Saller, R.P., *Personal Patronage under the Early Empire*, p.75.
67. Epictetus, *Discourses* 4.1.47.
68. Velleius Paterculus, *The Roman History* 2.101.1–3.
69. Velleius Paterculus, *The Roman History* 1.102.1; Tacitus, *Annals* 3.48, refers to Tiberius' speech in the Senate in AD 21; Pliny, *Natural History* 9.118, who states Lollius took poison.
70. Levick, Barbara, *Tiberius, the Politician*, pp.45–46; Seager, R., *Tiberius*, p.29; Suetonius, *Tiberius* 13.2; Dio, 55.10a.10.
71. Pliny, *Natural History* 6.32; Suetonius, *Augustus* 93; Everitt, Anthony, *First Emperor: Caesar Augustus and the Triumph of Rome* (John Murray, 2006), p.308.
72. Velleius Paterculus, *The Roman History* 2.102.2.
73. Dio 55.10.9; Tacitus, *Annals* 1.3; Velleius Paterculus, *The Roman History* 2.102.2 and n.332 p.119; Suetonius, *Augustus* 65.
74. For rumours suggesting Livia poisoned Gaius and Lucius, see Dio 55.10.10; Tacitus, *Annals* 1.3; Levick, Barbara, *Tiberius, the Politician*, pp.49–50; Seager, R., *Tiberius*, p.31.
75. Dio 55.32.1–2; Tacitus, *Annals* 1.3; Suetonius, *Augustus* 65; Pappano, Albert Earl, 'Agrippa Postumus', *Classical Philology*, Vol.36, No.1 (Jan., 1941), pp.30–45; Crook, J.A., 'Political History, 30 BC to AD 14', p.108.
76. Suetonius, *Augustus* 19, 51; Velleius Paterculus, 2.112.7; Pappano, Albert Earl, 'Agrippa Postumus', pp.30–45.
77. Suetonius, *Augustus* 19; Juvenal, *Satire* 6.158; Tacitus, *Annals* 3.24; Syme, R. *The Roman Revolution*, pp.432 n.4, 468; Wallace-Hadrill, Andrew, 'The Imperial Court', Cambridge Ancient History, Ch.7, p.304; Crook, J.A., 'Political History, 30 BC to AD 14', p.108; Holland, Richard, *Augustus, Godfather of Europe* (Sutton Publishing, 2004), p.264.
78. Tacitus, *Annals* 3.24,4.39; Levick, Barbara, *Tiberius the Politician*, p.159.

79. Suetonius, *Tiberius* 21; Josephus, *Jewish Antiquities* 18.181; Tacitus, *Annals* 6.9; Saller, R.P. *Personal Patronage under the Early Empire*, p.49.
80. Seager, R., *Tiberius*, pp.32–37; Levick, Barbara, *Tiberius the Politician*, pp.57–65.
81. Dando-Collins, Stephen, *Legions of Rome: The Definitive History of Every Imperial Roman Legion* (Quercus, 2010), pp.148, 172.
82. Millar, Fergus, *The Emperor in the Roman World*, p.102; Saller, R.P., *Personal Patronage under the Early Empire*, pp.48–49.
83. Tacitus, *Annals* 4.1.
84. Velleius Paterculus, *The Roman History* 2.127.3.
85. Dio 57.19.7.
86. Dio 57.19.5.
87. Tacitus, *Annals* 4.1.

Chapter 2 Crisis: AD 14

1. Levick, Barbara, *Tiberius the Politician*, pp.44, 53, 63–64; Syme, Ronald, *The Roman Revolution*, pp.433, 438; Syme, R., *The Augustan Aristocracy* (Clarendon Press, 1986), p.132; Wiedemann, T.E.J., 'Tiberius to Nero', *Cambridge Ancient History*, Vol.10, Chapter 5, p.206; Tacitus, *Annals* 6.40.
2. Tacitus, *Annals* 2.43.
3. Wiedemann, T.E.J., 'Tiberius to Nero', pp.200–01, argues that the transfer of power to Tiberius was a model of orderly and smooth transition facilitated by the fact that many opponents of Tiberius had been eliminated in the failed conspiracies of Julia the Elder and Younger in 2 BC and AD 8. This perception is, however, contradicted both by Tacitus and Dio.
4. Crook, J.A., 'Augustus: Power, Authority, Achievement', *Cambridge Ancient History*, Vol.10, Chapter 3, pp.135–36; Tacitus, *Annals* 1. 5; Dio 56.30; Zonaras 10.38; Pliny, *Natural History* 7.150; Victor, *Epitome* 1.27.
5. Pappano, Albert, 'Agrippa Postumus', *Classical Philology* Vol.36, No.1 (Jan., 1941), (The University of Chicago Press), pp.30–45; Wiedemann, T.E.J., 'Tiberius to Nero', p.202.
6. Velleius Paterculus, *The Roman History* 2.123.3, and Suetonius, *Tiberius* 21, describe a meeting between the two, whilst Dio 56.31.1 states Augustus was already dead by the time Tiberius returned. Tacitus, *Annals* 1.5.5, is undecided.
7. Tacitus, *Annals* 1.5.

8. Suetonius, *Tiberius* 24.
9. Epictetus, *Discourses* 4.1, 4.7.
10. Tacitus, *Annals* 1.10.
11. Velleius Paterculus, *The Roman History* 2.124.1.
12. Tacitus, *Annals* 1.7.
13. The manuscript has 'M Lepidum', who was inferred to be Manius Aemilius Lepidus, the consul of AD 11. However, Syme, R., *Roman Revolution*, p.433, identifies as Marcus Aemilius Lepidus, the consul of AD 6 whose daughter was married to a son of Germanicus, as by far the most powerful noble. Also see Syme, R., 'Marcus Lepidus, Capax Imperii', *Journal of Roman Studies* Vol.45, Parts 1 and 2 (1955), p.22–33.
14. Tacitus, *Annals* 1.13.
15. Syme, R., *The Roman Revolution*, pp.433–34; Syme, R., 'Marcus Lepidus, Capax Imperii', pp.22–33; Velleius Paterculus, *The Roman History* 2.114.5; Shotter, D.C.A., 'Tiberius and Asinius Gallus', *Historia*; Zeitschrift für Alte Geschichte, Rd.20, H.4 (3rd quarter, 1971), pp.443–57; Tacitus, *Annals* 11.7; Rogers, Robert Samuel, 'Lucius Arruntius', *Classical Philology* Vol.26, No.1 (Jan. 1931), pp.31–45
16. Tacitus, *Annals* 3.12–13; Seneca, *De Ira* 1.18–19; Shotter, D.C.A., 'Cneaus Calpurnius Piso, Legate of Syria', *Historia*: Zeitschrift für Alte Geschichte, Bd. 23, H. 2 (2nd quarter, 1974), pp.229–45.
17. Levick, Barbara, *Claudius* (Routledge, 2001), p.137; Barrett, Anthony A., *Caligula, The Corruption of Power* (B.T. Batsford Ltd, 1990), pp.82–83.
18. Syme, R., *The Roman Revolution*, p.425 n.2 and stemma V; Tacitus, *Annals* 2.27.
19. Tacitus, *Annals* 2.39; Suetonius, *Tiberius* 25; Suetonius, *Augustus* 19.
20. Tacitus, *Annals* 2.40.
21. Dio 56.31.2–3; Suetonius, *Augustus* 100.
22. Dio 57.2.2; Levick, Barbara, *Tiberius the Politician*, pp.69–70, calculates the arrival of the body in Rome based on the number of towns between Nola and Rome where the local populace would have been allowed the opportunity and privilege of paying their respects. These are listed as Suessula, Calatia, Capua, Casilinum, Urbana, Sinuessa, Minturnae, Formiae, Fundi, Tarracina, Tres Tabernae, Aricia and Bovillae; Suetonius, *Julius Caesar* 85; Velleius Paterculus, *The Roman History* 2.124.1.
23. Tacitus, *Histories* 1.18.1; Wellesley, K., 'The Dies Imperii of Tiberius', *The Journal of Roman Studies* Vol.57, Nos 1/2 (1967), pp.23–30; Levick,

Barbara, *Tiberius the Politician*, p.72, calculates that Tiberius received the news at Bovillae as he prepared to enter Rome.

24. Tacitus, *Annals* 1.17–18.
25. Tacitus, *Annals* 1.24.
26. Pliny, *Natural History* 19.137.
27. Tacitus, *Annals* 1.8.
28. Epictetus, *Disc* 1.10.
29. Dio 56.34.1–4.
30. Dio 56.42.1–4.
31. Dio 56.43.1; Tacitus, *Annals* 1.14.3; Wellesley, K., 'The Dies Imperii of Tiberius', pp.23–30.
32. Tacitus, *Annals* 1.12–13.
33. Tacitus, *Annals* 1.13.
34. Schmitt, H.H., 'Der panno nische Aufstand d. J. 14 und der Regierungsantritt des Tiberius', *Historia* 7 (1958), pp.378–83.
35. Tacitus, *Annals* 1.16–24; Dio 57.4.2.
36. Tacitus, *Histories* 2.89.
37. Tacitus, *Annals* 1.24.
38. Tacitus, *Annals* 1.25.
39. Tacitus, *Annals* 1.26.
40. Tacitus, *Annals* 1.27–29, 4.44; Seneca, *Moral and Political Essays* (trans. Cooper, John M.) (Cambridge University Press, 1995), pp.233–34; Seager, Robin, *Tiberius*, p.51; Syme, R. *The Roman Revolution*, p.400 n.4.
41. Tacitus, *Annals* 1.27–28.
42. Dio 57.4.4.
43. Tacitus, *Annals* 1.28.
44. Tacitus, *Annals* 1.29.
45. Tacitus, *Annals* 1.30.
46. Wilkes, J.J., 'A Note on the Mutiny of the Pannonian Legions', *The Classical Quarterly* Vol.13, No.2 (Nov., 1963), pp.268–71; Levick, Barbara, *Tiberius*, p.73; Tacitus, *Annals* 1.54; Dio 56.47.1.
47. Tacitus, *Annals* 1.7, 53–54; Shotter, David C., 'Agrippina the Elder: A Woman in a Man's World', *Historia*: Zeitschrift für Alte Geschichte, Bd. 49, H. 3 (3rd quarter, 2000), pp.341–57.
48. Tacitus, *Annals* 1.33–35; Drogula, Fred K., 'Who was watching whom?: A Reassessment of the Conflict between Germanicus and Piso', *American Journal of Philology* Vol.139, No.1 (whole number 541; Spring, 2015), pp.121–53.

49. Shotter, David C., 'Agrippina the Elder: A Woman in a Man's World', pp.341–57.

50. Wallace-Hadrill, Andrew,' The Imperial Court', *Cambridge Ancient History*, chapter 7, p.288.

51. Tacitus, *Annals* 1.3.

52. Dennison, Matthew, *Empress of Rome: The Life of Livia* (Quercus, 2011), pp.240, 259–61; Dio 57.12.1–4.

53. Tacitus, *Annals* 1.33.

54. Tacitus, *Annals* 1.69. Pliny the Elder's work on the German Wars has been lost.

55. Shotter, David, C., 'Agrippina the Elder: A Woman in a Man's World', pp.341–35; Levick, Barbara, *Tiberius the Politician*, p.37; Tacitus, *Annals* 1.14.

56. Suetonius, *Tiberius* 7.

57. Tacitus, *Annals* 1.69.

Chapter 3 His Rise: AD 15–20

1. Syme, R. *The Roman Revolution*, p.325.

2. Levick, Barbara, *Tiberius the Politician*, pp.95–96.

3. Saller, R.P., *Personal Patronage under the Early Empire*, pp.12–15, 30–35, 59, 78; Syme, R., *The Roman Revolution*, p.73; Millar, Fergus, *Emperor in the Roman World*, p.363.

4. Levick, Barbara, *Tiberius the Politician*, p.92; Suetonius, *Tiberius* 55.

5. Tacitus, *Annals* 1.6, 2.39–40; Dio 57.16.3–4; Suetonius, *Tiberius* 25; Syme, Ronald, *The Roman Revolution*, p.409

6. Seneca, *Ad Helviam* 19; Syme, Ronald, *Tacitus* (Clarendon Press, 1967), p.285; PIR2,4, G, 25.

7. Tacitus, *Annals* 3.30.

8. Tacitus, *Annals* 6.8.

9. Millar, Fergus, *Emperor in the Roman World*, pp.125–27; Saller, R.P., *Personal Patronage under the Early Empire*, p.59; Champlin, Edward, 'My Sejanus', *Humanities* 31.5 (Sept./Oct. 2010), pp.18–21,52–53, internet download.

10. Epictetus, *Discourses* 4.1.7.

11. Millar, Fergus, *Emperor in the Roman World*, p.209; Wallace-Hadrill, Andrew, 'The Imperial Court', p.289; Suetonius, *Vespasian* 21.

12. Pliny, *Natural History* 26.3; Valerius Maximus, xi.6.17; Suetonius, *Tiberius* 34,68, 72; Suetonius, *Vespasian* 2; Dio 57.11.1; Wallace-Hadrill,

'The Imperial Court', p.291; Saller, R.P., *Personal Patronage under the Early Empire*, p.61

13. Saller, R.P., *Personal Patronage under the Early Empire*, p.15; Tacitus, *Annals* 4.1, 13.20–22.

14. Seager, Robin, *Tiberius*, pp.78–83.

15. Syme, Ronald, 'Marcus Lepidus, Capax Imperii', pp.22–33.

16. Rogers, Robert Samuel, 'Lucius Arruntius', pp.31–45; Tacitus, *Annals* 11.6, 11.7.

17. Tacitus, *Annals* 3.48, 4.15, 4.58, 6.26; Pliny, *Natural History* 14.145; Seneca, *Epp* 83.14f; Syme, Ronald, *The Augustan Aristocracy*, p.345; Syme, Ronald, *The Roman Revolution*, pp.424, 432, 460; Syme, Ronald, 'History or Biography: the Case of Tiberius Caesar', *Roman Papers 3*, edited by Birley, Anthony R. (Oxford: Clarendon Press, 1984), pp.948–49; Levick, Barbara, *Tiberius the Politician*, pp.56, 207; Woodman, A.J., 'Tacitus' Obituary of Tiberius: Tacitus Annals 6.51.1–3', *Classical Quarterly* 39 (i) (1989), pp.197–205, based on Suetonius, *Tiberius* 65.1, where the emperor in a letter to the Senate denounces Sejanus as '*senex et solus*'.

18. Tacitus, *Annals* 6.20–21; Suetonius, *Augustus* 98.4; Suetonius, *Tiberius* 14; Dio 55.11.2–3.

19. Dio 57.15.7.

20. Suetonius, *Tiberius* 62.3; Dio 58.27; Levick, Barbara, *Tiberius the Politician*, pp.18, 174, 210.

21. Levick, Barbara, *Tiberius the Politician*, pp.174, 278 n.135; Tacitus, *Annals* 3.70.

22. Suetonius, *Tiberius* 34; Tacitus, *Annals* 1.76–77, 2.51; Dio 57.11.10; Cowan, Eleanor, 'Tacitus, Tiberius and Augustus', *Classical Antiquity* Vol.28, No.2 (October 2009), pp.179–210; Levick, Barbara, *Tiberius the Politician*, pp.96, 161, suggests D. Haterius Agrippa was married to the daughter of Agrippa and Marcella; de Bédoyère, Guy, *Praetorian: The Rise and Fall of Rome's Imperial Bodyguard*, pp.69, 295 n.14, suggests Haterius Agrippa may have been the son of a daughter of Agrippa and married to Demetria, a cousin of Germanicus.

23. Tacitus, *Annals* 1.76; Suetonius, *Tiberius* 52; Dio 57.14.10.

24. Suetonius, Augustus 49; Tacitus, *Annals* 4.2; Bingham, Sandra, *The Praetorian Guard: A History of Rome's Elite Special Forces*, p.69.

25. For presence of Praetorians at the games see Suetonius, *Augustus* 14, 43.3, 44.1, and as guards in city see Dio 56.23.4 and Suetonius,

Augustus 23, 32.1; Bingham, Sandra, *The Praetorian Guard in the Political and Social Life of Julio-Claudian Rome*, p.31.

26. Dio 52.37.2; Suetonius, *Augustus* 74; Bingham, Sandra, *The Praetorian Guard: A History of Rome's Elite Special Forces*, pp.89–90, citing for *speculatores Caesaris* or *Augusti* see CIL 6.1921a = ILS 2014 and CIL 3.4843 = ILS 2015, for Praetorian military diploma see CIL 16.21 = ILS 1993.

27. Tacitus, *Annals* 1.7.

28. de Bédoyère, Guy, *Praetorian: The Rise and Fall of Rome's Imperial Bodyguard*, p.70; Tacitus, *Annals* 1.51, 1.61, 2.16, 2.20; Bingham, Sandra, *The Praetorian Guard: A History of Rome's Elite Special Forces*, p.86.

29. de Bédoyère, Guy, *Praetorian: The Rise and Fall of Rome's Imperial Bodyguard*, pp.68–69; Rankov, Boris, *The Praetorian Guard* (Osprey Publishing, 2008), p.5.

30. Dio 56.25.5.

31. Suetonius, *Tiberius* 25; Tacitus, *Annals* 2.27–29; Dio 57.15.1–6; Seager, Robin, *Tiberius*, pp.74–76; Levick, Barbara, *Tiberius the Politician*, p.149; Syme, Ronald, *The Roman Revolution*, p.425 n.2; Flint, W.W., 'The Delatores in the Reign of Tiberius, as Described by Tacitus', *The Classical Journal* Vol.8, No.1 (Oct. 1912), pp.37–42.

32. Tacitus, *Annals* 2.27; Seneca, *Ep.* 70; Syme, Ronald, *The Roman Revolution*, p.358; Rutledge, Steven, H., *Imperial Inquisitions* (Routledge, 2001), internet download, loc. 530.

33. Tacitus, *Annals* 2.32; Velleius Paterculus, *The Roman History* 2.130; Dio 57.15.5; Marsh, Frank Burr, 'Tacitus and the Aristocratic Tradition', *Classical Philology* Vol.21, No.4 (Oct. 1926), pp.289–310; Shotter, D.C.A., 'The Trial of M. Scribonius Libo Drusus', *Historia* Zeitschrift für Alte Geschichte, Bd. 21, H. 1 (1st Qtr, 1972), pp.88–98.

34. Rutledge, Steven H., *Imperial Inquisitions*, loc. 487, 511; Saller, R.P., *Personal Patronage Under the Early Empire*, p.78; Rutledge, Steven H., 'Delatores and the Tradition of Violence in Roman Oratory', *The American Journal of Philology* Vol.120, No.4 (Winter, 1999), pp.555–73

35. Tacitus, *Annals* 2.29.

36. Tacitus, *Annals* 2.30.

37. Tacitus, *Annals* 2.30–31; Marsh, Frank Burr, 'Tacitus and the Aristocratic Tradition', pp.289–310.

38. Tacitus, *Annals* 2.32; Levick, Barbara, *Tiberius the Politician*, pp.183–84; Chilton, C.W., 'The Roman Law of Treason under the Early Principate', *The Journal of Roman Studies* Vol.45, Parts 1 and 2 (1955), pp.73–81.

39. Tacitus, *Annals* 2.32.

40. Tacitus, *Annals* 4.2, 4.13, 4.28–30, 4.36, 6.10; Rutledge, Steven H., 'Delatores and the Tradition of Violence in Roman Oratory', pp.555–73; Rutledge, Steven H., *Imperial Inquisitions*, loc 1178, 3822.

41. Saller, R.P., *Personal Patronage under the Early Empire*, pp.14–15.

42. Saller, R.P., *Personal Patronage under the Early Empire*, p.78; Rutledge, Steven H., *Imperial Inquisitions*, loc 119, 487, 651; Tacitus, *Annals* 4.66.2. In AD 24 the Senate sought to prohibit the confiscation of estates from those who committed suicide before formally convicted but Tiberius blocked this, arguing that the guardians of the state should be rewarded: Tacitus, *Annals* 4.30–34.

43. Epictetus, *Disc.* 4.1.91–97.

44. Tacitus, *Annals* 2.28, 3.19; Rutledge, Steven H., *Imperial Inquisitions*, loc 5414, citing AE 53.8 for Trio as governor of Lusitania; Rutledge, Steven H., 'Delatores and the Tradition of Violence in Roman Oratory', pp.555–73.

45. Dio 57.25.2; Tacitus, *Annals* 5.11, 6.4, 6.38.

46. Tacitus, *Annals* 2.56, 3.13, 3.19, 6.7.

47. Tacitus, *Annals* 1.70, 2.6, 2.74, 2.48, 3.10, 5.8; Suetonius, *Vitellius* 2; Syme, Ronald, *The Roman Revolution*, pp.83, 361, 386.

48. Tacitus, *Annals* 2.43, 3.10, 3.15–16; Suetonius, *Tiberius* 52; Rogers, Robert Samuel, 'A Tacitean Pattern in Narrating Treason-Trials', *Transactions and Proceedings of the American Philological Association* Vol.83 (1952), pp.279–311.

49. Tacitus, *Annals* 3.14–18, 6.26; Dio 58.22.

50. Tacitus, *Annals* 2.43, 4.12.5, 4.17.4.

51. Tacitus, *Annals* 4.4.

52. Seager, Robin, *Tiberius*, pp.99–100.

53. Seager, Robin, *Tiberius*, pp.100–01; Tacitus, *Annals* 3.29; Dio 58.1.5, 60.32.1; Suetonius, *Claudius* 27.1.

54. Talbert, Richard J.A., *The Senate of Imperial Rome* (Princeton University Press, 1984), pp.366–68.

55. Dio 57.19.6–7; Tacitus, *Annals* 4.2.

56. Tacitus, *Annals* 3.53–54; Meyer, Reinhold, Usurpation of Status and Status Symbols in the Roman Empire, *Historia*, Zeitschrift für Alte Geschichte, Bd. 20, H. 2/3 (2nd Qtr, 1971), pp.275–302; de Bédoyère,

Guy, *Praetorian: The Rise and Fall of Rome's Imperial Bodyguard*, p.72; Syme, Ronald, *Tacitus*, p.424.

57. Tacitus, *Annals* 2.87, 4.2; Suetonius, *Tiberius* 37; Juvenal, *Satire* 16.20–21 for antagonism between populace and soldiers.

58. Bingham, Sandra, *The Praetorian Guard: A History of Rome's Elite Special Forces*, pp.72–74; Bingham, Sandra, *The Praetorian Guard in the Political and Social Life of Julio-Claudian Rome*, pp.41–43, 153; Fields, Nic, *The Walls of Rome* (Osprey Publishing, 2008), p.13.

59. Bingham, Sandra, *The Praetorian Guard: A History of Rome's Elite Special Forces*, p.75; Bingham, Sandra, *The Praetorian Guard in the Political and Social Life of Julio-Claudian Rome*, p.44; Rankov, Boris, *The Praetorian Guard*, p.5; Drogula, Fred K., 'Who was watching whom?: A Reassessment of the Conflict Between Germanicus and Piso', pp.121–53.

60. Suetonius, *Tiberius* 37; Bingham, Sandra, *The Praetorian Guard in the Political and Social Life of Julio-Claudian Rome*, p.44 citing AE (1978) 286, and p.50.

61. Rankov, Boris, *The Praetorian Guard* (Osprey Publishing, 2008), p.6; de Bédoyère, Guy, *Praetorian: The Rise and Fall of Rome's Imperial Bodyguard*, p.73.

62. Tacitus, *Annals* 4.2.

63. Bingham, Sandra, *The Praetorian Guard in the Political and Social Life of Julio-Claudian Rome*, p.28; Bingham, Sandra, *The Praetorian Guard: A History of Rome's Elite Special Forces*, pp.60–63; Tacitus, *Annals* 4.4.2.

64. Tacitus, *Annals* 6.2; Juvenal, *Satire* 10, 90–91.

65. Wallace-Hadrill, Andrew, *The Imperial Court*, p.293; Champlin, Edward, 'My Sejanus', *Humanities* 31.5 (Sep./Oct. 2010), pp.18–21, 52–53; Tacitus, *Annals* 3.66.4, 6.14; Dio 58.10.8; Pliny, *Natural History* 7.129; Rutledge, Steven H., *Imperial Inquisitions: Prosecutions and Informants from Tiberius to Domitian*, loc 5575.

Chapter 4 The Right Hand of Caesar: AD 21–23

1. Tacitus, *Annals* 3.31.2; Suetonius, *Tiberius* 38; Rogers, Robert Samuel, 'Two Criminal Cases Tried Before Drusus Caesar', *Classical Philology* Vol.27, No.1 (Jan. 1932), pp.75–79; Levick, Barbara, *Tiberius the Politician*, p.158; Rogers, Robert Samuel, 'Notes on the Gallic Revolt, AD 21', *The Classical Weekly* Vol.36, No.7 (30 Nov. 1942), pp.75–76;

Rogers, Robert Samuel, *Studies in the Reign of Tiberius* (John Hopkins Press, 1943), p.126.

2. Tacitus, *Annals* 3.47.3, 3.49.1, 3.64.1; trial of Clutorius Priscus, see *Annals* 3.49.1–51.2; Dio 57.20.3, 57.21.1; Suetonius, *Tiberius* 26; Bellemore, Jane, 'Cassius Dio and the Chronology of AD 21', *The Classical Quarterly* (New Series) Vol.53, No.1 (May 2003), pp.268–85, citing CIL 6.2023b.

3. Tacitus, *Annals* 3.49; Dio 57.20.3–4; Rogers, Robert Samuel, 'Two Criminal Cases Tried Before Drusus Caesar', pp.75–79; Flint, W.W., 'The Delatores in the Reign of Tiberius, as Described by Tacitus', pp.37–42; Shotter, D.C.A., 'The Trial of Clutorius Priscus', *Greece and Rome* Vol.16, No.1 (April 1969), pp.14–18.

4. Tacitus, *Annals* 3.51.

5. Dio 57.20.4; Tacitus, *Annals* 3.51.2–3; Rutledge, Steven, H., *Imperial Inquisitions*, loc 2207.

6. Tacitus, *Annals* 3.66; Moore, Clifford H. and Jackson, John, *Tacitus Histories Books 4–5, Annals, Books 1–3* (Loeb edition), p.626 n.6.; Seneca, *Controversiae* 1.1.5, 1.3.11, 1.8.3, 2.1.33–35, 7.3.5, 7.7.15, 10.5.25; Rutledge, Steven H., *Imperial Inquisitions*, loc 5575.

7. Seneca, *Controversiae* 2.1.35–36, *Suasoriae* 6.20–21; Tacitus, *Annals* 3.66.5–6; Juvenal, *Satire 10* 83–88; Rutledge, Steven H., *Imperial Inquisitions*, loc 4768.

8. Tacitus, *Annals* 6.3.4–5, 6.4.1, 6.39.1; Courtney, Edward, *The Fragmentary Latin Poets* (Oxford University Press, 2003), p.343; Rutledge, Steven H., *Imperial Inquisitions*, loc 6126.

9. Saller, R.P., *Patronage Under the Early Empire*, p.46.

10. Tacitus, *Annals* 1.13.

11. Tacitus, *Annals* 3.31.6, 3.68.3, 6.29; Dio 58.24; Rutledge, Steven H., *Imperial Inquisitions*, loc 4376–4431, citing CIL 6.2023b, 4.1553 and for *frates Arvales* CIL 6.2023b; Seneca, *De Beneficiis* 4.31.3–5; Seneca, *Controversiae*, 1.2.22, 2.1.39, 9.5.17, 10.1.9, 10 pr.3.

12. Quintilian XI.98; Tacitus, *Annals*, 6.5.8, 11.13;,12.27; Tacitus, *Dial.13*; Syme, Ronald, 'Domitius Corbulo', *Journal of Roman Studies* 60 (1970), pp.27–39; Jackson, John, *Tacitus Annals, Books 4–6, 11–12* (Loeb), p.148 n.3.

13. Syme, Ronald, *The Augustan Aristocracy*, pp.298, 309 citing PIR2 C1390; Tacitus, *Annals* 6.30.2.

14. Suetonius, *Tiberius* 70.

15. Suetonius, *Tiberius* 32, 56, 70, Tacitus, *Annals* 4.58.1; Levick, Barbara, *Tiberius the Politician*, pp.16–17.
16. Levick, Barbara, *Tiberius the Politician*, p.17.
17. Mennen, Inge, *Power and Status in the Roman Empire, AD 193–284* (Brill, 2011), p.9.
18. Rutledge, Steven H., 'Delatores and the Tradition of Violence in Roman Oratory', pp.555–73; Tacitus, *Annals* 3.19.1, 6.38.1; Dio 48.2.12; Rutledge, Steven H., *Imperial Inquisitions*, loc 5414 citing AE 53.8 and PIR2 F 517; Syme, R. *The Augustan Aristocracy*, pp.330, 376; Syme, R., *The Roman Revolution*, see stemma V and p.424 n.1; Shotter, D.C.A., 'Cnaeus Calpurnius Piso, Legate of Syria', pp.229–45.
19. Saller, R.P., *Personal Patronage under the Early Empire*, pp.9–17.
20. Tacitus, *Annals* 4.3.5: Vibius Serenus the Younger charged his father with maiestas in AD 23, knowing that the Empire despised and hated Vibius Serenus the Elder. The charges were seen to be baseless, but Vibius Serenus the Younger unusually escaped prosecution for *calumnia* due to the protection of Tiberius.
21. Rutledge, Steven H., *Imperial Inquisitions*, loc 119, 511, 565, 827; Saller, R.P., *Personal Patronage under the Early Empire*, p.77.
22. Rutledge, Steven H., *Imperial Inquisitions*, loc 487, 1085.
23. Tacitus, *Annals* 4.1–2.
24. Tacitus, *Annals* 6.8.
25. Saller, R.P., *Personal Patronage under the Early Empire*, p.78.
26. Tacitus, *Annals* 6.8, 6.47.
27. Seager, Robin, *Tiberius*, pp.142–43; Levick, Barbara, *Tiberius the Politician*, p.132.
28. Tacitus, *Annals* 3.32.
29. Tacitus, *Annals* 3.35, 6.5; Velleius Paterculus, *Roman History* 2.114.5; Seager, Robin, *Tiberius*, pp.35, 96, 114, 133–34; Syme, R., 'Marcus Lepidus, Capax Imperii', pp.22–33.
30. Tacitus, *Annals* 3.35.
31. Tacitus, *Annals* 3.74; Velleius Paterculus, *The Roman History* 2.125.4; Seager, Robin, *Tiberius*, p.143.
32. Tacitus, *Annals* 4.26; Seager, Robin, *Tiberius*, p.144; Levick, Barbara, *Tiberius the Politician*, p.132.
33. Tacitus, *Annals* 3.56.
34. Tacitus, *Annals* 3.59.

35. Tacitus, *Annals* 3.64; Rogers, Robert Samuel, 'Drusus Caesar's Tribunician Power', *The American Journal of Philology* Vol.61, No.4 (1940), pp.457–59 citing CIL 12; Seager, Robin, *Tiberius*, p.103.

36. Freisenbruch, Annelise, *The First Ladies of Rome* (Vintage, 2011), p.111; Dennison, Matthew, *Empress of Rome: The Life of Livia* (Quercus, 2011), p.262.

37. Dio 57.12.5; Dennison, Matthew, *Empress of Rome: The Life of Livia*, p.263.

38. Tacitus, *Annals* 3.65–69; Dio 57.10.5; Rutledge, Steven H., *Imperial Inquisitions*, loc 119, 1608; Shotter, D.C.A., 'The Trial of C. Junius Silanus', *Classical Philology* Vol.67, No.2 (April 1972), pp.126–31.

39. Tacitus, *Annals* 3.72; Dio 57.16.2, 57.21.3; Suetonius, *Tiberius* 47, 48; Claridge, Amanda, *Rome, An Archaeological Guide* (Oxford University Press, 2011), p.239; Plutarch, *Life of Pompey* 40; Carandini, Andrea (trans. Halavais, Andrew Campbell), *The Atlas of Ancient Rome* (Princeton University Press, 2012), p.505.

40. Seneca, *cons. Ad Marc.* 22; Tacitus, *Annals* 4.6.

41. Dio 57.21.4.

42. Saller, R.P., *Personal Patronage under the Early Empire*, pp.11, 21, 61; Pliny, *Letters* 10.58.7–9; Tacitus, *Annals* 4.1, 13.20–22; Seneca, *De Beneficia* 6.33.3–8; Millar, Fergus, *Emperor in the Roman World*, p.112.

43. Dio 56.43.1, 57.11.1–5.

44. Dio 57.19.8.

45. Tacitus, *Annals* 4. 39.

46. Dio 57.19.7; Wiedemann, T.E.J., 'Tiberius to Nero', *Cambridge Ancient History*, p.213.

47. Suetonius, *Tiberius* 27.

48. Tacitus, *Annals* 4.67.

49. Dio 58.5.2–6.

50. Dio 57.22.1; Tacitus, *Annals* 4.1, 4.3.

51. Dio 57.21.3; Suetonius, *Tiberius* 37

52. Tacitus, *Annals* 4.4; Dio 57.22.1.

53. Dio 57.22.4; Levick, Barbara, *Tiberius the Politician*, p.158, citing *Fasti. Ant.; Viae dei Serpenti, Inscr. Ital.*, XIII, i, 329,214 f. = EJ2 P.53 see n.55 p.273; Suetonius, *Tiberius* 62. The Jewish historian Josephus, writing around AD 93, seems to suggest Drusus died a natural death, see *Jewish Antiquities* (Wordsworth Classics of World Literature, 2006), 18.206.

54. Dio 57.22.2; Tacitus, *Annals* 3.29, 4.3–4, 4.7, 4.40; Levick, Barbara, *Tiberius the Politician*, p.161; Syme, R., *Tacitus*, p.410; Seager, Robin,

Tiberius, pp.181–83; Syme, Ronald, 'History or Biography: the Case of Tiberius Caesar', *Roman Papers* 3, edited by Birley, Anthony R. (Oxford: Clarendon Press, 1984), p.942.

55. Suetonius, *Tiberius* 62; Dio 57.22.2; Tacitus, *Annals* 4.3, 4.8.
56. Marsh, F.B., *The Reign of Tiberius* (Oxford University Press, 1931), pp.163–64, 168, 177–78, 192, 198, which was based on the thesis of Willenbucher, H., *Tiberius und die Verschworung des Sejan*, *Gymnasial-Bibliothek* 25 (Gutersloh 1896). However, this view is contradicted by Koestermann, Erich, *Cornelius Taci* (Heidelberg 1965), p.41, and Meise, Eckhard, 'Untersuchungen zur Geschichte derjulisch claudischen Dynastie', *Vestigia* 10 (Munich, 1969), pp.49–50, and also Hennig, D.L., *Aelius Seianus. Untersuchungen zur Regierung des. Tiberius.* (Vestigia xxi) (Munich), p.39, n.24, who point out that nowhere in the existing books of the *Annals* does Tacitus suggest this motivation to Livilla. Also Sinclair, Patrick, 'Tacitus' Presentation of Livia Julia, Wife of Tiberius' son Drusus', *The American Journal of Philology* Vol.111, No.2 (Summer 1990), pp.238–56, asserts that Sejanus seduced Livilla as she was the most accessible and agreeable, and then cooperated in the plan to murder her husband. However, even Tacitus appears surprised that Livilla would make this choice, as 'instead of the respectable aspirations lying right before her, she preferred to await ones which were immoral and dubious of attributes of Sejanus'.
57. Tacitus, *Annals* 1.29, 3.23, 3.34; Dio 57.13.1, 57.14.9; Seager, Robin, *Tiberius*, p.155.
58. Tacitus, *Annals* 4.3.
59. Dio 57.22.4b.
60. Tacitus, *Annals* 4.3.
61. Tacitus, *Annals* 4.39; Levick, Barbara, *Tiberius the Politician*, p.274 n.72, divorce appears confirmed by PIR2 A 913 but date in AD 23 not certain.
62. Dio 58.11.6.
63. Dio 58. 11.6; Suetonius, *Tiberius* 62; Levick, Barbara, *Tiberius the Politician*, p.161 and n.71 p.274.
64. Tacitus, *Annals* 4.3, 4.7, 4.10–11; Dio 57.22.2; Pliny, *Natural History* 29.20; Rogers, R.S., *Studies in the Reign of Tiberius*, p.143; Feldherr, Andrew, 'The Poisoned Chalice: Rumor and Historiography in Tacitus' Account of the Death of Drusus', *Materiali e discussioni per l'analisi dei testi classici*, No.61, Callida Musa: *Papers on Latin Literature: In Honor of R. Elaine Fantham* (2009), pp.175–89; Seager, R., *Tiberius*, p.156.

65. Shotter, David, *Tiberius Caesar* (Routledge, 2000), p.40.
66. Suetonius, *Tiberius* 62; Dio 57.22.4b.
67. Dio 58.11.7.
68. Historians who consider the accusations of poisoning an invention include Wiedemann, T.E.J., 'Tiberius to Nero', p.213; Hennig, D.L., *Aelius Seianus. Untersuchungen zur Regierung des. Tiberius*, Chapter 3; Syme, R., *Tacitus*, Vol.1, pp 401–05, who believes the only conspiracy that we know for certain was Tiberius' against Sejanus in AD 31; Boddington, Ann, 'Sejanus. Whose Conspiracy?', *The American Journal of Philology* Vol.84, No.1 (Jan. 1963), pp.1–16; Eisenhut, Werner, *Der Tod des Tiberius-Sohnes Drusus*, Museum Helveticum, vii (1950), pp.123–28, casts doubt on the authenticity of the claims in Tacitus by questioning the dates of the executions of Sejanus' children and suicide of his wife; Seager, Robin, *Tiberius*, pp.154–57, struggles to understand what Livilla stood to gain, being already certain of the position of Augusta; Levick, Barbara, *Tiberius the Politician*, p.101, points to the many possible successors to Tiberius before the claims of Sejanus would have been recognized and, furthermore, Livilla needed Drusus to live in order to secure the succession for her own children, so only turned to Sejanus after the death of her husband. Historians who consider the poison plot credible include Bird, H.W., 'L. Aelius Seianus and his Political Significance', *Latomus*, T.28, Fasc.1 (Janvier-Mars 1969), pp.61–98; Rogers, R.S., *Studies in the Reign of Tiberius*, p.143; Balsdon, J.P.V.D., 'The "Murder" of Drusus, Son of Tiberius', *The Classical Review* (New Series) Vol.1, No.2 (Jun. 1951), p.75; Shotter, David, *Tiberius Caesar*, p.40, sees little reason not to believe the authenticity of Apicata's allegation as Livilla expected Sejanus to be emperor upon the death of Tiberius.

Chapter 5 The Inventor of all Villainies: AD 24–26

1. Dio 58.7.2.
2. Ovid, *Fasti 6* 270f; Syme, R., 'Seianus on the Aventine', *Hermes*, 84.Bd., H. 3 (1956), pp.257–66; Champlin, Edward, 'My Sejanus', pp.51–52.
3. Rogers, R.S., *Studies in the Reign of Tiberius*, p.30.
4. Tacitus, *Annals* 4.8.
5. Tacitus, *Annals* 4.9; Levick, Barbara, *Tiberius the Politician*, p.162.
6. Velleius Paterculus, *The Roman History* 2.128.4; Rogers, R.S., *Studies in the Reign of Tiberius*, p.30.

7. Tacitus, *Annals* 4.40.
8. Tacitus, *Annals* 4.10.
9. Dio 57.22.4a; Tacitus, *Annals* 4.12; Seneca, *Of Consolation to Marcia*, Create Space Independent Publishing Platform (May 2015), 15; Wiseman, T.P., 'Review of Sex, Power and Politics in the Early Empire by Anthony A. Barrett', *The American Historical Review* Vol.103, No.2 (April 1998), pp.492–93.
10. Dio 55.1.4; Seager, R., *Tiberius*, p.22.
11. Levick, Barbara, *Tiberius the Politician*, p.162; Seager, R., *Tiberius*, p.227.
12. Dio 58.11.7; Seager, R., *Tiberius*, p.108; Clark, Gillian, *Roman Women*, downloaded from www.cambridge.org/core.
13. Tacitus, *Annals* 2.43.
14. Tacitus, *Annals* 4.12.
15. Tacitus, *Annals* 4.1.
16. Tacitus, *Annals* 1.69.
17. Tacitus, *Annals* 2.72.
18. Tacitus, *Annals* 4.12.
19. Tacitus, *Annals* 4.12.
20. Levick, Barbara, *Tiberius the Politician*, pp.176–77; Tacitus, *Annals* 4.54, 5.1, 5.10, 6.10; Dio 58.4.
21. Tacitus, *Annals* 4.12.
22. Seager, Robin, *Tiberius*, p.27; Levick, Barbara, *Tiberius the Politician*, p.163; Rutland, L., 'The Tacitean Germanicus', *Rhien.Mus.*130 (1987), p.153.
23. Seneca, *ad Helviam* 14.2; Clark, Gillian, *Roman Women*.
24. Tacitus, *Annals* 4.17; Suetonius, *Tiberius* 54.1; Bird. E., 'Aelius Sejanus and his Political Influence', *Latomus* 28 (1969), pp.61–69; Barrett, Anthony A., *Caligula, the Corruption of Power* p.19.
25. Shotter, David C.A., 'Agrippina the Elder: A Woman in a Man's World', pp.341–57.
26. Mellor, R., *Tacitus* (London, 1933), pp.75–77, and Walker, B., *The Annals of Tacitus* (Manchester, 1952), pp.103–07, suggest Agrippina was conspiring against Tiberius but Tacitus ignores this in order to present Agrippina as the innocent victim of the tyranny of Tiberius and Sejanus. However, Shotter, David C.A., 'Agrippina the Elder: A Woman in a Man's World', dismisses this on the grounds that Tacitus presents Agrippina in his narrative as a bold, forceful personality rather than an innocent victim. Barrett, Anthony A, *Agrippina: Sex, Power*

and Politics In the Early Empire (Yale University Press, 1999), p.33, also rejects the assertion Agrippina was attempting to form a faction.

27. Shotter, David C.A., 'Agrippina the Elder: A Woman in a Man's World'.
28. Tacitus, *Annals* 4.18–19: Rogers, Robert Samuel, 'A Tacitean Pattern in Narrating Treason Trials', *Transactions and Proceedings of the American Philological Association* Vol.83 (1952), pp.279–311.
29. Tacitus, *Annals* 4.19.
30. Tacitus, *Annals* 3.33; Rutledge, Steven H., *Imperial Inquisitions*, loc 2056, 3403.
31. Tacitus, *Annals* 3.43, 6.8; Hennig, D., *L. Aelius Seianus: Untersuchungen zur Regierung des Tiberius* (Vestigia 21) München: Beck, 1975, p.48; Syme, R., *The Roman Revolution*, p.437; Syme, R., 'The Consuls of AD 13', *Journal of Roman Studies*, 56 (1966), pp.55–60; Levick, Barbara, *Tiberius the Politician*, p.53.
32. Tacitus, *Annals* 4.19–20; Seager, Robin, *Tiberius*, pp.160–61; Rutledge, Steven H., *Imperial Inquisitions*, loc 3422; Levick, Barbara, *Tiberius the Politician*, p.163.
33. Tacitus, *Annals* 4.21, 4.34; Seager, Robin, *Tiberius*, pp.161, 269 n.54; Rogers, Robert Samuel, 'A Tacitean Pattern in Narrating Treason Trials', pp.279–311; Marsh, F.B., *The Reign of Tiberius*, pp.290–93.
34. Tacitus, *Annals* 4.31.
35. Tacitus, *Annals* 4.13, 4.28; Rogers, Robert Samuel, 'A Tacitean Narrative in Narrating Treason Trials', pp.279–311
36. Tacitus, *Annals* 4.29; Rogers, Robert Samuel, 'A Tacitean Pattern in Narrating Treason Trials', pp.279–311.
37. Tacitus, *Annals* 4.30.
38. Tacitus, *Annals* 4.36.
39. Dio 57.24.8.
40. Tacitus, *Annals* 4.30; Chilton, C.W., 'The Roman Law of Treason under the Early Principate', pp.73–81.
41. Rutledge, Steven H., *Imperial Inquisitions*, loc 3882.
42. Tacitus, *Annals* 6.8; Epictetus, *Discourses* 4.1.91–97; Epstein, David, *Personal Enmity in Roman Politics; 218–43 BC*, Routledge Revivals (Oct. 2015), pp.92–95, for study of *inimicitae* during the Republic; Rutledge, Steven H., *Delatores and the Tradition of Violence in Roman Oratory*, pp.555–73, for the role of *delatores* under Tiberius.
43. Seneca, *De Consolatione ad Marciam* 22.

44. Seneca, *Consolatione ad Marciam* 1, 22; Seneca, *Dialogues* 6.22.4; Seneca, *Letters* 122.11; Dio 57.22.4a; Tacitus, *Annals* 4.34, 6.8; Seager, Robin, *Tiberius*, p.164; Rutledge, Steven, *Imperial Inquisitions*, loc 2272, 2291; Stewart, Zeph, 'Sejanus, Gaetulicus, and Seneca', *The American Journal of Philology* Vol.74, No.1 (1953), pp.70–85.

45. Tacitus, *Annals* 4.39.

46. Tacitus, *Annals* 4.39.

47. Syme, R., *Tacitus*, pp.170, 277–78, 288–89, 320; Syme, R., 'History or Biography: the Case of Tiberius Caesar', p.945; Suetonius, *Claudius* 4.1; Suetonius, *Tiberius* 61.1; Tacitus, *Annals* 4.53.2; Levick, Barbara, *Tiberius the Politician*, pp.165, 275 n.86; Bowen, Edwin P., 'Did Tacitus in the Annals Traduce the Character of Tiberius?', *The Classical Weekly* Vol.6, No.21 (5 April 1913), pp.162–66.

48. Seager, Robin, *Tiberius*, p.165, accepts the authenticity of the letter with little debate.

49. Tacitus, *Annals* 4.3; Syme, R., *The Roman Revolution*, p.358.

50. Juvenal, *Satires* 7.94; Horace, *Carmen Saeculare* 2.2; Pliny, *Natural History* 7.138; Syme, R., *The Roman Revolution*, p.236.

51. Velleius Paterculus, *The Roman History* 2.127.3.

52. Seager, Robin, *Tiberius*, pp.165–66.

53. Tacitus, *Annals* 4.40.

54. Tacitus, *Annals* 4.40.

55. Velleius Paterculus, *The Roman History* 2.127.1–2.

56. Taking their lead from Syme, R., 'History or Biography: the Case of Tiberius Caesar', pp.943–44, where he describes Tiberius as gently paring Sejanus' letter with hints of his future prospects, yet Sejanus' horror on reading the letter and his panicked response as described by Tacitus suggest at something far different.

57. Tacitus, *Annals* 4.41, 6.7, 6.40, 6.48; Dio 58.8.3; Rogers, Robert Samuel, 'Lucius Arruntius', pp.31–45.

58. Tacitus, *Annals* 4.44; Suetonius, *Nero* 4–5.

59. Suetonius, *Augustus* 53; Dio 54.30.1, 56.26.2–3, 56.41.5.

60. Tacitus, *Annals* 14.56; Talbert, Richard J.A., *The Senate of Imperial Rome*, Princeton University Press, 1984, p.75; Winterling, Aloys, *Caligula*, University of California Press, p.26

61. Tacitus, Annals, 4.40 and 41; Pliny, *Letters*, 3.7.4; Talbert, Richard, J.A., *The Senate of Imperial Rome*, p.74.

62. Tacitus, *Annals* 6.8; Seneca, *De Ben* 6.33.3; Epictetus, *Discourses* 4.1.148, 3.7.31, 4.7.19; Saller, R.P., *Personal Patronage under the Early Empire*,

pp.11, 61, 66; Winterling, Aloys, *Politics and Society in Imperial Rome* (Wiley-Blackwell, 2009), p.47.

63. Tacitus, *Annals* 4.41; Winterling, Aloys, *Politics and Society in Imperial Rome*, pp.28, 53.

64. Phaedrus, *The Fables of Phaedrus*, Fable 3, The Vain Jackdaw and the Peacock, StreetLib Write, Fable 3 pp.3,18 n.4, citing Scheffer.

65. Phaedrus, *The Fables of Phaedrus*, Fable 6, The Frogs' Complaint against the Sun, pp.4–5, 19 n.8, citing Brotier and Desbillons.

66. Phaedrus, *The Fables of Phaedrus*, Book 3, The Prologue To Eutychus.

67. Tacitus, *Annals* 4.36.

68. Dio 58.22.1–5, Tacitus, *Annals* 6.19.

69. Tacitus, *Annals* 3.11.2, 4.42.1; Seneca, *Controv* 7.5.1–12; Jerome, *Chron*, p.173b; Syme, R., *The Roman Revolution*, p.375 n.4; Seager, R., *Tiberius*, pp.168–69, 269, citing Tacitus, *Annals* 2.11 and ILS 2686; Rutledge, Steven H., *Imperial Inquisitions*, loc 2291, citing PIR1 V 446.

70. Tacitus, *Annals* 3.65.

71. Dio 57.24.5; Shotter, D.C.A., 'Agrippina the Elder, A Woman in a Man's World', pp.341–45.

72. Epictetus, *Discourses* 4.1.7, 4.7.

73. Tacitus, *Annals* 4.52; Rutledge, Steven H., *Imperial Inquisitions*, loc 5135; Syme, R., *The Roman Revolution*, p.44; Shotter, D.C.A., 'Tiberius and the Spirit of Augustus', *Greece and Rome* 13 (1966), pp.202–12.

74. Dio 59.19.2; Suetonius, *Tiberius* 53.

75. Tacitus, *Annals* 4.53.

76. Tacitus, *Annals* 1.13, 4.40, 6.25; Wiedemann, T.E.J., 'Tiberius to Nero', p.213; Rogers, Robert Samuel, 'Lucius Arruntius', pp.31–45; Shotter, D.C.A., 'Tiberius and Asinius Gallus', pp.443–57.

77. Tacitus, *Annals* 4.54, 4.68; Suetonius, *Tiberius* 53, 61; Shotter, D.C.A. 'Agrippina the Elder: A Woman in a Man's World', pp.341–57.

78. Suetonius, *Tiberius* 51; Dennison, Matthew, *Livia, Empress of Rome*, p.263.

79. Levick, B.M., 'Tiberius' Retirement to Rhodes in 6 BC', *Latomus*, T.31, Fasc.3 (Octobre-Décembre 1972), pp.779–813; Shotter, D.C.A., 'Agrippina the Elder: A Woman in a Man's World'.

80. Syme, Ronald, 'History or Biography: the Case of Tiberius Caesar', pp.940–50; Seager, Robin, *Tiberius*, p.171; Tacitus, *Annals* 4.57.

81. Dio 58.2.1; Tacitus, *Annals* 4.57.

Chapter 6 Regent: AD 26–30

1. Tacitus, *Annals* 4.57–58, 6.26; Dio 58.1.1; Suetonius, *Tiberius* 39; Justinian, *Digest*, 1,2,2,4; Levick, Barbara, *Tiberius the Politician*, pp.89, 276 n.100; Seager, Robin, *Tiberius*, p.171.
2. Tacitus, *Annals* 4.58, 6.19.1; Suetonius, *Tiberius* 56; Juvenal, *Satire* 10.94; Dio 58.15.3, 58.22.2, 58.27.2–3, 28.4; Dio 58.3.3, 58.3.7; Seneca, *Controv.* 1.9, 14, 21, 27.
3. Syme, Ronald, 'History or Biography: the Case of Tiberius Caesar', p.947; Shotter, D.C.A., 'Tiberius and Asinius Gallus', pp.443–57.
4. Tacitus, *Annals* 4.60, 5.1, 6.20; Barrett, Anthony R., *Caligula, the Corruption of Power*, pp. 20–21, 23, 27; Suetonius, *Caligula* 10.1; Suetonius, *Tiberius* 54.1; Dio 59.2.2; Levick, Barbara, *Tiberius the Politician*, p.175.
5. Phaedrus, *Fables* Book 2, Fable V, 'Caesar to the Chamberlain', pp.26–27.
6. Saller, R.P., *Personal Patronage under the Early Empire*, p.61.
7. Barrett, Anthony A., *Caligula, the Corruption of Power*, pp.84, 177; Philo, *leg.* 166–77, 181, 203, 206.
8. Josephus, *Jewish Antiquities* 18.6.1, 18.6.4; Pliny, *Natural History* 29. 93–94; Millar, Fergus, *The Emperor in the Roman World*, p.73.
9. Tacitus, *Annals* 6.38.
10. Tacitus, *Annals* 6.8, 6.10; Seager, Robin, *Tiberius*, p.74; Levick, Barbara, *Tiberius the Politician*, p.205; Rutledge, Steven H., *Imperial Inquisitions*, loc 5536.
11. Tacitus, *Annals* 4.53; Suetonius, *Tiberius* 39.
12. Suetonius, *Tiberius* 42, although Suetonius is in error in suggesting that Piso was made urban prefect after one such drinking party on Capri and Flaccus was rewarded with the governorship of Syria, as Piso had been in post since AD 13 and Flaccus would not become governor of Syria until AD 33. See Syme, Ronald, 'Diet on Capri', *Roman Papers* Vol. VI, edited by Birley, Anthony; Levick, Barbara, *Tiberius the Politician*, p.149; Seager, R., *Tiberius*, 107.
13. Seneca, *Letters* 83.15; Syme, R., *The Roman Revolution*, p.436; Levick, Barbara, *Tiberius the Politician*, p.202.
14. Velleius Paterculus, *The Roman History* 2.43 and n.135 p.62; Fasti Arvales, AE 1987, 163; Seager, Robin, *Tiberius*, p.108.
15. Tacitus, *Annals* 4.2.
16. Dio 58.4.2, 58.6.2.
17. Suetonius, *Tiberius* 40; Tacitus, *Annals* 4.67.

18. Suetonius, *Tiberius*, 38; Millar, Fergus, *The Emperor in the Roman World*, pp.31–32.
19. Suetonius, *Tiberius* 39; Tacitus, *Annals* 4.59; Champlin, Edward, 'My Sejanus', pp.18–21, 52–53: Seager, Robin, *Tiberius*, p.172; Platts, Hannah Frances Mary Landsbrough, *Art, Architecture and Landscape in 'Vila' Residences of Italy from c 1st century BC to 2nd century AD*, Ph.D dissertation (University of Bristol, 2006), pp.143, 155–56, 238.
20. Tacitus, *Annals* 4.59.
21. Levick, Barbara, *Tiberius the Politician*, pp.157, 163; Seager, Robin, *Tiberius*, pp.157–59.
22. Tacitus, *Annals* 4.59–60, 4.67, 6.27.
23. Tacitus, *Annals* 4.54, 4.59; Wiedemann, T.E.J., 'Tiberius to Nero', p.216.
24. Statius, *Silvae* 3, 5, I00.
25. Pliny, *Natural History* 9.172; Platts, Hannah Frances Mary Landsbrough, *Art, Architecture and Landscape in 'Vila' Residences of Italy from c 1st century BC to 2nd century AD*, p.86; Varro, *De Re Rustica* 3.17.5; Houston, George W., 'Tiberius on Capri', *Greece and Rome* Vol.XXXII, No.2 (October 1985); D'Arms, J., *Romans on the Bay of Naples: a Social and Cultural Study of the Villas and Their Owners from 150 BC to AD 400* (Cambridge, MA, 1970), pp.75–76.
26. Suetonius, *Tiberius* 60; Tacitus, *Annals* 4.67.
27. Suetonius, *Tiberius* 43–44; Suetonius, *Caligula* 16.1; Tacitus, *Annals* 4.67, 6.1; Champlin, Edward, 'Sex on Capri', *Transactions of the American Philological Association* (internet, 2011), Vol.141, pp.315–32; Booms, Dirk, 'The Vernae Caprenses: Traces of Capri's Imperial History after Tiberius', *Papers of the British School at Rome*, 78 (2010), pp.133–43.
28. Suetonius, *Tiberius* 43; FitzPatrick, Mary C.. 'Tiberius' Villa Jovis on the Isle of Capri', *The Classical Journal* Vol.45, No.2 (Nov. 1949), pp.66–70; Booms, Dirk, 'The Vernae Caprenses: Traces of Capri's Imperial History after Tiberius', pp.133–43.
29. Tacitus, *Annals* 4.67; Josephus, *Jewish Antiquities* 18.16; Seager, Robin, *Tiberius*, p.174.
30. Tacitus, *Annals* 4.62; Suetonius, *Tiberius* 40.
31. Tacitus, *Annals* 4.64.
32. Tacitus, *Annals* 4.60; Dio 58.14.4; Levick, Barbara, *Tiberius the Politician*, p.170.

33. Tacitus, *Annals* 4.66, 11.22 for Dolabella being alive in AD 47 proposed a gladiatorial show whilst Afer lived into old age, his oratorical powers much depleted, see Dio 59.19.1, 2.3, also Quintillian 12.11.3; Seneca, *Contr.* 3.10 for Varus' betrothal and possible acquittal; Rutledge, Steven H., *Imperial Inquisitions*, loc 3459; Seager, Robin, *Tiberius* p.173.

34. Tacitus, *Annals* 4.68–70; Dio 58.1.1–3; Rogers, Robert Samuel, 'A Tacitean Pattern in Narrating Treason Trials', pp.279–311; Rogers, Robert Samuel, 'The Conspiracy of Agrippina', *American Philological Association* Vol.62 (1931), pp.141–68; Rutledge, Steven H., *Imperial Inquisitions*, loc 5646, 5772, 5840; Levick, Barbara, *Tiberius the Politician*, p.168; Seager, Robin, *Tiberius*, pp.174–75; Levick, Barbara, *Roman Political Life, 90 BC–69 AD*, edited by Wiseman, Exeter Studies in History (1985), *The Politics of the Early Empire*, Chapter 4, p.56.

35. Tacitus, *Annals* 4.70.

36. Tacitus, *Annals* 4.71; Rutledge, Steven H., *Imperial Inquisitions*, loc 3494 Levick, Barbara, 'Roman Political Life, 90 BC–69 AD 3513; Pliny, *Natural History* 8.145; Flint, W.W., 'Delatores in the Reign of Tiberius, as Described by Tacitus', pp.37–44.

37. Tacitus, *Annals* 4.67; Rogers, Robert Samuel, 'The Conspiracy of Agrippina', pp.141–68.

38. Tacitus, *Annals* 4.70; Dio 58.1.3.

39. Morgan, Llewelyn, 'Tacitus, Annals 4.70: An Unappreciated Pun', *The Classical Quarterly* Vol.48 (2) (1998), pp.585–87.

40. Barry, William D., Exposure, Mutilation, and Riot: Violence at the 'Scalae Gemoniae' in Early Imperial Rome, *Greece and Rome* (Second Series) Vol.55, No.2 (Oct. 2008), pp.222–46.

41. Pliny, *Natural History* 8.145; Dio 58.1.3, 58.1.11; Tacitus, *Annals* 4.68–70, 5.9.

42. Dio 58.5.1–3.

43. Tacitus, *Annals* 4.71.

44. Dio 58.5.1.

45. Dio 58.4.2.

46. Pliny, *Letters*, 10.58.7–9; Tacitus, *Annals* 4.2, 4.3, 6.8; Saller, R.P., *Personal Patronage under the Early Empire*, pp.41–43, 69, 71–78; Rutledge, Steven, *Imperial Inquisitions*, loc 580, citing CIL 10.1129 for career of Natta; Epictetus, *Discourses* 4.10; Wallace-Hadrill, Andrew, 'The Imperial Court', pp.296–301; Winterling, Aloys, *Politics and Society in Imperial Rome*, pp.36–38.

47. Shotter, D.C.A., 'Elections under Tiberius', *The Classical Quarterly* Vol.16, No.2 (Nov. 1966), pp.321–32.
48. Bird, H.W., 'L. Aelius Seianus and his Political Significance', pp.61–98; Syme, Ronald, *The Augustan Aristocracy*, p.179; Tacitus, *Annals* 6.30; Stewart, Z., 'Sejanus, Gaetulicus and Seneca', *American Journal of Philology*, 74 (1953), pp.70–85. Sealey, Raphael, 'The Political Attachments of L. Aelius Seianus', pp.97–114, identifies fourteen consuls with links to Sejanus, but most of these links are tenuous and it is to be expected that as consuls they would have regular dealings with Sejanus as virtual head of state, especially after Tiberius left for Capri in AD 26.
49. Seager, R.. *Tiberius*, p.110; Bird, H.W., 'L. Aelius Seianus and his Political Significance', pp.61–98; Barrett, Anthony A., *Caligula, The Corruption of Power*, p.32; Syme, Ronald, *The Roman Aristocracy*, pp.188, 192; Levick, Barbara, *Tiberius the Politician*, pp.55–56, 202, 290 n.10.
50. Seager, Robin, *Tiberius*, p.107.
51. Tacitus, *Annals* 4.29, 12.1; Levick, Barbara, *Claudius* (Routledge, 2001), p.25; Suetonius, *Claudius* 26.
52. Tacitus, *Annals* 3.19; Seager, Robin, *Tiberius* p.108; Rutledge, Steven, *Imperial Inquisitions*, loc 5971; Syme, R., *Tacitus*, p.327, citing AE 1953, 88 dated to 22 January AD 31 for Fulcinius Trio's governorship of Lusitania.
53. Levick, Barbara, *Tiberius the Politician*, pp.136–37, 279 n.136; Brunt, P.A., 'The Administrators of Roman Egypt', pp.124–47; Wilson, Emily, *Seneca, A Life* (Allen Lane, 2014), p.61; Rogers, Robert Samuel, 'The Prefects of Egypt under Tiberius', *American Philological Association* Vol.72 (1941), pp.365–71; Seneca, *Cons. Ad Helvtiam* 19.4; Philo, *Legation to Gaius* 24.159–161, see also Eusebius, *Ecclesiastical History* 2.5; Smallwood, Mary E., 'Some Notes on the Jews under Tiberius', *Latomus* XV (1956), pp.314–29; Maier, Paul L., 'Sejanus, Pilate, and the Date of the Crucifixion', *Church History* Vol.37, No.1 (March 1968), pp.3–13; Dio 57.18.5; Tacitus, *Annals* 2.85; Suetonius, *Tiberius* 36, see also Josephus, Jewish *Antiquities* 18.3.5; Seager, Robin, *Tiberius*, p.125.
54. Tacitus, *Annals* 4.69, 73–74.
55. Tacitus, *Annals* 4.74–75.
56. Tacitus, *Annals* 4.74.
57. Dio 58.2.7–8; Suetonius, *Tiberius* 65.

58. Suetonius, *Tiberius* 48; Dio 58.4.4: Bird, H.W., 'L. Aelius Sejanus: Further Observations', *Latomus*, T.29, Fasc.4 (October–December 1970), pp.1,046–50.

59. Dio 58.2.5–6, 58.16.2; Tacitus, *Annals* 4.2; Saller, R.P., *Imperial Patronage in the Early Empire*, pp.71–73.

60. Dio 58.4.3–4.

61. Tacitus, *Annals* 5.1.2; Dio 58.2.1–6; Suetonius, *Caligula* 10.1, 16.3, 23.2; Barrett, Anthony A., *Caligula, The Corruption of Power*, p.22; Freisenbruch, Annelise, *The First Ladies of Rome* (Vintage, 2011), pp.94–95; Nicols, John, 'Antonia and Sejanus', *Historia: Zeitschrift für Alte Geschichte*, Bd.24, H.1 (1st Quarter 1975), pp.48–58; Wallace-Hadrill, Andrew, 'The Imperial Court', pp.288–89.

62. Tacitus, *Annals* 5.3.

63. Tacitus, *Annals* 5.3.

64. Philo, *In Flacc* 3.9; Shotter, David C.A., 'Agrippina the Elder: A Woman in a Man's World', pp.341–85; Rogers, R.S., 'The Conspiracy of Agrippina', pp.141–68; Rogers, R.S., *Studies in the Reign of Tiberius* (John Hopkins Press, 1943), pp.53–57; Allen Jnr, Walter, 'The Political Atmosphere in the Reign of Tiberius', *Transactions and Proceedings of the American Philological Association* Vol.72 (1941), pp.1–25.

65. Suetonius, *Tiberius* 53; Tacitus, *Annals* 5.4.

66. Decline, Tracy, 'The Criminal Charges Against Agrippina the Elder in AD 27 and 29', *The Classical Quarterly* 65 (2015), pp.766–72; Charlesworth, Martin P., 'The Banishment of the Elder Agrippina', *Classical Philology* Vol.17, No.3 (July 1922), pp.260–61; Rutledge, Steven H., *Imperial Inquisitions*, loc 3513.

67. Tacitus, *Annals* 5.4–5.

68. Levick, Barbara, *Tiberius the Politician*, p.169.

69. Suetonius, *Tiberius* 53–54, 64; Suetonius, *Caligula* 10; Seneca, *De Ira* 3.21.5; Cohen, Sarah T., 'Augustus, Julia and the Development of Exile "Ad Insulam"', *The Classical Quarterly* (New Series) Vol.58, No.1 (May 2008), pp.206–17; Barry, William D., 'Exposure, Mutilation and Riot: Violence at the Scalae Germoniae in Early Imperial Rome', pp.222–46.

70. Dio 58.3.1–7; Tacitus, *Annals* 6.25; Seneca, *Ep. Mor.* 55.3; Tuplin, Christopher J., 'The False Drusus of 31 AD and the Fall of Sejanus', *Latomus* T.46, Fasc.4 (Octobre–Decembre 1987), pp.781–805; Shotter, D.C.A., 'Tiberius and Asinius Gallus', pp.443–57; Rogers, Robert Samuel, 'The Conspiracy of Agrippina', pp.141–68; for *damnatio*

memoriae see ILS 97.165, 5050 line 168 Dessau. Bird, W., in 'L. Aelius Sejanus and His Political Influence', p.63ff, considers Asinius Gallus a political ally of Sejanus.

71. Dio 58.3.8; Tacitus, *Annals* 6.40; Syme, R., 'History or Biography: The Case of Tiberius Caesar' pp.940–50.
72. Seager, Robin, *Tiberius*, p.179; Wiedemann, T.E.J., 'Tiberius to Nero', p.216; Rogers, Robert Samuel, 'The Conspiracy of Agrippina', pp.141–68.
73. Suetonius, *Tiberius* 54, 61; Suetonius, *Caligula* 7; Tacitus, *Annals* 6.15, 6.24, 12.12.1; Rutledge, Steven, *Imperial Inquisitions*, loc 3513; Rogers, Robert Samuel, 'The Conspiracy of Agrippina', pp.141–68; Syme, R., *The Augustan Aristocracy*, p.306.
74. Tacitus, *Annals* 5.10; Dio 58.25.1; Suetonius, *Claudius* 3; Tuplin, C.J., 'The False Drusus of 31 AD and the Fall of Sejanus', pp.781–805; Seager, Robin, *Tiberius*, p.284 n.138; Levick, Barbara, *Tiberius the Politician*, pp.212–13, suggests this was an attempt by the supporters of Agrippina to save the life of Drusus, forcing the emperor to prove he was alive by releasing him from prison, or by Caligula to save the life of his brother. However, as Tuplin argues, Agrippina was imprisoned and unable to contact anyone. Furthermore, these actions would only serve to endanger the lives of Agrippina and Caligula. Caligula himself was on Capri, acting with great restraint and caution to avoid providing any ammunition for Sejanus' agents to persuade the emperor of his unsuitability.
75. Levick. Barbara, *Tiberius the Politician*, pp.170–71.
76. Dio 58.3.9, 58.19; Tacitus, *Annals* 5.6, 6.8; Suetonius, *Tiberius* 65; Seneca, *Consolation to Marcia* 22.4–7; Bellamore, Jane, 'The Wife of Sejanus', *Zeitschrift für Papyrologie und Epigraphik*, Bd.109 (1995), pp.255–66; Hennig, D, 'L. Aelius Seianus', p.78; Barrett, Anthony A., *Caligula, The Corruption of Power*, p.26; Seager, R., *Tiberius*, pp.179, 271 n.127; Bird, H.W., 'L. Aelius Sejanus: Two Observations', *Latomus* T.29, Fasc.4 (October–December 1970), pp.1,046–50; Stewart, Z., 'Sejanus, Gaetulicus and Seneca', pp.70–85. See also Wiedemann, T.E.J., 'Tiberius to Nero', pp.215–16, who identifies Livilla as Sejanus' betrothed. However, Syme, R., *Tacitus*, p.405, accepts Dio at face value, but in *The Augustan Aristocracy*, pp.170–71, considers the possibility Livilla was meant. See also Sinclair, P., 'Tacitus' Presentation of Livia Julia', *American Journal of Philology* 111 (1990), pp.250–53, for Julia. The fact the emperor ordered Gaetulicus to betroth his daughter seems to suggest that Sejanus was not related to the governor; see Bird, H.,

'L. Aelius Seianus and His Political Significance', p.77, and Sealey, R., 'The Political Attachments of L. Aelius Sejanus', pp.97–114, who convincingly argues for no familial relationship.

77. Suetonius, *Tiberius* 65; Dio 58.4.3–9; Syme, R., *The Roman Revolution*, p.94; Bingham, Sandra, *The Praetorian Guard in the Political and Social Life of Julio-Claudian Rome*, PhD Thesis (University of British Columbia, 1997), p.54.
78. Velleius Paterculus, *The Roman History* 2.127; Bowen, P., 'Did Tacitus in the Annals Traduce the Character of Tiberius?', pp.162–66; Cowan, Eleanor, 'Tacitus, Tiberius and Augustus', pp.179–210.
79. Dio 58.9.5; Suetonius, *Tiberius* 24.
80. Syme, R. *The Roman Revolution*, p 344–345, 389
81. Dio 58. 9.5; Wallace-Hadrill, Andrew, 'The Imperial Court', pp.301–02; Bird, H.W., 'L. Aelius Sejanus: Two Observations', pp.1,046–50; Bird, H.W., 'L. Aelius Seianus and his Political Significance', pp.61–98; Woodman, A. J., 'Tacitus' Obituary of Tiberius: Tacitus Annals 6.51.1–3', pp.197–205.

Chapter 7 His Fall: AD 31

1. Millar, Fergus, *The Emperor in the Roman World*, pp.31–32.
2. Dio 58.4.9; Suetonius, *Tiberius* 65.
3. Talbert, Richard J.A., *The Senate of Imperial Rome*, pp.200–02; Dio 58.5.5–58.6.1; Hölkeskamp, Karl-Joachim, *Consuls and Res Publica, Holding High Office in the Roman Republic* (Cambridge University Press, 2011), edited by Hans Beck, Antonio Duplá, Martin Jehne and Fransisco Pina Polo, p.173; Pliny, *Letters* 9.37.5.
4. Translation of ILS 6044 = EJ² 53, taken from Barbara Levick, *Tiberius the Politician*, pp.119, 261 n.12, 13.
5. Champlin, Edward, 'My Sejanus', pp.18–21, 52–53; Syme, R., 'Seianus on the Aventine', pp.257–66; Levick, Barbara, *Tiberius the Politician*, pp.119, 171, 261 n.12 and n.13; Braund, Susanna Morton, *Juvenal and Persius* (Loeb Classical Library, 2004), p.372 n.10.
6. Tacitus, *Annals* 4.1.3–4; Dio 58.4.1; Valerius Maximus 9.11; Suetonius, *Tiberius* 55; Boddington, Ann, 'Sejanus. Whose Conspiracy?' pp.1–16.
7. Syme, R., *Tacitus*, p.406; Sealey, Robin, *Tiberius*, p.181; Boddington, Ann, 'Sejanus. Whose Conspiracy?', pp.1–16.
8. Juvenal, *Satire 10* 73–77, Juvenal and Persius, Loeb Classical Library; Lawall, Gilbert, 'Exempla and Theme in Juvenal's Tenth Satire',

Transactions and Proceedings of the American Philological Association Vol.89 (1958), pp.25–31; Eichholz, D.E., *The Art of Juvenal and His Tenth Satire*, www.cambridge.org/core, pp.61–69; Fishelov, David, 'The Vanity of the Reader's Wishes: Rereading Juvenal's Satire 10', *The American Journal of Philology* Vol.111, No.3 (Autumn 1990), pp.370–82.

9. Dio 58.4.4, 58.6.1–2.
10. Tacitus, *Annals* 6.3; Winterling, Aloys, *Caligula*, p.38.
11. Tacitus, *Annals* 6.3.4–5, 6.4.1, 6.39.1; Rutledge, Steven H., *Imperial Inquisitions*, loc 6126; Courtney, Edward, *The Fragmentary Latin Poets*, pp.524.
12. For Manius Lepidus in Loeb translation, M. Lepidus in the Latin text, read Marcus Lepidus, see Syme, R., 'Marcus Lepidus, Capax Imperii', pp.22–33.
13. Tacitus, *Annals* 6.5; Juvenal, *Satire 5* 109, 7.94; Rutledge, Steven H., *Imperial Inquisitions*, loc 2385; Jackson, John, *Tacitus, Annals, Books 4–6, 11–12*, p.160 n.3.
14. Garner, Jane F. and Wiedemann, T., *The Roman Household: A Sourcebook* (Routledge Source Books for the Ancient World, 2013, Kindle edition), p.40.
15. epigraphy.packhum.org/text/248861, Ephesos 1139.
16. Tacitus, *Annals* 6.8
17. Tacitus, *Annals* 6.9; Suetonius, *Tiberius* 61; Levick, Barbara, *Tiberius the Politician*, p.173; Hennig, D., *L. Aelius Seianus, Untersuchungen zur Regierung des. Tiberius* (Vestigia xxi), pp.101–20.
18. Tacitus, *Annals* 6.18; Pliny, *Natural History* 7.39; Syme, R., 'Domitius Corbulo', pp.27–39; Levick, Barbra, *Tiberius the Politician*, p.290 n.10; Syme, R., *The Augustan Aristocracy*, p.308.
19. Antonia's guardianship of Caligula, see Seneca, *De Ira* 3.21.5; Pliny, *Natural History* 8.145; Suetonius, *Caligula* 10; Tacitus, *Annals* 3.3.
20. Josephus, *Jewish Antiquities* 18.180–182; Nicols, John, 'Antonia and Sejanus', pp.48–58.
21. Dio 66.14. On Antonia's role see Syme, R., *Tacitus*, p.406; Seager, Robin, *Tiberius*, pp.181–82.
22. Suetonius, *Vespasian* 3; Oost, S.V., 'The Career of M. Antonius Pallas', *American Journal of Philology* 79 (1958), pp.113–39; Weidemann, T.E.J., *Tiberius to Nero* (Cambridge Ancient History, Chapter 5), p.216.
23. Suetonius, *Caligula* 10; Winterling, Aloys, *Caligula*, p.38.
24. Seager, Robin, *Tiberius*, p.108; Shotter, D.C.A., 'Agrippina the Elder, A Woman in A Man's World', pp.341–55; Rutledge, Steven, *Imperial*

Inquisitions, loc 6467. Barrett, Anthony A., *Caligula, The Corruption of Power*, p.30, suggests Cocceius Nerva as one of the agents of Sejanus attempting to trick Caligula, but his survival at the side of the emperor suggests otherwise. A further suggestion the historian makes is the equestrian Curtius Rufus, who had a number of literary links, but there is little to support this.

25. Dio 58.6.2–4.
26. Seager, Robin, *Tiberius*, p.272 n.154, citing ILS 6124, contradicting Suetonius, *Tiberius* 26, who records that Tiberius resigned his third consulship on 15 May. The inscription also contradicts Bird, H.W., 'L. Aelius Seianus and his Political Significance', p.83, who states that Sejanus was replaced as consul by Faustus Cornelius Sulla at the end of March.
27. Dio 58.8.1–2.
28. Tacitus, *Annals* 6.9.
29. Dio 58.7.4–5.
30. Dio 58.7.5.
31. Suetonius, *Tiberius* 61.
32. Suetonius, *Tiberius* 54
33. Dio 58.8.3–4.
34. Tacitus, *Annals* 6.7, 6.48; Levick, Barbara, *Tiberius the Politician*, p.176; Rogers, Samuel Robert, 'Lucius Arruntius', pp.31–45; Syme, R., 'Personal Names in Annals I–VI', *The Journal of Roman Studies* Vol.39, Parts 1 and 2 (1949), pp.6–18; Bird, H.W., 'L. Aelius Seianus and His Political Influence', pp.61–98.
35. Dio 58.8.3; Tacitus, *Annals* 6.7, 6.40; Levick, Barbara, *Tiberius the Politician*, p.176; Rutledge, Steven, *Imperial Inquisitions*, loc 4696; Syme, R., *The Augustan Aristocracy*, p.298.
36. Suetonius, *Tiberius* 60; Dio 58.18.2–3.
37. Dio 58.6.2.
38. Dio 58.7.1–4; Champlin, Edward, 'My Sejanus', pp.18–21; Laurence, Ray, 'Rumour and Communication in Roman Politics', Greece and Rome Vol.LXI, No.1 (April 1994), pp.62–72.
39. Dio 58.10.4, 10.8, 12.3.
40. Dio 58.7.4.
41. Dio 58. 9.1.
42. Tacitus, *Annals* 3.13, 5.8; Suetonius, *Vitellius* 2–3.
43. Most of Tacitus' book 5, which covered the last years of Sejanus and his overthrow, is lost so historians are heavily reliant on the epitomized

history of Dio and the rather scurrilous account of Tiberius' life as presented by Suetonius. Dio says nothing of any conspiracy by Sejanus, whilst Suetonius suggests that it was Tiberius who used Sejanus to eliminate the family of Germanicus and then, his utility fulfilled, conspired to remove his Praetorian Prefect. Seager, Robin, *Tiberius*, p.182; Marsh, Frank Burr, *The Reign of Tiberius*, p.304, considers Sejanus' conspiracy was against Caligula, not Tiberius; Smith, Charles Edward, *Tiberius and the Roman Empire* (Louisiana State University Press, 1942), pp.152–53. Bird, H.W., 'L. Aelius Seianus and His Political Influence', pp.61–98, suggests P. Vitllius became an *amicus* of Sejanus, fearing retribution for his part in the prosecution of Calpurnius Piso.

44. Dio 58.9.2.
45. Tacitus, *Annals* 3.70; Dio 58.9.2; Birley, A.R., 'Sejanus: His Fall', in N. Sekunda (ed.), *Corolla Cosmo Rodewald* (Gdańsk, 2007), pp.121–50; Levick, Barbara, *Tiberius the Politician*, p.174, 278 n.134, citing PIR² E. 65; Barrett, Anthony A., *Caligula: the Corruption of Power*, p.261 n.67; de Bédoyère, Guy, *Praetorian, the Rise and Fall of Rome's Imperial Bodyguard* pp.83–85, 296 n.58 preserves name of Macro on inscription from amphitheatre at Alba Fucens AE (1957) 250 from latter part of Tiberius' reign, which describes him as a previous Prefect of Vigiles and Prefect of Praetorian Guard, but it fails to provide any dates. de Visscher, F., 'Macropréfet des vigilers et ses cohortes contre la tyrannie de Séjan', *Mélanges A. Piganiol* II (Paris, 1966), pp.761–68, suggests there was a power struggle on Capri between Sejanus and Macro, but Sejanus clearly trusted Macro as he accepted and trusted him when he was told Tiberius had given him *tribunicia potestas* before he entered the Senate.
46. Tacitus, *Annals* 6.26.
47. Levick, Barbara, *Tiberius the Politician*, p.278 n.134, citing PIR² G 202 and ILS 1336; Dio 60.23.3.
48. Levick, Barbara, *Tiberius the Politician*, p.177; Rogers, Robert Samuel, 'Lucius Arruntius', pp.31–45.
49. Suetonius, *Tiberius* 48, 65; Dio 58.18.2; Shotter, D.C.A., 'The Fall of Sejanus: Two Problems', *Classical Philology* 69 (1974), pp.42–46; Shotter, D.C.A., 'Agrippina the Elder, A Woman in A Man's World', pp.341–55; Rogers, R.S., *Studies in the Reign of Tiberius*, p.5.
50. Dio 58.9.3; Hennig, D., *L. Aelius Seianus. Untersuchungen zur Regierung des. Tiberius* (Vestigia xxi), p.153.

51. Dio 58.9.4–6, 10.3, 11.1; Barrett, Anthony A., *Caligula, The Corruption of Power*, pp.28–29.
52. Juvenal, *Satire 10* 70; Dio 58.10.1, 10.5.
53. Dio 58.10.6.
54. Suetonius, *Caligula* 30. See also Dio 59.4.3.
55. Dio 58.10.8.
56. Dio 58.11.3.
57. Claridge, Amanda, *Rome, An Oxford Archaeological Guide*, p.163.
58. Dio 58.11.5; Shotter, D.C.A., 'The Fall of Sejanus: Two Problems', pp.42–46.
59. Juvenal, *Satire 10* 61–68; Lawall, Gilbert, 'Exempla and Theme in Juvenal's Tenth Satire', pp.25–31.
60. Juvenal, *Satire 10* 81–89.
61. Dio 58.12.1; Tacitus, *Annals* 5.8; Barry, William D., 'Exposure, Mutilation and Riot: Violence at the "Scalae Gemoniae" in Early Imperial Rome', *Greece and Rome* (Second Series) Vol.55, No.2 (Oct. 2008), pp.222–46; Adams, Freeman, 'The Consular Brothers of Sejanus', *The American Journal of Philology* Vol.76, No.1 (1955), pp.70–76, suggests Aelius Gallus was the grandson of the former prefect of Egypt, but then it is difficult to understand why he was hiding from the mob that was hunting down those connected with Sejanus.
62. Dio 58.12.2–3.
63. Seneca, *De Ben.* 3.26.
64. Suetonius, *Tiberius* 65.

Chapter 8   The Terror: AD 31–37

1. Seneca, *De Beneficiis* 3.26.
2. Dio 58.12.3–8; Tacitus, *Annals* 6.2: Seneca, *De Tranquil* 11.11; Boddington, Ann, 'Sejanus. Whose Conspiracy?', pp.1–16, citing ILS 157 with name of Sejanus erased from consular *fasti*.
3. Bird, H.W., 'L. Aelius Seianus and his Political Influence', pp.61–98, citing Tacitus, *Annals* 3.66.1 and 13.45.1.
4. Sumner, G.V., 'The Family Connections of L. Aelius Seianus', pp.134–45; Braund, David C., *Augustus to Nero: A Sourcebook on Roman History 31 BC–AD 68* (Croom Helm, 1985), p.46; Bellemore, Jane, 'The Wife of Sejanus', *Zeitschrift für Papyrologie und Epigraphik*, Bd. 109 (1995), pp.255–66; Degrassi, A., *Inscriptiones Italiae* (Rome, 1947), Vol.13.1,

Fasti Ostienses; Sumner, G.V., 'The Family Connections of L. Aelius Seianus', pp.134–45; Adams, Freeman, 'The Consular Brothers of Sejanus', pp.70–76.

5. Dio 58.11.6; Tacitus, *Annals* 5.9; Levick, Barbara, *Tiberius the Politician*, p.161; Seager, Robin, *Tiberius*, pp.155–56, 188.
6. Dio 58.16.4–5; Tacitus, *Annals* 5.8, 6.3, 6.7, 6.18; Levick, Barbara, *Tiberius the Politician*, p.205; Rutledge, Steven, *Imperial Inquisitions*, loc 1122; Seager, Robin, *Tiberius*, pp.185, 191, 198; Levick, Barbara, *Tiberius the Politician*, p.201.
7. Dio 58.11.7.
8. Tacitus, *Annals* 5.9.
9. Seneca, *Consolatio ad Helviam* 10.
10. Tacitus, *Annals* 4.29.
11. Tacitus, *Annals* 5.8; Suetonius, *Claudius* 26.
12. Seager, Robin, *Tiberius*, p.201.
13. Tacitus, *Annals* 6.29, 6.48; Suetonius, *Tiberius* 62; Pliny, *Natural History* 29.20; Dio 58.24.5; Sinclair, Patrick, 'Tacitus' Presentation of Livia Julia, Wife of Tiberius' Son Drusus', pp.238–56.
14. Tacitus, *Annals* 6.47.
15. Tacitus, *Annals* 4.34, 6.8, 6.47; Dio 57.24.2–4; Seneca, *Dialogues* 6.1.2, 6.22.4; Rutledge, Steven, *Imperial Inquisitions*, loc 6075.
16. Tacitus, *Annals* 6.23–24; Suetonius, *Tiberius* 53–54; Dio 58.22.4, 25.4: Seager, Robin, *Tiberius*, p.196.
17. Tacitus, *Annals* 6.25; Seager, Robin, *Tiberius*, p.88.
18. Dio 58.15.3–4.
19. Suetonius, *Tiberius* 61.
20. Tacitus, *Annals* 6.19; Suetonius, *Tiberius* 61; Seager, Robin, *Tiberius*, p.196, dating mass execution of Sejanus' *amici* and clients to August AD 33, citing F. Osti (EJ p.43).
21. Tacitus, *Annals* 6.3–4, 6.39; Dio 58.24.2; Suetonius, *Tiberius* 61; Rutledge, Steven, *Imperial Inquisitions*, loc 6126; Chilton, C.W., 'The Roman Law of Treason under the Early Principate', pp.73–81; Seager, Robin, *Tiberius*, p.192.
22. Tacitus, *Annals* 4.30, 5.11, 6.4, 6.38; Dio 58.25.2.
23. Dio 58.15.4–16.2; Suetonius, *Tiberius* 61.
24. Tacitus, *Annals* 5.6.
25. Tacitus, *Annals* 5.7.
26. Tacitus, *Annals* 12.27; Stewart, Zeph, 'Sejanus, Gaetulicus, and Seneca', pp.70–85; Seager, Robin, *Tiberius*, p.199.

27. Tacitus, *Annals* 6.29; Brunt, P.A., 'The Administrators of Roman Egypt', pp.124–47; Rogers, Robert Samuel, 'The Prefects of Egypt Under Tiberius', pp.365–71.
28. Tacitus, *Annals* 1.13, 6.9.2, 6.14.1, 6.26; Wilson, Emily, *Seneca, A Life*, pp.61–62. For Fufius Geminus see Tacitus, *Annals* 6.10.1 = Vitia (PIR1 V 517) cited by Rutledge, Steven, *Imperial Inquisitions*, loc 2366. For Cotta see Tacitus, *Annals* 6.5. For Mam. Aemilius Scaurus see Dio 58.24.3–5; Suetonius, *Tiberius* 61; Seneca, *Suasoriae* 2.22; and Rogers, Robert Samuel, 'A Tacitean Narrative in Narrating Treason Trials', pp.279–311; Weidemann, T.E.J., *Tiberius to Nero*, p.219; Sealey, Raphael, 'The Political Attachments of L. Aelius Sejanus', pp.97–114; Bingham, Sandra, *The Praetorian Guard in the Political and Social Life of Julio-Claudian Rome*, p.144 n.67; Levick, Barbara, *Tiberius the Politician*, p.202–04.
29. Tacitus, *Annals* 6.48.
30. Tacitus, *Annals* 6.47–48, 11.10; Dio 58.23.8, 59.10.4, also 59.6.6, 59.10.4 for Caligula's punishment of those associated with prosecutions of members of his immediate family. Rutledge, Steven, *Imperial Inquisitions*, loc 2424; Weidemann, T.E.J., *Tiberius to Nero*, p.218; Levick, Barbara, *Tiberius the Politician*, pp.215–16.
31. Hennig, D., *L. Aelius Seianus. Untersuchungen zur Regierung des. Tiberius* pp.118–21, who suggests the senatorial infighting was born from Tiberius' position of weakness, meaning he was unable to decisively intervene.
32. Rutledge, Steven, *Imperial Inquisitions*, loc 119.
33. Braund, David C., *Augustus to Nero, A Sourcebook on Roman History 31 BC–AD 68*, citing EJ 52 from Gortyn, Crete.
34. Braund, David C., *Augustus to Nero, A Sourcebook on Roman History 31 BC–AD 68*, citing EJ 51 dated to AD 32 from Interamna, Umbria. The name of Lucius Arruntius Camillus Scribonianus was erased after his failed revolt in AD 42.
35. Braund, David C., *Augustus to Nero, A Sourcebook on Roman History 31 BC–AD 68*, citing EJ 85.
36. Valerius Maximus 9.11; Wardle, D., 'Valerius Maximus on the Domus Augusta and Tiberius', *Classical Quarterly* 50.2 (2000), pp.479–93; Ferguson, John, *The Religions of the Roman Empire* (Thames and Hudson, 1982), p.72.
37. For temporary amnesty on mourning see Suetonius, *Tiberius* 61; Dio 58.16.6–7. For mourning customs see Juvenal, *Satire 10* 245; Suetonius,

Augustus 23; Suetonius, *Julius Caesar* 67; Suetonius, *Caligula* 24. Seager, Robin, *Tiberius*, p.193, for mourning for those condemned under *maiestas*.
38. Tacitus, *Annals* 6.51.
39. Suetonius, *Tiberius* 61.
40. Suetonius, *Tiberius* 63, 67.
41. Tacitus, *Annals* 4.1; Suetonius, *Tiberius* 55.
42. Tacitus, *Annals* 4.1.
43. Dio 57.20.7; Tacitus, *Annals* 4.1.
44. Juvenal, *Satire 10* 90–96.
45. Epictetus, *Discourses* 4.1.60.

Appendix The Family, *Amici* and Clients of Sejanus

1. Seager, Robin, p.152; PIR ² A 157; Syme, R., *The Roman Revolution*, pp.400–01 n.6.
2. Westermann, W.L., 'Aelius Gallus and the Reorganization of the Irrigation System of Egypt under Augustus', *Classical Philology* Vol.12, No.3 (July 1917); Jameson, Shelagh, 'Chronology of the Campaigns of Aelius Gallus and C. Petronius'; Bird, H.W., 'L. Aelius Seianus and his Political Significance', pp.61–98; Syme, R., *The Roman Revolution*, p.409.
3. Adams, Freeman, 'The Consular Brothers of Sejanus', pp.70–76.
4. Suetonius, *Claudius* 26.
5. Adams, Freeman, 'The Consular Brothers of Sejanus', pp.70–76; Sumner, G.V., 'The Family Connections of L. Aelius Seianus', pp.134–45; Braund, David C., *Augustus to Nero: A Sourcebook on Roman History 31 BC–AD 68*, p.46; Tacitus, *Annals* 5.8.
6. Syme, R., *The Augustan Aristocracy*, pp.304–07; Badian, Ernst, *Oxford Classical Dictionary* (online publication, Dec. 2015); Ryan, F.X., 'The Praetorship of L. Aelius Tubero', *L'Antiquité Classique* T. 65 (1996), pp.239–42; Adams, Freeman, 'The Consular Brothers of Sejanus', pp.70–76.
7. Cornell, T.J., *The Fragments of the Roman Historians: L. and Q. Aelius Tubero*, p.363.
8. Tacitus, *Annals* 6.9, 6.29; Dio 58.243–45; Levick, Barbara, *Tiberius the Politician*, p.213; Rutledge, Steven H., *Imperial Inquisitions*, loc 2366, 2385.

9. Dio 58.19.1–2; Seager, Robin, *Tiberius*, p.143; Vàrhelyi, Zsuzsanna, *The Religion of Senators of the Roman Empire* (Cambridge University Press, 2010), p.68.
10. Dio 57.2.7, 58.3.1; Tacitus, *Annals* 1.13, 6.25; Shotter, D.C.A., 'Tiberius and Asinius Gallus', pp.443–57.
11. Seager, Robin, *Tiberius*, pp.116, 137; Sumner, G.V., 'The Family Connections of L. Aelius Seianus', pp.134–45.
12. Dio 58.11.6; Seager, Robin, *Tiberius*, pp.155–56, 186–88.
13. Martial, *Epigrams* 10.73; Pliny the Elder, *Natural History* 19.137; Seneca, *Consolatio ad Helviam* 10; Lindsay, Hugh, 'Who was Apicius?', pp.144–54.
14. Tacitus, *Annals* 6.7, 6.40; Syme, R., 'Personal Names in Annals I–VI', pp.6–18.
15. Levick, Barbara, *Tiberius the Politician*, p.206; Philo, *Embassy to Gaius* 3.
16. Tacitus, *Annals* 3.66; Juvenal, *Satire X* 81; Syme, R., 'Personal Names in Annals I–VI', pp.6–18; Seneca, *Controv.* 2.1.36; 7.5.9; 9.1.1; Seneca, *Suas.* 6.20–21; Rutledge, Steven H., *Imperial Inquisitions*, loc 1178, 4376, 4768.
17. Sumner, G.V., 'The Family Connections of L. Aelius Seianus', pp.134–45; Braund, David C., *Augustus to Nero: A Sourcebook on Roman History 31 BC–AD 68*, p.46; Bellemore, Jane, 'The Wife of Sejanus', pp.255–66; Degrassi, A., *Inscriptiones Italiae*, Vol.13.1, Fasti Ostienses; Sumner, G.V., 'The Family Connections of L. Aelius Seianus', pp.134–45; Adams, Freeman, 'The Consular Brothers of Sejanus', pp.70–76.
18. Levick, Barbara, *Tiberius the Politician*, p.277 n.116; Barrett, Anthony A., *Caligula: The Corruption of Power*, p.162.
19. Barrett, Anthony A., *Caligula: The Corruption of Power*, pp.33, 162; Suetonius, *Caligula* 57; Suetonius, *Nero* 37; Tacitus, *Annals* 12.11, 12.12, 16.7.3; Dio 59.29.3; Syme, R., *The Augustan Aristocracy*, p.173.
20. Dio 58.3.8.
21. Tacitus, *Annals* 6.30; Syme, R., *The Augustan Aristocracy*, p.298; Stewart, Zeph, 'Sejanus, Gaetulicus and Seneca', pp.70–85.
22. Adams, Freeman, 'The Consular Brothers of Sejanus', Tpp.70–76; Sumner, G.V., 'The Family Connections of L. Aelius Seianus', pp.134–45, citing CIL 11.7285; ILS 8996; Sealey, Raphael, 'The Political Attachments of L. Aelius Seianus', pp.97–114.

23. Tacitus, *Annals* 4.3, 4.7, 4.10–11; Dio 57.22.2; Pliny, *Natural History* 29.20; Rogers, R.S., *Studies in the Reign of Tiberius*, p.143; Feldherr, Andrew, 'The Poisoned Chalice: Rumor and Historiography in Tacitus' Account of the Death of Drusus', pp.175–89; Seager, R., *Tiberius*, p.156.

24. Tacitus, *Annals* 2.28, 3.19, 6.38.2; Dio 48.2.12, 58.25.2; Rutledge, Steven H., *Imperial Inquisitions*, loc 5414, citing PIR2 F 517 and AE 53.8.

25. Brunt, P.A., 'The Administrators of Roman Egypt', pp.124–47; Rogers, Robert Samuel, 'The Prefects of Egypt Under Tiberius', pp.365–71, who cites Dessau for suggesting Hiberus was a freedman of Antonia, with his full name being Marcus Antonius Hiberus, based on PIR H 118; Dio 58.19.6.

26. Tacitus, *Annals* 6.14.

27. Tacitus, *Annals* 6.7; Quintilian 10.118, 12.10.11; Seager, Robin, *Tiberius*, p.191.

28. Tacitus, *Annals* 4.58, 6.10; Rutledge, Steven, *Imperial Inquisitions*, loc 5646, 5536; Levick, Barbara, *Tiberius the Politician*, p.205.

29. Tacitus, *Annals* 4.12.

30. Tacitus, *Annals* 3.35, 4.26; Velleius Paterculus, *Histories* 2.127; Bird, H.W., 'L. Aelius Seianus and his Political Influence', pp.61–98.

31. Braund, David C., *Augustus to Nero: A Sourcebook on Roman History 31 BC–AD 68*, p.46; Dio 58.11.6; Tacitus, *Annals* 5.9.

32. Tacitus, *Annals* 1.16–30, 3.35, 3.72–73, 5.7; Dio 57.4; Syme, R., *The Augustan Aristocracy*, p.163.

33. Tacitus, *Annals* 1.19, 1.29, 6.27; Syme, R., *The Augustan Aristocracy*, p.163; Seager, Robin, *Tiberius*, p.201.

34. Tacitus, *Annals* 6.4, 6.27; Aelian, *Letters* Nos 113–14; Syme, R., *The Augustan Aristocracy*, pp.163, 304; Seager, Robin, *Tiberius*, p.201.

35. Rutledge, Steven H., *Imperial Inquisitions*, loc 5575; Tacitus, *Annals* 3.66, 6.47 and n.6 p.626; Seneca, *Contr.* 2.1.33, 2.1.34–35; Seager, Robin, *Tiberius*, p.201; Levick, Barbara, *Tiberius the Politician*, p.216.

36. Tacitus, *Annals* 2.43, 4.3, 6.2, 6.29; Dio 58.11.7, 58.24.5; Suetonius, *Claudius* 3; Pliny, *Natural History* 29.20; Bellemore, Jane, *The Wife of Sejanus*, pp.255–66.

37. Tacitus, *Annals* 4.71.1, 6.4.1; Rutledge, Steven, *Imperial Inquisitions*, loc 5772; Syme, R., *Personal Names in the Annals I–VI*, pp.6–18, citing PIR2 L 348 and IGRR 1.1032.

38. Tacitus, *Annals* 4.8, 4.10–11; Suetonius, *Tiberius* 62; Seager, Robin, *Tiberius*, pp.155–56.

39. Tacitus, *Annals* 6.7; Seager, Robin, *Tiberius*, pp.107, 191; Levick, Barbara, *Tiberius the Politician*, p.202.
40. Suetonius, *Nero*, 35.1; Griffin, Miriam T., *Nero: The End of a Dynasty*, (BT Batsford Ltd, 1984) pp.101–102; Holland, Richard, *Nero: The Man Behind the Myth*, (Sutton Publishing, 2000) p.96.
41. Tacitus, *Annals* 4.68–70; Seager, Robin, *Tiberius*, p.174; Levick, Barbara, *Tiberius the Politician*, p.276 n.106, citing *IG*, XIV, 719 (Naples).
42. Tacitus, *Annals* 3.67; Suetonius, *Tiberius* 61; Levick, Barbara, *Tiberius the Politician*, p.214.
43. Tacitus, *Annals* 4.68; Levick, Barbara, *Tiberius the Politician*, p.276 n.106, citing A. Birley, *Britannia* (1973), p.180; Rutledge, Steven, *Imperial Inquisitions*, loc 5840.
44. Seneca, *Consolatione ad Marciam* 1, 22; Seneca, *Dialogues* 6.22.4; Seneca, *Letters* 122.11; Dio 57.22.4a; Tacitus, *Annals* 3.72, 4.34, 6.8; Seager, Robin, *Tiberius*, p.164; Rutledge, Steven, *Imperial Inquisitions*, loc 2272, 2291; CIL 10.1129.
45. Tacitus, *Annals* 5.8, 6.8–9, 6.18, 11.13; Suetonius, *Tiberius*, 42; Dio 59.6.2; Syme, R., 'Domitius Corbulo', pp.27–39; Seager, Robin, *Tiberius*, pp.139, 198; Levick, Barbara, *Tiberius the Politician*, p.290 n.10, citing CIL XIII, 5201 and CIL XIII, 11515 (also PIR 2 P 754); Rutledge, Steven, *Imperial Inquisitions*, loc 580, 2366; Pliny, *Letters* 3.5, 7.17; Pliny, *Natural History* 7.39; Quintillian 11.98.
46. Tacitus, *Annals* 5.8, 6.9, 6.18; Dio 59.29.5; Rutledge, Steven, *Imperial Inquisitions*, loc 580, 2366, 5963; Levick, Barbara, *Claudius*, p.60.
47. Tacitus, *Annals* 4.68, 4.71; Frontinus, *De aquaeductu* 102; Levick, Barbara, *Tiberius the Politician*, p.276 n.106; Rutledge, Steven, *Imperial Inquisitions*, loc 5971, citing CIA 3.1.651, 871; Seager, Robin, *Tiberius*, p.108.
48. Syme, R., *The Roman Revolution*, p.384 n.6, citing ILS 914 and Propertius 3.12.1, and p.466.
49. Dio 58.8.3; Rogers, Samuel Robert, 'Lucius Arruntius'; Levick, Barbara, *Tiberius the Politician*, p.176; Syme, R., 'Personal Names in Annals I –VI', pp.6–18.
50. Tacitus, *Annals*, 4.34, 6.8, 6.47; Dio 57.24.2–4; Seneca, *Dialogues*, 6.1.2 and 6.22.4; Rutledge, Steven, *Imperial Inquisitions*, loc 6075 citing CIL 9.3091–2
51. Tacitus, *Annals* 6.7; Levick, Barbara, *Tiberius the Politician*, p.202.
52. Tacitus, *Annals* 1.7, 4.1; Suetonius, *Augustus* 66; Juvenal, *Satire X* 74–78; Adams, Freeman, 'The Consular Brothers of Sejanus', pp.70–76; Pliny,

Natural History 10.52; Syme, R., *The Augustan Aristocracy*, pp.301–08; Syme, R., *The Roman Revolution*, p.358, stemma VI; Sumner, G.V., 'The Family Connections of L Aelius Seianus', pp.134–45; Adams, Freeman, 'The Consular Brothers of Sejanus', pp.70–76; Hennig, D., *L. Aelius Seianus*, pp.5–12.

53. Tacitus, *Annals* 2.20, 4.29; Sumner, G.V., 'The Family Connections of L Aelius Seianus', pp.134–45; Syme, R., *The Augustan Aristocracy*, p.301; Syme, R., *The Roman Revolution*, p.307, whilst Seager, Robin, *Tiberius*, pp.108, 163, concurs with this conclusion.

54. Tacitus, *Annals* 2.56, 3.13, 3.19, 6.7; Seager, Robin, *Tiberius*, pp.85, 97, 99, 191; Levick, Barbara, *Tiberius the Politician*, pp.141, 156–57.

55. Tacitus, *Annals* 6.3.4–5, 6.4, 6.39; Levick, Barbara, *Tiberius the Politician*, pp.174, 192, 205, Seager, Robin, *Tiberius*, pp.191, 196; Rutledge, Steven, *Imperial Inquisitions*, loc 6126; Rogers, R.S., 'Criminal Trials and Criminal Legislation Under Tiberius', *American Philological Association* (1935), pp.141, 157.

56. Tacitus, *Annals* 6.9; Levick, Barbara, *Tiberius the Politician*, pp.196, 205; Powell, Lindsey, *Eager for Glory, The Untold Story of Drusus the Elder, Conqueror of Germania* (Pen and Sword, 2011), p.59.

57. Tacitus, *Annals* 6.46; Suetonius, *Tiberius* 62; Suetonius, *Caligula* 23.

58. Tacitus, *Annals* 6.8; Seager, Robin, *Tiberius* pp.191–92, 272 n.138.

59. Suetonius, *Augustus* 66; Syme, R., *The Augustan Aristocracy*, pp.301–08, conclusively argues that the inscription does relate to Strabo rather than Caecina Tuscus; Syme, R., *The Roman Revolution*, p.358, stemma VI; Sumner, G.V., 'The Family Connections of L. Aelius Seianus', pp.134–45; Adams, Freeman, 'The Consular Brothers of Sejanus', pp.70–76; Hennig, D., *L. Aelius Seianus*, pp.5–12.

60. Tacitus, *Annals* 2.28, 6.10; Dio 58.4.3; Seager, Robin, *Tiberius*, p.193; Levick, Barbara, *Tiberius the Politician*, p.205.

61. Tacitus, *Annals* 4.18–20; Seager, Robin, *Tiberius*, pp.160–61; Hennig, D., *L. Aelius Seianus*, pp.48–52.

62. Suetonius, *Vitellius* 2; Tacitus, *Annals* 1.70, 2.6, 3.13, 5.8, 6.47–48; Seager, Robin, *Tiberius*, p.107; Levick, Barbara, *Tiberius the Politician*, p.216.

63. Tacitus, *Annals* 5.6–7; Jackson, John, *Tacitus, Annals*, Books 4–6, 11–12 (Loeb), p.146 n.2.

Index